The Politics of Free Markets

The Politics of Free Markets

The Rise of Neoliberal Economic Policies in Britain, France, Germany, and the United States

MONICA PRASAD

THE UNIVERSITY OF CHICAGO PRESS CHICAGO AND LONDON

MONICA PRASAD is assistant professor of sociology at Northwestern University.

The University of Chicago Press, Chicago 60637
The University of Chicago Press, Ltd., London

Printed in the United States of America

15 14 13 12 11 10 09 08 07 06   1 2 3 4 5

ISBN: 0-226-67901-2 (cloth)
ISBN: 0-226-67902-0 (paper)

Library of Congress Cataloging-in-Publication Data

Prasad, Monica.
The politics of free markets : the rise of neoliberal economic policies in Britain, France, Germany, and the United States / Monica Prasad.
p. cm.
Includes bibliographical references and index.
ISBN 0-226-67901-2 (cloth : alk. paper) — ISBN 0-226-67902-0 (pbk. : alk. paper)
1. Free enterprise—United States. 2. Free enterprise—Great Britain. 3. Free enterprise—France. 4. Free enterprise—Germany. 5. Neoliberalism—United States. 6. Neoliberalism—Great Britain. 7. Neoliberalism—France. 8. Neoliberalism—Germany. I. Title.
HB95.P64 2006
330.12′2—dc22

2005021954

⊗ The paper used in this publication meets the minimum requirements of the American National Standard for Information Sciences—Permanence of Paper for Printed Library Materials, ANSI Z39.48-1992.

Contents

Preface

When I began this project in 1997, the tax cuts of the Reagan era were rapidly disappearing into the history books, and I thought enough time had passed to allow a dispassionate analysis of a controversial episode. In the years it took me to conduct that analysis, tax cuts, and the larger attempt to reduce the role of the state that they represent, jumped out of the history books and back onto the front pages: in the last four years we have seen an almost exact repetition of the attempt to cut taxes, deregulate, and cut welfare state spending that animated the early Reagan years. Critics of George W. Bush wonder how policies that seem so extreme to Europeans could be so successful in this country (and supporters wonder why Europeans consider these policies so extreme). Although in this book I do not comment on the policies of the George W. Bush administration directly, this historical analysis helps to put them in context. The story told in these pages shows that an adversarial politics established in the postwar period acquired its own momentum in contemporary America, pitting business against state and the middle class against the poor. I hope this book can help to explain how this happened and to identify the factors that prevent a similar dynamic in Europe.

It is a pleasure to thank the many people who have contributed directly and indirectly to this project. It began as a dissertation, and my thanks go first to my dissertation committee members. I am grateful to Andy Abbott for years of patient encouragement. He never forced me to take my research in particular directions, and yet he always saw exactly what I was trying to do and what I needed to do, even when I could not see it myself. I thank him for his outspokenness on behalf of a particular vision of sociology, for using his intelligence and force of personality to keep a space open at Chicago for a generation of students to try out risky topics, and most of all for the example he sets in his own work of intellectual curiosity and creativity combined with scientific rigor. To George Steinmetz I extend thanks for all the hours he spent providing detailed comments on successive drafts and for offering encouragement even when the project was in a very unformed stage. I still remember my excitement, my sense that here was something one could devote one's life to, when I took his "Sociology of the State" class more than a decade ago. The timely pragmatism of William Parish was crucial at many junctures, from choosing the dissertation project to preparing for job interviews, and I am grateful to him for his graciousness in matters large and small. I thank Lloyd Rudolph for his guidance as I first began to explore the parallel world of political science, and for anchoring a warm and lively intellectual community at Chicago. At the Michigan Society of Fellows, the kindness of Jim White sustains an extraordinary interdisciplinary community. Julia Adams gave extremely helpful and painstaking advice as I shaped some of this material for a job talk. Pierre Rosanvallon and Thomas Risse advised my efforts in France and Germany, and Chris Collins made very useful comments on the chapter on Britain. At Northwestern, Bruce Carruthers, Ann Orloff, and Kathy Thelen have commented on various parts of the work, and along with many others have welcomed me into an amazingly collegial academic environment. I have tried out parts of the argument presented in this work over the years at many campuses and professional meetings, and I am grateful to the dozens of audience members who have led me to rethink some of my conclusions.

I also thank Linnea Martin, Alta Goodwine, Billie Crawford, and Pat Preston for their years of help. Staff members at many campuses, institutes, and libraries provided crucial support, and I want to single out for thanks the librarians at the Bibliothèque Cujas, who went beyond the call of duty. Mina Yoo, Laurent Berthet, and Katharina Boerner provided expert research assistance.

Funding to conduct the research for this book came from the Division of the Social Sciences at the University of Chicago, the University of Michigan's Rackham Graduate School, the Deutscher Akademischer Austausch Dienst, and the Social Science Research Council/National Endowment for the Humanities Berlin Program for Advanced German and European Studies. None of these sources bears any responsibility for the contents of this book.

Doug Mitchell has been the sweetest editor anyone could hope for; I thank him as well as Tim McGovern, Christine Schwab, and the many others at the University of Chicago Press who have guided me through the process of publishing a first book. Comments from the anonymous reviewers led to major rethinking and reorganization and saved me from many mistakes; I thank them warmly. Nick Murray's copyediting has made the text immeasurably more readable and clarified the text citations and list of references. A version of chapter 4 first appeared in the *American Journal of Sociology*, and I am grateful for permission to reprint it here.

For the conversations that were the essence of my life over the last decade, I want to thank Andrés Villarreal, Steve Rosenberg, Karin Badt, Dee Ferron, Mike Rempel, Carlen Rader, Kushal Som, Jennifer Johnson, Sheba George, Jeremy Straughn, Tom Guglielmo, Jan Leu, Hanna Kim, Darcy Leach, Rachna Dhingra, Sujata Patil, and Anne Conway. Peter van der Poorten's strength of character and obsession with political economy were equally crucial elements of my days for many years, and I thank him for his gentle soul.

Finally, I would like to thank my family members. My brother's family grew from two to four during the time that I was writing this book. My sister, Leena Prasad, my fellow traveler through life, is the one person who has always supported all of my intellectual efforts, starting from when she taught me to read. I thank her for the example of openness with which she meets the world. Stefan Henning has brought vividness to my days. He argues with me about all of my assumptions, helps me see the humor and beauty in our everyday routines, and reminds me that there is more to life than neoliberalism. Every day I am newly amazed by his loving nature.

Last and most important, I thank my parents, Madhawi and Dinesh Prasad: for the confident feminism that led them to raise their daughters exactly as they had raised their son in a time and place when this was rare; for their resilience and resourcefulness in providing us with a safe haven from which to experience the drama of immigration; and for their spirited political engagements, to which I trace the roots of my own interests. My father wants to know when he will see me on C-Span's *Booknotes*; my mother is just relieved that the book is finished. I dedicate it to both of them.

Introduction

The dream of reason ended in 1973. In that year the oil crisis ended the world that the rich democracies of the West had taken for granted and brought inflation, unemployment, and recession into everyday life. After the Second World War, all the countries of the developed world had settled on a version of planned capitalism in which the state played a major coordinating role. They thought that it was possible to capture the benefits of the extraordinary productivity of capitalist systems while rationally avoiding their more brutal consequences and their instability. Moreover, they thought that without such steering from the state, capitalism could not work. "What was it that converted capitalism from the cataclysmic failure which it appeared to be in the 1930s into the great engine of prosperity of the postwar Western world?" asked Andrew Shonfield in 1965, in what quickly became one of the foundational texts of the analysis of modern capitalism. He believed the answer was intelligent economic planning. Shonfield argued that the secret to the success of capitalism included not only Keynesian demand-management policies, but also the vastly increased powers of public authorities who could control competition in the private sector in accordance with coherent, rational designs for growth. For this reason, his ideal economy was France, and he believed that countries with less developed planning systems would move inexorably toward the French pattern.

For three decades the policies of planned capitalism were so successful that mid-century observers thought they spelled the "end of ideology," for how could anyone argue with the peace and prosperity of the thirty years after the war? Even more surprising was that these prosperous states focused their attention on improving the welfare of their citizens, incarnating a new idea in the history of the world, a curious blend of communitarian

Christian ethics with the individualism and belief in progress of the Enlightenment: that the proper, the *moral* role of the community is to care for the individuals within it. Thus, along with the twentieth-century rise of democracy and the renaissance of nationalism in the world arose the idea of the state whose main role was to care for its citizens; and the extraordinary prosperity of the postwar period in Europe and the United States made this utopian idea the stuff of everyday politics. In Britain, T. H. Marshall (1950), as knowledgeable an observer as anyone at the time, thought he could see an evolutionary pattern in the movement toward a greater role for the state, and he predicted that the responsibility of the state would everywhere come to include providing economic security to all citizens. There was a natural progression, he thought, from "civic rights" like the rights of free speech and protection against tyranny to "political rights" like the right to vote and organize politically and, finally, to "social rights" like the right to minimum economic protection or even full economic equality. In the United States, Harvard professor Daniel Bell (1963) edited a book whose contributors concluded that those who objected to this economic system, whom they lumped together with groups like the Ku Klux Klan, were a fringe minority. Sophisticated critics of planning like the Austrian Friedrich Hayek were far out of the field of vision of mainstream scholars; in 1967 Eric Hobsbawm called Hayek—correctly—a "prophet in the wilderness" (cited in Cassidy 2000).

Of course, we know what happened next: the prosperity of the postwar period was founded to such a degree on oil that when the Organization of Petroleum Exporting Countries decided in 1973 to restrict output, the consequent fivefold increase in the price of this one commodity increased inflation throughout every developed economy. The higher costs of domestic goods reduced returns to investment, and a new economic phenomenon entered the world: "stagflation."

The economic crisis that resulted opened a space for political experimentation: "Crises pry open the political scene, throwing traditional relationships into flux. . . . Circumstances become less certain, and solutions less obvious. Crises thus render politics more plastic" (Gourevitch 1984, 99). But although the economic crisis did throw the political system of each country into crisis, the political responses diverged: in the United States and Britain the economic crisis led to a sustained and committed effort to cut taxes, spending levels, and the role of the state in overseeing industry—"neoliberalism." In West Germany and France, as in the majority of European countries, such efforts, when they were made, were not sustained.

Some observers think that the United States and Europe are developing into different models of civilization, underpinned by divergent understandings of morality. According to this argument the American model celebrates the creative powers of the individual and fears the tyranny of the collectivity, and so seeks to keep taxes and social spending low and government intervention minimal. The European model, despite differences between the individual countries, in general demands communities that care for their citizens, pooling risks through high taxes and spending, and attempting to make economics serve democratically determined ends. This argument builds on the "American exceptionalism" thesis, which holds that the particular circumstances of a settler society led to an individualistic and pro-market culture in America, and therefore the American Left has been unable to make a case for the more redistributive policies found in Europe and could not prevent more pro-business policies from taking hold in the wake of the oil crisis (Hartz 1955; Lipset 1996).

I argue in this book that the opposite is true. The United States and Britain embraced neoliberalism not because the Left in each country was weak, but because in the postwar period it had in some ways been so strong. American and British tax policies were more progressive, American and British industrial policy more adversarial to business, and the American and British welfare states more redistributive, and these structures (which defined the middle class in opposition to the poor and the interests of business in opposition to the general interest) proved fragile. In Britain, the catalyst for Thatcher's neoliberal reforms was the strength of labor: the unions displayed their muscle repeatedly over the course of the 1970s, bringing government after government down through strikes. But because the socioeconomic transformation of the postwar period had moved most voters out of the working class, the unions succeeded only in alienating voters and radicalizing the Conservative party. The reforms manifested themselves most fully in a series of privatizations that were more extensive than anything that had gone before. In both countries, the key was that postwar structures had defined the Left and Right as adversaries rather than as partners in a quest for national economic growth. In both cases, the key "adversarial" elements of the postwar structure had been implemented by governments of the Left (and in some cases in Britain, demanded by the labor unions). And in both cases, because the socioeconomic transformation of the postwar period had moved most voters to the other side of the adversarial divide, neoliberal reformers could find and take advantage of electoral dissatisfaction with the status quo.

In France and West Germany the situation was reversed: French tax structures were more regressive, French industrial policy was more concerned with helping business than punishing it, and the French welfare state redistributed risks within classes rather than across classes; meanwhile labor density remained even lower than in the United States, and France remained one of the most inegalitarian countries in the developed world. In West Germany, too, a tax structure less concerned with redistribution and industrial policies in which capital, labor, and the state were corporatist partners rather than adversaries produced a pro-business political economy. Moreover, a history of consultative wage agreements kept strike activity much lower than in Britain, and thus unions never hit the extreme of unpopularity that they did in Britain, ruling out an electoral appeal based on antagonism to the unions. In both France and West Germany the Left had been excluded from the highest office for two decades (France from 1958 to 1981; West Germany from 1949 to 1969), so postwar structures were built with the goal of aggregate economic growth rather than redistribution between classes. In both cases the ruling right-wing governments had concentrated on an overarching nationalist goal—turning an agricultural country into an industrial one in France and turning a war-traumatized country into a peaceful and prosperous one in West Germany—that led to business-friendly policies and universal rather than redistributive welfare states. And in both cases, neoliberal reformers made little headway in the wake of the oil crisis because the structure of policies and policymaking prevented the emergence of an electoral dissatisfaction with the status quo in which neoliberalism could be anchored.

By "free market" or "neoliberal" policies, I mean taxation structures that favor capital accumulation over income redistribution, industrial policies that minimize the presence of the state in private industry,[1] and

1. "Industrial policies" are policies through which the state seeks to influence the day-to-day operation of firms, whether indirectly through legislation and regulation or directly through state ownership. I examine deregulation in the United States and West Germany, but privatization in the United Kingdom and France. I have chosen this bifurcated strategy because deregulation was the main event in American neoliberalism, whereas privatization was the most important element of British neoliberalism. Because France did have a significant nationalized sector and also witnessed the beginnings of privatization in this period, it makes most sense to compare it with the United Kingdom in this case. And because West Germany did not have a significant nationalized sector but did have extensive regulations, it makes most sense to compare it with the American case and ask why a deregulatory movement never

retrenchment in welfare spending. The history of postwar neoliberalism can be divided into three periods. The first, the prehistory, began after the Second World War, when state intervention increased in many spheres, and neoliberals were confined to study groups on the fringes of politics. The second period, the experimental phase of neoliberalism, began in 1973, when the economic difficulties unleashed by the first oil crisis led governments all over the world to reconsider their basic political-economic foundations and to experiment with reducing the size of the state in various ways. And the third period, a period of consolidation, extends from the late 1980s, when the coming of European unification strengthened the hand of European neoliberals in ways that remain to be worked out, to the present.

In this book I examine the second of these eras, the nearly two decades from the first oil crisis to the beginning of unification—the experimental phase of neoliberalism, when it was not at all clear in which direction politics would move in any of the countries. In this phase a pattern of divergence between the countries evolved, and more recent developments in each country have followed this pattern rather than fundamentally challenging it.[2]

In retrospect it is easy to believe that neoliberalism was predestined in the United States, and impossible in continental Europe. It is easy to identify the differences between the United States and Europe, to exaggerate them, to trace them back through history, and eventually to discover an unchanging national culture of self-reliance in the United States or of community and solidarity in France or Germany. But at the moment of divergence itself, these patterns were not at all clear. For example, in the 1970s a concerted effort was made in the United States to pass a policy of full employment and national economic planning, wage and price controls had been implemented, and a guaranteed income plan was on the political agenda. Meanwhile, a pro-market French president was abolishing price

caught fire there. The drawback to focusing thus on the main event is that this work does not provide a comprehensive, four-country comparison of any one aspect of industrial policy. This also explains why I find a similarity in industrial policy between the United States and the United Kingdom, whereas Vogel finds divergence: Vogel looks at regulation in both countries and concludes that in Britain it is much less adversarial. But the major state intervention in industrial policy in postwar Britain was not regulation but nationalization, and in that context Britain was much more adversarial.

2. Germany after reunification is an exception. The conclusion to chapter 3 examines the different political patterns unleashed by reunification.

controls and systematically cutting state subsidies to industry in an attempt to roll back state intervention, and in West Germany the future president of the Bundesbank was ghostwriting a supply-side paper that helped to bring the Right back into power. In no country was there, nor is there now, a monopoly of ideas; in each country the struggle over the proper limits of the state is a central political struggle, and it is a real struggle, with conflicted public opinion, ambivalent cultural rhetorics and practices, opposed interests, and minority traditions so strong that in each case solid scholarship suggests that the minority tradition is much more influential and vibrant than we think. Therefore, if we can identify enduring patterns of national practice, we need to ask what mechanisms in each country make it more likely that the struggle will be resolved in one direction rather than another.

The incorrect predictions of some of the most sophisticated scholars of an earlier generation should teach us first that our own moment may also be temporary. The divergence in patterns examined here may well end, as some predict, with the European states reforming their taxation and spending along American lines; it is also possible, as others argue, that the different models are different and equally stable "varieties of capitalism," or that pressures we do not yet fully understand will swing the United States toward a more interventionist mode. Nevertheless, whatever the outcome of the current struggles, the divergence examined here has lasted for a generation and is a historical phenomenon worthy of investigation in its own right. Even if it is not permanent, it has set the stage for whatever comes next, and it contributes to the current atmosphere of ambivalence in relations between the United States and Europe.

These four cases provide a range of settings on both the independent and dependent variables under consideration, and together the cases present a series of theoretical anomalies: First, federal states are usually less able to steer through great changes, because a multiplicity of veto points—sites in the decision-making process where actors can block change—makes it difficult to pass legislation that hurts anyone. Centralized states, on the other hand, are thought to be able to oversee great change because those who would resist such change lack access to any institutional means of blocking it. But in these four cases, the greatest degree of change was in a federal state (the United States) and the least in a centralized state (France). Second, the power of labor is one predictor of social democratic policies; but one of the "strong labor" countries among these four saw a great degree of neoliberal change (the United Kingdom), while the other did not (West Germany), and one of the "weak labor" countries saw great change (the United States), while the other did not (France). Finally, the two countries that saw the most capital flight and the most rhetoric of globalization during their neoliberal periods (France and West Germany) did not see the kind of neoliberal change experienced in countries where globalization was not yet part of the rhetoric during their neoliberal periods (the United States and United Kingdom).

Obviously these counterinstances by themselves do not "disprove" the theories of veto points, power resources, or capital flight, since these are all probabilistic theories. But, as Paige (1999) writes, the historical investigation of theoretical anomalies—cases that do not fit the pattern predicted by a theory—can be a fruitful method of conducting historical research that is informed by the attempt to learn from history, and that in turn sharpens our theoretical understandings: Anomalies show us that there is something else going on that we need to understand.

What Has Changed?

Despite the rhetoric of "the Reagan Revolution" and "the Thatcher Revolution," there has been little "retrenchment" of the welfare state and very little "rolling back of government." What has changed is that the *growth* of the size of the state has been halted: this is, as we will see, a considerable achievement, given the many pressures toward growth. Figures 1–5 present data on government size as measured by (1) tax revenue as a percentage of gross domestic product (GDP); (2) government consumption as a

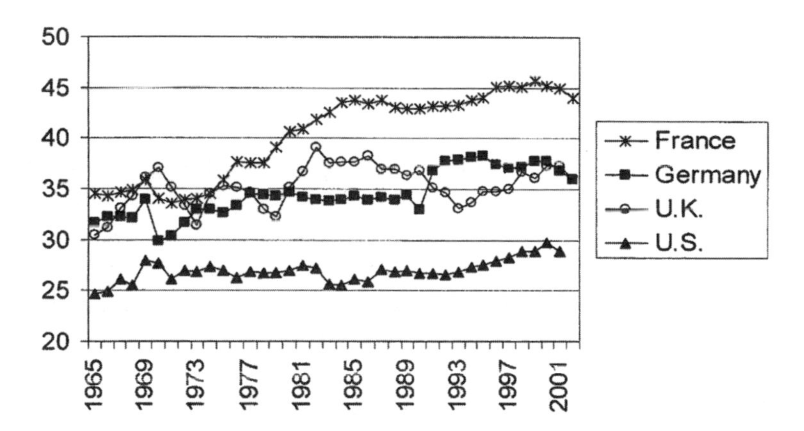

FIGURE 1. Total tax revenue (% GDP)
Source: Organization for Economic Cooperation and Development (OECD) 1965–2002 (*Revenue Statistics of OECD Member Countries*).

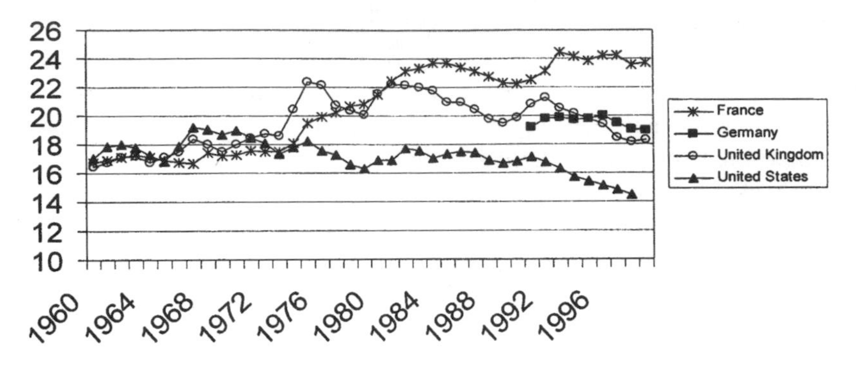

FIGURE 2. General government final consumption expenditure (% GDP)
Source: World Bank 1960–1999 (*World Development Indicators*).

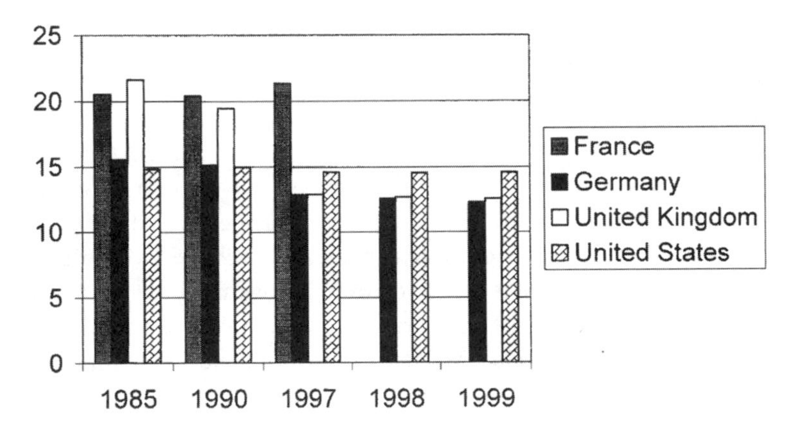

FIGURE 3. Public-sector labor force (% total labor force)
Source: OECD 2001 ("Public Sector Pay and Employment Data").

percentage of GDP (all goods and services that the government purchases directly, plus wages and salaries of all government employees and fixed capital costs); (3) public sector labor force as a percentage of the total labor force; (4) an Organization for Economic Cooperation and Development (OECD) index of government control of industry (summarizing public ownership and state involvement in business operations); and (5) social policy spending levels as a percentage of GDP.

These figures reveal the following facts. (1) The growth of taxation levels has been steady in France but volatile in the United Kingdom and United States, resulting in significantly higher tax levels in France. (2)

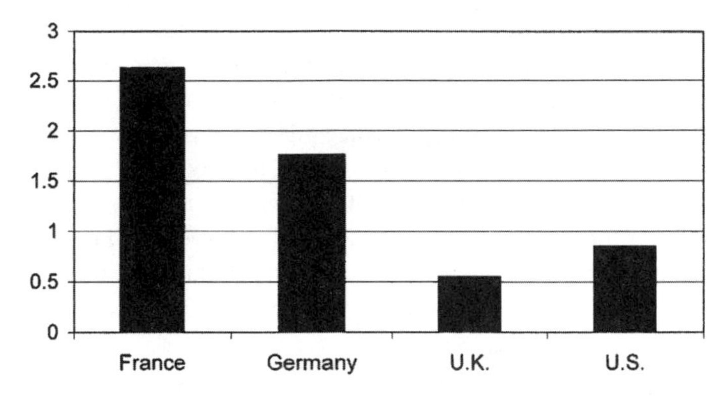

FIGURE 4. OECD index of state control in industry
Source: Nicoletti, Scarpetta, and Boylaud 2000.

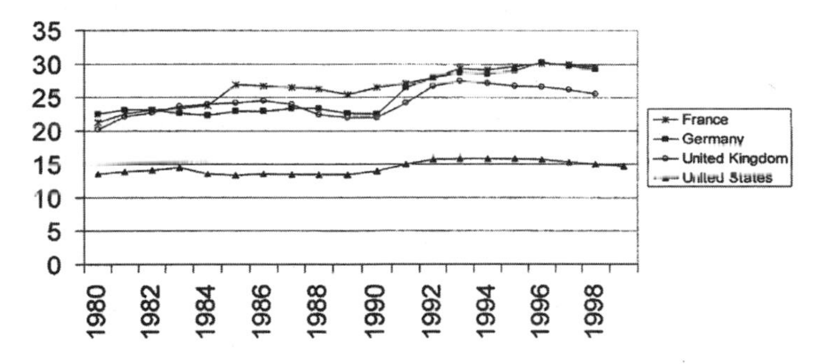

FIGURE 5. Public social expenditure (% GDP)
Source: OECD 1980–1999 (*Social Expenditure Database: Public Expenditure*).

Tax revenues had been holding steady in West Germany, but the costs of unification pushed them up. (3) The presence of government in industry, as measured by its expenses, has declined in the United States and, to a lesser degree, in the United Kingdom, while it has remained stable in Germany during the years for which data are available and has gone up in France. (4) France continues to have a larger public-sector labor force than the others, and the British public-sector labor force has seen the largest decline, so that the figures for Britain, Germany, and the United States are now similar.[3] (5) France scores highest on an index of public ownership and state involvement in business, while the United States and

3. Note that these figures include defense: excluding defense, the United States would have the smallest public-sector labor force relative to the total labor force.

United Kingdom are lowest. (6) Public social expenditure as a percentage of GDP has risen the most in France, from around 20 percent of GDP in 1980 to around 30 percent two decades later, and it has risen in the United Kingdom from 20 percent to 25 percent, while holding steady in the United States at around 15 percent of GDP. (7) In Germany, social expenditures had been keeping pace with the United Kingdom until the moment of unification; after that the German pattern has followed the French.

There is much debate in the literature on how to measure the degree of rollback of state intervention, particularly in welfare policy. Although the amounts spent on welfare policy have not significantly decreased (Esping-Andersen 1999; Huber and Stephens 2001; Pierson 1994), there is debate over whether stability in the measures is, because of an inherent bias toward growth or because of increasing demand, actually evidence of retrenchment. For example, Esping-Andersen (1999) argues that in the face of new social risks, lack of growth in social spending indicates that the welfare state is less of a force for security and stability than it has ever been—that is, that welfare provisions have not kept up with the need for them (see also Clayton and Pontusson 1998). Korpi and Palme (1998) argue that, with regard to a traditional goal of welfare state policy—full employment—the rise of large-scale unemployment in Europe without a corresponding rise in spending indicates substantial retrenchment. Rhodes (1996; see also Rhodes and van Apeldoorn 1997) argues that if we control for the "inflationary pressures" on the welfare state—particularly the demographics of an aging labor force driving up spending on pensions and health care, and the "trading" of inflation for unemployment—then there has, in fact, been substantial retrenchment. As Esping-Andersen puts it, there is a "growing disjuncture between existing institutional arrangements and emerging risk profiles" (1999, 146). Despite maintaining levels of spending, the welfare state is a different thing today than it was thirty years ago, because it does not attempt to cover the new risks that have arisen in the last decades, including the increasing "flexibility" and insecurity of the labor market, workers' need for greater technological training to be able to compete in the labor market, and the consequences of an unstable work history for the accumulation of pensions. Finally, Hacker (2004) shows that changes in policy implementation can add up to a much weaker welfare commitment even when explicit attempts to change policy have failed.

As Pierson comments, "measuring the extent of [welfare state] retrenchment is a half-empty/half-full question" (1994, 5). Although this debate on measurement has been conducted primarily with reference to the welfare state, it applies equally well to questions of taxation: the amount of tax revenue that a state collects increases automatically when GDP is growing, because economic growth pushes people into higher tax brackets and allows them to purchase more luxury goods, which are more heavily taxed. Moreover, in inflationary periods taxes that are calculated in nominal terms automatically increase the percentage of revenue as a proportion of GDP. For these reasons, rising tax revenue is automatic under economic growth or inflation, and an absence of increase in the tax revenue measures is evidence of active tax cuts. Similar automatic pressures may exist in industrial policy (once states begin to regulate or subsidize industries, interest groups may arise—the regulators, or the industries themselves—that can fight for ever-greater state intervention, but this is difficult to prove and certainly not as automatic as the inflationary pressures in the other two domains), but it is not necessary to belabor the point. The attempt to define how much change has occurred is interpretive, depending on a series of analytical judgments upon which there is no consensus.

As if this did not complicate the matter enough, we must bear in mind that the aggregate figures hide important qualitative distinctions: first, the most important legacy of the neoliberal period under Reagan was the introduction of large-scale deficits as a sustained feature of American politics. The recent performance of George W. Bush's administration underscores the degree to which major deficits have become routine in the United States, and the fact of deficits can make discussion of spending increases more difficult.

Second, the aggregate figures show that West Germany posted figures similar to those of Britain in almost all policy domains until the years of reunification. This indicates that West Germany, too, had a weak neoliberalism, as discussed in chapter 3. However, the figures hide two facts: the change in *shape* of the British tax structure under Thatcher (it was made more regressive), and the remarkable degree of privatization that has taken place in Britain. Privatization is the policy most closely associated today with the term "Thatcherism," and was the one policy that has not, to date, been rolled back; indeed, it has been copied all over the world. But because West Germany never had a large nationalized sector, comparative figures miss this aspect of British neoliberalism.

Although the figures show France as posting high levels of state presence in all dimensions, France too has embraced a slow neoliberalism, the hallmark of which has been the privatization of a large part of the

TABLE 1 **Policymaking episodes examined in tax policy, industrial policy, and welfare state policy**

	Tax policy	Industrial policy (deregulation in U.S. and West Germany; privatization in Britain and France)	Welfare state policy
United States	1981 Economic Recovery Tax Act	Environmental deregulation	Omnibus Budget Reconciliation Act
United Kingdom	1981 budget	Privatization of British Telecom	Council house sales
West Germany	1987 tax cut	Shopping hours deregulation; labor market deregulation; (lack of) environmental deregulation	Health care reform
France	No major tax cut attempts in this period.	Chirac: privatizations; Giscard: punitive industrial policy	No major attempts to cut social spending in this period

nationalized sector. The difference is that the privatizations in Britain occurred more rapidly and were more market-oriented. France has been selling off its state holdings, but it has taken twenty years to accomplish what Britain did in three years; and many of those privatizations were conducted in remarkably "statist" ways, with the state deciding who was allowed to purchase how much.

Because of these difficulties in measuring neoliberalism, in this work I focus on *policymaking episodes* rather than global statistics. Within each country, I identify a period in which a government of the Right did initiate a series of neoliberal reforms, and I focus within that period on the policies that were the most important as judged by historians of the period. I then trace the process by which these specific policies arrived on the political agenda, and whether they were eventually passed or were defeated. Table 1 identifies the episodes within each country that are the focus of the following chapters.[4]

Much of the existing work on neoliberalism is split into separate streams concentrating on one particular policy domain. The welfare state as a distinct object of study has received the lion's share of attention, and the literature on that topic is comprehensive and sophisticated. A smaller but

4. I examine the 1981 ERTA rather than the 1986 tax cut because the latter was intended to be revenue-neutral; it was the former that was instrumental in widening the deficit and inaugurating the American era of deficit spending.

still considerable body of work examines industrial policy. The politics of taxation is remarkably little understood, despite the centrality of taxation to modern politics, and understanding all three domains—taxation, industrial policy, and welfare state policy—as part of an integrated whole is rare.

In this book I examine all three together, as all three realms are analytically linked: taxes and spending are obviously related, not only because taxes pay for the welfare state and the welfare state justifies taxes (not all of which are spent on purchases as popular as social policy), but also in more subtle ways: for example, the *manner* in which revenue is raised (and not just the total amount of revenue) can have a significant influence on whether spending can be cut. A decoupled process, where spending and taxing decisions are conducted separately, is much more fragile than a coupled process, because it allows politicians committed to welfare cuts to cut taxes first in order to constrain spending later (Steinmo 1989, 1993). Thus, considering taxation can significantly alter our understanding of welfare state retrenchment and its potential path: for example, Pierson (1994) argues that welfare states are resilient because cutbacks in spending impose losses on targeted groups who then protest the cuts, forcing politicians into strategies of "blame avoidance" rather than "credit claiming." But as Pierson himself acknowledges, in the domain of taxation, politicians can engage in the usual politics of credit claiming by offering tax cuts; given certain political circumstances, this is an easy and popular strategy, and can create financial pressures on the welfare state that would not otherwise have existed (as was the case in West Germany and seems to be the case in the United States today). Therefore, if we include taxation in our field of vision, we begin to doubt the resilience of the welfare state and to look for the broader political circumstances that determine what happens when the popularity of the welfare state meets the unpopularity of taxes. If we understand that the politics of taxation and the politics of welfare states are empirically linked, our attention shifts from investigations of the inherent features that make welfare states popular, to questions of when and why the popularity of welfare states is *salient*.

Aside from the causal links, looking at the welfare state through the lens of taxation can change our entire perspective on the welfare state. Scholars of taxation have long known what students of the welfare state are only now starting to discuss: that the most generous welfare states, such as those of France and Sweden, are based on regressive taxes. The American tax structure, on the other hand, is based on income taxes and is therefore more progressive than those of most European countries. This simple observation, if followed to its logical conclusions, forces a reconsideration not only of the implicit moral ranking in much welfare state literature, but also of the political strategies of the contemporary Left and Right.

Less obvious but equally pertinent are the links between industrial policy and the other two realms: changes in labor laws that make the exercise of labor power more difficult can cut away the political sources of support for the welfare state, and privatization of public assets can create a class of small property holders with a stake in lower property taxes. Taking this interlinked view again changes our perspective on how to judge recent developments. For example, scholars often cite the extensive privatization of the French economy over the last two decades as evidence that France, too, has embraced the free market. But from a broader perspective, it is not at all clear that this shift of ownership has had much effect on the actual conduct of economic activity in France: taxation levels and "social costs" still make France one of the most expensive places to run a business, whether it is state owners or private entrepreneurs paying those costs.

In addition to these theoretical and analytical reasons for considering the development of free market politics as a whole, there is a strong substantive reason: The politicians involved in these efforts themselves saw their goals as reaching across policy domains; although cuts in the welfare state were a central part of the stated agenda, they were supported by a theory of economic growth that extended to tax and industrial policy realms.[5] For all of these reasons, the movement toward halting the growth of state intervention should be conceptualized as one phenomenon in the evolution of modern capitalism, which manifested itself in several policy domains.

Finally, as I argue below, examining all three domains together reveals a remarkable feature of postwar American and European political economy: at the level of policy, America and Great Britain saw a much greater degree of "class war" in the postwar period than did France and West Germany. Because the Left was out of power for long stretches of time in the latter, these countries engaged in a nationalist project of rebuilding that stretched across all three domains examined here; meanwhile, the United States and Britain saw adversarial policies in all of these domains.

5. In the British case, it also extended to monetarist policy, which chapter 2 examines in connection with tax policy.

Previous Explanations

The empirical literature attempting to explain the rise of free market policies in one or several countries is large. In general, we can identify four clusters of explanation: (1) those that point to globalization, particularly capital flight, as causing a "race to the bottom" in social protections; (2) class-based explanations, such as those that point to business-group power, arguing that the crisis and the resulting decline in profits mobilized business actors to define themselves as a class and push for policies that preserved their class interest; (3) explanations that identify the rise of neoliberal ideas, particularly monetarism and supply-side economics, as causing the rise of neoliberalism; and (4) explanations that ascribe the differences in the patterns of the different countries to differences in "national cultures."

Although the globalization and the business-group explanations may apply to developments at later periods, for the time period we are examining—the two decades from the oil crisis to the coming of the European Union (EU)—the weight of the empirical evidence is clearly against these explanations. I define the globalization argument to consist of two claims: first, that increase in cross border capital flows forces state actors to decrease taxes on capital in an effort to attract mobile capital; and, second, that trade openness increases the pressure on state actors to decrease taxes and regulations on domestic firms so that these firms will be able to compete with low-cost imports.

The effect of globalization has been studied most systematically with regard to policies of taxation and the welfare state, and although debate is ongoing, a consensus seems to be emerging that globalization has not had the effect of undermining revenue collection or social protections. A thorough review is found in Hay (2001),[6] who notes that several assumptions in the thesis that capital will seek lower taxation are not borne out, including the assumption that the greatest returns to capital are to be found where labor costs are lowest, and that welfare states have no positive externalities for investors. Clearly investors would prefer lower taxes, all else equal; but the services those taxes purchase *make* all else unequal, in that they create stable government, paved roads, cooperative unions, and healthy and educated workers, and investors may decide that these benefits are worth the higher taxes. Indeed, some scholars (e.g., Rodrik 1997; Garrett 1998) argue that globalization may lead to *increased* welfare spending, because

6. See also Boix 1998; Genschel 2002; Hicks 1999; Locke and Kochan 1995; Swank 1998.

the risks associated with an open economy will lead to political demands for greater protection; Katzenstein (1985) shows through a historical examination that Scandinavian governments did increase welfare spending in response to trade openness (but see Iversen and Cusack 2000).

Although the debate is not yet resolved for the general question, it is easier to resolve for the specific time period we are examining here and for the four countries we are considering, because the *timing* of the variables as required by the theory is incompatible with the evidence: capital flight did not precede but followed Reagan's and Thatcher's periods in office (in the Reagan case, investors clearly fled because of the large deficits), and capital was "flying" France in the early to mid-1970s but did not trigger neoliberal policies (see figs. 6–8). As for trade openness, imports have constituted only about 10 percent of the American market, and most imports in Europe come from other "high cost" countries.

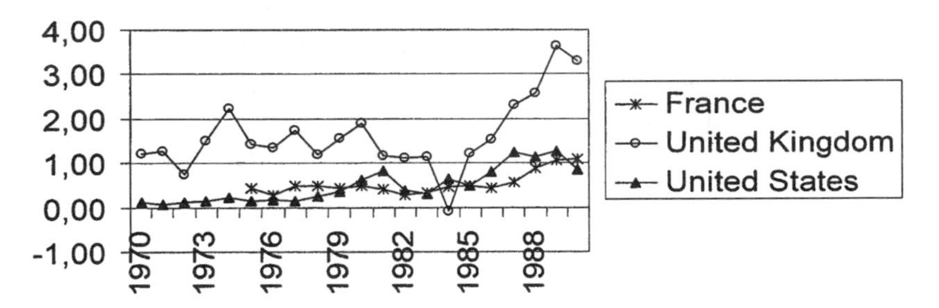

FIGURE 6. Foreign direct investment, net inflows (% GDP)
Source: World Bank 1960–1999 (*World Development Indicators*).

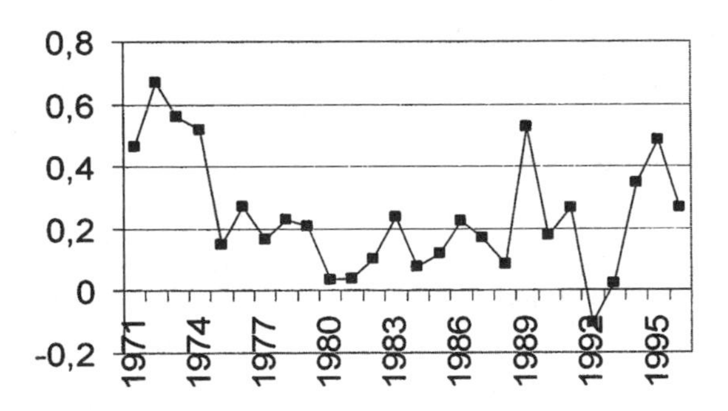

FIGURE 7. Foreign direct investment in Germany (% GDP)
Source: International Monetary Fund (IMF) 1971–1996 (*Balance of Payment Statistics Yearbook*); OECD 1974–1997 (*National Accounts*).

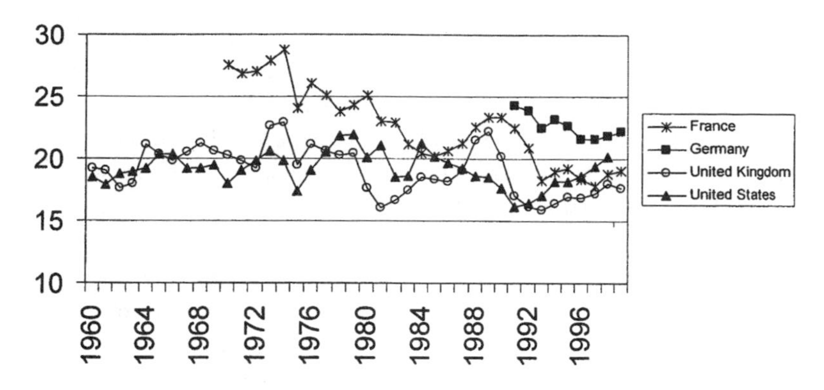

FIGURE 8. Gross capital formation (% GDP)
Source: World Bank 1960–1999 (*World Development Indicators*).

Hay (2001) argues that although globalization may not have caused retrenchment, impressions of the need for international competitiveness did. On this, we can turn to the historical record: Reagan and (especially) Thatcher did point to the experience of other countries, particularly, at the time, Germany and Japan, but they made these comparisons in general terms of economic competition, not in specific terms of capital flight or trade openness. In general, impressions of economic competitiveness were important, particularly in the European countries, which constantly compared themselves to each other; but these were not linked to policies of capital flight and trade openness until a few years *after* the bulk of the Reagan and Thatcher reforms. The rhetoric of globalization, and appeals by politicians to globalization, are phenomena of the late 1980s and 1990s, partly a result of decreasing regulations regarding capital mobility. This meant that this rhetoric was much more prominent during West Germany's neoliberal moment in the late 1980s than it had been under Reagan or Thatcher, whose neoliberal moments came in the early 1980s—even though Kohl's neoliberalism was much less successful.[7]

The business-groups explanation has been elaborated most systematically for the United States. Because chapter 1 is largely devoted to assessing this explanation in the U.S. case, I simply summarize the argument here:

7. Of course, the fact that the oil crisis of 1973 was the trigger for many of these events points to the importance of the globalization *of production* (if not the globalization of investment or trade) in the phenomena under investigation. But note that all four countries felt the effects of the oil crisis, yet only two moved in a sustained neoliberal direction.

business-group influence was important at several moments, but business groups in the United States did not want the large, across-the-board income tax cuts that were passed (they too feared the deficits the cuts would produce), and they were not pushing the cuts in means-tested programs that were implemented (because the antipoverty programs that were cut were such a small portion of the budget). The area where business groups had the most influence is in deregulation, but even here, the timing of the policies suggests that business-group power cannot explain the whole story (because deregulation started before business groups began to organize and ended at the height of their power); moreover, the circumstances under which and manner in which business groups gained the victory were limited and unusual.

A recent variant on the business-groups argument is the "varieties of capitalism" thesis, which argues that high taxation, high welfare state spending, and an interventionist industrial policy can add up to an equally efficient and equally stable alternative form of capitalism (Hall and Soskice 2001). This literature sees firms as the central actors in generating persistent differences across countries; the argument is that firms in countries specializing in high-quality, high-tech, high-cost products that require highly skilled labor need, above all, a predictable political-economic environment. Firms in such countries will agree to the welfare protections and labor regulations necessary to convince labor to invest in the years of training necessary for such production. The varieties of capitalism thesis is a powerful and provocative synthesis of institutional and political-economy approaches; however, at least for the countries and the time period examined here, the empirical evidence for this thesis based on the behavior of employers is not strong. Not only were business interests opposed to the income tax cuts in the United States (the paradigmatic "liberal" market economy), but they largely wanted *more* neoliberalism in West Germany (the paradigmatic "coordinated" market economy). I discuss the varieties of capitalism thesis and the problems of its economic determinism further in connection with the German case (see chapter 3).

Another version of the class-based argument might suggest that the strength of labor is the crucial variable. Transformations in class structure do have much to do with the emergence of neoliberalism, and the different ways in which a strong labor movement was incorporated in West Germany and excluded in Britain are crucial to the developments there (as explained further below; see Collier and Collier 1991); nevertheless, there is no straightforward link between the strength of labor and policy in

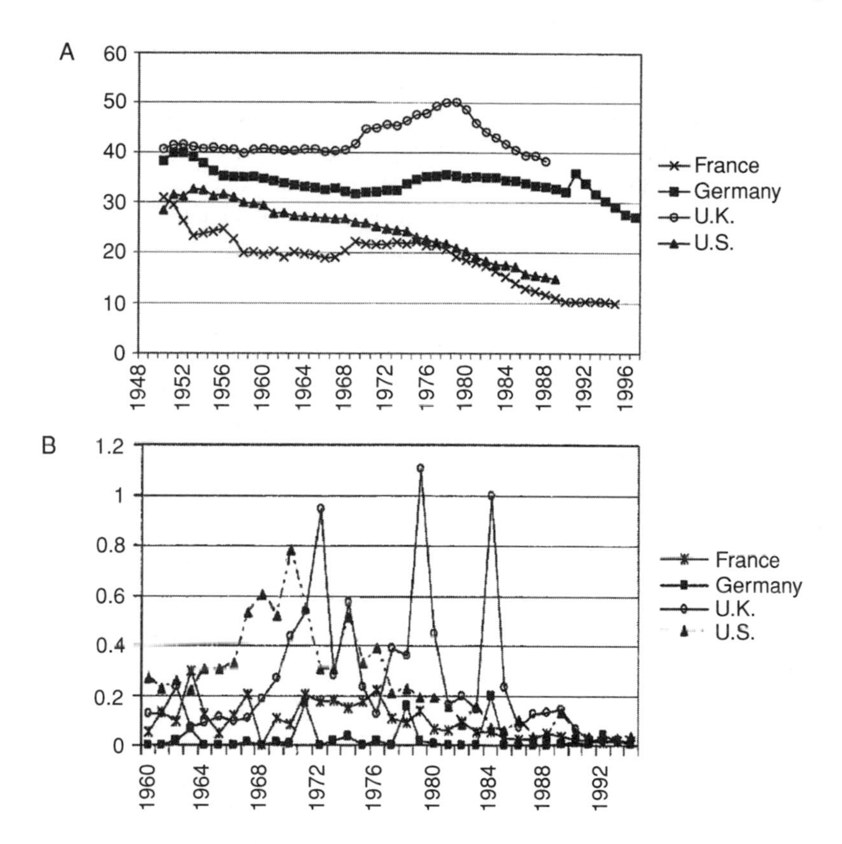

FIGURE 9. (A) Net union density; (B) working days lost per thousand workers
Sources: (A) Golden, Lange, and Wallerstein 2002; (B) Huber, Ragin, and Stephens 1997, from data provided in International Labour Organization 2002.

these countries in this time period. The two panels of figure 9 show that, as measured by (A) union density and (B) workdays lost, labor was strongest in Britain, where there was a great degree of neoliberalism, and weakest in France, where there was very little—the opposite of the expected pattern. Similarly, the explanation that social democratic parties sustain interventionist policies cannot explain these cases, because all four countries saw extended periods in which parties of the Right, favorable to free market measures, were in power after the oil crisis: France from 1974 to 1981; the United Kingdom from 1979 to 1997, the United States from 1981 to 1992; and West Germany from 1982 to 1998. Each party made some attempt at neoliberal reform, but in France and West Germany the attempts did not go as far as in the United States and United Kingdom.

As to the "neoliberal ideas" explanation—that ideas of monetarism and supply-side economics carried the day—a look at the historical record shows that most economists rejected the ideas that the Thatcher and Reagan administrations advocated. For example, in the United Kingdom, as Thatcher was about to pass monetarist policies in 1981, 364 academic economists—a large sector of the British academic economics establishment—signed a letter urging her not to do it. Supply-side economics and the kind of monetarism practiced by Thatcher were doctrines that most economists did not subscribe to. Thus, the "ideas" explanation by itself cannot take us very far, because we must still explain why ideas that very few people actually believed became so politically powerful.

One of the most sophisticated recent exponents of the argument that ideas are important in politics is Mark Blyth (2002), who argues that the rise and fall of Keynesianism in both the United States and Sweden are best explained through an examination of economic ideas. But Blyth's own evidence does not fit this thesis. The U.S. case, with its adoption of Keynesianism in the 1920s and 1930s, and its rejection in the 1970s, provides evidence that the particular ideas won because they provided political benefits to politicians who adopted them. For example, Blyth notes that Hoover called a conference of economists to suggest policies to deal with the Depression, and that the conference produced laissez-faire ideas. But as Blyth writes, "[G]iven that the depression showed no signs of curing itself, and the idea of the depression as a therapeutic smacked of being patronizing, the deployment of such *laissez-faire* economic ideas confined American academic economists to the margins of debate and influence for most of the 1920s and 1930s. Given the *practical inadequacy* of such ideas, Hoover *sought a rationale* for a more active policy" (52; emphasis added). And, as chapter 1 shows in greater detail, the *ideas* of supply-side economics never convinced more than a handful of people in the 1970s and early 1980s in the United States; the real question is why this small number of people acquired such disproportionate power. This is an argument closer to the structural argument of Skocpol and Weir's (1985) analysis, which found that particular structures were more or less conducive to experimenting with Keynesian policies during the Great Depression—that is, that structures determine whether ideas will be successful. Blyth writes, "[R]emove the ideas of business from the practices of the Conservatives in the 1990s, and the policy responses . . . make no sense" (261). But this is too easy; what we actually need to show, when arguing for the importance of ideas, is that if we could "remove" the ideas, they would not be regenerated from the structural settings (as seems to have happened in the Laffer curve episode under Reagan as well as the monetarism episode under Thatcher, discussed below). The materialist argument, after all, is not that people act *without* ideas—as if they were robots—but that certain material structures prove advantageous to the spread of certain ideas.

The ideas explanation has been quite popular in explanations of Thatcherism, and so chapter 2 considers in more detail what we can learn from looking at ideas and what the limits of such strategies of explanation are. My argument, briefly, is that even quite narrowly defined economic ideas are polyvalent and even self-contradictory, so that the same idea may come to mean quite different things at different times or to different audiences. In this situation, material and institutional incentives often determine which version of an idea prevails and is implemented, and this is indeed what happened in the Thatcher episode. There is a folk theory of the neoliberal revolution that places academic economists at its center, but the historical record shows that academic economists overwhelmingly rejected the policies that both Reagan and Thatcher actually implemented. Instead, the process involved politicians settling upon specific policies for their own reasons and then seeking out those who could provide intellectual legitimacy for those policies, even if they were at the fringes of their profession (see Reay 2004, for a thorough analysis of the American economics profession and the place of neoliberal ideas within it).

Finally, a word about the "national culture" explanation, which holds that the United States and United Kingdom saw neoliberal changes because their national cultures were more receptive to free market claims, whereas the cultures of solidarity and egalitarianism in France and Germany resisted the free market. This explanation has been most popular among analysts attempting to explain why the French welfare state resists reform—indeed, there seems to be an elective affinity between studying France and favoring culturalist explanations—so I examine it most systematically in chapter 4. In brief, I argue that national culture arguments are problematic because, despite differences between the countries, there is no empirical evidence for the hegemony of a particular cultural strain in any of these countries, and diffusion across national boundaries has been a persistent postwar trend. We see this diffusion, for example, in the international origins of the Mont Pèlerin Society, the scholarly group founded by Austrian Friedrich Hayek that represents the formal beginnings of intellectual neoliberalism. The society's members included scholars and political actors from not only America (Milton Friedman, Frank Knight) and Britain (Lionel Robbins) but also Germany (Walter Eucken, Wilhelm Röpke, Ludwig Erhard) and France (Bertrand de Jouvenel, Jacques Rueff), among other countries. The networks through which neoliberalism as a movement was built were international, and they brought the ideas of neoliberalism to all four countries.

Moreover, the scholars who think most carefully about culture—literary theorists, cultural critics, and anthropologists on the one hand and psychologists on the other—are themselves skeptical of the idea that culture is a coherent whole pushing in one or another direction. The consensus developed among literary scholars over the last thirty years seems to be that cultural objects (values, beliefs, norms, symbols) are subject to interpretation, that it is not possible to settle upon one "correct" interpretation, and that therefore multiple interpretations of the same cultural object will proliferate. Culture is reproduced through symbols, and the link between a symbol and what it symbolizes is historically and culturally variable; this means that culture is never like the unambiguous blueprints of engineers, but more like the polysemic expressions of poets, and can underpin a wide variety of actual policies. (The phenomenon of shifting signifiers appears most clearly in the story of deregulation in the American case, where the meaning of the word *deregulation* changed in line with the interests of the powerful.) Cognitive psychologists, too, have moved away from a totalizing view of culture. As chapter 4 discusses in more detail, recent research "refutes the notion that people acquire a culture by imbibing it (and no other) through socialization; . . . explains the capacity of individuals to participate in multiple cultural traditions, even when those traditions contain inconsistent elements; . . . [and] establishes the capacity of people to maintain distinctive and inconsistent action frames, which can be invoked in response to particular contextual cues" (DiMaggio 1997, 267–68).

The national culture arguments rely on a thin notion of culture that cultural critics and psychologists have rejected. Perhaps the most convincing refutation of these arguments, however, is the simple fact that the political-economic structures of these four countries were quite different from what the national culture argument predicts: the United States had the most progressive tax structure and the most antibusiness industrial policy of the four, and France had the most regressive tax structure and the most reverse-redistributive welfare state of the four.

Institutions and Neoliberalism

The lack of fit between the predictions of these various theories and the historical record results from a limitation that these frameworks share: Explanations of neoliberalism are still dominated by a "society-centered" perspective, that is, a perspective in which the institutions of public decision-making themselves play no role (Skocpol 1985). Despite the quite different locus of pressure identified by each of the arguments above—the pressures of global economic integration, the rise of new ideas, the power of social interests, and so forth—all of these explanations share the assumption that the process of policymaking itself is a straightforward conveyor of interests, preferences, or ideas. This is surprising, as over the last two decades we have learned a great deal about how institutions, particularly the institutions of the state, are central to social and policy change. "Historical institutionalist" scholars have shown that (1) institutions structure the incentives of actors in ways that cannot be reduced to the social origins of the actors, and institutions aggregate social preferences and pressures in ways that cannot be predicted from the strength of those preferences and pressures; and (2) institutions generate feedback effects: previous policies set up a structure of incentives and resources that has an independent causal effect on later policies ("policies create politics"), and, at the extreme, patterns established during moments of crisis can influence events long afterward, evidencing "path dependence."[8]

This book offers an explanation of neoliberalism built on these two concepts. (1) In the immediate postwar period, France and West Germany, ruled by politicians of the Right, developed decision-making structures that subordinated political conflict to either *academic expertise* (in the case of France) or *corporatist decision-making structures* (in the case of West Germany). These institutions allowed the two governments to resist and transform the new social pressures arising from the oil crisis. In the United States and United Kingdom, however, which saw a greater degree of alternation between Left and Right in government, political conflict was instantiated in the political parties, and (in Britain) in the labor movement. In the United States, political conflict intensified when the weakening of party systems created a system of "entrepreneurial politicians" (Aldrich and Niemi 1996) who sought out new issues with which to mobilize electoral and financial resources, even when no social group was doing so—that is, the autonomous incentives of politicians within a changed institutional setting contributed an independent causal effect to the outcome. In the United Kingdom, an increasingly militant and

8. See Laitin 1985; Mahoney 2000; Pierson 1993, 1994, 2000; Pierson and Skocpol 2002; Skocpol 1985, 1992; Skocpol and Weir 1985; Steinmo 1993; Steinmo, Thelen, and Longstreth 1992.

unincorporated labor movement alienated the public and moved the Conservative party to the right. The adversarial political structures in both countries meant that politicians jumped on the conflicts arising from the oil crisis for their own purposes.

In addition, (2) in the postwar period the United States and Britain implemented *adversarial policies*—policies that punish business and divide the middle and working classes from the poor—and these proved fragile. By adversarial policies I mean in the American case progressive taxation, antibusiness regulation, and targeted welfare policies; and in the British case, progressive taxation, political steering of the nationalized industries, and targeted welfare policies. In contrast, France implemented policies of regressive taxation, nationalization in the interest of modernization, and welfare policies that actually gave a greater proportion of transfer payments to the more wealthy—what I call "pro-growth" policies, because they represent the strong state's commitment to an overarching nationalist project of modernization rather than redistribution. West Germany had a taxation structure that was less regressive than that of France, but more regressive than those of the United States and Britain. Some regulatory policies were adversarial, but in one crucial domain—environmental regulation—the pre-1973 structure was marked by self-regulation by business. The West German welfare state, however, was almost as redistributive as the British. In accordance with this intermediate position between the extreme pro-growth policies of France, and the extreme adversarial policies of Britain and the United States, West Germany saw a greater degree of neoliberal change than France, but a lesser degree than Britain and the United States. In the early postwar years West Germany, like France, was also for many years ruled by a Right that was intent on a nationalist project of rebuilding; however, the right-wing party included a strong and influential leftist segment. Out of this mixed political pattern came policies and a decision-making structure that were adversarial enough to generate neoliberal proposals, but pro-growth enough that these proposals were by and large defeated.

I characterize the two postwar models of political economy that resulted as "political economy as justice" versus "political economy as nation-building." In the United Kingdom and the United States, where the postwar period saw regular alternations of power between two major parties, decisions on taxation, industrial policy, and welfare state policy were often made by politicians from the party more committed to economic redistribution and followed the logic that the goal of political economy is justice: to redistribute from rich to poor, to protect workers and consumers, to lift people from poverty. The underlying model of redistribution was *charity*—those not at risk protecting those at risk. In France and West Germany in the postwar period, where the Left was excluded from power for twenty years,[9] decisions on taxation, industrial policy, and welfare state policy were made largely by politicians from the party less committed to economic redistribution and followed the logic that the goal of political economy was to rebuild the nation after the war. Their decisions, therefore, led to taxation structures that favored productive investment, nationalized industries managed with the goal of efficiency rather than full employment, and welfare states that redistributed within rather than across classes. The underlying model of redistribution was *insurance*: collective protection against risks that affect everyone. Although both countries followed this logic, for reasons examined below, the pattern was stronger in France than in West Germany.

The argument that the United States had more progressive and antibusiness policies is not new, but it always seems to come as a surprise: Sven Steinmo (1989, 1993) recorded his wonder at discovering that the United States had a more progressive tax regime, resting on progressive income taxes and taxing capital more heavily than Britain or even the welfare paradise of Sweden. In this he was following up an insight of Harold Wilensky (see Steinmo 1989) that other scholars have continued to confirm. Most recently, Peter Lindert has collected evidence showing that the European welfare states tax capital and property more heavily than the "liberal" regimes of Britain and the United States, and that while the large welfare states rely on regressive sales taxes, the United States relies to a much greater extent on capital and income taxes, which are progressive. The four panels of figure 10 depict the tax structure in the four countries, and those of figure 11 show that, comparatively, the United States and United Kingdom rely to a greater extent on progressive taxes—income and property taxes—while West Germany and France rely to a greater extent on regressive taxes—sales taxes and payroll taxes (OECD, various years; Lindert 2004; see also Kato 2003). Tables 2 and 3 present figures on

9. Note that the strength of the Communists divided the French Left between Socialists and Communists, so that the right ruled from 1958 to 1981. Thus, in France, the preference of a minority of voters for an extreme Left position in fact contributed to the hold of the Right on power. This is a stunning demonstration of part of the institutionalist insight that the procedures by which preferences are aggregated into power can be more important to the final outcome than the preferences themselves.

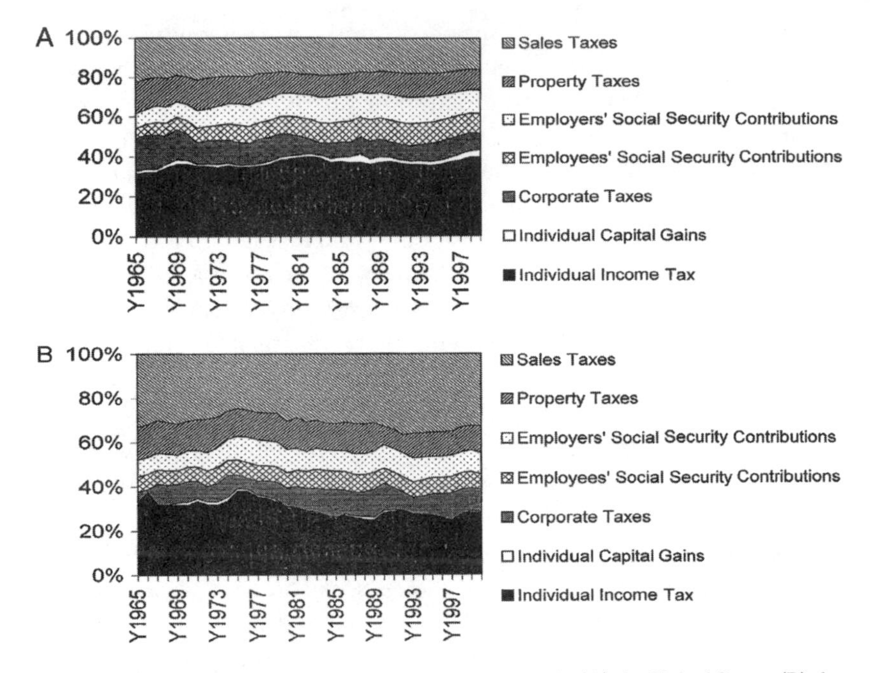

FIGURE 10. Tax types as a percentage of total tax revenue in (A) the United States; (B) the United Kingdom; (C) France (individual capital gains taxes are so proportionately small that they are invisible in the figure); and (D) Germany (no individual capital gains tax in this period)
Source: OECD 1965–2002 (*Revenue Statistics of OECD Member Countries*).

effective tax rates and tax ratios (see also Swank and Steinmo 2002). Although the methods of calculation and the results are slightly different, the tables show that the United States and Britain tax capital at higher rates, and labor and consumption at lower rates, than France and Germany, and that personal income taxes are much lower in France than in the other three countries.[10] (All data include state, local, and federal taxes.)

In industrial policy, David Vogel's study of regulation notes that "[t]he United States remains exceptional, but, at least with respect to [regulation], this exceptionalism is precisely the opposite of what

10. Effective tax rates and tax ratios take exemptions and refunds into account. I do not present simple tax rates here because they can be highly misleading. A tax structure is composed of three elements: tax rates (how much is taxed), the tax base (who must pay the tax), and tax exemptions (any special circumstances in which the tax does not apply). When rates are high, the politics of taxation is largely the politics of obtaining exemptions. Simple tax rates can therefore become meaningless symbols, and effective tax rates and tax ratios are

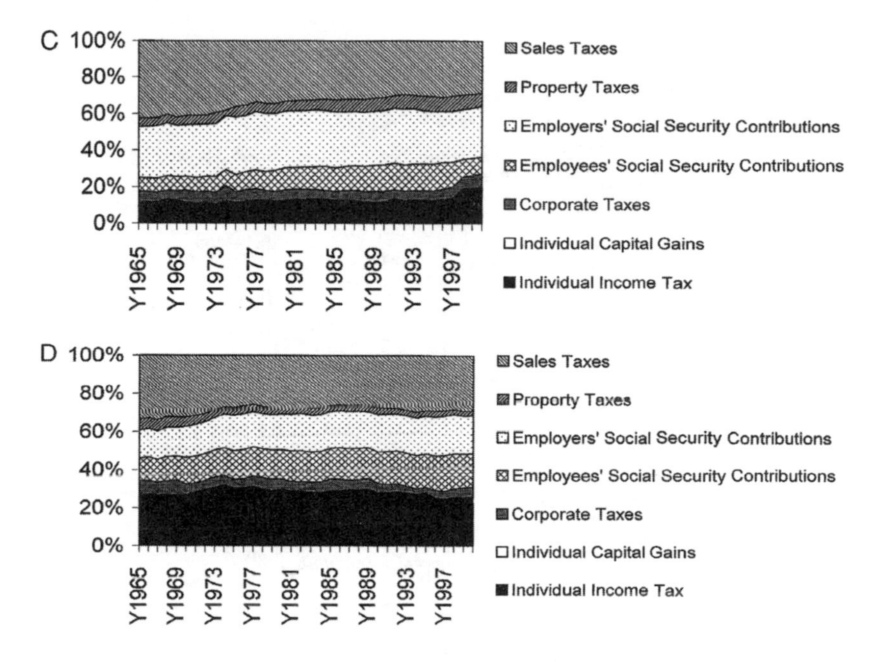

much of the literature on American politics would have led one to expect.... Far from occupying a uniquely privileged position,... industry has been forced to struggle harder to resist additional government restrictions on its prerogatives in the United States than in any other capitalist nation" (Vogel 1986; see chaps. 3 and 4 for comparisons of industrial policy in the United States and Germany, and in Britain and France, respectively).

In the domain of welfare policy, Korpi and Palme (1998) describe the United States and United Kingdom (among other countries) as having "a *simple egalitarian strategy* with equal benefits for all, but in relative terms giving more to low-income earners than to the better off," while France and Germany (among others) "follow the *Matthew principle* of giving more, in absolute terms, to the rich than to the poor, and also, in relative terms, having limited low-income targeting" (671–72; emphasis in original). Data from the Luxembourg Income Study show that in France the wealthier segments of the citizenry actually receive proportionately more in transfer payments than the poorer segments (fig. 12)—that is, there is less targeting in France, and, as many analysts have shown, the middle

a much better gauge of tax incidence. Note, however, that in this case the general conclusion would be the same if we compared simple tax rates across countries.

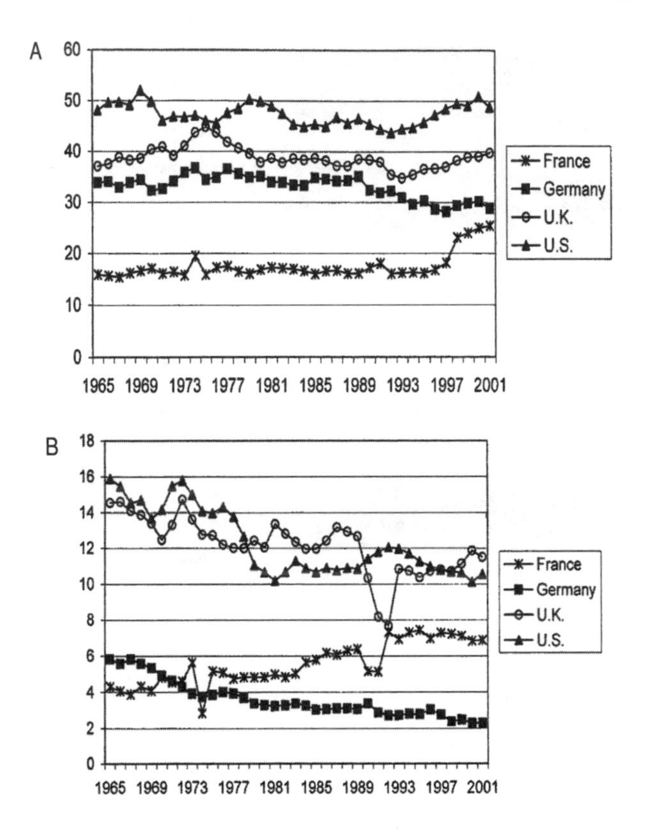

FIGURE 11. (A) Income, profits, and capital gains taxes; (B) property tax; (C) social security contributions; (D) taxes on goods and services (all panels show taxes as a percentage of total tax revenue)
Source: OECD 1965–2002 (*Revenue Statistics of OECD Member Countries*).

and upper classes benefit more from universal education, universal health care, and universal old-age pensions (see the discussion of this issue in chapter 4 for more detail). Britain is the most redistributive of the four, and Germany is nearly as redistributive.[11] The data show a trend toward less targeting in the United States, but unfortunately the series does not

11. Note that there is a discrepancy between the Mahler and Jesuit (2004) study and the Korpi and Palme (1998) study on whether the German welfare state is redistributive. For the post-1989 period, the level of redistribution has probably increased. For the pre-1989 period, it remains to be understood how the German welfare state could be redistributive in the absence of targeted programs. Future research might consider differences between France and Germany on rate of takeup of public spending (likely to be affected by the availability of

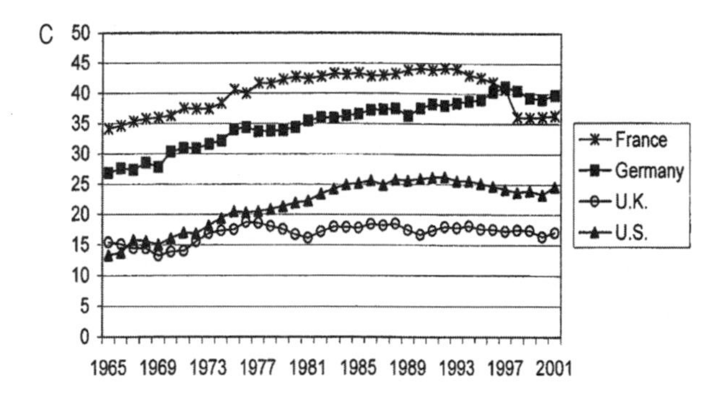

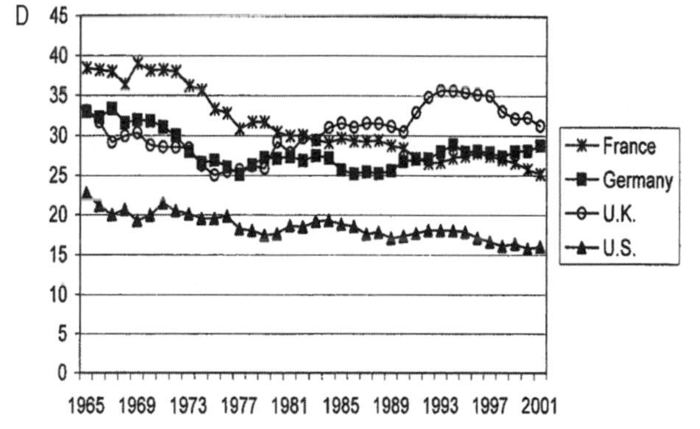

extend to the earlier period that we are interested in. Given that the data describe the period after Reagan's welfare cuts, it is likely that the degree of targeting was in fact higher before those cuts.

In short, in taxation policy, industrial policy, and welfare state policy, we find the opposite of what the American exceptionalism thesis would predict. What is it that the thesis of American exceptionalism misses? First, it is based on the *size* of the state (the level of tax revenues or welfare spending, resources expended in direct government intervention in industry), and misses the importance of the *shape* of structures. But as Korpi (1989) writes, it is also important to examine types of programs, program structure, and whom programs benefit, for the great irony—hidden by the broad brush of the American exceptionalism thesis—is that every one of these progressive American measures has backfired: progressive taxes generate

private alternatives) as well as on whether some universal programs are more intensely utilized by the middle and upper classes than others.

TABLE 2 **Average effective tax rates**

	Capital			Labor			Consumption		
	1965–75	1975–85	1985–94	1965–75	1975–85	1985–94	1965–75	1975–85	1985–94
France	17	25	25	29	37	43	19	18	17
Germany	21	29	26	29	35	37	14	13	15
United Kingdom	50	60	52	24	25	21	12	13	14
United States	42	42	40	17	21	23	6	5	5

Source: Genschel 2002, 250.

TABLE 3 **Tax ratios**

	Capital income			Labor income			Consumption			Personal income		
	1973	1979	1989	1973	1979	1989	1973	1979	1989	1973	1979	1989
France	17.39	23.06	25.44	32.63	39.01	45.99		22.94	21.07	6.45	8.22	8.85
Germany	25.88	29.33	28.56	36.02	38.03	41.64	16.79	15.85	15.32	16.43	16.40	17.15
United Kingdom	45.88	53.19	61.54	23.22	24.52	24.99	11.79	12.25	16.25	14.75	15.69	13.59
United States	42.77	44.59	41.77	22.59	26.94	29.14	6.20	5.31	4.43	12.08	14.25	13.53

Source: Volkerink and de Haan 2000, 63–74. I have drawn on the first four data tables in the paper, which are the most complete. Note that the different methods of calculation do not affect the main comparative point.

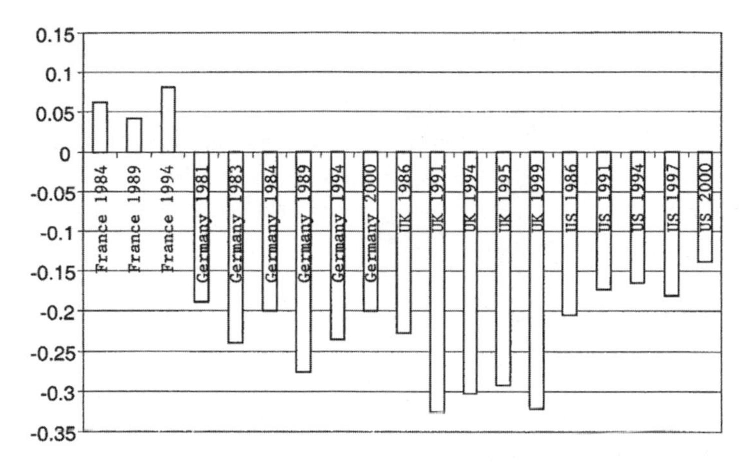

FIGURE 12. Index of concentration of welfare benefits (lower number = greater proportion of benefits going to poorest; zero = all income groups receive equal proportions)
Source: Mahler and Jesuit 2004.

resentment from taxpayers, antibusiness industrial policy leads business to organize against the state, and targeted welfare measures are subject to the fluctuating goodwill of those who pay for them. Thus, the *shape* of the American state has restricted its *size*.

Second, the American exceptionalism thesis captures only part of the picture. Certainly there are vast areas where the United States refuses the kind of government intervention taken for granted in Europe: health care is only the most obvious example. My aim here is not to replace the American exceptionalism thesis with an argument that the United States is *more* accepting of state intervention. Instead, I intend to show that what the thesis of American exceptionalism misses is that *because of* the areas of pro-market dominance in some areas of American policy, there have always been moments of backlash in American policymaking in other domains. Antitrust legislation in the late nineteenth and early twentieth centuries and social regulation in the 1960s are two examples. These moments of backlash in turn set up their own backlash, of which the Reagan period was one. The American experience is not one of an overarching pro-market consensus, but of swings toward and away from pro-market policies, whereas other countries have seen a more stable pattern.

In Britain, the degree to which the pre-Thatcher political structure was remarkably antimarket has been forgotten. Tanzi (1969) examined British tax policy in comparison to other industrial countries, and concluded,

> The burden of [individual income tax] was higher in the United Kingdom than in any other country;...most of the revenues were collected from the higher income classes with high marginal rates while the lower income classes paid very little.... [Meanwhile, i]n Italy and France... only a small part was collected from high income brackets.... These two countries [Italy and France] as well as Japan may have been able to achieve higher growth rates at the cost of greater equity. (124–26; see also Crafts 2001)

The Thatcher experiment received early inspiration from West Germany. Indeed, on the eve of Thatcherism, the *Frankfurter Allgemeine Zeitung* (*FAZ*) lauded the British government for finally bringing into Britain the market principles that were accepted as "common sense" everywhere else; for example:

> Whereas on the Continent the steel industry long ago saw the writing on the wall, and has persistently reduced its [surplus]capacity, workers in England preferred to march the streets in their thousands and demonstrate for the maintenance of their jobs. The nationalised British steel industry was compelled to continue to work its old plants and to return enormous losses. The cuts that now, belatedly, have to be made are that much more painful. A much larger number of jobs must be lost. Those who conserve uneconomic plants are not ready to see that such delay always leads to Kapitalvernichtung [destruction of capital]; they haven't even got a word for that in England.... A famous London stockbroking firm—of all people—has today lent its name to the demands for a wage and price freeze as the only possible way of fighting inflation. This demonstrates how little confidence the people in this country have in market forces. (*FAZ*, 21 Jun 1980, translation from Macauslan to Unwin, 14 Jul 1980, Conservative Research Department file 4/4/32, Conservative Party Archives, Bodleian Library, Oxford University)

Although measuring productivity in the nationalized industries is difficult, it appears that French nationalized industries were more productive than British nationalized industries throughout the postwar period, except for the decade of 1958 to 1968 (see Pryke 1971, 1981). Estrin and Pérotin (1987, 1991) suggest that this is because productivity depends not on ownership so much as how the firm is managed, and they discuss various mechanisms that ensured that French nationalized firms were managed with the goal of productivity, unlike British nationalized firms. Kuisel (1981) writes,

> The [French] nationalized companies [in the 1950s] were expansionist in their own operations and in their effect on the French economy. Electricité de France

> (EDF) and the state railways led the way in applying econometric techniques. The uniform purchasing procedures of state firms fostered the standardization of equipment supply. In a few instances a public enterprise, such as Renault, served as a model for private firms and sharpened competition. The directors of the nationalized companies successfully pressed for higher productivity, new technology, and more investment. The result was a large expansion of capacity (e.g., EDF) and rising productivity (e.g., coal mines and railways).... The example of public enterprise contributed to leading private industry toward a pattern of high investment and a decisive break with prewar behavior. An economist surveying the machine tool industry of Renault, the Caravelle jet, and EDF's high-voltage power grid, concluded that "much of the stimulus for technological change came from nationalized industry." (266)

Chapter 4 investigates this issue in more detail. Finally, capital, income, and property taxes as a proportion of total tax revenue were also higher in Britain than in France and Germany, and British unions did not moderate their wage and employment demands as German unions did.

These adversarial structures opened a space for an electoral appeal based on neoliberalism in the United Kingdom and United States when the socioeconomic transformation of the postwar period moved the majority of voters from one side of the adversarial divide to the other. In the United States, the majority of voters became taxpayers and began to resent the intrusions of taxation, particularly because the benefits were much less immediately visible than the costs of the taxes, and entrepreneurial politicians exaggerated the resentment against targeted welfare programs. In Britain, the majority of voters moved out of the working classes that the postwar policies, underpinned by labor power, had sought to help, and when the trade unions struck, the populace turned against them. Although the majority also experienced this socioeconomic transformation in France and West Germany, the pro-growth policies and structures did not provide space for an electoral appeal in the same way. An invisible taxation structure, pro-business industrial policies, and universal welfare policies generated little electoral dissatisfaction in France, and the moderate nature and pro-growth structure of decision making in West Germany meant that unions struck much less often, which in turn meant that neither the radicalization of the Conservative party nor the unpopularity of the unions seen in Britain occurred in West Germany. In addition, an institutionalized Left faction within the right-wing party prevented even moderate neoliberal proposals from being implemented.

To understand why the adversarial policies persisted in the first two cases and the pro-growth policies in the latter, and also to understand why the adversarial policies led to neoliberalism in the first two cases, we must rethink our understanding of "path dependence." Path dependence has become a popular explanatory tool in the social sciences. The basic idea is that certain identifiable features of complex systems can make reversal of a system decision much more difficult and unlikely than the original choice of the decision had been. Thus, practices that may once have been efficient, or that were simply chosen accidentally, can persist long after their inefficiency has become evident. Economists have used this insight to explain, for example, why some countries remain poor. Arthur (1994) notes four particular features that make causation "one-way": startup costs, learning costs, coordination costs, and adaptive expectations. Once a particular path is chosen, investments must be made in this path, and if the path is later altered, those investments, the startup costs, would be lost. Similarly, once a path is chosen, individuals begin to learn how to navigate it; if the choice is altered, their efforts at learning would be lost, and learning would have to begin again. For these reasons, chosen paths tend to persist. Coordination costs occur when the benefits of a technology multiply as more people use it; to switch to a different technology would mean sacrificing those additional benefits. And adaptive expectations are the self-fulfilling predictions that individuals make when, aware of coordination costs, they attempt to choose the technology that will attract the most users. Coordination costs and adaptive expectations mean that the first technology out of the gate may gain a lasting advantage, even if it is demonstrably inferior to later competitors. Pierson (2000) builds on Arthur's work and adds the insight that path dependence is much more likely in the social world, because certain features that "correct" path dependence in economics—competitive pressures and learning processes, both of which reduce the persistence of inefficiency—are attenuated outside of the economic sphere. Scholars have developed a theoretical arsenal around the claim that moments exist (particularly moments of crisis) when action is contingent, but that once a particular decision is made during this contingent moment, the costs of change make reversal difficult (see especially Mahoney 2000, 2001).

This model of path dependence, based on the costs of change, has been quite successful. But the basic fact of representative democracy is that those who decide whether or not to adopt policy changes are not the ones who bear the costs of those changes: politicians externalize the costs of change, in that the startup costs, learning costs, and coordination costs are borne by those who must implement the policy and those who are the subjects of the policy. Politicians' own cost-benefit calculations are based on criteria that are partially independent of the question of the costs of adopting the new policy. Thus, we can find a better framework for understanding how political paths persist (and when they change) by looking at what policies do for and to the incentives of state actors. I suggest that adversarial policies do three things to structure the consequent path of policy development: They (1) define categories of opposed combatants; (2) structure information flows to reinforce these categories; and (3) strengthen the coalitions that struggled to get them passed. These dynamics provide opportunities for political gain to politicians who exploit the resulting divisions.

First, as many analysts have noted, adversarial policies make coalitions across the adversarial line difficult: "Because marginal types of social policy programs are directed primarily at those below the poverty line, there is no rational base for a coalition between those above and those below the poverty line. In effect, the poverty line splits the working class and tends to generate coalitions between better-off workers and the middle class against the lower sections of the working class" (Korpi and Palme 1998, 663). Adversarial business regulations in the United States provide another example: Social regulations, which affected business in general, called forth a businesswide countermobilization. And labor relations that defined capital and labor as adversaries rather than partners in a quest for national economic growth created opportunities to exploit sentiment against labor.

Second, adversarial and pro-growth policies set up very different kinds of bureaucracies for collecting and disseminating information. Sales taxes are the classic example of a kind of tax collection that obscures its incidence, and income and property taxes are classic examples of highly visible tax-collection procedures. Sales taxes are regressive, but because of the piecemeal, long-term nature of the collection, this information is not immediately visible to taxpayers; whereas income taxes, because they require accurate information about income status to determine the appropriate rate, have the effect of disseminating accurate information to taxpayers about how much they are paying. As another example, states that target welfare benefits invest large amounts of resources in identifying who is eligible for them, and patrolling that boundary takes a great deal of information-collection effort.

Finally, states make policies, but policies also make states (Skocpol 1992). The struggle to get a policy passed creates a coalition that can last long after the policy has been implemented. In France, because de Gaulle was part of the postwar coalition that nationalized large parts of the French economy, the French Right never seriously considered privatization; but as soon as Mitterrand broke that implicit coalition, the Right immediately revised its ideology and embraced privatization. Ideology was much less stable than the political coalition formed during the Resistance.

All of these dynamics mean that adversarial policies open up spaces for political entrepreneurship and demagoguery. *Demagoguery* is generally used as a term of disapprobation. Here I want to give it a precise technical definition in order to use it as an analytical tool. In this work, *demagoguery* is understood to happen when (1) a politician, in an effort to gain political power, mobilizes support for a position or issue for which voters have not shown any spontaneous concern, *and* (2) evidence shows that main elements of the appeal are demonstrably false, or evidence shows that the majority of voters do not actually favor the position when they are given more information about it. If (1) can be shown, but not (2), I call the phenomenon *political entrepreneurship*.

Both of these phenomena can be seen in the example of Ronald Reagan's story of the "welfare queen" who allegedly used multiple aliases to live like a queen on welfare, cheating the government of $100,000–$150,000 (the story is discussed in chapter 1). This story shows elements of both political entrepreneurship and demagoguery. First, welfare fraud clearly does exist, and clearly outrages citizens when they learn of it. When he first used this story in 1976, Reagan was engaging in political entrepreneurship; that is, he was simply mobilizing an issue by bringing it to the attention of voters. However, when he continued to use the unproven $100,000–$150,000 figures after the woman in question had been convicted of fraud worth $8,000—and especially after news media had pointed out the facts of the case—he engaged in demagoguery, using false claims to mobilize an issue. Moreover, in not presenting the anecdote in the context of the actual extent of welfare fraud and the costs versus the benefits of fighting it, he exploited the information asymmetry between voter and politician that is the basis of the possibility of demagoguery. If Reagan had noted in his speeches that this woman was an extreme case (instead of implying, as he did, that her scenario was usual), or that policing welfare fraud would mean that even less of taxpayers' money would get to the poor and more would be spent on policing costs, or if he had qualified his story by noting that reduction in welfare benefits could translate to increased risks for poor children, certainly the political effects of the story would have been reduced.

These observations are not meant as aspersions on the character of Ronald Reagan; the point is to characterize the normal process of politics across the political spectrum under certain circumstances, because politicians who engage successfully in such processes (whether they do so out of sincere belief or out of a wish for power) have a competitive advantage over those who do not. Similar dynamics are seen by politicians who seek to gain power by exploiting, for example, vague anxieties caused by globalization, as John Kerry and John Edwards did in the Democratic primary of 2004 when they attacked an economic adviser to President Bush who had praised the outsourcing of jobs as a source of economic growth—a fairly noncontroversial position among academic economists from across the political spectrum. All politicians are demagogues sometimes, and some structures make demagoguery more possible and successful than others.

Finally, the analysis that follows shows the usefulness of recent attention in historical sociology to the importance of specific *transformative events* in structural change (Abbott 1992, 1997, 2000; Sewell 1996a, 1996b): social change is nonlinear because a specific event can quickly change opinions, reveal or highlight elements of a phenomenon, spread information or misinformation, and transform how characters conceive of their own goals. Although earlier theorists of the event insisted that "social relations are profoundly governed by underlying social and political structures" (Sewell 1996a, 842), more recent work tends to take this observation in a direction that emphasizes contingency and the inability to draw strong conclusions about the social world. I hope in this work to define a theoretical space between absolute determinacy and absolute contingency by showing how events are rooted in social structure. In particular, I show here that although neoliberal policies were suggested in all four cases, only particular structural settings led to the events that *exaggerated* the neoliberal impulse: in the United States, the dissatisfaction with progressive taxation allowed an anchor for neoliberalism; in Britain, the success of the first privatization recast the Thatcher effort in moral terms and gave it a coherence that it was in danger of losing because of the lack of success of monetarism. In both cases particular state structures also encouraged the mobilization and exaggeration of policy issues—entrepreneurial politicians in the American case, and, in Britain, extreme political competition combined with a mechanism for policy rethinking while in opposition. Eventually, exaggeration itself becomes a political fact, yielding backlash, defining coalitions, and providing opportunities to politicians, so that the dynamics may continue even if the original structure producing them is removed. In France neither the policies nor the state structure could support the neoliberal impulse; and in Germany the state structure dampened conflict rather than exaggerating it. The importance of transformative events is another factor explaining why seemingly similar variables in different contexts can represent quite different phenomena, as many sociologists have argued (Abbott 1997, 2000).

In making this argument about the effects of adversarial policies and state structures I am particularly indebted to the work of Harold Wilensky (2002), who argues that the United States and the United Kingdom are part of a group of six "rich democracies" that are "least consensual" in their conduct of politics and whose adversarial structures have produced many dysfunctional outcomes. I am indebted as well to the work of Walter Korpi and Joakim Palme (1998), which shows the political implications of the structure of welfare policies.[12]

Together, these points lead to the following argument: Free market, or neoliberal, policies did not result from any pragmatic or rational analysis showing that they were the best way to manage the crisis; nor were they the result of globalization, business-group pressure, or national culture. Rather, they arose where the political-economic structure was adversarial. States in which the political-economic structure defined labor and capital as adversaries and the middle class and the poor in opposition to one another (the middle class paying for policies that benefit the poor) provided the potential to ally the majority of voters with market-friendly policies, and certain structural changes provided incentives to politicians to mobilize this potential.

In the United States, postwar tax structures, industrial policy, and welfare state policies defined the middle class in opposition to the poor and business interests in opposition to the general interest. Furthermore, in the United States, social pressure to give "power to the people" in the 1960s and 1970s led to a series of changes that weakened the power of congressional committees and the importance of seniority in congress. Combined with weaker parties and a resulting "candidate-centered" political system, this change produced a class of "entrepreneurial politicians" (Aldrich and Niemi 1996) who were dependent on social sources to develop their power bases and actively sought out issues on which to develop stable followings.

12. In addition, the work of Reimut Zohlnhöfer (1998, 1999, 2001a, 2001b, 2001c) has been crucial to my understanding of the German experience.

This resulted in a dynamic of legislators who were particularly sensitive to issues that would be popular with large majorities. Making the state more responsive to society thus made state actors more responsive to *nonpoor majorities* and sources of campaign financing, and less able to protect the interests of disadvantaged minorities—an ironic outcome, given the leftist motivations of the 1960s changes in state structures that were intended to give politics back to the people. Because economic policies such as targeted programs put the interests of majorities at odds with the interests of the poor, giving power to the people meant weakening autonomous state structures that had served as a bulwark against social sources of power, and these social sources of power led to the enactment of politically salable market-friendly policies.

In Britain postwar politics had been driven by goals of social justice and by class resentment, and the decision-making structure excluded the strong unions, whose recourse to power was to strike. Moreover, a highly competitive party system ensured the continuous renewal of political innovation, and the dealignment of voters from parties led to the rise of a politics of appealing to the floating voter. But policies that did not create exploitable divisions, like the universal elements of the welfare state, proved resilient (as in the United States). In France, meanwhile, invisible and targeted taxation, a middle-class welfare state, and a postwar industrial policy that put the state at the service of capital all combined to create a highly resilient political-economic structure, and in Germany corporatist institutionalization of business and labor power dampened conflict. Moreover, in France, innovation during this period came from moderate sources, and there was no dynamic of politicians seeking out policies potentially popular with the majority. More neoliberal innovation occurred in Germany because of the role of a small libertarian party, but resistance within the right-wing party blocked most of these innovations from becoming policy.

This work also seeks to focus attention on a problem that arises at the heart of the meeting of democracy and late capitalism: how to protect the interests of the poor when the majority is not poor, and the majority rules. When the majority of citizens become taxpayers and move out of the working class, especially under certain economic and decision-making structures, support for redistribution to the poor (as opposed to redistribution from the rich) is fragile. If politics is particularly competitive, politicians will take advantage of this fragility in their quest for power. This is the story of neoliberalism in the United States and, in a different way, in Britain. The comparison with France and Germany shows that the divergent outcomes arose not because of cultural differences but because the nonadversarial political-economic structure in France and Germany meant that there was less room for an electoral appeal to neoliberalism.

The role of the majority in determining policy—and especially the fear of the tyranny of the majority—was a classic concern of early democratic theoreticians. Tocqueville wrote, "What is a majority, in its collective capacity, if not an individual with opinions, and usually with interests, contrary to those of another individual, called the minority? Now, if you admit that a man vested with omnipotence can abuse it against his adversaries, why not admit the same concerning a majority? Have men, by joining together, changed their character? By becoming stronger, have they become more patient of obstacles?" (1969, 251). Indeed, one of the primary motivations of the American Constitutional Convention was the fear that a poor majority was taking advantage of the extensive egalitarianism of the Articles of Confederation. John Adams recalls the happiness of a client of his, a debtor frequently hauled before court, at the closing of the Massachusetts courts just before the Revolution:

> Is this the object for which I have been contending? said I to myself. For I rode along without any answer to this wretch. Are these the sentiments of such people, and how many of them are there in the country? Half the nation for what I know; for half the nation are debtors, if not more, and these have been, in all countries, the sentiments of debtors. If the power of the country should get into their hands, and there is great danger that it will, to what purpose have we sacrificed our time, health and everything else? Surely we must guard against this spirit and these principles, or we shall repent of all our conduct. (quoted in Kramnick 1987, 24)

Adams had cause to worry: all over the young country, the powerful state legislatures were filled with representatives of the 70 to 90 percent of white males who had been given suffrage between 1776 and 1789, the majority of whom were of moderate means, if not actually poor: "This presence of new men, common men, in the politics of revolutionary America was one of the most striking features of the years preceding the Constitutional Convention. It was continually noted by the traditional leaders of American life" (Kramnick 1987, 23). More alarming still, these new men were passing redistributive policies such as acts of debtor relief and debt postponement, confiscation of property, printing of paper money, and other policies that worked to the interest of those without property. It was precisely this problem that led Madison to complain in *Federalist 10* of "the superior force of an interested and overbearing majority" (Madison, Hamilton, and Jay 1987, 123). Madison specifically believed that a new Constitution would prevent "a rage for paper money, for an abolition of debts, for an equal division of property, or for any other improper or wicked project" (quoted in Kramnick 1987, 26). This fear of a poor majority seizing the wealth of a productive minority is encapsulated in the old libertarian joke about democracy being two wolves and a sheep voting about what to have for dinner.

The problem of the tyranny of the majority was a pressing empirical possibility in the eighteenth century and received careful scrutiny from early theorists. In the nineteenth and twentieth centuries, however, this question came to be eclipsed by research traditions that investigated the power of organized groups. A curious feature of the historical development of democracy has thus remained unexamined: since Tocqueville and the Federalists worried about the "tyranny of the majority," the characteristics of that majority have dramatically changed.

The tyranny that was once feared was of a poor majority rising up and seizing for itself the fruits of the labor of a productive minority, but in the advanced industrial countries of the Western world, the majority has increasingly been brought to an unparalleled level of prosperity, and under certain circumstances, associates this prosperity with the free market. Under certain conditions, the majority may benefit from—and see itself as benefiting from—market-friendly policies. The majority can therefore be aligned in favor of the market—in favor of property rights, debt collection, the enforcement of contracts, sound money, and all of the other principles that the brahmins of Boston feared would be lost if power were extended too widely.

The conclusion takes up these theoretical issues more systematically. The following chapters present the evidence for the empirical argument, which we are now in a position to summarize very briefly: Different decision-making structures and policies mobilized the electorate in different ways in the two sets of countries, so that in West Germany and France, pro-growth policies and state structures meant that politicians were neither forced to make neoliberal appeals to the electorate to stay in power, nor able to find issues that would appeal to a broad segment of the electorate. In the United States and Britain, in the wake of the 1973 oil crisis, the adversarial structure of previous policies led to the potential popularity of neoliberalism, and adversarial state structures led to a greater need for politicians to mobilize populist appeals to acquire or maintain power.

Chapters 1 and 2 tell the stories of the Reagan and Thatcher cases, guided by the insights of the "faces of power" research tradition: to be enacted, a policy must be thought of, brought to the political agenda, and win in the decision-making arena (Bachrach and Baratz 1962; Crenson 1971; Lukes 1974; Gaventa 1980). Policies can fail at any of these three stages. I trace tax, regulation/privatization, and welfare state policies in those two countries through the stages of their first conceptualization (third face), their arrival onto the political agenda (second face), and their victory or defeat in the decision-making arena (first face). I pay particular attention to the transformative events of each episode. Chapters 3 and 4, on West Germany and France, are more explicitly comparative: I contrast the attempts made in both cases with the Reagan and Thatcher cases, and with each other. Unless otherwise indicated, translations from French and German are my own, and I have aimed for literal translations rather than elegant ones.

CHAPTER ONE

Power to the Middle Classes: Entrepreneurs and Ideologues in the Reagan Revolution

In the early 1980s the administration of President Ronald Reagan passed a series of policies—broad tax cuts, deregulation of industry, and cuts in government programs—to reduce the presence of the state in the market. These policies seemed so significant at the time and were passed in such quick succession that many observers called the episode the "Reagan Revolution." The most consequential policies were passed in a concentrated burst of legislation during the first two years of the administration. After that, for various reasons, the momentum dwindled. The deficits created by the tax cuts forced the administration to raise taxes, deregulation caused a backlash among the public, and other events in the second term, such as the Iran-Contra affair, hampered the administration's ability to make policy. Reagan's immediate successor raised taxes, at great political cost, as did the Democrat Bill Clinton. The single delayed success of the Reagan Revolution was the replacement, in 1996, of Aid to Families with Dependent Children (AFDC; "welfare") by the more time-limited Temporary Assistance for Needy Families (TANF). The administration of George W. Bush has been quite active in cutting taxes and regulations, leading another neoliberal period.

In retrospect, it is hard not to see the Reagan Revolution as inevitable, a natural outgrowth of the radical individualism and distrust of government that are supposed to be ingrained in the American character. This sense of inevitability is itself part of Reagan's success. There is indeed some truth to the argument that Reagan's policies intensified trends that had begun before his term, but it is important not to underestimate the context in which Reagan came to office. The economic crisis of the mid-to-late 1970s had led political actors to discuss with some seriousness measures that we would today consider hopelessly radical, such as shortened workweeks, nationalization of key industries, large public works projects, and wage and price controls.[1] In this context, attempting to reduce the size of government was one among many proposals for dealing with the economic crisis.

Moreover, although Reagan had worked out a general antigovernment credo by the mid 1970s, the *specific* policies that made up the Reagan Revolution were not formulated until just before and just after Reagan's 1980 victory. A battle raged in the early days of the administration between those who supported the large tax cuts and those who feared the deficits they would produce; the spending cuts were a product of intense and occasionally incoherent political dealing. Nothing in the mid-1970s could have led to a confident prediction of the extensiveness of the changes that took place a few years later.

This chapter concentrates on that early burst of legislation during the first two years of the Reagan period—the first significant break with the postwar consensus—and particularly on three events: the Economic Recovery Tax Act (ERTA) tax cuts of 1981, which created the deficits; deregulation, particularly at the Environmental Protection Agency (EPA)—the largest regulatory cutbacks in monetary terms; and the implementation of cuts in antipoverty programs (but not in middle-class programs like Social Security) in the Omnibus Budget Reconciliation Act (OBRA) of 1981. I aim to show that the tax cuts were rooted in those elements of the American tax structure that were most progressive (income and property taxes), that business encouraged deregulation, but it could only be implemented because of a strange helping hand from the Left, and that the targeted nature of welfare policy caused it to appear on the agenda. In all three domains, the size or degree of policies was not as important as their shape: visible income and property taxes; adversarial regulations; and targeted welfare policies. In all three domains, entrepreneurial politicians found issues that hit a nerve. Moreover, certain political structures (weak parties, integration

1. See Bourgeois 1978; Galbraith 1977; Levitan and Belous 1977; Martin 1977; Shultz and Dam 1977; U.S. Congress 1977, 1978b, 1978c; Vaughan 1976; Vernez 1977; Whiteman 1978; as well as "Short Weeks, Pay Cuts Aim at Avoiding Layoffs," *Industry Week* 184, no. 8 (1975): 15–16; "Unions Campaign to Shrink Work Time," *Business Week*, 24 Apr 1978, 30–31; and "Will Wage-Price Guidelines Work? Yes: Interview with Charles Schultze, Chairman, Council of Economic Advisers; No: Interview with Alan Greenspan, Former Chairman, Council of Economic Advisers," *U.S. News & World Report*, 13 Nov 1978, 29–30.

of interest groups in politics, lack of a permanent state bureaucracy) increased the quantity of innovations that would be brought onto the agenda, but only those innovations that did not violate majority opinion survived.

Taxation

The Economic Recovery Tax Act of 1981 (ERTA) was the largest tax cut in American history; the deficit it produced generated a climate of penny-pinching that was partly responsible for the popularity of cuts in social spending in the 1980s and 1990s. The Reagan administration's later attempts to reduce the deficit did not restore pre-1981 levels of financing, and by the time these later attempts were instituted, the deficit had already ballooned. Herbert Stein calls 1981 the year of the "Big Budget Bang": "Fiscal policy in all the years since . . . was dominated by efforts to deal with the consequences of that event" (Stein 1996, 266; see also Stein 1990).[2] The tax increases under George Bush and Bill Clinton eventually brought the budget back into balance, but George W. Bush has reintroduced sustained deficits as a feature of American political life. Approximately 12 percent of the budget went toward interest on debt in 1996 (Brownlee 1996a).

Two stories circulate about the tax cuts: that business groups were responsible for their passage and that they represented a spontaneous revolt by the majority against excessive taxation. The evidence that the majority of voters wanted tax cuts is unconvincing: respondents agreed that taxes were too high when specifically asked about taxes, but the tax issue was not a high priority, and the support for tax cuts dropped dramatically if they were seen as leading to a deficit or to cuts in social spending.

Polls showed that 33 percent of respondents blamed "poor governmental leadership" for economic decline, and only 4 percent blamed "high business taxes"; that respondents thought a balanced budget (49 percent) was a better means of fighting inflation than reducing taxes (14 percent); and that in 1980, 63 percent favored a balanced budget, and only 30 percent favored

2. The increases in military spending in the early 1980s were also necessary to the creation of the deficit. But military spending had also skyrocketed in the 1940s, when it led not to a deficit but to a vastly expanded state structure; the taxes used to finance military spending for the Second World War did not come back down to prewar levels after the war, and therefore effectively financed the new American welfare state (Steinmo 1993). The two outcomes differ not because of different patterns of military spending but because of the different tax policies enacted.

Reagan's tax cut (all reported in *Public Opinion*, August–September 1980). Never has more than a small percentage of respondents answered Gallup's long-term question, "What is the most important problem facing the nation today?" by saying "high taxes," even in the period when most respondents were saying that taxes were "too high" (*Public Opinion*, August–September 1980). The editors of *Public Opinion* summed up the tax attitudes in the late 1970s as follows: "These figures do not suggest that taxpayers are opposed to tax cuts. Many surveys indicate that tax cuts per se are popular. The public seems to be saying, 'We want to balance the budget by cutting spending, and if we can cut taxes, too, that's even better. But start by putting the government's house in order'" (*Public Opinion*, August–September 1980). That is, tax cuts were popular, but not particularly salient. Citizens did not in this period ascribe the nation's ills to high tax rates, and they showed fiscal conservatism, a preference for "putting the government's house in order," over tax cuts.

Citizens did, however, clearly and actively reject one set of taxes in the 1970s: a series of "tax revolts" against property taxes occurred across the nation, beginning with the passage of California's Proposition 13. This episode has passed into legend as the beginning of the turn to the Right, "conveniently separating the New Deal-Great Society era from a newer, leaner period that finds the public far stingier with tax dollars and increasingly skeptical about government's basic competence to solve problems" (Kuttner 1980, 7). But Lo (1990) notes that even though working-class and middle-class homeowners were active in the beginning, the property tax revolt was largely "a movement of suburban businesses and professionals who used their skills, resources, and influence in their community to organize a campaign directed against the higher levels of government and other corporatist institutions" (197). Business interests saw to it that "business property received most of the benefits from Proposition 13" (21) and that the eventual result was an upward redistribution of income. Moreover Proposition 13 addressed property taxes, which are local, not federal, and had risen to much higher levels than income taxes.

Nevertheless, Proposition 13 did put taxes on the map; the momentum of the California victory created a "bandwagon effect" (Martin 2003), so that property tax limits quickly spread across the nation. The passage of Proposition 13 brought the issue of taxes into the vision of policymakers, as we will see below. In general, however, citizens supported tax cuts when offered, but they were not clamoring for them; they were passive in accepting the cuts, rather than active in demanding them.

The other story that gets told about the tax cuts is that they were caused by the lobbying efforts of business groups. Akard explicitly formulates this thesis in terms of the "instrumental Marxist" paradigm, and adds that business interests unified on a classwide basis, *as a group*, because they perceived growing social spending as a common threat: "A general consensus emerged between big and small business, industrial and finance capital... based on a common perception of the costs imposed on capital by labor and the state. From the perspective of business, thirty years of government expansion had absorbed a growing share of the nation's economic resources for unproductive social expenditures that created a shortage of capital for private investment and fueled inflation" (Akard 1992, 601). This common threat led the business community to override its usual fragmentation, and even its occasional direct conflicts of interest. They combined in groups such as the Business Roundtable, the Carlton Group, and the Chamber of Commerce to lobby for cuts in corporate income tax (Akard 1992; Martin 1991). Business groups were instrumental both in bringing the specific details of the tax cuts they wanted to the agenda and in pushing them through: the Carlton Group, in association with others, drafted the proposal for business tax cuts that was eventually adopted, and the same group successfully threatened to rebel in order to keep those business tax cuts from being reduced at a later stage in the negotiations (Akard 1992).[3]

The historical record shows that business groups were indeed instrumental—in bringing about *corporate* income tax cuts. But the ERTA was not limited to corporate income tax cuts. In fact, those tax cuts produced only a minority of the ERTA's total revenue losses, less than 22 percent by 1990 (fig. 1.1). The quantitatively more important pieces of the legislation were the individual income tax cuts: both the across-the-board reduction in individual taxes over three years and the tax indexation, which began in 1984. By fiscal year 1990, the individual tax cuts and the indexation had produced losses in revenue of $164.3 billion and $57.4 billion respectively; the corporate tax cuts meanwhile had produced a loss of $47.9 billion (Steuerle 1992, 186–87). The Reagan administration's 1982 tax increases made up two-thirds of the revenue lost in individual and corporate cuts, but indexation was not repealed.

Business groups were not behind the individual income tax cuts: "The Roundtable and the financial community were... wary of the possible

3. See also Piven and Cloward 1982; Edsall 1984; Ferguson and Rogers 1986; Himmelstein 1990; Martin 1991.

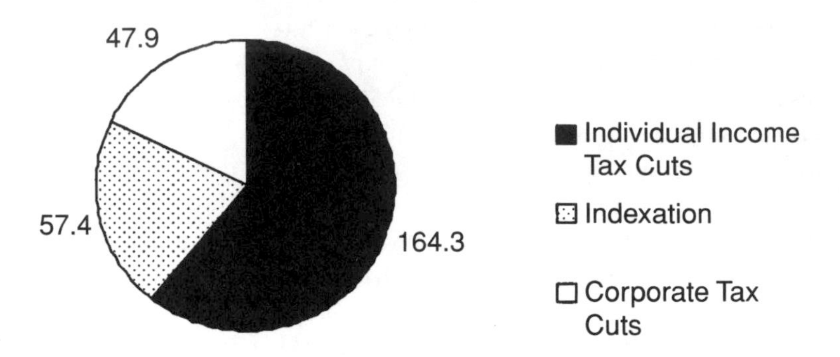

FIGURE 1.1. Revenue loss caused by the ERTA in the United States as of 1990 (billions of dollars)
Source: Steuerle 1992, 186–87.

inflationary and deficit-enlarging effects of the Kemp-Roth 30-percent cut in individual income tax rates. . . . Though ambivalent about the proposed tax cuts for individuals in the Reagan plan, the [Carlton] Group agreed to support them in return for the inclusion of accelerated depreciation" (Akard 1992, 607–8). Business groups did not stand to gain from these cuts, and stood to lose from their possible deficit-generating and inflationary effects; consequently they offered only acquiescence, not support. The head of the Business Roundtable said in February 1981,

> Kemp-Roth is political rhetoric. Neither Kemp nor Roth are economists or students of the economy. They're politicians. And they arrived at a formula that had a ring to it, and it played politically, and they milked it. But it ought to be discarded now . . . the intelligent people [in the administration] have to recognize that you can't really commit the country to 30 percent tax cuts for individuals and believe that the Laffer curve is going to save you. (Pine 1981)

Scholars often note the role of business groups in Reagan's victory: corporate donations to PACs grew from $89 million in 1974 to $1,204 million in 1980, compared with labor union PAC donations to political candidates of $201 million in 1974 and $297 million in 1980 (Alexander 1983, 126). Moreover, "ideological" PACs, which donated $38,613,000 in 1980 (of which $27,275,000 came from conservative PACs), spent more than 40 percent of the money they spent on behalf of Republican candidates on Reagan (Alexander 1983, 128–29; Clawson, Neustadtl, and Weller 1998; Robinson 1981). This PAC spending may have been important *after* Reagan won the Republican nomination, but before he won the nomination, most business groups favored John Connally or George Bush (some groups did prefer Reagan, but they did not in the end actually spend the large amounts of money that they had planned to spend for him [Maxwell 1980; Perry 1980]). Reagan won the nomination because his campaign—organizationally mature from his 1976 run for president—managed to target *individuals* more successfully. Reagan had raised more money than Bush, more even than Carter for his primary campaign, and National Election Studies data show that in 1980 Republican voters in the highest income brackets were more likely than in any previous campaign to have contributed money to a political campaign, suggesting that wealthy *individuals* were contributing to the Reagan campaign more than they had to any previous campaign (National Election Studies Cumulative Datafile, 1952–1992). The importance of this fund-raising effort can again be traced to the weakness of parties. After the nomination, Reagan did benefit from business-group donations, but it is not clear that his victory can be attributed to this. Most examinations of the 1980 election agree that people were voting against Carter's economic record, rather than in favor of Reagan's platform (Harwood 1980; Schneider 1983)—but the business-group donations may have helped Reagan to portray the deficiencies of Carter's economic record more efficiently.

The more important point here, however, is that even if business groups did manage to get Reagan elected, once elected, *he did not do what the business groups wanted*: that is, he pushed a large tax cut for the middle classes that business groups feared. Thus, scholars may be correct in noting the central role of business groups in helping Reagan win and in getting any kind of tax cuts passed, but the groups involved had to be talked into supporting the individual income tax cuts, the quantitatively more important piece of the legislation, because they were wary of the deficit that would likely ensue. Who talked the business groups into it, and why?

The original proposal for income tax cuts arose from both traditional and new right-wing sources. Although the idea was "in the air" generally in the early 1970s (Roberts 1984), most accounts trace its precise formulation to a specific meeting between the economist Arthur Laffer and the *Wall Street Journal* journalist Jude Wanniski (Himmelstein 1990; Stockman 1986). Laffer demonstrated to Wanniski the tenets of supply-side economics, particularly the idea that taxes create disincentives to work. While this is a standard principle of microeconomics, Laffer's elaboration claimed that taxes in the United States were so high, creating such major disincentives, that cutting taxes would lead to greater work effort, greater economic growth, and therefore higher tax revenues for the government. Mainstream economists dismissed this idea, pointing out that no one knew at what point the disincentive effects of high taxes become so large that cutting taxes will increase government revenue; most economists agreed that the United States had not reached that point (Stein 1994, 245–48). Nevertheless, Wanniski popularized the supply-side view on the pages of the *Wall Street Journal*, and, funded by the American Enterprise Institute, the Smith Richardson Foundation, the Scaife Foundation, and the Olin Foundation—think tanks that increasingly supported conservative causes—Wanniski and Laffer and other supply-siders brought their ideas to political elites, notably Congressman Jack Kemp and presidential candidate Ronald Reagan (Himmelstein 1990).

The Laffer curve is an astonishing example of the power of structure, and the weakness of ideas: in essence, a progressive tax structure (with highly visible income and property taxes) combined with the increasing receptivity of politicians to new ideas to *generate an idea* that had not previously existed and probably would not have come into being without the structural supports. The structure called forth the necessary ideology. The opposition to it among economists (see U.S. Congress 1978a) suggests that the Laffer curve idea would have died a quiet death if not for the way entrepreneurial politicians sought it out and nurtured it.

Kemp's commitment to the cause of tax cuts was reinforced by his experience as an adviser to the 1978 Senate campaign of Jeffrey Bell, a political newcomer who pulled off a stunning upset against an incumbent senator in New Jersey. Bell attributed his success to his embrace of the Kemp-Roth tax-cut plan: "It's a dynamite issue.... This is what people care about; I find I'm dealing largely with a one-issue electorate" (Hunt 1978). Although Bell lost the general election to Bill Bradley, his success in the primary solidified Kemp's convictions that the issue of tax cuts could transform the Republican Party, and Kemp worked tirelessly to convince the party of this. The degree to which he was successful can only be appreciated in retrospect: according to 1978 poll results, "more people ... believe *Democrats* are more likely to deliver tax reduction" (Miller 1978, 18; emphasis added). The most recent tax cut, after all, had been undertaken by President Kennedy, whose line about a rising tide lifting all boats Kemp made his own. The Republicans in 1978 were still the party of balanced budgets, but a Republican strategist hoped that with the new focus on tax cuts, "The Republicans, who have always preached fiscal prudence, suddenly could become the party of more, the party of hope and opportunity, while the Democratic message seems to be that people will have to lower their expectations and get by with less" (quoted in Miller 1978, 18).

The role of Jack Kemp is the first notable curiosity in the story. Elected in 1974, Kemp was relatively low on the House totem pole and did not hold seats on either the Budget or Ways and Means Committees, the two areas in the House where tax issues are handled. As a newcomer, what he should have been doing is quietly aiding his district and managing his networks to be able to win reelection until he had climbed into a more powerful position. Instead, he was setting the national agenda.

Kemp's role in the issue reflects the rise in the late 1970s of a new breed of legislator, the "policy entrepreneur." The weakening of party structures in the 1960s increasingly forced candidates to turn away from dependence on parties and to oversee their own campaigns. For most of the century, the mass party was the medium through which politicians acquired and used power; by the 1970s, however, parties were no longer financially strong enough to continue in this role, and so politicians increasingly turned to social sources of support to be able to build their own personal campaign machines and conduct their campaigns themselves. In this system, candidates are "in business for themselves" (Davidson 1981, 131) and more beholden to voters to keep them in power than to party elites. This vulnerability to voters increases dependence on media outlets that can help a candidate attract voters, which in turn increases vulnerability to sources of campaign funding who can help a candidate finance an expensive media onslaught. One of the techniques for ensuring visibility in voters' eyes is immediate engagement with substantive issues. The Congressmen elected in the mid-1970s were significantly more likely to become immediately involved in substantive issues than their predecessors (table 1.1) in order to maintain their position in the public eye, which was newly crucial to political success.

TABLE 1.1 **Percentage of new members participating in U.S. House leadership activities, 1965–76**

	89th Congress (1965–66)	91st Congress (1969–70)	94th Congress (1975–76)
Floor manager of major bill or amendment	0	—	37
Offered floor amendments	12	40	86
Offered committee amendments	[illegible]		90
Served on conference committees	6	17	69
Made "major" floor speech	30	—	72

Source: Loomis 1988, 40.

Thus, the weakening of party structures created a generation of legislators who actively *sought out* issues on which to make their names, one of whom was Jack Kemp. There is no question that Kemp benefited from the early exposure: "The ambitious author of the tax-cut idea has rocketed out of the back benches of the House to become a star attraction at GOP gatherings around the country" (Miller 1978, 1). Kemp's success in setting the national agenda on supply-side policies made him one of very few legislators to be able to mount a bid for national office from the House. A large number of such "policy entrepreneurs" creates a state structure more open to society, and as those legislators seek out new policy issues in order to establish and maintain an ideological and political base, they will address numerous social issues that are potentially popular with the majority. Even in the absence of democratic *pressure* to enact certain policies, in the presence of a large number of policy entrepreneurs, the suspicion that an issue has *potential* appeal may be enough to bring it onto the agenda. These changes were directly responsible for the proliferation of attention to new issues and the movement of some of these, such as the Laffer tax-cut idea, onto the policy agenda, in this case through the medium of junior Congressman Kemp.

Thus, Kemp's interest and personal ambition brought the issue into the national spotlight, where a conservative president supported it. But given the proliferation of issues that were being brought into the national consciousness by "policy entrepreneurs," why was this particular issue selected for inclusion in a presidential agenda? We can begin to answer this by comparing the fate of the tax-cut proposal to that of another supply-side idea, the return to the gold standard. This comparison is quite revealing: the two cases hold *almost* everything constant except the policy itself. First, both the gold standard and the tax-cut issues arose at the same time and in the same political context: Reagan adopted both of them in his 1980 campaign platform, but while the tax cut became law, the gold standard issue was first referred to a commission (see Paul and Lehrman 1982), then dropped entirely. Second, the same actors responsible for the successful movement of the tax cut onto the agenda—Arthur Laffer, Jude Wanniski, and Jack Kemp—were also pushing for a return to the gold standard. Third, the majority of mainstream economists were against both developments. Fourth, both issues offered "ideological" benefits from an antigovernment standpoint: reducing tax revenues would put pressure on government spending, while returning to the gold standard would reduce governmental ability to manipulate the market. Finally, both issues were strongly supported by business groups; but while PAC financing played a role in getting the tax-cut issue onto the agenda, heavy lobbying from "gold bug" groups did not manage to move the gold standard issue onto the agenda.

The theoretical justification for the gold standard is that it prevents governments from taking short-term measures in their individual interest that interfere with long-term domestic and international economic growth: if governments tie their currencies to the amount of gold reserves available domestically, they will not be able to print paper money to cover short-term debts and thus drive up inflation. In addition, because gold reserves are fixed, different currencies will be automatically tied to each other, preventing governments from manipulating exchange rates in their favor and thus stabilizing the risks of rapid exchange-rate fluctuations for investors. These anti-inflationary and antifluctuation benefits should, in theory, lead to a domestic and international economic environment more conducive to investment and growth. Market mechanisms—the supply and demand for gold and other goods—rather than the politically motivated decisions of individual governments will determine the rates of individual currencies (Eichengreen 1985). As the economy grows, demand for goods other than gold will increase, causing a fall in the price of gold and (equivalently) an increase in the effective money supply without inflation.

A gold standard was in effect internationally from 1880 until the outbreak of World War I. Empirical evaluations give no clear evidence of its superiority in terms of price stability, but the prewar gold standard period is clearly associated with a period of exchange-rate stability for countries at the center of the world economy. The interwar gold standard did not work so well, because in this period governments were more likely to devalue their currencies to attain export advantage. After the Second World War the international economy entered the Bretton Woods period, when only the dollar was pegged to gold, and other currencies floated against the dollar. However, because the dollar was held internationally, foreign reserves of dollars outgrew U.S. reserves of gold: "The system relied on dollars for liquidity, but . . . the very accumulation of dollars abroad was undermining confidence in the dollar's convertibility" (Eichengreen 1985, 27). Fearing a run on the dollar, the Nixon administration officially ended the system in 1971, and the world entered a period of floating exchange rates.

The economic consensus in the late 1970s was against a return to the gold standard, even the modified version of it in place before 1971. Several practical problems with a gold standard were presented: the price of gold would not necessarily be determined by market forces, since Soviet Union and South African gold reserves were likely to be subject to political will; if other countries did not follow suit, the anti-inflationary and antifluctuation benefits to the United States of pegging itself to gold would be swallowed by cross-border flows; and new discoveries of gold would lead to inflation. But the main argument against a return to the gold standard was political rather than technical: gold would not bring about the benefits of price and exchange-rate stability, it was argued, because governments always had the option of going off the gold standard by devaluing their currencies against gold. In other words, to stay on a gold standard is a political decision—as political as the decision to print money or manipulate exchange rates: "Imposing a gold standard is like a dieter putting a lock on the refrigerator door. If one has self-discipline, it isn't necessary. If one does not, there is always a way to find the key" ("Handcuffs of Gold," editorial, *New York Times*, 23 Aug 1981, sec. 4). Economist Herbert Stein echoed others who pointed out that a gold standard had not prevented price swings in the pre–World War I period, nor did it prevent the Great Depression, and it may actually have contributed to prolonging the Depression by tying governments' hands.

However, Laffer, Wanniski, and Kemp were successful in making themselves heard in the Republican Party in 1980, and they were supported by Robert Bartley, editor of the *Wall Street Journal*, Robert Mundell of Columbia University (later a winner of the Nobel Prize and the only professional economist who also supported the tax cuts), and particularly Congressman Ron Paul and businessman Lewis Lehrman, who both served on President Reagan's Gold Commission. The argument of this group was that the inflation of the early to mid-1970s had been caused by the 1971 abandonment of the gold standard and could only be remedied by a resumption of fixing the dollar to gold. If the United States should do so, Wanniski argued, other countries would have no choice but to follow, since if they did not, investments would flow into the United States because of the anti-inflation properties of the fixed dollar. New discoveries of gold would get absorbed into the price rate through regular market mechanisms, the supporters argued, and the Soviet Union and South Africa had only 1 percent of the world's gold reserves. The supporters could not answer the political objection, but they argued that the benefits of a gold standard were so great that governments *ought not* to politically manipulate adherence to the gold standard, and that if they did not do so, then the gold standard would work. Of course, it is easy to argue that governments ought not to print money in the first place or manipulate exchange rates for local gain, and if they did not do so, a gold standard would not be necessary.

But even if it was not airtight (perhaps no more or less so than the case for a massive tax cut) the case for gold had strong financial backing. In 1983, the lobbying group that spent the most money on Capitol Hill was the Free the Eagle National Citizens Lobby, whose "goals were to restrict Federal authority, to deregulate the economy, to balance the budget and to return to the gold standard" ("Natural Gas and Insurance among Big-Spending Lobbyists," *New York Times*, 27 Nov 1983, sec. 1). The case for the gold standard had strong institutional backing, with supporters at the highest reaches of Congress and the administration as well as in the media, the academy, and the business communities. It was an implicit part of the Republican Party platform in 1980, though not as important a part as the tax cuts. And the case for gold had ideological benefits from a neoliberal standpoint: it would lessen governmental ability to manipulate the market, at least until further positive government action could be taken to undo it. Moreover, the gold standard had one major advantage that tax cuts did not: while a return to the full gold standard required legislative action (which Reagan could probably have gotten in 1981), opening a "gold window" *required only administrative decree.* As Nixon had unilaterally taken the dollar off of gold, Reagan could unilaterally put it back on gold by committing the government to buy and sell gold at a fixed dollar price.

Despite all of these advantages, the gold standard did not become law and is no longer a serious political issue, while the issue of tax cuts has transformed the Republican Party and remains a centerpiece of American politics. Thus, comparing the two cases draws attention to the causal role of the differences between the two issues: the case for gold never aroused much public enthusiasm. This seems to be the only real difference between the issues—in terms of ideological elaboration and backing, they are equivalent.

John Kingdon's analysis of agenda-setting in politics (1995) suggests that in the competition for political attention, proposals, no matter their sources of support, must be marketable to voters; moreover, proposals are moved rapidly onto the agenda in response to "focusing events," sudden crises in the political or social environment that seem to call for a response from policymakers. These concepts help us explain why tax cuts rather than the gold standard moved onto the political agenda: tax cuts have an appeal to voters that a return to the gold standard does not. In addition, tax cuts tapped into what was *perceived* as a taxpayer revolt:

> The passage of Proposition 13 . . . became symbolic of a perceived restiveness among taxpayers, a shift in public opinion. Politicians had felt something like a taxpayer revolt coming for some time, but Proposition 13 became their shorthand way of referring to it. They would refer in an offhand way to a "Proposition 13 mentality" or a "Proposition 13 atmosphere," meaning a severe public opinion constraint on government spending, higher taxation, and new, expensive programs. Indeed, the symbol diffused very rapidly, probably because it captured the mood rather convincingly, at least as politicians saw it. Proposition 13's passage came in the midst of my 1978 interviews. It was discussed by name as being important in only 2 of the 26 interviews conducted before its passage. But 15 of the 38 postpassage interviews (39 percent) contained a spontaneous, mention of Proposition 13 by name—quite a remarkable diffusion of a symbol among policy elites over a short period of time. (Kingdon 1995, 97)

Politicians interpreted Proposition 13 as a symbol of a general citizens' revolt against taxation. As noted above, there was not actually much pressure from citizens to cut taxes. But the drama of Proposition 13 led politicians to suspect the potential to exploit antitax sentiment. Taxation in the United States is highly visible and dispersed; on the other hand, the benefits received from taxation are largely invisible and taken for granted. Compared to the French system, for example, in which the benefits of taxation are highly visible and widely dispersed, while taxation is invisible and/or concentrated, the American tax structure is much more amenable to political change because it *uncouples* the process of taxation from the process of expenditure (Steinmo 1993). Thus, a dramatic focusing event, and the possibility of framing the tax-cut issue in such a way as to demobilize opposition to it, led to politicians' perceptions that the issue of tax cuts could be a political winner; no such event happened to bring the gold standard issue to public attention.

One additional kind of evidence supports the idea that the political appeal of the tax cuts brought them onto the agenda: the precise timing of the start of Ronald Reagan's campaigning for the cause. Before 1976, Reagan, like most Republicans, was squarely in the "fiscal austerity" wing of the party, those who argued that spending cuts should precede tax cuts; as late as 1978 he was quoted as saying, "Frankly, I'm afraid this country is just going to have to suffer two, three years of hard times to pay for the binge we've been on" (quoted in Akard 1989, 108). But he began endorsing Kemp-Roth that year, it seems on the advice of his campaign manager John Sears, who saw in the Proposition 13 issue a hook on which to hang a successful campaign (Blumenthal 1986, 198). Reagan did not begin pushing the tax-cut idea vigorously, however, until immediately after his primary loss to George Bush in 1980 (Stein 1994); but once the primary nomination was secured, the emphasis on tax cuts declined, and advisers began to tell the press that Reagan "has begun to listen to other economists, such as Alan Greenspan and George Shultz, who argue that, given a substantial tax cut, Federal spending must be reduced if higher rates of inflation are to be avoided" (Lindsey 1980)—a position that contradicted the Laffer curve idea. There is no doubt that the issue of tax cuts was central to the eventual presidential campaign. Hansen (1983) has formulated a rough measure of the importance of tax issues in campaigns by counting sentences devoted to tax issues in campaign platforms. She finds that taxation issues were more central to the Republican campaign in 1980 than they had been for either party in this period—indeed, her data, which go back to 1844, show that the issue had *never* before been so central.

Once it moved onto the agenda, the victory of the ERTA could by no means be taken for granted. Congress was controlled by Democrats, who had a comfortable margin in both houses. When the tax-cut bill first arrived on the scene, commentators predicted a sure defeat for the president. "Ronald Reagan's $48 billion package of budget cuts is steaming through Congress, but his three-year 10-percent tax cut proposal seems to have run aground," said *Newsweek*; the Speaker of the House thought, "There's no support out there, even among the Republicans," and a Republican Congressman worried that "the administration is in the ditch on tax cuts" (all quoted in Stockman 1986, 232). So the victory, when it came, was even sweeter for Reagan and his supporters. In July 1981, forty-eight Democrats "defected" to vote for the tax cuts, while only twelve Republicans voted against. The outcome was much more lopsided in the Senate: eighty-nine of the hundred senators voted in favor.

The victory in the House was particularly significant, as the House had been much more hostile to the original idea than the Senate. Crucial to the House victory were the Southern Democrats: 45 percent of the 80 Southern Democrats in the House of Representatives voted in favor of the tax cuts, compared to only 7.3 percent of the 160 Northern Democrats. The Southern Democrats provided the swing votes; without them, the 12 Republican defectors exactly canceled out the 12 Northern Democratic

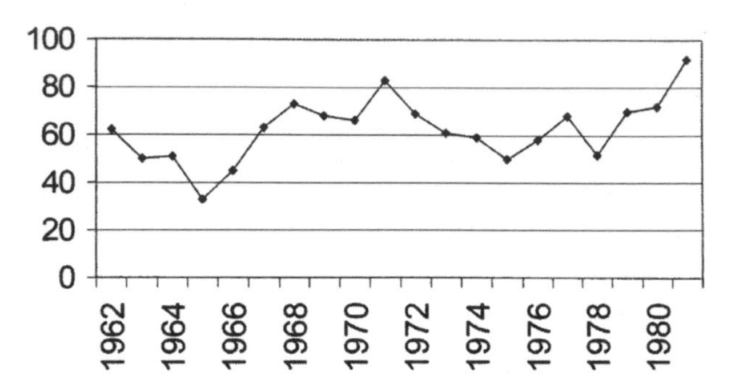

FIGURE 1.2. Conservative coalition victories, 1962–80, United States (%)
Source: Congressional Quarterly 1982, 38.

defectors. The 36 Southern Democrats who voted in favor of the tax cuts provided a margin large enough to overwhelm the Democrats' numerical advantage.

Why did the Southern Democrats vote in favor of the Republican-led tax cut? And why did they do so in such overwhelming numbers when their northern counterparts by and large voted the party line? There is both a historical and a policy-specific answer. First, although the south had been solidly Democratic since the Civil War (because of the Republican Party's role in abolishing slavery and imposing a punitive Reconstruction on the south), the region's attachment to the Democratic party had been weakening since the 1940s and dropped precipitously beginning in the 1960s because of the Democratic Party's increasingly receptive stance on civil rights for blacks and the beginning of racial gerrymandering, which lessened the pressure for Southern Democrats to take progressive stances (Bass and DeVries 1995). This was reflected first in the rise of Republican candidates and successful officeholders in the South and second in the increasing detachment of the Southern Democrats from the national party organization. Figure 1.2 shows the percentage of votes on which a coalition of Republicans and Southern Democrats outvoted Northern Democrats in the always Democratically controlled Congress of the 1970s on issues on which Southern Democrats and Republicans were opposed to Northern Democrats. This figure is well above half for the entire period since the late 1960s, signaling the rise and importance of the coalition; but note also the sharp rise in 1981, when the conservative coalition won 92 percent of issues on which it cooperated. What happened in this year to make the Southern Democrats vote so often in the Republican president's favor?

TABLE 1.2 **Voting for 1981 tax cut in House of Representatives by party and constituency, United States**

	Total	Number voting for ERTA	Percentage voting for ERTA
All Democrats	244	48	19.7
Northern Democrats	164	12	7.3
Southern Democrats	80	36	45
Southern Democrats from nonfarm districts[a]	46	16	34.8
Southern Democrats from farm districts[a]	34	20	58.8

Source: Barone and Ujifusa 1982; author's calculations.
[a]Farm districts are defined as southern districts where the percentage of residents involved in farming is greater than the southern district average.

To attract swing supporters to the tax cuts, Reagan and his Republican supporters in both the House and the Senate increased the scope of the tax bill by adding eleven separate, major amendments that benefited particular constituencies, including tax cuts on unearned income, estate taxes, interest and dividend income, and for high-technology industries, married couples, persons employed overseas, contributors to IRAs, the self-employed, oil-royalty owners, and "persons rehabilitating old buildings" (Cohen 1981, 1061). Other additions included tax relief for owners of oil land, deductions for trucking companies, and special allowances for six distressed industries. Politicians who were "in business for themselves" took action to protect their constituencies, and were not bound by the discipline of the Ways and Means Committee that had kept earlier tax cuts, such as the Kennedy-Johnson tax cuts of 1964, within budgetary bounds.

Of the provisions added, one turned out to be crucial in its effect on the votes of the Southern Democrats: the raising of the exemption ceiling on estate taxes, which affected family farms and small family businesses. Table 1.2 shows the rate of voting for the tax cut broken down by party and constituency. Southern Democrats from farm districts, in particular, were more likely to vote for the ERTA than Northern Democrats and all other Southern Democrats: only 7.3 percent of Northern Democrats voted for the ERTA, while more than a third of Southern Democrats from nonfarm districts did, and almost 60 percent of Southern Democrats from farm districts did.

The dynamic of legislators needing to be individually attracted to vote for the legislation with benefits for their particular constituencies shows the influence of a territorially instantiated democratic process on the victory of the ERTA. The *reason* that legislators had to be individually attracted, and how they were attracted, again has to do with recent changes in the structure of the state. The congressional budget reforms of 1974 had weakened the power of centralized budget-making committees. The result was lack of careful review or deliberation on the ERTA by the Ways and Means committee:

> The reforms had a devastating effect on Ways and Means. As its autonomy was diminished, the committee was weakened. Without its function of assigning members to committees and the virtually automatic closed rule, Ways and Means had few resources for imposing its will on the House. The committee was opened up, not only by opening its meetings to the press but also by enlarging its membership and altering its composition. It now has a larger proportion of members from unsafe districts, who are more responsive to constituency-based interest groups than to the chairman or the ranking minority member. Since many members feel electorally insecure, the absence of committee constraints has had an adverse effect on the entire membership, not only on those who have experienced close elections. With the power of the chairman significantly curtailed, the inclination of members to pursue their own goals rather than those of the committee or their party has been encouraged. (Rudder 1983, 204–5)

The 1970s reforms thus resulted in "change in the direction of less carefully crafted decisions that reflect greater attention to servicing clientele groups and more distribution of particularistic benefits to members' constituencies" (Strahan 1990, 55). The dynamic of members pursuing their own goals, particularly the goals of their constituencies, had two effects on the passage of the ERTA. First, it further unlinked tax issues from spending issues by removing the power of the Ways and Means committee to bring these issues out of the sphere of public influence; second, by removing the committee's power to set the *terms* upon which tax and budget issues would be decided, it opened the way for appeals from individual entrepreneurs to seek particular favors for their constituencies.

In the case of the ERTA, then, changes in the structure of the state meant that state actors were increasingly oriented toward short-term, populist causes benefiting their particular constituencies. With regard to the 1981 tax cuts, state actors who were "in business for themselves" needed to be individually attracted to the tax cuts because of the absence of a centralized decision-making and -enforcing body like the Ways and Means Committee in the House. Once a "big tax bill" was on the agenda, it could only be pushed through by adding tax breaks to attract more and more of these individual political entrepreneurs. The result has been characterized as a "bidding war"; the final bill included eleven separate major amendments intended to attract particular constituencies, especially the Southern Democrats. The need to attract more votes explains the size of the tax cuts: they grew in response to the need to attract more and more supporters in the legislature. Indeed, indexation—the issue that more than any other gave the 1981 tax cuts a permanency not seen before or since—was passed in the House because of this frantic bidding activity, without receiving *any* debate or committee consideration. It was included as part of a Republican package that "reflected less a consistent philosophy than the result of a fierce bidding war between the administration and House Democrats to demonstrate who controlled the floor of the House" (Weaver 1988, 203) by offering alternative proposals that outbid each other in the size and particular distribution of tax cuts offered. Notice the neat political reversal in the floor dynamics of the 1981 tax cuts: in the postwar period this has usually been the dynamic of "pork barrel" politics, gaining support by giving each representative something for her or his district. Because of the declining influence of the Ways and Means Committee, the President could offer tax cuts as pork in reverse.

The story of the 1981 tax cuts argues against the business-groups explanation. Business groups were wary of the deficits that such a large tax cut would produce. Instead, the tax cuts originated in, moved onto the agenda, and were passed because of certain changes in state structure and certain interactions of state and society: the weakening of parties and the consequent rise of entrepreneurial politicians such as Jack Kemp; the political appeal of the tax cuts when they were presented outside the context of the issue of balanced budgets; and the "pork in reverse" use of the decentralized state structure to exaggerate the scope of the tax cuts. At each step, politicians did not simply respond to majority demands, but actively sought to anticipate, discover, and even generate them. The visible nature of progressive income and property taxes helped them in this: progressive taxes are levied in accordance with income; consequently they require that information be collected to determine what a taxpayer's income is and what the appropriate rate should be, and this puts detailed information on how much is being paid into the hands of the taxpayer. Taxpayers expressed their dissatisfaction with property taxes in one state, and politicians thought they sensed dissatisfaction with income taxes and responded accordingly.

Industrial Policy: Deregulation

Direct regulation of economic activity is as old as the American state. The early state was aggressively interventionist on a local level in matters that affected the "public interest," such as the operation of public utilities. It was only with the arrival of railroads, however, and the creation of the Interstate Commerce Commission (ICC) in 1887 to regulate them, that regulation became a major national issue. The Federal Exchange Commission and the Federal Reserve followed in the second decade of the new century, and then the Depression spurred another round of regulatory reform designed to stabilize capitalism, which included the creation of major regulatory agencies such as the Securities and Exchange Commission and the Federal Deposit Insurance Corporation. In the 1960s legislators began to pass a new type of "social regulation" that attempted to protect the public from the "externalities" of private production such as industrial risk and environmental pollution (Eisner 1993; Novak 1996; McCraw 1984).

The 1960s burst of regulation was quickly followed by a developing critique of regulation, and the issue of deregulation remained on the political agenda for the entire decade of the 1970s. Even as he signed into law the Environmental Protection Act, which would create the largest single regulatory agency to date, the EPA, President Richard Nixon indicated a desire to contain "regulatory sprawl." President Gerald Ford took up the banner of deregulation as an anti-inflationary measure and passed an Executive Order that new regulations be assessed for their impact on inflation before being implemented. It was in President Jimmy Carter's term that deregulation first began to make headlines. Following a series of dramatic congressional hearings led by Senator Edward (Ted) Kennedy, the Civil Aeronautics Board (CAB) was deregulated out of existence, and Carter established the Regulatory Analysis Review Group (RARG) to examine and comment on the effect of regulations on the economy. When Reagan took office, airlines, railroads, and interstate trucking had all been deregulated; Reagan's contribution was to implement cost-benefit analysis as a standard for all new regulations, put the Office of Management and Budget in control of regulatory oversight, and create a Task Force on Regulatory Relief chaired by the vice president (Friedman 1995). These innovations extended the Carter-era economic deregulations into the sphere of social regulation, most particularly into the Occupational Safety and Health Administration and the Environmental Protection Agency.

The puzzle in the story of deregulation is why it was supported by Democrats as well as Republicans. Ted Kennedy is not usually associated with right-wing policies; indeed, in the latter part of the twentieth century he has been one of the most reliable standard bearers for the Left in American politics. The picture becomes more puzzling still when we realize that Kennedy's involvement was partly a result of consumer advocate Ralph Nader's activism. Nader is generally considered to be on the extreme Left of American politics and has been one of the Left's most successful social activists. Existing explanations of deregulation do not take this oddity into account, and, as I will show, they therefore miss the key dynamic in the process of deregulation as it worked out in the 1970s and 1980s. Deregulation in the 1970s was a populist phenomenon, protecting consumers at the expense of particular industries; that is, deregulation in the 1970s was *not* in the interest of business, and was not meant to be. Presidents Ford and Reagan turned the deregulatory movement in a pro-business direction. Existing explanations ignore this important difference between deregulation in the 1970s and deregulation in the 1980s, and they therefore also miss one of the key elements in the rise and eventual decline of deregulatory policy: the role of the "new social movements" in the "old" class struggle of regulation and deregulation.

Two themes are common in scholarly investigations of the rise of deregulation. Many analysts see it as the result of the rise and classwide coordination of business in the late 1970s and early 1980s.[4] The problem with this explanation is one of timing. As Patrick Akard notes, business lobbying between 1974 and 1978 was primarily defensive, attempting "to block a number of legislative initiatives proposed by labor and liberal groups" (Akard 1992, 603). Business moved into the ideological and policy offensive in 1978, but by then, deregulation had already been endorsed and implemented in varying degrees by three presidents. Table 1.3 presents a measure of business concentration and a chronology of the major deregulatory initiatives, and figure 1.3 presents an aggregated measure of cutbacks at the top regulatory agencies. Economic regulatory agencies are charged with making the market function better and fostering competition; social regulatory agencies are charged with limiting the functions of the market in the interests of protecting citizens and workers.

Table 1.3 and figure 1.3 show that economic deregulation was already being considered and implemented before the big wave of corporate mobilization in the late 1970s: the CAB and the ICC in particular had already begun to lose budgets and personnel by the late 1970s. On the other hand,

4. See, e.g., Akard 1992; Edsall 1984; Eisner 1993, 174–78; Ferguson and Rogers 1986; Himmelstein 1990; Pertschuk 1982; Piven and Cloward 1982.

TABLE 1.3 **Chronology of corporate mobilization and deregulation, 1968–1992, United States**

Year	Membership of U.S. Chamber of Commerce	Chronology of deregulatory initiatives	Agencies and industries deregulated
1968	32,000		
1969			
1970	34,000		
1971		Nixon: "Quality of Life" regulatory review process	
1972	40,000		
1973	40,000		
1974		Ford: Council on Wage and Price Stability, Executive Order No. 11821, "Inflationary Impact Statement"	
1975	40,000		
1976	40,000		
1977	56,000		Civil Aeronautics Board
1978	64,000	Carter: Regulatory Analysis and Review Group, Executive Order No. 12044, "Unnecessary Burdens on the Economy"	Airlines
1979	69,000		Air transportation
1980	77,000		Railroads, freight trucking, financial services, natural gas
1981	96,000	Reagan: Presidential Task Force on Regulatory Relief, Executive Order No. 12291, "Cost-Benefit"	EPA, OSHA, mining
1982	200,000		
1983	250,000		
1984	200,000		
1985			
1986			
1987			
1988		Bush: Council on Competitiveness	
1989			
1990			
1991			
1992		Bush: moratorium on new regulations	

Source: Encyclopedia of American Associations 1959–1989; Derthick and Quirk 1985; Eisner 1993; McCraw 1984.

corporate mobilization alone was not enough to initiate social deregulation, which only picked up steam with the arrival of Ronald Reagan: although the small Consumer Product Safety Commission (CPSC) was in a slow decline, the large social regulatory agencies—the Food and Drug Administration (FDA), Equal Employment Opportunity Commission (EEOC), Occupational Safety and Health Administration (OSHA), EPA,

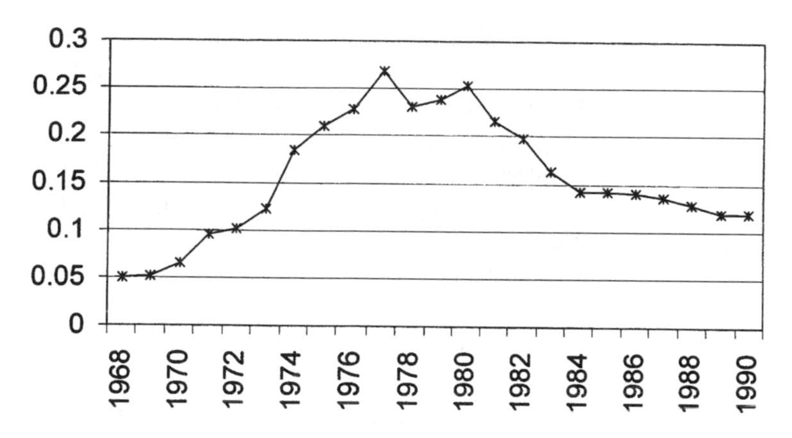

FIGURE 1.3. Total budget of major regulatory agencies (% GDP)
Source: Office of Management and Budget, *Budget of the U.S. Government*, 1968–1992; OMB, *Historical Tables*, 1968–1992; author's calculations.

and the National Labor Relations Board (NLRB)—were all holding their own before 1980. Despite intensive business-group lobbying, Carter remained a supporter of social regulation. A final problem with the business-group explanation is that it does not explain the end of the deregulatory push. Business-group pressure intensified in 1981 and 1982, but deregulatory initiatives ended in 1983, and by the late 1980s several agencies were witnessing increases in budgets and personnel.

Some scholars argue that deregulation represents the triumph of the "politics of ideas," particularly of academic economic analysis: "Our cases demonstrate the role that disinterested economic analysis can play in the formation of public policy" (Derthick and Quirk 1985, 246). But ideas alone cannot have been enough. If they were, we would have seen another measure move onto the political agenda in the 1970s: the use of effluent taxes (247). Economically, measures that distort incentives in a desired direction are as useful as regulatory measures in bringing about certain behaviors. But deregulation had advantages that effluent taxes did not: "Both liberals and conservatives found in the proposals the opportunity to assert their principles; . . . these intrinsically rather obscure proposals could be linked rhetorically to larger public concerns—inflation and big government—which gave them potential to be widely noticed" (247). Effluent taxes, on the other hand, were repellent to *both* liberals and conservatives—to liberals because they could be portrayed as licenses to pollute, and to conservatives because they could be seen as punishing the most successful businesses. The examination of why deregulation moved onto the agenda when other microeconomics-approved measures did not also highlights the necessity of political marketability. Also, like the business-group explanation, the "ideas" explanation cannot explain why the deregulatory movement ran out of steam in 1983. The "ideas" and the economic arguments were the same as they had been a few years ago, but deregulation as a sustained policy effort petered out. To explain this, we must again investigate the different appeals of ideas at different times.

The rise of deregulation is well understood. All scholars who have examined the issue agree that the deregulatory movement "was produced by a five-part coalition consisting of consumer advocates in Congress, a new strain of entrepreneurial congressional staff members, advocacy journalists, organized labor, and private not-for-profit issue entrepreneurs, of whom the most prominent was Ralph Nader" (Derthick and Quirk 1985, 10–11).[5]

The important attribute of this early phase of the movement is that it advocated a *specific kind* of deregulation: deregulation of economic regulatory agencies only. As noted above, *regulation* has two distinct meanings: *economic regulation* is the regulation of one particular industry in the interest of preventing any one company from gaining a monopoly in that industry; *social regulation*, on the other hand, is regulation that extends to *all* industries, such as legislation concerning the environment and worker safety intended to protect others from the "externalities" of market production in general.

In the postwar period economists and social scientists began to argue that economic regulatory agencies were inevitably "captured" by the industries they purported to regulate: daily contact, revolving doors from government to industry, and mutual interest in survival created "iron triangles" of association between agency, industry, and representatives in Congress that functioned to the benefit of industries and the disadvantage of consumers (Friedman 1995). According to the theory, these "captured" agencies encouraged the passage of laws that kept prices artificially inflated, directly contributing to corporate profit at consumers' expense.

Thus, when deregulation first moved onto the political stage, it was *not a free-market issue*. The aim was not to "get the government off the back

5. See also Creighton 1976; Friedman 1995; Hammond and Knott 1988; MacAvoy 1979; Mayer 1989; Meier 1988; Moe 1985; Nadel 1971; Pertschuk 1982; Teske 1991.

of industry," but to prevent the government from giving *unfair advantage* to industry at the expense of consumers. The economists who first developed this critique came from the populist Left as well as the neoliberal Right. Consider the colorful Alfred Kahn, an economist by training and a liberal Democrat by temperament, President Carter's choice to head the Civil Aeronautics Board and then the Council on Wage and Price Stability. In a memorable debate with a member of the Air Line Pilots Association who accused him of being antilabor, Kahn snapped, "If I'm anti-anything, I'm anti-excessive government interference.... And I am *particularly* against government being used to protect powerful business interests by giving them special grants of monopoly privilege.... Lower prices induced by more competition mean *more* jobs, not fewer: don't you forget that when you say it is you who speak for labor, and not I" (quoted in McCraw 1984, 288). Because they agreed that regulation meant that government was being used to protect powerful business interests, advocates for consumers and the Left in general supported deregulation in the early 1970s.

Deregulation emerged as a central political issue primarily because of the work of three men: Edward Kennedy, the senator from Massachusetts; Stephen Breyer, a law professor at Harvard and later a Supreme Court Justice; and Ralph Nader, the head of the consumers' movement. All three are on the Left of the American political scene: Breyer has been a reliably (though not radically) left-wing voice on the right-wing Rehnquist Court, voting on the progressive side of almost every issue; Kennedy has for three decades championed causes identified with the Left, such as expanded access to health care; and Nader has been the most important force in getting consumer protection legislation implemented against the wishes of large corporations, even running for the presidency on an anticorporate platform in 2000 and 2004.

In the early 1970s, the consumers' movement took up the cause of pro-consumer deregulation. The movement's investigations and condemnations of regulatory agencies, published as a series of books in 1971, were widely disseminated in the media and may have helped to mobilize public opinion in favor of deregulation (Derthick and Quirk 1985). Nader and groups affiliated with him testified in Congress in favor of deregulation many times (Bykerk and Maney 1991–92). Nader himself was the first to propose, at a Congressional hearing, the abolition of the Civil Aeronautics Board, which he believed artificially inflated airfares; this measure was eventually adopted and became the most drastic symbol of deregulation

(Derthick and Quirk 1985). Scholars of the era agree that Nader's influence was instrumental in the rise of deregulation. Louis Harris, for example, attributes a 50 percent drop in trust in the nation's major companies to the influence of the consumers' movement. In addition to making deregulation a salient issue and contributing to the dissemination of a populist critique of economic regulation, the consumers' movement prodded Ted Kennedy to adopt deregulation as a cause in "his" Congressional subcommittee, the Senate's Subcommittee on Administrative Practice and Procedure (AdPrac). Kennedy became involved when Breyer, an expert in administrative law and one of Kennedy's aides, called the issue to his attention.

A revealing aspect of the transformation of deregulation from a left-wing to a right-wing issue is that those who participated in deregulation in the early years were retrospectively redefined as conservatives. For example, on the occasion of Breyer's appointment to the Supreme Court several years later, many commentators interpreted his role in deregulation as a clue that he was generally conservative (Kuttner 1994, 15A). Kennedy himself, when considering a presidential run in 1988, succeeded in positioning himself as a "centrist" by referring to his role in deregulation (Balz 1985; "Kennedy for U.S. Senate," *Boston Globe*, 2 Nov 1994): "As he has shown on several issues in recent years—including leadership of airline deregulation and support for President Reagan's proposed presidential line-item veto of federal spending—Kennedy has an innovative and sometimes independent streak. He does not quite fit the big-spending caricature of partisan Republican attacks" (Cohen 1986).

To call Breyer and Kennedy's participation in deregulation an indication of their underlying conservatism or eclecticism is a misreading of history, in light of what deregulation *became*. In the early to mid 1970s deregulation was not a conservative idea, but a liberal populist one, against big business in the interest of consumers. That Breyer himself saw the issue in these terms—and *not* in conservative terms of getting the government out of industry—is apparent in two memos that he wrote for Kennedy in 1974, urging Kennedy to push deregulation of the airlines.

The first memo explains that "The major issue in these hearings is whether the CAB should allow more price competition among airlines" (Breyer quoted in Simon 1977, 22). Breyer does not frame economic deregulation as an issue of "getting the government out of industry." Indeed, he suggests that government oversight of industry is necessary, but that regulation is the wrong instrument in this case. The fundamental issue that the deregulation hearings would be part of, Breyer notes, is how the government should best address industrial "problems": "The government has four sets of weapons at its disposal: (1) antitrust, (2) classical regulation (prices, allocations), (3) *forms of nationalization*, (4) systems of taxes and subsidies. Which weapon suits which problem?—a basic question over the next 20 years, which AdPrac would set out to explore" (22; emphasis added).

Implicit in this discussion is that the government has a role to play in shaping industry. Moreover, Breyer goes on to say that the expertise the committee develops in these hearings can be used in the future to address "more complicated problems, involving energy shortages, possible nationalization, etc." He again clarifies what the main purpose of the hearings would be: "The ultimate statute should lead to lower prices." He thinks the hearings would not get much publicity, because "the consumer, the main beneficiary, is not very interested in the issue; the industry knows only too well what is going on." He speculates on some possible themes for the hearings: "'Help the consumer?' 'Free the captive agency?' 'More competition?'" (Simon 1977, 23). While Breyer tries out antigovernment themes in speculating on how to sell the hearings, he sees the real purpose of deregulation as benefiting consumers and is suspicious of industry—the same position (though less extreme) as that of Nader and the consumers' movement. A subsidiary benefit of the hearings, according to this memo, is that they would provide expertise on industrial policy that would be useful for AdPrac in the future, when it addressed other issues where government needs to intervene in industry—such as "possible nationalization," a far cry from the conservative position ascribed to him by later commentators!

The second, longer memo is similar. It begins as follows: "An investigation of the CAB would focus upon the question whether existing CAB regulatory policies or increased competition is more likely to *produce lower prices*" (Simon 1977, 25; emphasis added). Breyer devotes eight of the eleven pages of the memo to discussing "the price issue," that is, the question of whether more deregulation would lead to lower prices or would harm the airline industry (25–33). He also addresses other consumer issues, such as overbooking flights and lost luggage.

Thus, at its debut on the political stage, deregulation was framed as being in the interest of the consumer—a populist issue rather than a promarket one. Kennedy's opening statements in the hearings continued this framing: "Regulators all too often encourage or approve unreasonably high prices, inadequate service, and anticompetitive behavior. The cost of this regulation is always passed on to the consumer. And that cost is astronomical" (U.S. Senate 1977).

Although it had emerged on the Left as a pro-consumer issue, by the end of the 1970s deregulation had become a free-market issue pushed most heavily by the Right. In particular, the *meaning* of deregulation had changed: instead of economic deregulation (deregulation involving agencies that regulate one industry in the interest of preventing monopoly but have become "captured" and are giving unfair advantages to that industry), deregulation now referred to social deregulation (deregulation involving agencies such as the EPA and OSHA that regulate all industries in the interest of consumers, workers, and the environment). By 1985, Nader was commenting, "Deregulation is a code word meaning no more law and order for corporations" (Sinclair 1985).

To capture these shifts in the framing of deregulation, I analyzed and coded articles about regulation from periodicals in the 1970s. All articles indexed in the *Readers' Guide to Periodical Literature* under the heading "independent regulatory commissions" (1969–79) and "regulatory agencies" (1979–81)[6] were analyzed, as well as those under headings cross-referenced under those two headings. The total population of 144 articles was drawn from thirty-six different periodical titles.[7] The articles were read once to identify the themes that dominated discussion of deregulation. All but fourteen of the articles fit nine specific themes that may be formulated as answering the questions "Whom does regulation hurt?" (consumers, everyone, or business) and "How does regulation hurt its victims?" (costs, inefficiency, or abuse of government power). I coded the articles according to whether the particular theme was present or absent. Articles were allowed to have multiple themes. The nine themes were then divided into three frames—a pro-consumer frame, an intermediate frame, and a pro-business frame, depending on the perceived victim of

6. In the 1979–80 volume, the heading "regulatory agencies" is designated as equivalent to the earlier heading with this italicized note: "For material before this volume, see heading Independent regulatory commissions." The *Readers' Guide* indexes articles in general-interest U.S. publications; it has been published since 1900, annually since 1965.

7. *America, American Academy for the Advancement of Political and Social Science, American Heritage, Aviation Week and Space Technology, BioScience, Business Week, Congressional Digest, Conservationist, Consumer Reports, Current, Duns Review, Environment, Farming Journal, Forbes, Fortune, Harper, Human Behavior, Intellect, Nation, Nation's Business, National Review, New Republic, New York Times Magazine, Newsweek, Reader's Digest, Saturday Review, Saturday Evening Post, Science, Senior Scholastic, Successful Farming, Technology Review, Time, Transaction, U.S. News & World Report, Vital Speeches,* and *Washington Monthly.*

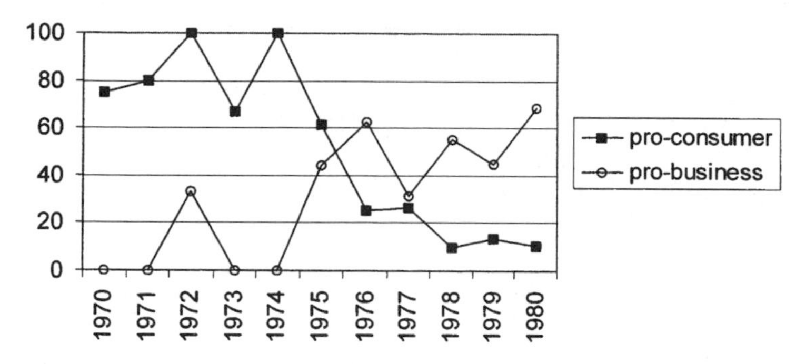

FIGURE 1.4. Pro-consumer and pro-business articles (% of total articles on regulation)

regulation—and an article's dominant frame was determined according to the number of themes of each frame that were present. For example, if an article included one theme from the "pro-consumer" frame and two from the "pro-business" frame, it would be coded as a "pro-business" article; if the same number of themes appeared from each frame, the article would get both a pro-consumer and a pro-business coding.

Figure 1.4 shows the results of the analysis. In the early part of this period, deregulation was framed as in being in the interest of consumers and against the interest of business. By the end of this period, deregulation was framed as being in the interest of business. Three issues are continuously present throughout this period in the discussion of regulatory agencies: the high costs they generate, their inefficiencies, and the abuse of government power that they allow. However, as table 1.4 shows, these three issues are deployed in quite different ways at the beginning of the 1970s than at the end.

At the beginning of the 1970s, these issues are articulated under a pro-consumer frame: the high costs referred to are costs to consumers, the inefficiencies are generated by the coziness of regulators with the industries they regulate, and the abuse of government power refers to its use in the interests of business: "Critics contend that the regulators of business have stopped being champions of the average citizen and have become the defenders of the industries they are supposed to oversee."[8] The result of this absorption (what the economists had called "capture") is regulations

8. "Federal Agencies under Fire," *U.S. News & World Report*, 9 Nov 1970, 82. To conserve space, the articles in the data set have not been included in the references. Those quoted directly in the text are cited in footnotes, as here. A list of all the articles, with complete citation information, is available from the author.

TABLE 1.4 **Pro-consumer, intermediate, and pro-business frames.**

	Pro-consumer frame (dominant in early 1970s)	Intermediate frame (dominant in mid-1970s)	Pro-business frame (dominant in late 1970s)
Whom does regulation hurt?	Consumers	Everyone	Business
How does regulation hurt its victims?			
Costs	Regulation causes high costs to consumers.	Regulation causes inflation.	Regulation causes high costs to business.
Inefficiency	Regulatory agencies are inefficient because captive agencies choose mediocre regulators.	Regulation produces paperwork, red tape, and silly regulations.	Regulation causes hassles to businesspeople.
Abuse of government power	Regulatory agencies use government power to protect big business.	Regulation is unchecked government power; leads to government surveillance.	Regulation is government intervention in the free market.

that benefit the regulated industry, such as artificially inflated prices and barriers to competition, at the expense of the consumer. Therefore, an antitrust lawyer advocating change comments "We want to suggest to the Congress that they should have less consideration for special interests and more consideration for the consumer. . . . We're going to lay this right at the door of the Congress and ask them if they shouldn't reconsider basically Depression-style regulations which were set up to protect industry not the public."[9] In short, the hallmark of the dominant frame in the early 1970s is that regulatory agencies have been "captured" by the industries they are supposed to regulate, and this situation represents an abuse of government power at the expense of consumers.

In contradiction, by the end of the period, the same three issues—costs, bureaucratic inefficiency, and abuse of government power—are articulated in a quite different way, under a pro-business frame. The high costs are costs to business, particularly small businesses, the inefficiencies are "silly regulations" and demands that hassle business, and the abuse of government power is governmental intervention in the free market: "The facts that

9. Rosalind K. Ellingsworth, "Close Scrutiny, Legal Challenges Face CAB on Regulatory Policy," *Aviation Week and Space Technology*, 11 Nov 1974, 27.

some zealous agencies have carried regulation to excess and that the burden frequently falls on small business, which is least equipped to handle it, are no longer debatable."[10] The CEO of Prudential complains about "the nitpicking reporting requirements, the endless reviews, the red tape and harassment" and proudly proclaims that "our case shows that companies... can stand up to government intimidation... can fight government harassment and win."[11] Democratic Senator Lloyd Bentsen is quoted as saying that "Congress should give business 'a little breathing room.'"[12] By the late 1970s, the dominant frame was that regulations cost business more than the value of their benefits, that the regulatory agencies harassed businesses incessantly, and that the abuse of government power involved is government intervention in the free market.

The transformation of the pro-consumer frame to the pro-business frame was buffered by the rise in the mid-1970s of an intermediate frame, which speaks of deregulation in terms of the "national interest," or in vague terms that refer neither to consumers nor to business but to society as a whole. In this frame, the high costs are generalized as the problem of inflation; the inefficiencies are paperwork and red tape, which are seen as bad in themselves; and the abuse of government power is referenced by the problem of government surveillance. The CEO of Gulf Oil complains that the regulatory agencies are "fueling our current double-digit inflation,"[13] and President Ford is quoted as wanting to dismantle "excessive Government regulations that stifle productivity, eliminate competition, increase consumer costs and contribute to inflation."[14] In this frame, red tape and paperwork are often referred to in terms of the *size* of the regulatory machine: "Last year... the *Federal Register*—carried almost 46,000 pages of single-spaced fine print!";[15] "The number of approved Government forms... has risen to 5,146."[16] And a virtual subgenre arises of articles

10. Michael Thoryn, "Converting the Regulators to the Rule of Common Sense," *Nation's Business*, Sep 1979, 54.

11. Robert A. Beck, "The Misuse of Power by Regulatory Agencies," *Vital Speeches of the Day*, 1 Nov 1980, 38.

12. "Putting Regulation on a Tight Budget," *Nation's Business*, Aug 1980, 17.

13. Z. D. Bonner, "The Abuse of Power by Regulatory Agencies," *Vital Speeches of the Day*, 15 Jan 1975, 194.

14. "The 'Regulators': They Cost You $130 Billion a Year," *U.S. News & World Report*, 30 Jun 1975, 24.

15. James H. Sammons, "Federal Regulation versus Professional Judgment," *Vital Speeches of the Day*, 1 Sep 1975, 694.

16. "Getting Government Off People's Backs," *U.S. News & World Report*, 6 Oct 1975, 28.

ridiculing silly regulations: that OSHA "recently undertook to instruct a company on the exact size of the partitions separating the stalls in the factory washrooms,"[17] or that "the U.S. Department of Agriculture has decided to reduce the minimum acceptable size for Norgold variety Irish potatoes grown in the State of Washington and shipped from Districts 1 through 4 from 2 1/4 to 2 1/8 inches in diameter."[18] A parody in the *Saturday Evening Post* considers how the American Revolution would have unfolded under the purview of regulatory agencies.[19] In this period fear of government surveillance is a commonly mentioned theme.

This intermediate frame is characterized by complaints that regulation contributes to inflation, leads to paperwork and red tape, and leads to government surveillance of every aspect of the lives of citizens. The articles often explicitly invoke nationalist terms—that is, regulation is bad not only because it hurts consumers or business specifically, but because it hurts all Americans. The *Saturday Evening Post* parody suggests there is something unheroic, perhaps un-American about regulation. This intermediate, general frame bridges the transformation from the pro-consumer frame to the pro-business frame.

One primary source gives a remarkable glimpse into an active moment of this public redefinition of deregulation that focuses especially on the question of the abuse of government power. On September 11, 1975, Eileen Shanahan of the *New York Times* hosted a round table discussion on regulatory reform whose panel members included Ralph Nader and Ronald Reagan. A telling moment comes when Reagan agrees with the capture theme and uses it to enter an antigovernment tirade, which Nader enthusiastically seconds:

REAGAN: I agree with you about business and the fact that business is responsible in part for going along with regulations that finally have led to some advantages for them such as preventing entry of new businesses into the field, competition, price fixing, and so forth. I still think those businesses are wrong. And I think it's led to what I call an interlocking bureaucracy. That the bureaucracy in government is now being matched by a bureaucracy employed by business to do business with the bureaucracy here and now you have two bureaucracies feeding on each

17. William F. Buckley Jr., "Mr. Carter's Discovery of Human 'Rights,'" *National Review*, 1 Apr 1977, 403.

18. "All in a Day's Work," *Fortune*, 25 Aug 1980, 32.

19. Maynard Good Stoddard, "Our Floundering Fathers," *Saturday Evening Post*, Jul–Aug 1980, 64–65.

other and neither one of them wants the other to go away because then they wouldn't have a job.

NADER: If you make that your campaign theme next year you'd be making a major contribution to the American dialogue.

REAGAN: Well. I—

NADER: Speaking out against corporate socialism and government subsidies of big business where big corporations are so big they can't be allowed to fail; only small businesses can go bankrupt, but if you're big like Lockheed and those other companies you can go to Washington instead.... Massive outflow of the taxpayer's revenue into the coffers of these giant corporations... people who say they're conservatives do not speak out enough against monopolistic practices, highly concentrated industry; they don't speak for the enforcement of the antitrust laws for beefing up the Justice Department's budget; they don't speak against the massive, inflated contracts and subsidies that pour out of Washington which makes up the bulk of government.... And if you speak out against that, politics will be enriched.

REAGAN: I've been speaking out against that for a long time.

NADER: The press isn't coverin' ya.

REAGAN: I know! [laughter]

Notice the specific use that Reagan makes of the "capture" thesis: government has been captured by business, he acknowledges, agreeing with the critique from the Left, but then he uses the capture thesis to criticize the size of bureaucracies. The solution to this *is not to reduce business control of government, but to reduce government.* This solution, only implied in the quotation above, is made explicit during the question and answer session immediately following the panelists' debate. An audience member says to Nader,

AUDIENCE MEMBER: I was struck in listening to the conversation that just occurred suggested the best way you can hear all the people, or there is one thing that can hear all the people most of the time and that's the marketplace. And that of course suggests that we ought not to have as much government regulation that we have and ought to place a greater degree of reliance on market forces. That leads me to the question that I wanted to ask Mr. Nader. He asked Governor Reagan to provide a list of the subsidies to business that the governor would get rid of, and then in response to the governor's point that the proliferation of laws and regulations that we have seen occurring in this country particularly on the federal level has led to a disrespect if not for a contempt for the law

Mr. Nader said many of these laws and regulations should be repealed. Now I assume from looking at things that Mr. Nader has said in the past that he would agree that perhaps the Civil Aeronautics Board and the Interstate Commerce Commission should be abolished for starters. But I would like Mr. Nader to give us a list of other government agencies and other government regulations that he would get rid of and why.

NADER: What, now? [laughter]

AUDIENCE MEMBER: Yeah.

NADER: The Maritime Administration, a good deal of the Department of Commerce, a good deal of the Department of Interior, a good deal of the Department of Defense. Portions of the GSA. I mean we can go on forever.

[Senator Hubert Humphrey, another member of the panel, intervenes. Another audience member asks another question, Humphrey responds. Reagan intervenes, then adds:]

REAGAN: . . . Now Mr. Nader responded to the challenge by naming some of the agencies and I thought for a minute there he and I had become blood brothers, uh, that he was going to eliminate. I have a proposal as to how we might find out what we could eliminate. I have a sneaking suspicion after eight years in public office that if all of us in government just quietly some day sneaked home and shut the door, it'd be weeks before the people ever missed us. [laughter] Then—

HUMPHREY: Governor, that's exactly what I thought those two years I was out of office. [laughter] (Shanahan 1975)

Deregulation had made Ronald Reagan and Ralph Nader "blood brothers." The "capture" thesis—that government is giving unfair advantages to business—is turned in a pro-market direction and used to suggest that government is too big. Nader had agreed that government should be cut back, and although we can surmise that his reasoning is that the particular departments and agencies he mentions are captives of business and raise costs to consumers, Reagan extends the argument into a general antigovernment argument.

This is a concrete example—involving two of the key players in the drama—of how, although deregulation was brought onto the agenda in the 1970s by left-wing groups, certain elements of the left-wing deregulatory idea were reinterpreted to resonate with a right-wing frame in the mid-1970s.

President Ford's main contribution to the effort was Executive Order 11,821, which required that "[m]ajor proposals for legislation, and for the promulgation of regulations or rules by any executive branch agency must be accompanied by a statement which certifies that the inflationary impact of the proposal has been evaluated" (Gerston, Fraleigh, and Schwab 1988, 44). This extended the deregulatory push to *all* regulatory agencies, including social regulatory agencies like the EPA and OSHA. At the time, critics suspected that the Ford administration's use of the issue of economic deregulation to push social deregulation was intentional, but they could not provide concrete evidence of this (Burnham 1975). With the opening of the Ford Presidential Library in Ann Arbor, Michigan, such evidence has become available. In the mid-1970s, inflation was named the most important problem by the vast majority of respondents in Gallup's annual assessment of this question, and Ford aides were aware of the potential of using this concern in particular ways. A memo from Stan Morris, the head of the Office of Management and Budget's (OMB's) regulatory policy staff, notes,

> During the past several years, Federal Government anti-inflation restraint measures of a structural nature have focused primarily on short-run "supply actions" which could be translated immediately and directly into an impact on prices and which could be implemented for the most part administratively, without legislative action. The time is ripe to consider a strategy which is broader in nature—*one which assumes that widespread public concern over inflation could build a consensus for action that might otherwise meet with powerful opposition* (among outside economic interests as well as in the Executive Branch and the Congress). (Morris 1974; emphasis added)

Morris lists five options as part of this broader strategy, the third of which is "Encourage in-depth review and reform of structural impediments to competition in more complex areas (environmental, safety, labor standards)." This seems to be the first documented coupling within the Ford administration of social deregulation as a strategy to fight inflation, and the memo suggests that the public's approval of anti-inflation policies be used strategically to pass "action that might otherwise meet with powerful opposition."

These events set the stage for the Reagan administration's cutbacks in 1981 and 1982; the largest of these cutbacks, in monetary terms, was at the EPA (fig. 1.5). Reagan was able to implement a more extreme environmental policy than would have been expected given the high public support for environmentalism because of the centralization of environmental policy in the executive branch. As Moe writes, within the executive branch "[presidents] can organize and direct the presidency as they see fit,

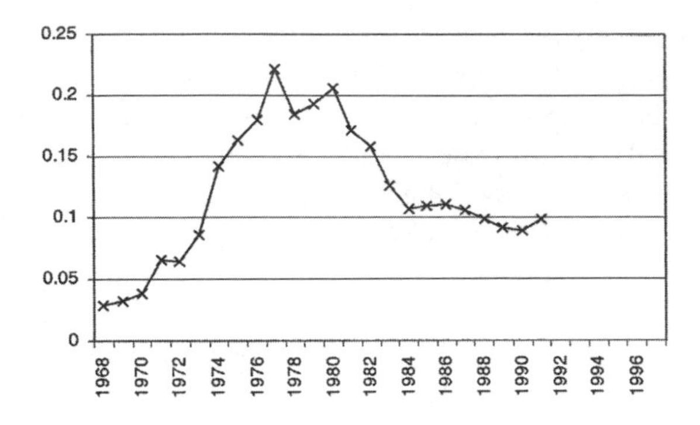

FIGURE 1.5. Budget for the EPA (% GDP)
Source: Office of Management and Budget 1968–1997b.

create public agencies, reorganize them, move them around, coordinate them, impose rules on their behavior, put their own people in top positions, and otherwise place their structural stamp on the executive branch" (Moe 1993, 366). Particularly important to environmental deregulation was the ability to avoid the veto points of the American political system by using executive orders and creating task forces with real power. The ability to appoint regulatory heads was also useful, although these appointments had to be confirmed by Congress.

Executive orders have been a significant source of presidential power. Mayer (1999) points out that between 1936 and 1995 several of the most historically important policies were carried out by executive order, including internment of Japanese-Americans, integration of the armed forces, the requirement that government contractors implement affirmative action policies, unilateral unfreezing of Iranian assets in exchange for a release of American hostages, and imposition of weak sanctions on South Africa to head off much stronger sanctions—significant policy accomplishments, even in foreign policy, carried out without input from any of the "checks and balances" structured into the American system. Reagan used an executive order to authorize the OMB to oversee the regulatory agencies and perform cost-benefit analyses on proposed regulations. The OMB

> was given enhanced authority to grant final approval to regulatory proposals, and by 1985 it was authorized to approve initial action as well. Sometimes these moves sidetracked regulations already under way.... Others... were modified more in accordance with the wishes of the business community. Some proposed

rules that the administration favored, such as the prohibition of local restrictions on the transport of nuclear waste, were permitted to proceed. (Hays 1987, 495)

Decision making through the OMB could therefore short-circuit the checks and balances of more traditional policymaking. Moreover, the regulatory agencies began to censor themselves: "OMB statistics indicate that agencies took the probability of OMB review into consideration *before* issuing any rules.... Perhaps hundreds of regulations were dropped *before* the preliminary proposal stage because the agencies anticipated their rejection by OMB" (Gerston, Fraleigh, and Schwab 1988, 56).

In addition to executive orders, Reagan reorganized the executive department to enforce his goals at the level of implementation—that is, to enact through delays and budget-cutting an anti-environmental agenda. The administration created a Task Force for Regulatory Relief, headed by Vice President George Bush, which forced delays in the implementation of environmental regulations and worked out so many loopholes for industries that offshore drilling and timber cutting actually increased and new wilderness areas were sold and opened to industry (Sale 1993, 52). Other reorganizations within the executive branch eliminated those offices opposed to the president's agenda, such as the EPA's Office of Enforcement (the abolition of which was probably the main factor in the 84 percent decline in cases referred by the EPA to the Department of Justice) and the Interior Department's Office of Surface Mining, while creating new organizations to advance the president's agenda, such as the Office of Information and Regulatory Affairs, which was given the important power to delay the implementation of regulations indefinitely (Kraft and Vig 1984).

Finally, one of the most important tools in Reagan's anti-environmental push was the presidential power to appoint heads of regulatory agencies sympathetic to the president's views on the proper extent of regulatory interference. Reagan appointed only agency heads who agreed with the need to cut back environmental protections, particularly personnel from business and the regulated industries. The most significant enforcer of environmental protection—the Environmental Protection Agency—is under direct jurisdiction of the executive branch; Reagan placed at its head Republican legislator and environmental skeptic Anne Gorsuch. James Watt, head of a business lobbying organization with explicit anti-environmental ideas, was appointed to lead the Department of the Interior, and immediately announced that he wanted to change regulations so drastically that no successor "would ever change them back because he won't have the determination that I do" (quoted in Hays 1987, 495). This was also the strategy followed for OSHA (Noble 1986).

These three strategies—executive orders, reorganization, and appointment of sympathetic agency heads—allowed the president to avoid the time-consuming process of building Congressional support for his environmental policies; they are examples of powers that have accrued to the presidency as a result of the rise of the "administrative state" (Waterman 1989). Instead, because of the way in which decisions that did not require wide approval could be kept under wraps, for a time the president could slip environmental deregulation into policy on the back of the popularity of economic deregulation. However, the deregulatory push lasted only until 1983. Although the EPA cutbacks were never reversed, reform of the Clean Air Act—the one measure costing business more money than any other, the one measure which all three major business groups were heavily lobbying against, the one measure which even environmentalists and nonpartisan groups conceded was inefficient and needed to be reformed—had not been accomplished.[20] In the 1984 campaign, deregulation played no significant role, and Reagan gave no more attention to deregulation in his second term.

The administration abandoned the effort because Reagan's early efforts against environmentalism had generated a strong, highly visible backlash brought about by clashes with organized environmentalist groups and may even have precipitated the resurgence of support for the environment among the public. In particular, the administration's attack of the EPA and the anti-environmentalism of the Department of the Interior under James Watt were highly unpopular and highly salient. In 1983 crises at the EPA and the Department of the Interior kept the issue on the front pages for several weeks, which led to a public perception that the administration was reckless with the environment, seen in every poll taken on the subject (Shabecoff 1983; Schneider 1983). Reagan's own comments did not help (e.g., in response to why environmentalists did not support him: "Well, there is environmental extremism. I don't think they'll be happy until the White House looks like a bird's nest" ["Transcript of President's News Conference on Foreign and Domestic Matters," *New York Times*, 12 Mar 1983, sec. 1]). In March "nine House Republicans wrote to Reagan, suggesting that he appoint [at EPA] 'someone who has a strong record

20. Hornblower 1979; Lave and Omenn 1981; Malone 1980; McDowell 1981; Shabecoff 1981; Vogel 1989.

of experience and interest in environmental protection'" (Peterson 1983) and according to the *New York Times*: "The aspect [of the controversy] that White House officials fear the most is that, amid all the confusion, there may be a general suggestion of favoritism to polluters in the Reagan Administration. That, they fear, could cost Mr. Reagan and the Republicans dearly in 1984 if Democrats succeed in pinning on them a label of playing politics with something as deadly as toxic waste" (Weisman 1983).

Reagan defused the issue by appointing a moderate at the EPA and disbanding the Task Force on Regulatory Relief (Smith 1983; Kraft and Vig 1984, 371). Ralph Nader commented, "They read the same polls we do," and suggested that the administration was looking for a way out of its antiregulatory image, given that polls consistently found high support for environmental measures, as well as for consumer protection and workplace safety measures (Tolchin 1983). Vogel quotes one administration official as explaining, "There's an election coming, and how can we be for cancer or be seen as being in the pocket of big business?" (1989, 268).

Public opinion in favor of the populist consumers' movement, and this movement's late-1960s to mid-1970s salience (see Lipset and Schneider 1979; Shapiro and Gilroy 1984a, 1984b), lit the torch under the deregulatory effort. Executive control of deregulation and the "frame ambiguity" of the cultural Left allowed Ronald Reagan to shift this effort in favor of business. A renewed focus on the negative effects of deregulation generated by the environmental movement brought deregulation to a halt. The history of the rise and fall of deregulation is a lesson in the relation of state institutions to societal trends as well as in the interaction of new social movements with economic policy. Reagan's "old" class effort to help business was generated, and ultimately defeated, by the new social movements of the 1960s, '70s, and '80s. The history of deregulation thus shows both the ways in which business can exercise power and the limits to that power: in the case of environmental cutbacks, what business wanted clearly opposed majority opinion. Business power could only be exercised on this issue because it was amenable to executive control, and it could only be exercised as long as the issue was kept under the radar through a process of symbolic politics that exploited confusion over the meaning of the term *deregulation*. Once that confusion cleared, the process ended.

Would the cutbacks at the EPA have happened if Nader and his activists had not put economic deregulation on the agenda? It's possible: the business community was increasingly unified against social regulation and may have convinced Reagan of its cause even without the laying of the groundwork done by the Ford administration's reappropriation of the deregulation symbol. On the other hand, Smith (1999, 2000) has shown that the issues on which business is most unified are precisely the ones that arouse the most political resistance and on which business is *least* able to get its way. Issues that unify business trigger the attention of watchdog groups and the public. Because the public was so firmly opposed to environmental cutbacks, it is clear that some kind of rhetorical obfuscation would have been necessary, or else the issue would have had to be kept out of the limelight. The concrete benefit of the economic deregulation movement was that it provided an easy means of obfuscation and allowed social deregulation to be moved ahead as part of the normal political agenda—since, after all, both Ford and Carter had been involved in "deregulation." If the stylistic missteps of Watt and Gorsuch had not brought public attention to the policy changes, it is quite possible that the cutbacks would not have stopped where they did. It seems that both the obfuscation provided by the efforts of Nader, Kennedy, and others *and* the fact that business had been lobbying the Republicans to do something about regulation were necessary. As we will see more clearly when we discuss the West German case, the adversarial structure of environmental regulation in the United States was conducive to cross-industry business mobilization, but this mobilization had to be under the radar to be effective.

Welfare State Policy

The Reagan administration's attack on the welfare state was much less successful than its implementation of free market policies in taxation and deregulation; it was also less successful than—but paved the way for—the attempts of Republicans in the next decade to transform antipoverty policy. Despite the political benefits of the image of the welfare queen, there is no historical evidence that the Reagan administration planned to single out means-tested programs for attack. Rather, the administration attempted to cut spending on *all* welfare state policies, including costly universal policies—targeting "weak claims rather than weak clients," as David Stockman put it—but was successful only in achieving marginal cutbacks in means-tested policies. This failure to rein in spending on universal policies is what the name of Stockman's memoir, *The Triumph of Politics*, refers to: the ability of the politically powerful to resist the Reagan cuts, while the politically powerless could not. William Greider would later ask, "What was new about the Reagan Revolution, in which oil-royalty owners win and welfare mothers lose?" (1982, 60). But there *was* something new, and that was the attempt itself to cut the highly popular universal programs. Thus, we need to address two separate elements of the welfare state cuts: the rise of attempts to make cuts in all social policies, and the resilience of universal programs and the weakness of targeted programs.

The largest segment of the American welfare state is old-age pensions and medical care for the elderly, constituting approximately a third of the entire budget since the 1970s (Office of Management and Budget 1968–1997a). This portion of the welfare state is not means-tested, and, as pension benefits are indexed to lifetime earnings, this portion of the welfare state reproduces the class structure rather than undermining it. For these reasons—universality and reinforcement of the merit ethic—old-age pension benefits generate widespread support.

Support for the second part of the welfare state, means-tested benefits, is considerably more ambivalent. These programs provide benefits for the poor and the unemployed, though in fact they also disproportionately benefit the elderly (including two-thirds of by far the most costly program, Medicaid). In the 1980s Medicaid hovered at 3 percent of the budget, but in the 1990s it shot up to about 7 percent of the budget (driven by increasing health care costs for the elderly). The percentage of the budget devoted to unemployment insurance has been quite volatile because of its links to the business cycle; in the postwar period it reached 5 percent of the budget once, but it has most often been between 2 and 4 percent. Family support payments (including AFDC and, after 1996, TANF) peaked at 3 percent of the budget in the early 1970s and then remained at approximately 1 percent throughout the 1980s and 1990s. (All figures are from Office of Management and Budget 1968–1997a.) Polls measuring support for this second part of the welfare state produce widely varying results depending on how questions are phrased: the American public feels warmly toward "poor people," but not toward "people on welfare" (Cook and Barrett 1992; Gilens 1999). Finally, spending on education is a large portion of the American welfare state, but it is conducted at the state level; there is little national commitment to public education.

The Reagan administration's most significant changes came in the Omnibus Budget Reconciliation Act of 1981 (OBRA), which tightened program eligibility and time limits for AFDC, disallowed work-related expenditure deductions, and allowed states to implement a "workfare option"; this cut AFDC expenditures by 14 percent. In addition to cuts in AFDC, the act achieved cuts in the food stamp program and Medicaid as well as smaller cuts in subsidized housing, the school lunch program, child care and housing assistance, public mental health and counseling services, legal aid, and other smaller means-tested programs (Nathan and Doolittle 1985; Rochefort 1986; Trattner 1999). The average disposable income (counting income, benefits, and food stamps) of families on AFDC who had working income fell from 101 percent of the poverty line to 81 percent (Joe 1982).

That these cuts were not larger has led some scholars to conclude that the conservative attack was not successful: "These programs remained substantially larger in 1985 than in 1966—the Reagan Revolution was a skirmish when viewed in its historical context" (Gottschalk 1988). Expenditure levels on most programs either held steady or climbed back up after the Reagan years. However, *need* for spending had increased during the Reagan years because of the increase in poverty in the 1980s, which was caused by several factors. A "skill mismatch" had developed between the jobs being offered in the American economy—high-tech, high-skill jobs—and the low skills that those most at risk of becoming poor could offer. Technological innovations had largely eaten away the low-skill jobs that once afforded a livable wage, and the low-skill jobs that did open up were being created in the outlying suburbs of large cities, far from the inner-city or rural residences of the chronically poor, who were mostly without means of transportation. The rising incidence of divorce in American society increased the number of families with only one worker, and especially the number of families headed by low-skilled women (though this was only a minor part of the increase in poverty), and because of the large influx of low-skilled women into the workforce, the wages for low-skill jobs have tended to become even lower, making it difficult for a worker to rise out of poverty (Blank 1997).

These factors combined to detach the poor from the rising tide that lifted the economic fortunes of the rest of the population in the 1980s. In not meeting this "new poverty" with new antipoverty policies such as federally funded child care, more public transportation, or comparable worth programs, the Reagan administration not only missed the chance to reduce poverty in the 1980s, but actually increased it, since what would have been the minor effects of the new OBRA rules were magnified in the new situation to become major poverty-generating policies, accounting for about half of the rise in poverty (Gottschalk 1988, 132; Joe 1982). Note that this is quite different from what happened in the mid-1990s: Bill Clinton ended AFDC at a time of decreasing poverty. The Reagan administration did, then, achieve a limited degree of success in implementing its convictions by avoiding new social expenditures at a time of growing poverty.

Explanations for the success of antipoverty policies can be placed into two camps: (1) scholars like Michael Katz (1989) emphasize the importance of the rise of a new set of *ideas* that legitimized the attack on welfare by questioning both the state's right to tax some to provide for others and the moral effects of welfare on its recipients; (2) some analysts, primarily Jill Quadagno (1994), have pointed to the role of *race* in the unraveling of the New Deal coalition.

As in the deregulation case, scholars identify the emergence of a new set of ideas as a central variable in the rise of the attack on the welfare state, including philosophical critiques of redistribution (e.g., Nozick 1974), sociological critiques of the nonreciprocal nature of welfare (e.g., Mead 1986), and the rise of the popular idea that welfare creates disincentives for work and marriage (e.g., Murray 1984). As in the taxation and deregulation cases, however, the ideas criticizing welfare were not hegemonic: vigorous challenges developed quickly. Nozick's formulation was, and continues to be, criticized for its assumption that the original appropriation of property by any individual can be shown to be just; if it cannot, his philosophical structure based on property and its unbroken just inheritance collapses (Kymlicka 1991). Mead's citizenship model and Murray's disincentives argument both assume that jobs are available for welfare recipients to take and that welfare recipients are on welfare for cultural reasons. But some scholars argue that unemployment and inequality have been generated by unscientific Federal Reserve decisions on interest rates rather than by impersonal market forces or individual effort (Galbraith 1998), and others argue that the data do not seem to show large disincentives for work and that for the majority of poor people spells of poverty begin and end not because of the dissolution or formation of marriages, but because of the availability or unavailability of jobs (Ellwood and Bane 1984; Blank 1997). In 1993 Murray himself concluded that a relationship between welfare and illegitimacy exists among whites, but not blacks, and that for blacks the strongest correlation with illegitimacy is with segregation (Murray 1993; see also Moffitt 1992).

The point here is not to delve into the specifics of the arguments so much as to note the prevalence in American scholarship of mutually contradictory ideas, and that the antistate ideas have by no means been proven to be true. Thus, if "ideas" drove the attack on the welfare state, we still need to show why one particular set of *contested* ideas gained ascendance. As in the cases of the ERTA and deregulation, a business-group explanation might be suggested, as extensive social costs cut into the profit rates of business. But the means-tested programs that were cut were such small parts of the budget that business groups were not lobbying against them. AFDC peaked at 3 percent of the budget in the 1970s and has been declining since then. For this reason, business groups concentrated their efforts on trying to get corporate tax cuts and social deregulation.

One very common argument is that the decline of welfare state spending is the outcome of the curiously American brand of racialized politics. Jill Quadagno (1994) has written the most elaborate defense of this perspective (see also Gilens 1999; Kinder and Sanders 1997; Lieberman 2001). In broad terms, the argument is that Republicans benefited from a racialized division among the poor: the numerically larger working poor, especially in Southern states, who were largely white, resented the nonworking poor, who were disproportionately (though not majority) black. This division was seen not in class terms, but in terms of race, and it was politically mobilized first by George Wallace, then by Barry Goldwater, and then most successfully by Richard Nixon.

These scholars are quite correct to note the political benefits of exploiting racial divisions: Reagan inherited this politics of racial division, but his genius was in discovering a way to crystallize it that would allow the "Southern Strategy" to be generalized across the country by linking racial hostility to the work ethic. He did this through a remarkable rhetorical invention, the story of the "welfare queen." In his presidential campaigns in 1976 and 1980, Reagan told this story over and over. There was in Chicago, he said, a woman who "has 80 names, 30 addresses, 12 social security cards and is collecting veterans' benefits on four nonexisting deceased husbands; . . . she is collecting welfare under each of her names. Her tax-free cash income alone is over $150,000." A *New York Times* reporter followed Reagan to eighteen "citizens' press conferences" in southern New Hampshire and noted that Reagan told this story at every single one: "Mr. Reagan had hit a nerve" ("'Welfare Queen' Becomes Issue in Reagan Campaign; Hitting a Nerve," *New York Times*, 15 Feb 1976).

The story of the welfare queen became a bone over which the Left and Right tussled for years afterward. To Reagan's supporters, it encapsulated everything that was wrong with state intervention. As Bo Rothstein (1998) points out, the phenomenon of welfare fraud infuriates citizens in many contexts, even in the welfare paradise of Sweden. A remarkably similar story of a "welfare scrounger" began to receive a great deal of coverage in Britain at almost the same time. The theme of the lazy taking advantage of the hardworking is a common political trope; originally used by leftists, who complained (and still do) of the lazy rich taking advantage of the hardworking masses, it became a staple of the Right with the arrival of the welfare state. It may have given Ronald Reagan an edge in the 1984 election, during which those who considered "social welfare" the most important national problem were more likely to vote Republican than Democratic for the first time (National Election Studies Cumulative Datafile 1952–1992).

Reagan's detractors complain that the welfare queen was a myth: the newspaper reporter who reported the story noted that the woman in question "is now charged with using not 80 aliases, but four. The amount that the state is charging that she received from her alleged fraud is not $150,000, but $8,000" (*New York Times*, 15 Feb 1976). She was eventually found guilty of using two aliases to collect twenty-three different checks totaling $8,000, which was all that the state's attorney investigating the case felt that he could prove. A commission investigating welfare fraud had suggested the higher amount of between $100,000 and $150,000; it is not clear how they reached those figures, but the head of the commission complained that the welfare department would not cooperate in the investigation. These higher amounts were reported in newspapers that Reagan read, although he clearly embellished the accounts by reporting only the highest figures and implying that she had received even more. Finally, although the woman involved in this case was only charged with fraud worth $8,000, she did indeed own a Cadillac, which the state seized upon discovery of her welfare fraud ("'Welfare Queen' Loses Her Cadillac Limousine," *New York Times*, 29 Feb 1976).

However, although the story of the welfare queen was quite useful for electoral purposes, there is no evidence that the specific legislation to cut means-tested programs under Reagan (the OBRA of 1981) was driven by racial animus or by political calculations that attacking means-tested programs would be popular, nor does any analysis of the legislation make that argument. Indeed, polls showed that the majority disapproved of Reagan's spending cuts immediately after they were implemented (Shapiro et al. 1987).

The process by which the OBRA originated and was implemented is very curious: although the Office of Management and Budget usually spends most of each year preparing the budget, during the first year of a presidency the budget-making process takes place in only a few months.

This was especially true in 1981, because the head of the OMB, David Stockman, was seen in the administration as thoroughly knowledgeable on the issues, and there was little opposition to him: "Thus President Reagan's first-stage budget proposal in 1981 was conceived and born in the OMB" unlike any of the administration's later budgets (Hartman 1982, 382). And unlike the issue of tax cuts, the issue of spending cuts did not have a long gestation period. An analysis of the OBRA therefore begins with the role of Stockman.

In what follows, I rely heavily on a single source: William Greider's interviews with David Stockman, the director of the OMB, published as an article in the *Atlantic Monthly* in December 1981. The article is an extraordinary document. Greider, a journalist at the *Washington Post*, held a series of interviews with Stockman when he took over as head of the OMB. As we have noted above, the budget-making procedure for that year was concentrated in the OMB, and no one contradicted Stockman's authority, so Greider had a view of the budget-making process from the man most responsible for it. There was some confusion about whether Stockman was giving Greider these interviews for immediate publication: Greider says Stockman knew the results would be published in the *Atlantic Monthly*; Stockman says he thought he was giving these interviews off the record, and was upset when the article was published (Weisman 1981).

Can we trust Greider's account? That is, did Greider report Stockman's revelations accurately, and did Stockman tell Greider the truth? As a historical source, this account meets very high standards for credibility. First, despite the trouble that it brought him, Stockman confirmed that Greider's quotations were accurate at a press conference immediately after the publication of the article, and he has never disavowed them; and second, the political costs of Stockman's confessions were staggering, nearly ending his political career.

In contexts such as this one, where testimony is not lacking (in addition to extensive contemporary media coverage, many participants in the events have published retrospective memoirs, and the scholarly literature on the events is large) and where participants may have incentives to falsify their testimony (to make themselves look better or to help their political cause), one of the primary criteria that historians and social scientists use to judge the worth of statements is their *costs* to the speaker. Statements that carry low or no cost, "cheap talk," are not necessarily reliable. (On judging the reliability of evidence in political contexts, Moravcsik [1998] notes that political statements—if repeated often enough in the echo chamber of biographies that repeat newspaper reports that repeat unnamed sources—can come to be accepted as true even if no check of reliability is performed on the original source.)

The verifiable costs to David Stockman of the Greider article are, in increasing order of severity: (1) loss of information, resulting from the revelation that Stockman had a spy among the Democrats, Congressman Phil Gramm. This hurt Stockman because it gave Gramm's enemies a "technical hook" with which to get rid of him ("The theme of party betrayal dominated the response of the Democratic leadership to Gramm's resignation from the House and his vow to return as a Republican" [Baker 1985, 324]), so that Stockman no longer had inside information. (2) Stockman's revelation that he and others in the administration did not believe in the supply-side program gave the Democrats an opportunity to criticize the administration and the program as well. Democratic House Speaker Tip O'Neill said, "His credibility and the credibility of the program he supports [are] in serious doubt" (Weisman 1981). Republican Majority Leader Howard Baker said, "Of course, we're unhappy with the prospect that the Democrats get a free shot. They get a lick at our heads every time we see a microphone or a camera, and we're going to have that fed back to us ad nauseum [*sic*]" (Lescaze 1981). (3) Because of the revelations in the article, Stockman lost his prime role in budget-making (Hartman 1982). One Reagan aide was quoted as saying in 1982, "There are very few members of the White House or the Cabinet who continue to hold him in awe.... Last year, Dave was more of an advocate in the budget process. This year, he's more of a presenter of options. Put it this way: If you're at a luncheon meeting, and he says the sun's out, everybody checks" ("For David Stockman, It's Round 3," *New York Times*, 28 Nov 1982, sec. 3). Finally, (4) Stockman was almost dismissed from his position at the head of the OMB: top aides, including Ed Meese and Michael Deaver, thought he should be dismissed, and he offered his resignation, but Reagan decided to keep him on. Kessel (1984, 243) reports a White House staff member saying, "I wasn't over here [on the White House staff] when the *Atlantic* article ... broke, but I said that they'd have to keep him because they didn't have anyone else who had a fraction of his knowledge about the budget." In other words, Stockman was kept on *despite* the article because of his substantive expertise.

For these reasons, Stockman's revelations are not "cheap talk"—they are quite expensive talk—and the fact that he nevertheless confirmed Greider's account means that the article meets very high criteria of reliability.

No scholarly work or historical evidence that I know of has appeared during the intervening twenty years to contradict Stockman's account (other memoirs interpret Stockman's role quite differently—as arrogant and naive, for example, rather than as heroic—but do not disagree with his basic factual account of events). I therefore rely on it for details of the budget-making process that led to the OBRA. For our purposes, the following revelations in Greider's account are relevant:

The process of budget-making at OMB was surprisingly chaotic. When computer estimates predicted that Reagan's policies would lead to deficits, Stockman simply reprogrammed the computers to include an assumption of productivity increase (the new forecasts and the assumptions they incorporated were made public when the budget was announced). Stockman used the fact that agency heads were just getting settled into their positions to rush through cuts. Stockman himself was confused by the budget accounts: "None of us really understands what's going on with all these numbers. You've got so many different budgets out and so many different baselines and such complexity now in the interactive parts of the budget between policy action and the economic environment and all the internal mysteries of the budget, and there are a lot of them. People are getting from A to B and it's not clear how they are getting there" (Greider 1981, 38).[21] He dismissed projections of future deficits of over $60 billion with a device dubbed the "magic asterisk" (39), which stood for budget cuts to be identified at a future date, allowing him to postpone difficult decisions. Stockman admitted that the speed of the process had led to major miscalculations:

> The defense numbers got out of control, and we were doing that whole budget-cutting exercise so frenetically . . . you were juggling details, pushing people, and going from one session to another, trying to cut housing programs here and rural electric there, and we were doing it so fast, we didn't know where we were ending up for sure; . . . we should have designed those pieces to be more compatible. But the pieces were moving on independent tracks—the tax program, where we were going on spending, and the defense program, which was just a bunch of numbers written on a piece of paper. And it didn't quite mesh. That's what happened. But, you see, for about a month and a half we got away with that because of the novelty of all these budget reductions. (40)

Stockman knew that the OBRA cuts were based on false premises. Stockman said,

21. This article is subsequently cited in the text by page number alone.

> There was less there than met the eye. Nobody has figured it out yet. Let's say that you and I walked outside and I waved a wand and said, "I've just lowered the temperature from 110 to 78." Would you believe me? What this was was a cut from an artificial CBO base. That's why it looked so big. But it wasn't. It was a significant and helpful cut from what you might call the moving track of the budget of the government, but the numbers are just out of this world. The government never would have been up at those levels in the CBO base. (51)

Stockman considered the large income-tax cuts as camouflage for tax cuts for the top bracket. Stockman said, "The hard part of the supply-side tax cut is dropping the top rate from 70 to 50 percent—the rest of it is a secondary matter. . . . The original argument was that the top bracket was too high, and that's having the most devastating effect on the economy. Then, the general argument was that, in order to make this palatable as a political matter, you had to bring down all the brackets. But, I mean, Kemp-Roth was always a Trojan horse to bring down the top rate . . . " (46). "It's kind of hard to sell 'trickle down,' . . . so the supply-side formula was the only way to get a tax policy that was really 'trickle down.' Supply-side is 'trickle-down' theory" (47).

Stockman repeatedly tried to cut politically protected programs, and politicians repeatedly thwarted him. When the team was looking for budget cuts, Ronald Reagan declared defense and universal programs (particularly the central benefits of the two most expensive, Social Security and Medicare) off-limits. Stockman insisted on cutting funding for the Export-Import Bank, whose main beneficiaries were major corporations, saying "how in the world can I cut food stamps and social services and CETA jobs and EDA jobs and you're going to tell me you can't give up one penny for Boeing? . . . I've got to take something out of Boeing's hide to make this look right" (35)—but he offered no resistance when Senators, led by a Republican Senator from a major Boeing-beneficiary state (Nancy Kassebaum of Kansas), reinstated the bank's subsidies. Stockman attempted, and Reagan rejected, cutbacks in tax deductions for the oil industry. Stockman did not cut the subsidy for the Clinch River nuclear reactor in Tennessee, even though he had long criticized it, because he feared the resistance that it would provoke from the senior Senator from Tennessee, who happened to be the majority leader ("A very poor reason, I know" [36]). Finally, Stockman attempted to close the deficit gap by identifying cuts in areas that had hitherto been off limits—Social Security, Medicare and Medicaid, defense, and the tax cuts—but the Senate (controlled by Republicans) unanimously opposed cutbacks in Social Security, elderly constituents across the nation complained, and the president himself eventually went on television to insist that Social Security would not be cut, and that even small cuts would be postponed until 1983. In the end, political realities trumped the effort to reduce the deficit, because "[t]he power of these client groups turned out to be stronger than I realized. The client groups know how to make themselves heard. The problem is, unorganized groups can't play in this game" (52).

Several points in the story demonstrate differences between the United States and other countries in the operation of politics. First, there is the presence of Stockman himself, a man whose professional training was in theology rather than economics, as head of the OMB; second, the lack of a rational budget-making process based on budget numbers that were arrived at separately from processes of political expediency (rosy scenario, magic asterisk; see Schulman 1988 for an interesting attempt to understand such policymaking); and, third, the political inability to cut universal programs, even at the expense of creating a deficit. All of these points demonstrate the same underlying characteristic of U.S. politics: the *permeability of the American state* to policymaking based on social interests rather than on technocratic or academic analysis.

In his memoir, Stockman describes his entry into the OMB thus:

> Kemp and I launched a campaign to secure me a position in the new Cabinet. The odds were long. I was young and relatively inexperienced. . . . [Fellow supply-sider newspaper columnist Bob] Novak wrote a column saying there was a movement growing to put Stockman in at the Office of Management and Budget. At the time he wrote it, it was a movement of three or four, if you included the minority of my staff that favored the idea. But after his column appeared, it did become a movement of sorts. (Stockman 1986, 69–70)

Stockman quickly put together a document making the case that unless various supply-side measures were taken, the U.S. economy would experience dramatic recession. Buried among these measures was a call for reduction of "Non-Social Security Entitlements"; although AFDC was not mentioned by name, the genesis of its end was in this measure. The paper impressed Reagan enough that Stockman could hold out for the top job at OMB—and thus was Stockman installed: with the help of well-placed journalists and policymakers favorable to supply-side ideas and looking for a bright, hard-working fellow traveler.

Stockman's remarkably quick entry into government was made possible by a unique feature of the political structure: its extraordinary permeability to the rapid ascent of "outsiders." Greider writes,

> One striking quality of Stockman's career is the ease and swiftness with which he moved from an obscure and unpretentious background to the highest circle of power in the federal government.... This pattern is not at all unusual in modern Washington; the channels of power are much more accessible to new participants than one might think.... In administration after administration, obscure Americans who are essentially political technicians have been anointed with awesome power. (1982, 83–85)

This is characteristic of public administration in the United States:

> In Western Europe, beginning with the absolutist monarchies of the seventeenth and eighteenth centuries in Prussia and France and continuing in the nation-states of the last two centuries, the emphasis has been on "career" staffing in some form, with individuals customarily entering the service at an early age and remaining throughout their careers until retirement. In the United States, on the other hand, the orientation has been toward shorter-term or "program" staffing. (Heady 1988, 405)

In the United States the top levels of the bureaucracy are especially vulnerable to politically motivated staffing—such was the case with the EPA and the Department of the Interior under Reagan, as we saw in the previous section, and such was also the case with the OMB (the one large exception to this rule is the Federal Reserve).

This permeability and lack of technocracy clearly is beneficial in resisting the rigid canalization of careers that one sees, for example, in France and in allowing input from outside sources. But it also hinders the separation of policymaking from political considerations and leads to the chaotic process seen in the OBRA case with its manipulations such as the "magic asterisk" and the politically motivated choice of budget projections.

Two recent changes in the structure of the state had made rational decision making less likely. First, the Civil Service Reform Act of 1978 further weakened the autonomous basis of the government bureaucracy, making it "easier to fire civil servants and to provide for direct partisan control of the civil service" (Thayer 1997, 97) and thus reducing the number of trained professionals preparing the budget. Second, in 1974 Congress had passed the Budget Control and Impoundment Act, which attempted to coordinate budget decisions by consolidating them into one up-or-down vote rather than having them made individually in isolated committees. Ironically, this attempt to introduce rationality in the budget-making procedure had the opposite effect: it allowed Stockman to hurry OBRA through Congress, and because the budget-making was not delegated to a nonpartisan technocracy, it allowed spending decisions to be made on partisan bases (Mackay and Weaver 1983). Because only one vote was taken, it had clear symbolic significance, which worked to the Republicans' advantage for political reasons. One of the enduring features of American public opinion is that the public is ideologically conservative but pragmatically liberal: Americans are against big government but in favor of all of the particular programs that constitute it. Thus, one symbolic vote on "government spending" was more likely to go the Republican way than several small votes on particular programs. More important, at this moment Reagan was very popular, and members of Congress did not want to vote against him (Joe and Rogers 1985, 55). Stockman made the maximum use of these political advantages by rushing the vote, to such an extent that members had not even had time to read what they were voting for. Speaker Tip O'Neill complained, "There is no doubt that there is utter confusion. And why should there not be? Copies of the amendment are now available for the first time, and most of the Members have not even seen the bill. The truth of the matter is, the front page of the [Washington] *Star* today says that the author of the bill has not seen it himself" (quoted in Joe and Rogers 1985, 54).

Despite these political and organizational advantages, however, Stockman did not achieve all of his goals. Although he was a consistent antigovernment ideologue—"more Reaganite than Reagan," as Noble (1997) says—his attempt to push through a full, across-the-board reduction in government spending failed. Instead he achieved cuts in means-tested spending, the smallest part of the budget, while the largest programs, particularly Social Security, escaped the budget ax. When he introduced cuts in means-tested programs, he secretly planned to present further budget-cut packages in the near future, which would include cuts in Social Security, Medicare, federal pensions, and "corporate welfare," but the plan to cut middle-class entitlements was stymied by opposition. When Senator Pete Domenici proposed a plan to save Social Security, Reagan's top advisers advised him against it, because this could be interpreted as an attack on Social Security (Cannon 1991, 246; Meese 1992, 136), although in retrospect this would be seen as a mistake. Two months later, Reagan (pressed by the ever-present deficit projections and perhaps misinformed by Stockman about the extent of the proposal) did approve a plan of Stockman's whose centerpiece was removing early Social Security retirement benefits, but the Senate unanimously rejected it, and it became a political embarrassment for the president (Cannon 1991, 251). After that, the administration did not again try to attack the universal programs.

Thus, although Stockman planned an across-the-board reduction in government, he quickly discovered that middle-class entitlements are difficult to cut because they are so popular that legislators are unwilling to cut them. This is Stockman's conclusion about the "triumph of politics"—middle-class beneficiaries were automatically protected by their representatives in Washington, who feared the unpopularity of cuts in universal programs, and wealthy minorities could mobilize political protection with implicit threats of withdrawing financial support. The only group whose interests were not protected were the poor minorities who felt the influence of OBRA most directly. Of course, means-tested programs are such a small part of the budget that cutting them did little to stop the generation of the deficit; to actually balance the budget, cuts in the large, middle-class programs would have been necessary, and although a rational process of budget balancing would have pointed this out, these cuts were politically impossible.

The entrance of a nonprofessional to the head of the budget-making process, the rushed and chaotic nature of that process, and the protection of Social Security and middle-class entitlements even while means-tested programs were cut, were all made possible by the same phenomenon: the U.S. government's lack of a permanent staff of trained bureaucrats at the highest levels of the state. The United States has on occasion attempted to put its government on the rational bureaucratic footing common in Europe, but this has been counterbalanced by a populist skepticism of elite bureaucrats, so that on the whole the United States remains the only country whose highest levels of office are staffed by party elites rather than career bureaucrats. This openness of the American bureaucracy allows rapid access to outsiders who have not been trained for their work. The chaos and mistakes of the budget-making procedure are only possible under such a circumstance. And the lack of a permanent bureaucracy means there is no rational matching of programs that are cut with the savings that are necessary, so that small, unpopular programs are cut while the most expensive programs, the ones where the savings are possible, are off-limits: populist politics trumps rational budget decisions.

The U.S. government's weakness and openness allowed market reform in the direction of cutting welfare spending. Our investigation of tax reduction showed that new changes in the structure of the state had turned politicians into entrepreneurs looking for issues with majority appeal, and the issue they discovered was latent dissatisfaction with adversarial taxes. In the section on deregulation we saw the role that broad-based social movements played in influencing economic policy, and the way in which this allowed business dissatisfaction with adversarial regulations to influence policy. This analysis of cuts in welfare spending traces the effects of the U.S. government's "weakness" in one final measure: its lack of a strong, permanent government bureaucracy. The lack of a permanent bureaucracy makes the U.S. state more permeable to social developments, and made possible the chaotic and uninformed calculations of the Reagan team that directly led to deficits. And the lack of rational budgeting meant that means-tested programs—an insignificant fraction of the annual budget—could be cut, while large programs like Social Security, which really needed to be cut in order to balance the budget, were protected because legislators feared the reaction of their constituencies. A more open government—more open to ideologues of one stripe or another, to ideologically motivated accounting procedures, and to majority interests—allowed the cuts in means-tested programs. The story of the welfare queen and the dissatisfaction with adversarial welfare policies that it tapped may have helped Reagan acquire or retain power, but the process by which antipoverty programs were actually cut also required a chaotic budget-making procedure combined with well-defended middle-class entitlements.

Conclusion

The Reagan tax cuts, deregulation, and welfare spending cuts were rooted in the adversarial structure of American policies—visible and progressive taxes, antibusiness regulations, targeted welfare policies—which opened up an electoral dissatisfaction with the status quo. A movement against property taxes had brought the issue of taxation to politicians' attention, and entrepreneurial politicians sensed dissatisfaction with income taxes. Businesses had been complaining about the burden of regulations for years, and the Republican party saw a way to satisfy business lobbies by capitalizing on the popular consumers' movement. And politicians saw political capital to be made from exploiting resentment of targeted welfare policies, although the actual implementation of welfare cuts was largely a story of a nonprofessional bureaucratic process meeting politically protected middle-class entitlements. In all three realms, the adversarial nature of the policies had opened up a potential dissatisfaction, and the competitive and individualized nature of politics had made mobilizing electoral dissatisfaction a stable route to power.

The Reagan Revolution has become, at least for now, an integrated part of American politics. Reagan's two immediate successors, George H. W. Bush and Bill Clinton, both raised taxes, but their fortunes suggest the limits of the politics of taxation in the United States. Bush lost his bid for reelection partly because of the tax increases, and Clinton's increases were concentrated on a small, wealthy minority. Tax increases for the middle classes essentially became unthinkable. George W. Bush has used the model of the Reagan tax cuts to cut taxes again, despite agreement among economists not working for the president that tax cuts are unlikely to help the economy in the long term. The presidency of the second Bush is a replay of the politics of demagoguery: for example, in campaigning for his first tax cut, Bush and his advisers repeatedly proclaimed that the tax cuts would benefit the "average" family—not making it clear that this referred to the mean family and not the median family. The actual distribution of benefits was highly skewed, so that the majority of the benefits went to families in the top percentiles of the income distribution. Although the first President Bush presided over a great expansion of regulation—the introduction of the Americans with Disabilities Act—the second President Bush returned to deregulation, having learned well the lessons of the Reagan experience with environmental deregulation. Attacks on environmental protection have gone underground, and the administration has avoided the kind of controversy over style that brought the Reagan cuts to public attention. And finally, Bill Clinton's presidency saw the largest change in American social policy in decades, introducing time limits on welfare payments and allowing states to pass more stringent welfare requirements, but welfare cuts have not been a major concern of the second Bush.

Thus, the essential features of the Reagan changes—the middle-class tax cuts, cuts in funding for environmental protection, and cuts in social spending for the poor—have not been undone, and in a few cases have been extended.

CHAPTER TWO

Populist Revolutionary: Margaret Thatcher and the Transformation of the British State

Scholars often juxtapose the Reagan and Thatcher administrations as two examples of the same phenomenon, and, indeed, the parallels are striking: both Reagan and Thatcher were political outsiders in terms of their social background (Reagan the son of an alcoholic shoe salesman, Thatcher a grocer's daughter and a woman in the male world of politics) who had achieved material prosperity and ascribed this to hard work and the virtues of the free market in rewarding it. Like the middle-class voters who voted for them, they both equated the planned capitalism of the postwar period with an elite political establishment. They both challenged this establishment in the name of the virtues they thought their own lives embodied, and voters appreciated them for doing so. Both headed movements that were intellectually nourished by the various groups affiliated with Friedrich Hayek and the Mont Pèlerin Society. They both attempted to "roll back the state" and were successful to such a degree that both the Democrats and Labour have more or less renounced economic redistribution. Under Reagan, the American political establishment discovered that deficits and increasing poverty did not make the president unelectable; under Thatcher, British politicians learned that three times as many unemployed as in previous administrations did not make the government unelectable.

But the differences in the way neoliberalism was implemented in the United States and Britain are as revealing as the similarities in the political dynamics that led up to it. Many of the political elements that led to Thatcherism are quite similar to the elements that led to Reaganism—adversarial structures, the socioeconomic transformation of the majority, the presence of an unpopular minority that could be demonized as the enemy within—but the results of the two episodes are quite divergent. In the United States, it is clear that tax cuts were popular, but not at the expense of balanced budgets; that deregulation was popular, but not environmental deregulation; and that cutting "welfare" was popular, but not cutting aid to the poor. It is also clear that politicians mobilized the issue of cuts in taxes and welfare because they thought it would help them get into power, but the policies that were actually passed in all three domains were not particularly popular.

This was not the case in Britain. First, as in the United States, income tax cuts were popular in Britain if they did not come at the expense of spending or a balanced budget, and this is exactly what the government eventually produced: income tax cuts without spending cuts or a large deficit. Spending increased slightly over the course of the Thatcher administration despite income tax cuts and despite Thatcher's stated intentions, and a deficit on the American scale was avoided through increased sales taxes and the proceeds of privatization and sales of public housing stocks (council houses). In industrial policy, the political dynamics were almost the opposite of those seen under Reagan. There, the popular symbol of deregulation was used to implement unpopular cuts in environmental protection; under Thatcher, the proposed privatizations were unpopular until they were implemented, and then they turned out to be quite successful (if not exactly as popular as the administration thought). And in welfare state policy, the main achievement—council house sales—was supported by the vast majority of the population from the start. In all other areas of social policy the changes produced by Thatcher were minor, reflecting the popularity of the welfare state with voters.

The American context led to a chaotic process by which policies were implemented that the people did not clearly desire. The British political context channeled the innovations into less chaotic lines, on some occasions despite the best intentions and efforts of the Thatcher team. Certainly there were major elements of the Thatcher episode that went awry—privatization was rushed and not performed in the best way possible, and the administration only managed to control inflation at the cost of a rise in unemployment that devastated British manufacturing (Branson and Baily 1981; Buiter and Miller 1981, 1983; Layard and Nickell 1989; Sachs and Branson 1983).[1]

In the terms of this book, however, the Thatcher episode shows political entrepreneurship (politicians getting into or staying in power by mobilizing issues that are popular with the public) rather than demagoguery (politicians getting into or staying in power by mobilizing issues that are demonstrably false or that would not be popular if voters had more information). The administration did not make demonstrably false claims, either before or after getting into power, regarding tax policy, industrial policy, or welfare state policy as the Reagan team did in both tax (e.g., Stockman's magic asterisk) and welfare (e.g., the story of the welfare queen) policy. And although pushing popular framings of issues is an exercise in which all politicians engage to some degree, in Britain it never went to the extreme of using popular framings to disguise policies that were clearly unpopular, as in the deregulation episode under Reagan.

This is an important difference, and in the conclusion to this chapter I discuss how Britain's responsible party government channeled the neoliberal impulse in ways in which the fragmented American state could not. But whether it was political entrepreneurship or demagoguery, the main story of Thatcherism, as of Reaganism, is of politicians mobilizing an increasingly prosperous majority that had moved across the class divide of the adversarial policies. Thatcher rode a wave of popular disgust with the trade unions into power, and she stayed in power because, although voters had moved away from extreme leftist positions, the Labour Party in the 1980s was having a difficult time doing so; and, at least in the domains of taxation, industrial policy, and welfare state policy, the popular elements of Thatcherism were radicalized, and the unpopular ones dropped out.

In this chapter I concentrate on three particular policies of the Thatcher episode: the 1981 budget; the privatization of British Telecom; and the sale of council houses. All three of these are famous, or notorious, episodes in the history of Thatcherism. The anti-Keynesian 1981 budget provoked the

1. Proponents of the policy argue that only this severe constraint could force British industry to shape up—that unemployment and bankruptcies were the result of previous overstaffing and previous soft budget constraints—and moreover that the future of Britain lay in financial services. Critics like Jim Prior argued at the time that "we were not just wiping out the fat of British industry and making British industry leaner, we were actually knocking out quite a bit of the lean meat as well" (*Thatcher Factor*, Prior, box 5). The interviews conducted for the documentary *The Thatcher Factor* (Brook Lapping Productions 1991/1992) are collected in the archives of the London School of Economics. They are subsequently cited parenthetically in the text.

famous letter of protest from 364 academic economists, raising taxes as it did in the middle of a recession (although the 1981 budget followed the policy lines on taxation set by the two earlier budgets, so I consider all three here). The unexpected success of the privatization of British Telecom significantly accelerated the privatization movement and led to its being copied all over the world. Finally, the sale of council houses was Thatcher's most visible and successful attack on the British welfare state.

Many scholars believe that the rise of a set of free market ideas caused the turn to the right: that Thatcherism was essentially the political embodiment of an intellectual counterrevolution against the Keynesian consensus. This is one of the most common explanations of Thatcherism. Richard Cockett, in a wonderful history of those ideas, writes "The 1979 election victory was thus the culmination of nearly forty years of intellectual and political work.... Unusually in British politics, the 1979 election victory signalled the victory of an idea—the idea of economic liberalism" (1995, 286).

The role that ideas play in historical causation has begun to receive considerable attention from scholars (Blyth 2002). But although the ideas were one factor, they cannot have been central for several reasons. First, the "intellectual counterrevolution" never convinced most intellectuals—the 364 economists who signed the letter of protest represented the majority of the British academic economics establishment, which remained Keynesian until well into the 1980s. In the mid-1970s only a minority of economists was convinced by monetarism, and almost none were convinced by the way in which the administration was implementing it. The real question is how this small number of intellectuals who were convinced by the idea gained enough power to put their ideas into practice. The answer, I hope to show in this chapter, is that the ideas appealed to the political needs of state actors to provide a challenge to the reigning policy.

Second, the main elements of the Thatcherite agenda—privatization, council house sales as part of a broader resistance to the welfare state, a shift from direct to indirect taxation, and "sound money" and balanced budgets rather than Keynesian countercyclical measures—had been favorites of a minority of Conservatives throughout the postwar period and had been present in embryonic form in previous manifestos. Moreover, the previous Labour government had put in place a tight monetary policy and had also implemented the first sales of British Petroleum shares, and council house sales had been conducted as far back as Macmillan. Thus, the main elements of the Thatcherite agenda represent intensifications of one branch of postwar politics rather than a complete repudiation based on new ideas.

Third, the monetarist intellectuals had not worked out how to implement the policy. In attempting to do so, the Thatcher team had little guidance from the ideas, and, in a curious process explored below, turned the idea of "monetarism" into the idea of "balanced budgets"—a position Milton Friedman himself disavowed.

Most important, although in the run-up to the 1979 election the main element of the "intellectual counterrevolution" was monetarism, it turned out that monetarism was Thatcherism's enduring failure. The central assumption of the experiment—that the government would be able to define and control the money supply—proved to be incorrect. In retrospect, it is clear that Thatcherism's great success was privatization—an element that the policy groups had not made central to their propaganda efforts before the election. Indeed, privatization on a *major* scale arrived on the political agenda for reasons that were not ideological—as a way to raise capital for one of the nationalized industries, British Telecom. That privatization was seen to be so politically popular that it was quickly repeated, until eventually nearly half of the state's holdings had been sold over the course of the administration, and privatization had become a movement carried on by Thatcher's successors and copied all over the world.

The story of the failure of monetarism, and the success of privatization, is a story of the primacy of the political in the history of Thatcherism. Monetarism as political policy (as opposed to monetarism as academic theory) was developed as an answer to the political problems of the mid- to late-1970s. It proved unequal to the complexities of the modern British economy. Instead, an element of the intellectual counterrevolution that had not been central became, because it was perceived to be politically popular, the major success story of the decade, the policy identified most closely with "Thatcherism" today. The process of converting imprecise ideologies into concrete policy proposals was driven in the United Kingdom, as in the United States, by the needs of state actors and the opportunities open to them, not by a set of predetermined ideologies; the ideologies were one causal element, but not the major one.

The following sections, in tracing the course of taxation, industrial policy, and welfare state policy, therefore carry a dual thesis: It was not ideas that drove the Thatcherist experiment; rather, electoral considerations did (as Hall [1993] also argues), and one consequence was that those elements that seemed to the government to resonate with the public, such as cuts in progressive taxes, were radicalized. At the stage of formation of ideas (third face), all of the components of Thatcher's policies had been suggested and some even implemented in embryonic form long before Thatcher took office—either by the previous Labour government or by Conservative governments before that. They arrived on Thatcher's agenda (second face) as part of a coherent right-wing program and as a direct result of the electoral defeats of 1974, which led one faction of the Conservative Party to set up a wide range of policy discussion groups with a mandate to develop and argue for policies to the right of the previous, discredited Conservative government. The implementation (first face) of taxation policy shows mainly confusion and electoral incentives, and the implementation of radical versions of privatization and council house sales was the result of actual or perceived public support. In short, Thatcherism was a democratic phenomenon—not the result of the hijacking of the party by a faction under the grip of an extreme economic ideology. It is not the case that all elements of Thatcherism represent the "will of the people," however, and, indeed, the Thatcher government was not very popular for most of its time in office; but in taxation, industrial policy, and welfare state policy, the main policy measures that were actually implemented were shaped by the broad outlines of public opinion, and public opinion was in turn shaped by adversarial policies and an adversarial state structure.

Finally, the Thatcher episode shows the power of transformative events to create effects that extend far into the future. In particular, the sale of British Telecom was the key event that led to the coherence of the economic project of Thatcherism. Before this event, Thatcherism threatened to dissipate because of the failures of the monetarist strategy. The sale of British Telecom broadened the horizon of political possibilities because it changed the *meaning* of privatization: it created a moral justification for privatization as implementing a "property-owning democracy" that the political actors then carried into other political domains. It changed the actors' understanding of the project on which they were embarked.

Taxation and the 1981 Budget

The early Thatcher budgets shared some similarities with the U.S. budget of 1981 but also had some telling differences. The main similarities are that taxation had been an important part of the electoral promises of both British Conservatives and U.S. Republicans during their respective elections and that opinion polls in both countries showed that majorities favored tax cuts—at least when this option was presented in isolation, not when it was counterposed to spending cuts (Young 1989; Butler and Kavanagh 1980; Clemens 1983; CCO 180/9/10/5, "Attitudes to Taxation").[2] In addition, Britain under Thatcher also saw a mild version of the permeable bureaucracies seen in the American case, in that business and media figures played important roles in developing the arguments and strategies of Thatcherism. The main structural difference was that there were no "policy entrepreneurs" (actors at the margins of the political system working to get into power by mobilizing an issue) and no local elections or coalition partners mobilizing the popularity of tax cuts. The main difference in outcome was that, although both top and average income tax rates were cut in Britain, the resulting shortfall in revenue was made up by, first, increasing indirect (sales) taxation, and, second, by selling parts of nationalized industries, so that there was no deficit of American proportions—indeed, total tax revenues *increased* in the first years of the Thatcher administration, a pro-cyclical measure that helped to wring inflation out of the system at the cost of increasing unemployment. Faith in the supply-side principle that cutting taxes would automatically increase revenue by increasing work incentive did not take hold in Britain. Although total tax revenues as a share of GDP declined in later years, the effect of the early increase was decisive: Britain avoided the "Big Budget Bang" that hit America in 1981.

A comparison of the British and American cases is particularly revealing on the question of the influence of ideas. The comparison of the British and American budget-making processes shows what ideas can and cannot do. Both processes were inspired by the same broad set of free market, anti-state ideas, and the intellectual lineages of both contain many of the same elements. Both acknowledged each other as influences. Nevertheless, the two budget processes resulted *in opposite policies*: the American budget of 1981 was a deficit-creating budget, lowering taxes and increasing spending, while the British budget of the same year was pro-cyclical, raising taxes in the midst of a recession. The same set of free market ideas led to directly opposite policy results.

2. The references ACP, CCO, CRD, LCC, SC, and KJ are to the papers of the Conservative Party Archive in the Bodleian Library, Oxford; they refer respectively to the papers of the Advisory Committee on Policy, the Conservative Central Office, the Conservative Research Department, the Leader's Consultative Committee, the Steering Committee, and the Keith Joseph papers. The numbers in the parenthetical text citations are the catalog numbers (analogous to standard call numbers) of the documents.

The key difference was that, although income tax rates were cut in both countries (and had been important parts of the campaign in both countries),[3] in Britain sales taxes were raised to make up for the revenue shortfall. Without this, the British deficit would have been similar in proportion to the American deficit. Thus, this section traces the history of the decision to raise sales taxes in the early budgets.

I intend to show in this section that much of the recent work arguing for an "ideational" turn ignores the fact that ideas are malleable. Just as "culture" does not map very well onto action, so "ideas" are nothing like clear blueprints for policy. An idea can be instantiated in many ways, and the process of instantiation usually has little to do with ideas and everything to do with political interest. In the American case, the idea of rolling back the state led to a process that decreased total tax revenue as a share of GDP; in Britain, the same idea led to a process that increased total tax revenue as a share of GDP.

Thatcher's tax policy in the early years—the notorious pro-cyclical (anti-Keynesian) policy that refused to reflate in the middle of a recession—is bound up with the monetarist experiment. Monetarism is the idea that inflation arises because the supply of money is increasing faster than the supply of goods and services, and not because wages or other costs increase; consequently, the government should be able to control inflation by controlling the money supply. Neither the public at large, nor Parliament in particular, had been convinced by monetarism, or even particularly attentive to it in the run-up to the 1979 election. William Keegan quotes an MP who summarizes the 1975 leadership election in the statement, "We voted against Ted [Heath], and then we found we had monetarism" (1984, 42)—that is, the election was a referendum on Heath's performance rather than a positive preference for monetarism. Although recent research has shown that a substantial minority viewed Thatcher's program positively, it does not deny that the majority of MPs were voting against Heath rather than for Thatcher (Cowley and Bailey 2000). Similarly, during the General Election of 1979 voters had heard little of the monetarist agenda, and still believed that incomes policy was the only way of controlling inflation; they preferred lower inflation and more jobs, but did not hold informed opinions on whether Labour or the Tories had the best plans for both. The public voted Conservative because voters, particularly the floating voters,

3. Already in 1975 individuals within the party were making references to "the coming 'revolt of the tax payer'" (KJ 16/3, Della Nevitt to Keith Joseph, 10 Jan 1975).

preferred lower taxes and a tougher stance on trade unions; the experience of the two previous governments had convinced them that without attacking the power of unions, an incomes policy would not work. It was this—rather than the new idea of monetarism—that got the Conservatives in. Nevertheless, the monetarist idea did allow the right-wing opposition to form a fairly cohesive faction.

Two steps occurred in the transformation of the idea into policy: the particular problems of British political economy guided the choice of monetary policy (rather than steep income tax cuts) as the policy to emphasize; and then officials chose M3 as the relevant monetary measure to target partly because it was linked with the Public Sector Borrowing Requirement (PSBR), a measure of the deficit (on the assumption that a higher deficit raises interest rates, and higher interest rates increase the money supply), and the government wanted to keep the budget deficit low. The result was that the issue of "rolling back state intervention" *became* the issue of keeping the deficit low. The government took two steps to implement monetarism: it increased sales taxes and published a target range for the money supply. The point of publishing the target range was that it would reduce inflationary expectations and bring home to workers that the government would not inflate its way out of excessive wage demands, thereby helping to reduce inflation (a point at odds with the strict monetarist teaching that wage demands are symptoms, not causes, of inflation). On this score the government's innovation was to publish a "Medium Term Financial Strategy," because a clear statement of intent "Allows others—decision-makers, etc.—to work with grain of strategy, understand limits imposed, opportunities offered" (CRD 4/4/10; "Background Briefing on Budget") and the more "companies, unions, borrowers and lenders can anticipate the monetary environment . . . the less the cost of monetary stringency in terms of unemployment, bankruptcy etc." (CRD 4/4/11; Lilley, 4 Feb 1981, "Ten Questions"). "Only when those operating in the real economy understand that the fiscal and monetary framework will not be relaxed to accommodate irrational behaviour, will that behaviour itself change" (Centre for Policy Studies Papers, box 7, Westwell Report, 16).[4] As Lawson put it, all actors would know "that inflationary impulses, whatever their origin, will not be accommodated" (CRD 4/4/11, Lawson, 14 Jan 1981, "Thatcherism in Practice"), and so high wage claims would only

4. The Centre for Policy Studies Papers are collected in the archives of the London School of Economics and are cited, as here, parenthetically in the text.

cause unemployment.[5] But aside from this psychological intervention, the only thing the government actually *did* to try to hit its monetary targets was to increase the sales tax. The rest of this section describes this unfolding process—the focus on monetary policy, the choice of M3, and finally the raising of sales tax—in more detail.

Monetary policy promised an alternative method of controlling inflation that would allow the government to avoid dealing with trade unions; as Keith Joseph and Angus Maude wrote in 1975, "By not trying 'incomes policy' we avoid mass confrontation" (LCC 75/57, "Notes Toward the Definition of Policy"). The previous attempt to control inflation had been by implementing an incomes policy, with the intention of imitating the German method of controlling inflation. But the fact of inflation set up a vicious circle: inflationary expectations led British unions to reject moderate wage increases, particularly in profitable industries. The consequence was a series of strikes that discredited the Labour government and helped to bring in Thatcher. But the abandonment of incomes policy did not mean that the government could give up trying to fight inflation. According to a 1977 Shadow Cabinet paper that advocated the abandonment of price controls, "The political reality is that prices are the single most important matter of concern to the electorate and one of the major influences affecting the way they vote at any election.... It is crucial, therefore, that we should have a policy for prices that is distinctive and one which does not attempt to adapt or build on failed Socialist policies. It must be clearly shown to be an advance and not a retreat" (LCC 77/162, "A Policy for Prices"). In this context, an alternative approach to fighting inflation that would allow the government to sidestep the unions was welcome, and monetarism promised to provide a policy that was "distinctive" and that did not "build on failed Socialist policies." It also had the advantage of being able to be characterized as "sound money," as not "printing money to pay for a deficit" (see, e.g., KJ 10/14, letter from Enoch Powell, 18 Oct 1976), "the money that fuels the inflation" (CRD 4/4/10, Chancellor's Budget Broadcast, 26 Mar 1980), or as that old standby, "too much money chasing too few goods" (Centre for Policy Studies Papers, box 6/2, "Speaking Module—Economic Policy, 29 Mar 1979").

5. But as critics pointed out, "They've said well we're laying down tight monetary guidelines, we're raising interest rates, now it's up to you, you can price yourself out of a job. In practice, of course, what happens is that you price someone else out of a job, not yourself" (CRD 4/16/18, "Interview on Monetary Policy").

But the simplicity of the approach turned out to be deceptive, because the various actors who had pushed the monetarist approach did not agree on how to turn the idea into policy. It was not clear how best to define the money supply: Is it cash only (M0), or cash plus current accounts (M1), or cash, current accounts, and all interest-bearing deposits (M3)? Does it include foreign currencies? Moreover, it was not clear how to control the money supply. One subgroup of monetarists, of which Milton Friedman was a member, favored "monetary base control," which meant that the Bank of England would set the rates at which it lent to other banks at levels designed to decrease (or increase, as necessary) the supply of money. Gordon Pepper, one of the men most responsible for thinking about how to implement monetarism in Britain, also favored this approach (their critics called this the "theological" school [*Thatcher Factor*, Biffen, box 1]). Another subgroup favored a more indirect method of exerting downward pressure on the money supply by keeping interest rates and the value of the pound high. The Confederation of British Industry (CBI), the main business association, thought that fiscal and monetary means would only work after a time lag, and therefore supported "realistic pay settlements" and reform in bargaining structures and procedures, but it also supported reduction of the PSBR to help reduce interest rates (CRD 4/4/10, "CBI Representations").

In the decisions to target M3 and reject monetary base control the seeds of the 1981 budget were sown, because both decisions led to a fixation on reducing the budget deficit (the PSBR); government budget-making in the next years consequently shifted to a determined focus on fiscal policy. The first of these decisions was influenced by Treasury officials, and the second was taken entirely because of the opposition of the Bank of England to monetary base control.

First, M3 was chosen for three reasons: it had done better at predicting recent inflation than M1; the preceding Labour government had used M3 to implement its monetarist policy; and because a large component of the growth in M3 was the PSBR, so Treasury officials "liked the emphasis on £M3 precisely because of its close links with the PSBR. They felt that this helped them to control public spending, which was what most concerned the Treasury" (Lawson 1992, 78). Both Milton Friedman and Gordon Pepper, as well as many hard-core monetarists, were against this: Friedman had testified to the House of Commons concerning his belief that there is "no necessary relation between the size of PSBR and monetary growth," and in fact that an emphasis on controlling PSBR would draw attention away from "the really important aspects of government fiscal policy," that is, controlling money supply directly through monetary base control (quoted in Gilmour 1992, 28). During an extraordinary televised debate in 1980 between Friedman, Howe, and the previous Labour Chancellor Dennis Healey (at that time a potential future Prime Minister), moderated by the monetarist journalist Peter Jay, Friedman explicitly disavowed the need to control public spending to control inflation:

> I have never argued that deficits are the cause of inflation. Except if the deficits are financed by printing money. The source of inflation is too much money. Countries like Germany may well have large borrowing requirements provided they finance it either from abroad or from real savings at home it does not contribute to inflation [and although borrowing can crowd out investment and reduce productivity]. That's not the question of inflation, but I have never argued that for inflation borrowing is a requirement.

Healey responds, "With respect, I think you are making a point which I hope Sir Geoffrey [Howe] is listening to. The fact is that cutting the PSBR is not necessary for controlling the money supply providing you finance it from outside the banking system, which is what Sir Geoffrey has done." Howe does not answer this point—indeed, he seems completely overmatched by the other two (CRD 4/16/18, "Free to Choose: How to Cure Inflation," BBC-2, 22 Mar 1980). Healey, the chancellor under the previous Labour government who had first published monetary targets,[6] had elsewhere criticized the focus on PSBR because, he argued, the British savings rate was unusually high (18 percent), and if the government did not borrow and spend that money, it would cause a recession. This too remained unanswered, Howe saying only that too much was being spent on interest on the debt (CRD 4/16/17, Healey Interview; CRD 4/16/18, Chancellor Interview, Peter Hobday report).

Gordon Pepper, the other key figure in the spread of the idea of monetarism, has written as follows:

> I argued for the strategy to include the variables that were under, or should be under, the authorities' control, for example, the money supply and public expenditure. The PSBR is not under a government's control, because it alters according to the phase of the business cycle. . . . I argued that the PSBR should be

6. Much later, however, Healey would say, "I was described by the most acute observer—Sam Brittan of the *Financial Times*—as an unbelieving monetarist, and I published the targets because the markets had been carried away by these exotic new theories of Professor Friedman" (*Thatcher Factor*, box 3).

> adjusted for the business cycle, [but others] thought that a constant-employment PSBR would be too complicated for public consumption and that the strategy would not be credible without inclusion of the PSBR itself.

He concludes, "A rise in the PSBR in a recession is offset by a fall in bank lending in the private sector, . . . and in a boom the automatic fall in the PSBR is needed to compensate for a rise in bank lending. The PSBR should be allowed to act as one of the economy's self-stabilisers" (Pepper 1998, 24–25).

Academics also criticized the focus on the PSBR and

> the way in which the public sector borrowing requirement has actually taken over an extraordinary importance which it doesn't have in any other country and where Governments get obsessed by guesses of £700 million being needed to cut the borrowing requirement. Now the Treasury itself said that its estimate, the borrowing requirement, can be £3,000 million out at any time. So it's absolutely absurd to be obsessed by doing it in any case. But the fact is that the Government can, and probably should, be borrowing more money at the moment. . . . It would be worth it because it would be investing for our future. (CRD 4/16/19, David Blake, "Interview on Alternative Economic Strategy")

The emphasis on the PSBR, and consequently on M3, seems to be due to its potential use as a tool with which to control public expenditure, a traditional Conservative and Treasury concern—despite the advice of the key monetarist figures. As far back as 1974 the urge to keep the PSBR down as a response to the economic crisis was common, as was the link between monetary policy and the PSBR: "It is important to close negative fiscal drag by cutting spending or making buoyant some indirect taxes. . . . Any wage freeze should be accompanied by a firm declaration of a government programme to reduce the growth rate of money supply, with target figures including the borrowing requirement stretching a few years ahead" (see, e.g., SC 74/22, "Minutes of Eighteenth Meeting, 9 Dec 1974"; and SC 74/20, "Prospects for Economic Policy"; see also ACP 75/3). Geoffrey Howe noted in 1975 that "our argument, that excessive public expenditure was helping to cause inflation and was squeezing the private sector, was coming across in the Press" (SC 75/41/34), and in 1975 Howe also used the PSBR as a weapon with which to criticize the current government: "Sir Geoffrey Howe said he was arranging for all items of Government expenditure to be scrutinized and suggested that the Government borrowing requirement should be emphasised at every stage in debates on the

Bills of the following week" (LCC 75/59, "Minutes of the 59th Meeting of the Leader's Consultative Committee, 23 Apr 1975").[7] Even though M3, seen on its own terms as a predictor of inflation, had met with skepticism as far back as 1976, the overriding concern with controlling government spending was accepted almost across the board. The only hesitation came from Adam Ridley of the Conservative Research Department, who noted in 1975 that "the [public sector deficit] does not affect the money supply in a direct, constant or automatic way; . . . the savings behavior of the private sector is what determines 'par for the course,' and there is no case for pursing a smaller public sector deficit than that." He concludes that cutting the deficit would lead to unemployment and lack of business confidence (KJ 10/11, Ridley to Thatcher and Howe, 8 Apr 1975). By 1976, Ridley notes that "prior changes in M3 were a bad guide to changes in prices in the years 1969–72, which fell and rose in magnitude from one year to the next in inverse relationship to what the M3 trend predicted. Price increases in 1973–75 were very much less than the relevant M3 increases suggested, though the rises and falls are properly matched." Nevertheless, he concludes that "the size of the public sector deficit in prospect is not compatible with a low rate of monetary growth for much longer, particularly if economic activity revives" (LCC 76/113, "The Monetary Approach to Forecasting Inflation"). The conclusion is curiously detached from the evidence. Once the party is in government, this pattern continues. Peter Lilley of the Conservative Research Department, for example, writes in two notes on the adequacy of M3 that "£M3 has expanded far more rapidly than either the narrow measure of money M1 or broader aggregates. . . . There is quite a strong case for using [a broader aggregate] as the target variable" (CRD 4/4/11, Lilley, "Ten Questions") but nevertheless concludes that "the broader aggregates are less volatile but also less closely related to spending and the PSBR" (CRD 4/4/12, Lilley, "Review of MTFS").

That the commitment to reduce government spending was *independent* of any of the monetarist teachings is evident in an interesting letter in the Keith Joseph papers. In 1975 the *Times* (London), in an editorial probably written by the more "pure" monetarist Peter Jay, had attacked Joseph's identification of reduced government spending with monetarism, stating,

7. In June 1975 there is discussion of a paper on inflation arguing that rising inflation "dictates a programme for reducing the Public Sector Borrowing Requirement, which is the major determinant of money supply." The issue is considered important enough for the minutes to note that "it was agreed to amend the penultimate line to read 'a major determinant'" (SC 75/38/31, "Minutes of the 31st Meeting, 30 Jun 1975").

"No monetarist could have said that" (Denham and Garnett 2001, 290). In response, Joseph prepared a speech to be given at Stockton defending his position, and while composing it he wrote the following letter to a businessman in January 1976:

> I am giving next week the Stockton lecture which is, in brief, arguing that monetarism without diminution of the public sector simply strangles the private sector—except when the private sector is relatively inactive as now.... I am convinced that the growth of the public sector and the high taxation, high interest rates and climate that have at least in part resulted, must have reduced the private sector below what it would otherwise have been.
>
> *This is a difficult case to argue.* All I can find as evidence is that as the public share in G.N.P. has risen the surplus of the corporate sector has plunged—and indeed turned into a deficit. Thus, the growth of the public sector appears to have reduced the capacity of the corporate sector spontaneously to renew and expand itself.
>
> *But is there any other proof of this?*... Can you and your allies give me any guidance? (KJ 10/3, Keith Joseph to Patrick Evershed Esq of Fielding, Newson-Smith & Co., 7 Jan 1976; emphasis added)

Apparently Joseph had concluded that public-sector spending was necessary in addition to control of the money supply—despite monetarist teachings to the contrary—and then looked for evidence of this, sticking to the theory even when such evidence was not forthcoming.

Joseph had clearly been concerned about public spending for other reasons; for example, in his correspondence in 1975 and 1976 with various high-level executives from Unilever, Joseph states the reasons why public-sector spending must be cut, but he never mentions monetarism (KJ 10/5). The famous series of speeches that he made between the autumn of 1974 and the end of 1975, which first brought monetarism to the attention of the wider, informed public, assumed that public spending was part of the problem of inflation:

> Our inflation has been the result of the creation of new money—and the consequent deficit financing out of proportion to the additional goods and services available. (KJ 30/2, Preston speech, 5 Sep 1974)

> It is government overspending which is maintaining and accelerating inflation; it is government overspending which is causing prices to rise; it is government

> overspending which puts us so heavily into balance of payments deficits: it is government overspending and its consequences which are now breeding unemployment and bankruptcies. (KJ 30/2, Edinburgh speech, 10 Jan 1975)

> The ultimate cause of too much money has—in this country at any rate—usually been the excessive rise in government spending . . . whatever the purpose of the expenditure, it is this government overspending which prevents us getting on top of the long term causes of inflation. . . . That is the choice: printing money on a large scale—with consequent worse inflation and unemployment next year—or cutting government spending drastically. (KJ 30/2, Oxford speech, 14 Jun 1975)

Cutting public spending was already a traditional Tory concern, and monetarism fit into it—or was forced to fit into it even when it did not.

In other words, the *concern with controlling spending defined what monetarism came to mean*. Instead of defining and implementing monetarism independently, the government defined it in order to reach other goals, and by choosing M3 the government turned "monetarism" into "balanced budgets." Then it looked around for supporting evidence and sought out monetarists who would support the focus on balanced budgets, such as Brian Griffiths of the London School of Economics and Robert Thomas of Greenwells (KJ 10/14, John Nott to Howe, 28 May 1976). In choosing M3, they were, as Nigel Lawson noted, "like our [Labour] predecessors, but unlike most other countries" that had attempted monetary policies (CRD 4/4/11, Lawson, "Thatcherism in Practice").

Second, monetary base control was rejected because, despite support from some of the most important monetarists, as well as from Thatcher herself, and a receptive ear from Howe and Lawson (e.g., CRD 4/4/11, Lawson, "Thatcherism in Practice"), the Bank of England and the Treasury were completely opposed to it (CRD 4/4/31, Treasury, "Consultative Document on Monetary Control"). Lawson concluded that in addition to the technical problems raised, the fact of the bank's opposition was the main reason it could not work: "Above all I was convinced that such an experiment had a chance of success only if those responsible for its implementation wished to make it a success. Given the Bank's profound antipathy, it would all too likely have proved the disaster they predicted. Certainly the risk was too great to take" (Lawson 1992, 81). Certain technical changes were made that were meant to make an eventual evolution toward monetary base control possible (CRD 4/4/32, "Budget Snapshot"), but the recommendations of the monetarists by whom the Thatcher team is said to have been influenced were decisively rejected. In both cases a traditional prejudice in favor of controlling public spending and the practical questions of implementation led the government to take measures favored by the bureaucracies, namely, the Treasury and the Bank of England—a quite subtle causal influence that, in fact, determined the outcome of the monetarist experiment.[8]

Once the PSBR had been selected in this way as the key figure in the early budgets, the tactical question became how to reduce it—a difficult problem, since the recession was causing it to rise steadily. Spending had proved impossible to control because, in addition to the increase in social services and unemployment caused by the recession, the government had pledged during the campaign to honor public-sector pay increases that the Labour government had committed itself to as one response to the winter of strikes. But these increases turned out to be quite high, and Thatcher was later criticized for giving in to electoral pressure. Geoffrey Howe wrote later, "I can think of no other democratic leader who would have resisted for as long as she did" (Howe 1994, 115). In the middle of an election campaign, and with even some of her free-market advisers, such as Peter Thorneycroft, suggesting they accept the commitment, it was simply impossible not to do so. Thus, the only way to reduce the PSBR was to increase taxes. The government was hesitant to do this, but—and this was the real triumph of the 1981 budget—finally figured out how to do so in a way that was politically possible.

A war of memoirs has erupted regarding how the 1981 budget was produced. The early budgets increased unemployment, but more embarrassing for the government was the fact that the stated targets for M3 were not met. At this point, the government commissioned an independent monetarist economist to examine the policy, who concluded that monetary policy was too tight; the 1981 budget therefore cut interest rates and

8. The Bank of England's ambivalence about monetarism is evident in correspondence between Keith Joseph and Geoffrey Howe: Joseph tells Howe that a Bank of England functionary told him that "no-one knew how to control money," but later the same day the same functionary speaks to Howe, who says that "to me at least, he took a slightly different line to the effect that the Bank and the Treasury did know more than you imply about the technicalities" (KJ 10/11, Joseph to Howe, 24 Jun 76; Howe to Joseph, 2 Jul 76). The fingerprints of the Treasury are also visible in some of the publications of the "independent" right-wing think tanks that use the Treasury's data and consequently its interpretation of inflation as partly caused by a high PSBR and are thus led to adopt certain conclusions over others (see, e.g., "Step by Step against Inflation," Cockett Papers, in the archives of the London School of Economics, box 1/6).

made the monetary targets more flexible while tightening fiscal policy despite the deepening recession. This represented the beginning of the end of the monetarist experiment, while the PSBR and the exchange rate became the main criteria guiding policy. Monetarists criticized this move, but the Bank of England clearly favored it (Riddell 1989, 19).

Early accounts described this change as an instance of outsiders gaining the upper hand over bureaucrats; Keegan (1984) finds the catalyst to the whole process in a study commissioned by the Institute for Economic Affairs, blaming the pound's high exchange rate on a monetary policy that was too tight and the government's own incorrect definition of the proper monetary measure to target. As Keegan points out, "The episode also illustrated the degree to which the Tories were badly prepared in the one economic policy area where they were supposed to be so radically different—namely monetarism" (160). Keegan sees Alan Walters and John Hoskyns, two outsiders, as using the commissioned study to press their case, successfully, to Thatcher. Hoskyns supports this view: "The shape of the Budget first emerged at an advisers' meeting in my office on 21 January. It was fiercely resisted on 13 February by both the Prime Minister and the Chancellor—and who could blame them? Douglas Wass, the head of the Treasury, supported their position, not ours. But, in the end, Margaret and Geoffrey took the outsiders' advice rather than Whitehall's" (Hoskyns 2000, 285).

But two of the key players—Chancellor of the Exchequer Geoffrey Howe and Financial Secretary Nigel Lawson—minimize the role of the outside advisers and insist that they determined the shape of the budget. And, indeed, all published accounts agree that the key innovations of the 1981 budget—raising taxes in politically acceptable ways—were Howe's and Lawson's. Hoskyns and Walters wanted to raise the income tax; Hoskyns's diary entry for February 13, 1981, reads, "We said put up income tax, grasp the nettle now. They [Thatcher and Howe] said such a tough budget was simply not on politically" (2000, 273). As far back as 1976 the party in opposition had foreseen that "any savings on public expenditure in the foreseeable future will be taken up in the need to reduce the enormous borrowing requirement. . . . An all-round lowering of taxation will have to wait. The political taxes must come first" (LCC 76/116, "Policy Group on Taxation Second Interim Report"). Moreover, the 1979 and 1980 budgets had also reduced income tax, and internal party polling research had shown that "76 percent were aware that the standard rate of income tax had been reduced. . . . Amongst those who were aware of the reduction, it was a universally popular aspect of the [1979] budget" (CCO 180/9/3/11, "Report on a Post-Budget Survey," 25 Jul 1979). It had also shown that "increases in the duties on alcohol and tobacco were quite clearly approved" in the 1980 budget (CCO 180/9/3/12, "Report on a Post-Budget Survey," May 1980). Presumably Howe did not want to increase the general income tax rates because reducing them had been the centerpiece and the most popular part of his 1979 budget. He had proudly announced, "In total we have carried through the biggest cut in income tax in British history" (CRD 4/16/16, "Background Economic Briefings") and may have considered it humiliating to backpedal. Moreover, the 1979 budget had also nearly doubled the value-added tax (VAT), and it would be impossible to take it any higher. Thus, what he came up with was a severe increase of the excise taxes (sales taxes on specific goods, in this case alcohol, tobacco, gas, and diesel fuel), and a decision not to index tax allowances for inflation for the next year. Criticism from backbenchers caused a slight adjustment—less tax increase on diesel fuel, more on tobacco, on which Howe comments: "Such is the success of the anti-smoking lobby that the tobacco duty is the one tax where an increase commands more friends than enemies in the House of Commons" (Howe 1994, 97).

Although none of the memoirs explains why an income tax increase was "not on politically" but excise tax increases were, it seems likely that the "invisibility" of sales taxes was on the minds of the politicians. The Conservative Party's own public opinion research had concluded as early as 1976 that

> income tax was more frequently thought to need decreasing than any of the other forms of taxation. 62 percent of respondents thought it very important that income tax should be reduced, a further 25 percent thought it 'important.' 30 percent thought [income tax was] unfair ... [while the b]etting tax, tax on tobacco, and tax on drink were not thought to need reducing, were seldom considered unfair and were the only taxes thought to need increasing by more than a very small minority. (CCO 180/9/10/5, "Attitudes to Taxation")

Because Britain, unlike most other countries, still receives nearly a fifth of all tax revenue from excise taxes (Daunton 2002; Grant 1994), this increase represented a more substantial tax rise than it would in other contexts, but the only one of the excise taxes to cause grumbling was the tax on petrol. In fact, the petrol tax seems to have made the budget as a whole extremely unpopular: nine out of ten electors agreed that "most people will be worse off as a result of the Budget," but the only proposals that drew specific criticism were the petrol tax and, secondarily, the increase in car licenses; a slim majority approved the increased tobacco tax, and the electorate was divided over alcohol tax (CCO 180/9/3/13, "Attitudes to the March 1981 Budget"). There was also some right-wing opposition to the policy of moving to indirect taxes, for example, from journalist Sam Brittan, who wrote,

> A shift from direct to indirect taxation is a way of concealing from the public the extent to which income is withdrawn from their pay packets and devoted to collective consumption. If I wished to enlarge the share of the state sector, I would recommend such a shift. It is no accident that the great 19th Century exponents of a market economy, such as Peel, Cobden and Gladstone, were intensely suspicious of consumer taxes, while modern Communist countries have low income taxes and high turnover taxes. (KJ 10/21, quoted in David Howell to Joseph, 5 Aug 1975)

The rise of indirect sales taxes and decline of direct income tax made the tax structure more regressive, and, in the early years, increased the overall tax burden (Taylor-Gooby 1989, Wicks 1987). Rose and Karran thus call Thatcher "a spectacular example of the inadequacy of the politician's will to introduce big tax cuts when confronted by the government's need for big sums of money" (1987, 4), but although total tax revenue did decline as a percentage of GDP in the second and third terms, the regressivity of the structure did not. In 1983 Dilnot and Morris wrote, "The period since 1979 has seen a rise in the overall tax burden for the majority of taxpayers; . . . overall marginal rates have risen steeply, . . . [and] the progressivity of the tax system has declined" (54). The effects were even greater by the end of the decade: "For those on half national average incomes the proportion paid in tax has risen from 2 to 7 per cent, for those on three-quarters from 30.5 to 34 per cent, and for those on average incomes from 35 to 37 per cent; for those on twice average incomes it has fallen from 27 to 25 per cent, and for those on five times average incomes from 49 to 35 per cent" (Taylor-Gooby 1989, 441–2). Wealth distribution, however, became slightly more equal even as income distribution became more unequal.

The sequence of events that led to the rise in indirect taxation in the early Thatcher years can be summarized thus: the symbol of monetarism provided an alternative method of controlling inflation around which a new political coalition could form;[9] in practice, however, monetarism became defined as controlling the budget deficit because of the influence of the Treasury and the Bank of England. Spending could not be controlled because of a promise made during the election campaign; therefore, the only way to control the budget deficit was to increase taxes, and since income tax cuts had been part of the election manifesto, the government was more comfortable taking sales tax increases. Monetarism became sales tax increases. Indeed, monetarism seemed to have become simply Keynesianism in reverse: not a distinct policy paradigm at all, but simply a strategy of lowering the budget deficit to lower inflation by increasing unemployment. "In the end . . . one has found that some of the more classic theories of . . . depression, for squeezing inflation have perhaps, ah, been really what it was all about" (*Thatcher Factor*, Heseltine, box 3).

The key difference from the U.S. case is that tax increases were seen to be necessary because the "Laffer curve" never caught on in Britain. Although Howe and Lawson were quite radical in their rejection of Keynesian attempts, neither seriously considered that it was possible to balance the budget without raising taxes. Howe simply dismissed it in these words: "My Treasury team and I had never succumbed . . . to the mistaken interpretations of Lafferism, which have led some U.S. policymakers so far astray. . . . Every penny I chose to knock off the rate payable by 19 million taxpayers would cost the Revenue almost £500 million" (Howe 1994, 128–29). Instead, he explained his reason for wanting to cut income taxes thus: "Not just because [the taxpayer's] income was more highly taxed than that of most of our overseas competitors. Not just because he or she felt demotivated. But, most important of all, because it would be politically impossible to make the large cuts in top rates that were necessary without achieving some compatible reduction in the direct tax burden of the average citizen" (129). The parallel to Stockman's "Trojan horse" is striking: the main goal was to cut top rates, and income tax cuts were added to make the package politically palatable.

Nigel Lawson was more reflective. He wrote that the government did not want to run a deficit because of its effect on interest rates. He

9. That it was an empty symbol was politically important: it allowed the discrepancies between the camps to be hidden from sight and made criticism difficult. For example, it was hard for Labour—which had implemented a monetarist policy—to criticize the government's monetarism, even though the implementation was quite different (*Thatcher Factor*, Biffen, box 1, and Howe, box 3).

reproduced a 1980 article in which he had written that a high deficit necessarily increases interest rates and said, "Later I became sceptical of the link between Budget deficits and interest rates in a world of free capital movements. Even in 1980, I had my doubts about how strong the link really was. But in so far as a link existed, it could only be in the direction the Treasury alleged" (Lawson 1992, 70). This observation is important for its suggestion that the link between budget deficits and interest rates was put forth by the Treasury. But at the time, no one seriously questioned this link, and markets did respond to the size of the government deficit by demanding higher interest rates. Thatcher also puts forward this argument in her memoirs.

Why did this argument not convince Stockman and the U.S. budget-makers? Primarily Stockman seems to have convinced himself that the tax cuts would not create a deficit because they would force spending cuts. But this reasoning—tax cuts now to force spending cuts later—does not make sense in the British case, where responsibility for tax and spending decisions is borne by the Prime Minister and Chancellor of the Exchequer: if they want tax cuts, they must be able to find the spending cuts or take the blame for the deficit (Steinmo 1993).

The different outcomes in the United States and Britain were due not to differences in ideas—both governments had similar ideas about free enterprise and state intervention—but to differences in *practice*, specifically, in the way the budget deficit was interpreted as relating to the goal of reducing the size of government, and whether taxation and spending were coupled or decoupled. In this process, bureaucracies and electoral considerations played the key role; the role of "ideas" was secondary. Hall writes, "Thatcher was able to resist massive pressure from inside and outside the government to reverse the course of policy in 1980–81 in large measure because she could draw on the monetarist paradigm to explain what others saw as unanticipated events and to rationalize her resistance to demands for change" (1992, 97). But monetarists themselves did not agree on what role the PSBR played, and the monetarist paradigm turned out in practice to be quite plastic. The tight reduction of PSBR was not dictated by the idea of monetarism, but it was this and the raising of taxes during a recession that it required that were the most radical elements of the first Thatcher budgets. The emphasis on controlling money supply was not a big change from the previous government's practice; as the Conservative Research Department liked to point out when the government was attacked, the contraction of the money supply was only half as severe as

Labour's in 1973–74 (CRD 4/4/31, Lilley, "Need to Explain"). The emphasis turned into a rather flexible and ad hoc policy, quite a departure from the monetarism advocated by Friedman.

In the years after the episode examined here, the government repeatedly failed to hit the M3 target, despite successively redefining it to make it easier to hit, and then abandoned the attempt to hit targets altogether without recourse to any other monetarist mechanism. As early as 1981, voices within the party were calling the policy "a shambles," noting that "the publication of precise monetary targets had made political life more difficult than would otherwise have been the case" and suggesting at the least wider targets—"The excuse can be that the Government has had to take account of the recession" (CRD 4/4/11, Mockler, 5 Feb 1981; Bulloch, 5 Feb 1981). In fact, informed observers had predicted exactly this:

> If £M3 is evidently such a poor guide to policy this year [1980], why should things be different in 1981/82 or 1982/83? Probably, in the event, they will not be different, and the Government will again show the flexibility which it has shown this year by abandoning the £M3 growth range as a guide to policy well before the end of each future year; . . . the commitment to the medium-term financial strategy can only be interpreted, at best, as an indication of the Government's good intentions with respect to curbing inflation. In the circumstances, as we argued in our *Gilt-Edged Research* comment of 8 September this year, it is unfortunate that these intentions should have been expressed in terms of control over a statistical measure which is so unreliable and which the Government must now feel, after the recent easing of inflationary pressures, is not essential to the ultimate objective of price stability. . . . The current volatility in the £M3 figures provides clear evidence for the impracticality of basing economic policy on £M3 targets. (CRD 4/4/11, Phillips and Drew, "Gilt-Edged Research," 8 Dec 1980)

Government policy in the later years was more ad hoc and pragmatic. Moreover, the government did increase public spending immediately preceding the 1983 and 1987 elections in classical Keynesian manner and then finally settled down to "inflation-constrained growth management" (Riddell 1989, 26), fairly standard and nonradical goals.

Thus, the most important legacy of the *monetarist* experiment in Britain was a *fiscal* policy—increase in indirect taxation—that the original proponents of monetarism disavowed, and in 1998 a monetarist could plausibly claim that "far from monetarism having failed, it has not been tried" (Robinson 1998, xx). (For this reason, I disagree with Hall's [1993] conclusion that monetarism represented a third-order change—although, as I argue below, *privatization* did.) In addition, there were political reasons why income tax cuts did not become the centerpiece for Thatcher that they were for Reagan. In the centralized system, there were no provincial elections to bring income tax cuts dramatically to attention, and no political entrepreneurs mobilizing the issue. The upshot was that in Britain, despite the popularity of income tax cuts, the implementation of neoliberalism did not see the arrival of persistent budget deficits.

The Privatization of British Telecom

If the case of taxation shows how standard practice overwhelmed ideological commitment to produce a result that was the opposite of what happened in the United States, the case of privatization shows another way in which the process of implementing neoliberalism in Britain constrained the ideology. Although the privatization effort was ideologically motivated, its implementation was constrained by political factors. The effort began hesitantly because of the fear that it would be unpopular. It moved into a new phase because the government needed to raise money to finance the modernization of a large public utility, and when this privatization turned out to be popular, the privatization movement was accelerated and became a centerpiece of the program. Indeed, if monetarism was supposed to be what Thatcherism was all about before the fact, twenty years later Thatcherism is identified most closely with privatization instead.

Privatization has been an issue for the Conservative Party throughout the postwar period. Defense and energy-related industries had been placed under state control during the first World War, but the Second World War and its aftermath saw nationalization on a wide scale: coal mines, telecommunications and transportation, electricity and gas, and the iron and steel industries were all nationalized in quick succession between 1946 and 1949. Increasing disillusionment with the performance of the nationalized industries, coupled with the Tory Party's ideological suspicion of state ownership, led to several attempts at denationalization. When Churchill won the election of 1951, he immediately tried to return road transport and steel to private hands, managing to reduce the share of the state in both sectors, but not completely in transport, and only temporarily in steel. Throughout the postwar period, attempts were made to increase efficiency in the nationalized industries, with little permanent result (Pollard 1992; Saunders and Harris 1994; Zahariadis 1995).

Thatcher's privatizations were thus not a new idea. What was new was the extreme to which privatization was carried under her tenure: at the end of the Thatcher-Major period, fully half of the state's assets in industry had been sold, making privatization one of Thatcher's chief successes.[10] Privatization on this scale was a new phenomenon in the history of the world, and remains unique in the development of capitalist states; the Thatcher experiment attracted worldwide attention (Craig 1990, 273; Swann 1988; Saunders and Harris 1994).

In particular, the Thatcher effort extended privatization to the public utilities, which most observers thought should remain in public hands because of their natural monopoly characteristics. In the early years of the Thatcher administration, the effort concentrated on the "narrow" goal of returning nationalized industries to the private sector; however, large sales of public utilities—the "broad" privatization program—began in 1983, starting with British Telecom. This movement of a policy from a narrow goal upon which there is consensus to a broader, contested goal is similar to the dynamic of deregulation in the United States—which moved from economic deregulation, on which there was wide consensus, to social deregulation, on which there was much difference of opinion. However, whereas social deregulation, particularly environmental deregulation, was actively and widely unpopular in the United States, public opinion on privatization in the United Kingdom was more ambivalent. In 1979 support for privatization was rising in the electorate, although supporters were still in the minority. The majority preferred the status quo: neither more nationalization nor more privatization (Särlvik and Crewe 1983). Once the privatizations were accomplished, the Thatcher team saw that they were popular. The way in which the privatizations were implemented probably helped, because small investors received favorable terms. Thus, whereas the evidence seems to indicate that American politicians were actively using the popularity of the deregulation symbol to implement unpopular policies, the Thatcher government seems to have moved to large-scale privatizations despite a fear of unpopularity; only in retrospect, when large-scale privatization was seen to be popular with the public, did it take off.

10. Chris Collins comments, "Privatization was not a new idea, true; doing something about it *was* new. This could be said to be the essence of Thatcherism, in a way. 'When you want something *said*, ask a man. When you want something *done*, ask a woman'" (personal communication, 31 Mar 2004). The quotation is from a speech given by Thatcher on May 20, 1965, at the National Union of Townswomen's Guilds Conference; see Collins 1998.

Although the Conservative Party had been studying the problem of the nationalized industries closely in opposition, privatization was not a central element of the 1979 manifesto. There, the main concern is resistance to further nationalization; privatization is mentioned only in regard to recently nationalized industries, and some government intervention is accepted in order to impose clear financial disciplines on those industries that remain nationalized. Nicholas Ridley had led a policy group on denationalization in 1968 and then again in 1978, but his group had not mentioned privatizing the public utilities, and the party—under Thatcher's leadership—had decided not to include privatization on the 1979 manifesto because of fear that it would frighten the "floating voter."

Because the privatization program was not heavily advertised in the 1979 manifesto, early accounts concluded that the Thatcher team had stumbled on the privatization program almost by accident and largely because of a need to raise money to keep down the PSBR (Riddell 1989; Feigenbaum and Henig 1994). Thatcher herself writes, "Over these [early] years privatization had leapt from fairly low down to somewhere near the top of our political and economic agenda" (1993, 678). She ascribes the initial hesitation to the lack of any precedent, and the gathering momentum to the administration's learning from its own early successes. Others have suggested that privatization got a boost when the sale of council houses brought the attention of the Treasury to the profits to be made from privatization (*Thatcher Factor*, Heseltine, box 3). On the other hand, Nigel Lawson writes,

> The limited and low-key reference to denationalization in the 1979 manifesto has led many commentators . . . to suppose that privatization was not part of our original programme and emerged as an unexpected development into which we stumbled by happy accident. They could not be more mistaken. The exiguous references in the 1979 Conservative manifesto reflected partly the fact that little detailed work had been done on the subject in Opposition; partly that the enthusiasts for privatization were Keith Joseph, Geoffrey Howe, John Nott, David Howell and me, rather than Margaret herself; and, perhaps chiefly Margaret's understandable fear of frightening the floating voter. But privatization was a central plank of our policy right from the start. (1992, 199)

Although helping to keep down the PSBR was one reason for the early privatizations, "denationalisation," as it was then called, had clearly been an important element of the policy rethinking of 1975–79 (Cockett 1995) and such thinking was becoming increasingly bold. In 1969 Ridley had noted that

> Denationalisation is an unpopular word. The electorate think that it is 'playing party politics.' To talk about it is said to be bad for the 'morale' of those who work in Public Industry. Nevertheless, a substantial number of people, particularly Tories, (as evidenced by our public opinion poll) believe that we should do some denationalising. The politics of the matter appear to suggest that we should denationalise some industries but avoid using that word. (ACP 69/65, Ridley, "Denationalisation")

Between 1975 and 1979, privatization moves more and more centrally onto the agenda, but the line of proposing the privatization of public utilities was never crossed. In 1974 Michael Heseltine, in a paper entitled "A New Industrial Charter," had concluded that "there is no real prospect of significant de-nationalisation" and thought that it would be a major step—"grasp[ing] the nettle"—to simply "offer a new deal to the nationalised industries" (LCC 74/32). In 1975 Keith Joseph wrote to a correspondent, "I fear the nationalisation bug will not be as easy to demolish as you think. But certainly, events must be increasing disenchantment, and we shall do our best to reinforce this" (KJ 17/6, Joseph to G. R. James, 6 Aug 1975). Nevertheless, Joseph and Angus Maude are a bit less categorical than Heseltine had been a year earlier:

> Presumably we do not think that denationalisation is practicable. Who would buy under Labour threats? Can we go half-way—BP [British Petroleum]? We must study. Anyway, I assume—but I may be wrong—that we are agreed to manage them at arm's length, phasing out subsidies, and seeking to cut overmanning as hard as we can. I am very conscious of a reservoir of disenchanted experience among our colleagues, and hope that suggestions will be made for fruitful thought and study. (LCC 75/57, "Notes Toward the Definition of Policy")

In 1976 Heseltine produced a comprehensive look at the nationalized industries, concluding,

> Our discussions have brought us to the conclusion that there are inherent defects in Nationalised Industries which exist because they are nationalised and which cannot be overcome.... The only solution which would have dramatic effect would be to return the industries to the private sector. We are aware of the difficulties of doing this: the shortage of buyers, particularly under a threat

> of 'renationalisation,' the difficulty of legislating, and the possibility of bitter industrial action to frustrate us. We do not therefore favour a policy of wholesale denationalisation by legislation of the old fashioned variety. (LCC 76/132, "Nationalised Industries")

He then outlines a policy of "gradual erosion of the public sector" but notes that "the scope for such a policy is not enormous. We doubt if it can apply to the great utilities like posts, gas, electricity, and the railways—at any rate in the first instance. But it might succeed in those industries where there is room for greater efficiency" (LCC 76/132). The paper also includes a table of various pre-privatization options (whether monopolies can be broken up, whether units can be sold, etc.) and whether they apply to various industries, but the answer is no for all the possibilities for Telecom, Electricity, Gas, Posts, and Transport. In British Rail, only "Catering, Hotels, Ships, etc. can be sold off," and only marginal industries like shipbuilding and the bus company are unequivocally labeled yes (LCC 76/132). In the meeting at which Heseltine's paper was discussed, however, a more open-ended view prevailed

> We should not commit ourselves to de-nationalise only the National Bus Company. Our de-nationalisation programme was designed to start with selling off the Felixstowe Docks, nationalised aircraft and shipbulding companies and other companies taken over by the NEB, but all these were subject to the need to find buyers at a reasonable price.... The proposals to break up the nationalised industries into smaller units, more amenable to disposal, and to remove statutory monopolies... was perhaps the most fertile area of approach, and these should be further examined. (LCC 76/126)

In 1977 David Howell explicitly mentions the privatizations under Labour as setting a precedent: "Now that the Labour Government has set an example with the sale of BP shares there seems every reason for pursuing this policy of giving industries back to the people. The rest of BP could go and this would be a possible route to follow with BNOC.... The policy group on nationalised industries is making detailed recommendations on possible sales" (KJ 10/17, in George Cardona to Joseph, 29 Jul 1977). By 1978 Ridley's paper on "Policy for the Nationalised Industries" notes, "The scope for achieving [denationalization] will vary widely. The objective must be pursued cautiously and flexibly, recognising that major changes may well be out of the question in some industries such as the utilities" (SC 78/71). Norman Lamont's response to this report is interesting, as it notes both the political risks of denationalization, uses the still uncommon word "privatisation," and suggests for perhaps the first time the privatization of telecommunications for the purpose of raising capital:

> You say that de-nationalisation should not be attempted by frontal attack, and yet the list of de-nationalisation proposals is really very comprehensive. You are proposing a degree of 'privatisation' of eight or nine different nationalised corporations. It does not seem to me that there will be much 'stealth' in such a comprehensive approach, and I would have wondered whether it really was very practical politically. Rather than tinkering about with so many different industries, I would prefer a substantial degree of 'privatisation' in one or two of them. We would thus avoid a clash with the unions across a broad front, and we would be able to demonstrate that de-nationalisation can work. Personally I would confine myself to de-nationalising British Aerospace, British Shipbuilders, forcing B.S.C. to undertake more joint ventures with the private sector, and the telecommunications side to raise its capital on the private market. (KJ 8/19, Lamont to Ridley, 20 Feb 1978)

By 1978 the denationalization group had proceeded far enough in its work to consider its strategic aspects, such as the need to stockpile coal if coal miners were provoked to strike (KJ 8/19, Ridley, Confidential Annex, "Countering the Political Threat"). Thus, denationalization crept from having "no real prospect," to being firmly, if carefully, on the agenda. But despite the occasional mention, the privatization of public utilities was not a substantial part of the proposals.[11]

What is also clear from the archives is that one reason the privatization effort had not been heavily advertised is that the Conservatives did not want to be pinned down to any specific policy promises; over and over

11. There was some debate over the possibility of taking any action on the utilities. Ridley writes, "The utilities are clearly the least likely candidates—partly because they are big and unlikely to be saleable, and partly because they might need 'regulating' if they were sold back. In any case it is suggested they are in a lower category." Then, in considering whether action can be taken in various industries, he lists telecommunications and writes, "Consider converting to a B.P., selling part of the equity." But this was evidently a second thought, as it is written on liquid paper: under the liquid paper the words "No action" are visible (KJ 8/19, Ridley, "Denationalisation"). Conservative party sympathizers were often more radical than the party itself: a "Prospective Conservative Candidate for South Battersea" forwards a letter written to the *Daily Telegraph* considering the privatization of British Telecom as early as 1975, which Joseph esteems enough to pass on to Heseltine of the denationalization group (KJ 17/6, Theo Wallace to Joseph, 31 Jul 1975; Joseph to Wallace, 7 Aug 1975).

again they say they want to include in the manifesto only "absolutely necessary pledges" (LCC 74/22, Howe, "Minutes of 22nd Meeting"). They fear "the danger of being over-committed to a detailed blue-print of our actions in Government" (LCC 76/98 "The Political Prospect and Strategy"), and a Manifesto Background Brief of 1978 states quite explicitly that "there are of course numerous borderline cases of statements which we know are actually intended as pledges, even though for obvious reasons they are tentatively worded" (LCC 78/203, "Manifesto Background Brief"). To a friendly correspondent wanting to know more details about what the party planned to do in government, Keith Joseph refused to provide any specifics, saying, "We are not in office, and we do not know what the conditions will be when we shall be in office" (KJ 10/5, Keith Joseph to A. V. Duncan, 28 Oct 1975). This is the reason why the commitment to privatization is not evident in the manifesto: the party did not want to limit its own course of action in government by election pledges,[12] and carefully kept the denationalization proposals out of the public eye, leading early commentators to think that not much work had been done on the issue. But as the work of the various groups shows, denationalization was on the agenda in increasingly bold terms.[13]

The first Thatcher administration actually privatized much more than the manifesto promised: five major state-owned firms and twenty smaller ones. In addition to aerospace and the National Freight Corporation, it sold off Cable and Wireless, Amersham International, and Britoil. Comparing these early privatizations to what came afterward helps to explain why outside observers believe the party stumbled onto privatization, whereas those on the inside insist it was always a part of the platform. These early, narrow privatizations were much larger than anything that had ever gone before and mark a clear break with the history of postwar industrial policy, but those that followed in the second administration were so large—on a

12. It was common political wisdom that parties in opposition should avoid making extensive specific pledges. A constituent writes, "I know that it is normally regarded as politically unwise to declare one's hand too far in advance, and for this reason you may be judging it wrong to elaborate too much policy of what you will do" (KJ 17/5, Viscount Trenchard to Joseph, 13 Aug 1975).

13. It is also clear that much of the work of the policy groups was out of sight of even backbenchers, much less the public. James Douglas writes to Keith Joseph concerning Terence Higgins and the Trade group: "It might also be a good idea if you could have a word with him about the policy work as a whole since, as he is not a member of the Shadow, neither he nor his Trade Parliamentary Committee have been kept very closely informed of what is going on" (KJ 17/7, Douglas to Joseph, 9 Jun 1975).

world-historical scale—that they dwarf the privatizations of the first administration. As John Campbell writes, "only by comparison with what came later" (2003, 96) can we consider the early privatizations as not marking a major implementation of free market policy.

The key episode that led to a significant acceleration of privatization was the sale of British Telecom. The privatization of British Telecom was neither the first nor the largest privatization of the Thatcher period; but it was the one that, by most accounts, transformed privatization from an ad hoc program helping to bring in more money to an ideologically coherent pillar of the "popular capitalism" Thatcher saw herself as installing. As one minister said at the time, "The sale of British Telecom had proved to be a great success. The marketing campaign which accompanied the flotation won people's attention to such an extent that, in my view, it had transformed the ground rules for further privatization measures" (John Moore, quoted in Cockett 1995, 303).

The sale of British Telecom (BT) was qualitatively different than anything that had gone before for several reasons: BT was a company that the mass public interacted with, so everyone was paying attention; the value of the sale was of an order of magnitude greater than any of the others; and it was a public utility, thus moving beyond what everyone agreed on and into the kind of privatization about which many economists had doubts. It was much more successful than anyone had thought possible. Lawson recounts a party with "captains of industry and pillars of leading City merchant banks," all of whom, apart from the government's own adviser, "roundly declared that the privatization was impossible: the capital market simply was not large enough to absorb it" (1992, 222). The number of people who purchased small amounts of shares, in particular, was spectacular: two million shareholders participated, one million of them buying stock for the first time.

Before 1979 there had been no serious systematic consideration of the idea of privatizing telecommunications. Rather, the main problem discussed was that a report on telecommunications had concluded that British services were among the worst in the industrialized world in terms of number of telephones per capita, investment in telecommunications, and productivity in the telecommunications sector (Zahariadis 1995, 84). Large amounts of capital would be necessary to bring the service up to par (CDR 4/4/32, Ridley to Shepherd, 26 Jun 1980), but the government—committed to reducing its PSBR—was not enthusiastic about providing these funds. So the original aim was to raise capital to improve services as well as to replace a part of the subsidies provided to BT by the Treasury with capital raised on the financial markets, so that the Treasury could lower PSBR. But it quickly became clear that the financial markets would judge a loan taken out by a nationalized industry to be, in effect, a loan backed by the government, and therefore would not scrutinize it as they would a loan to a private company—setting up the possibility of a government bailout down the line and defeating the whole purpose of trying to increase the efficiency of the company. Under its dynamic leader, George Jefferson, BT was committed to finding the necessary funds, but it was boxed in: higher user charges were unpopular and would not raise enough; bonds for an inefficient monopoly would attract buyers only at very high interest rates or those anticipating government bailout; and the Treasury, committed to lowering the deficit, did not want to provide the capital (Zahariadis 1995).

It was in canvassing and rejecting these other options that the privatization idea first came up. Curiously, it does not seem to have been debated very much ahead of time. It received backing primarily because Jefferson had made BT salable: it had achieved a substantial profit margin at a moment when demand for telecommunications was set to soar. In addition, by this point the government had a record of having successfully privatized many small firms and the council houses.[14] The original plan, however, was to sell only 51 percent of British Telecom shares; the government would retain 49 percent. The motivation was to "convert British Telecom . . . into a dynamic private company; fully responsive to market demands, free from Government restraints and able to raise investment capital on a commercial basis and on a scale which will allow it to make full use of the coming opportunities" (J. Butcher, quoted in Zahariadis 1995, 88). But as David Steel pointed out, if the government remained the single largest shareholder, capital markets would still assume a governmental guarantee (Zahariadis 1995).

The discussion therefore turned to the possibility of breaking up BT as AT&T had been broken up in the United States, but the conclusion was that this would take too long and that a single company would be most attractive to stock purchasers. This decision has been criticized in retrospect as putting haste above proper surveillance. Because BT was

14. The money from the sale may also have been a consideration: "Scope for really substantial savings and a corresponding improvement in the relationship between Government and the citizen may lie in the direction of privatisation," including getting local governments to privatize (CRD 4/4/32, Howarth, "Notes on Strategy").

a monopoly, economists have argued that ownership did not matter as much as the regulatory structure; and, indeed, complaints about BT's post-privatization performance put a damper on the privatization effort after 1987. But in 1983, the political reasons for selling the company off as quickly as possible were paramount. The sale was a great success, attracting two million customers and doubling the number of Britons who owned stocks (Riddell 1989).

At this point privatization began to come unmoored from the original reasons put forth for it, and new rationales were developed to support it. The original argument for privatization was that companies in the public sector were inefficient because of lack of competition and the soft budget constraint, knowing the government would always bail them out. But these concerns do not clearly apply to natural monopolies, for even if they are moved into the private sector, the government must retain significant control to prevent them from abusing their monopoly power, and their monopoly position allows them to remain inefficient. Thus many observers argued that ownership was irrelevant; what mattered was the structure of regulation. But at this point, officials began to argue as follows: "We will encourage competition where appropriate but where it does not make business or economic sense we will not hesitate to extend the benefits of privatisation to natural monopolies" (Zahariadis 1995, 88). As Zahariadis points out, this was directly contradictory to the original reason given for privatization—increasing efficiency. Political actors at the time pointed this out as well: Lord Weinstock protested that the company had, in public hands, become quite efficient, and that the regulatory structure set up to control it was weak (Zahariadis 1995).

The case for increasing efficiency by taking BT into the private sector—the original reason given for privatization—was not strong, but the case for raising capital by doing it was overwhelming, and the Treasury was convinced this was the only way to do it. Thus, despite the potential problems and concerted opposition by the unions, the government backed it. Their reward was considerable: it was hailed as an instant success in ways that had not been foreseen.

Heath et al. (1991) have shown that, in fact, privatization was not a vote-winner among the general public, nor even among those who had bought shares for the first time when the state firms were privatized. However, their data do show an increase in Conservative voting among those who bought these shares and also held other shares, as well as among those who did not buy these shares but held other shares. What privatization seems to have done is energized the Conservative base. And since it did not cause other voters to switch their votes *away* from the Conservatives, it was a net electoral gain.

More important, however, is the question of how the government, and particularly Thatcher herself, saw the popularity of privatization. Even if privatization was on the agenda from the beginning, "broad" privatization was not, and Thatcher was worried about "frightening the floating voter," so we must still ask how that worry was overcome. We know that Thatcher was wary at the beginning, but at the end of the privatization process she clearly believed that privatization was popular—indeed, by the end of her term in office, privatization had been taken further than anywhere else in the developed world. This would hardly have been possible if Thatcher had continued to fear the response of the floating voter.

There is no direct evidence on what changed her mind, but the indirect evidence from Thatcher's speeches is quite clear: before the sale of British Telecom, every mention of the organization involves its inefficiency, and the impending privatization is justified in terms of increasing competition, efficiency, and benefits to the consumer. In every single speech in the six months directly after the sale, however, the privatization is justified in terms of increasing public ownership of shares. Here are the relevant passages from Thatcher's speeches directly before the sale: "We need much greater efficiency from British Telecom and from every other industry. We need to reduce overmanning and restrictive practices" (MTF: Hansard HC [27/144–48], 6 Jul 1982).[15] (This was the standard government line; the Secretary of State for Employment, Norman Tebbit, gave the nationalized British Telecom as a prepared example of "the overmanning and inefficiency which have characterised much of British industry in the past [but] have been largely rooted out now in the private sector" [MTF: Hansard HC [16/902–18], 27 Jan 1982].) When a Labour MP mentions BT in another context in a House of Commons debate, Thatcher takes the opportunity to answer, "With regard to competition, it serves the British consumer better than nationalised monopolies" (MTF: Hansard HC [29/498–502], 21 Oct 1982). On another occasion, she says, "Innovation, more responsive services, and a better deal for customers all spring from the spur of competition. That is why we have ended the monopoly of British Telecom" (MTF: "Speech Opening Conference on Information Technology," The Barbican

15. Citations followed by the initials "MTF" were examined on margaretthatcher.org, the official website of the Margaret Thatcher Foundation. Citations give a short version of the original source and the date. A preservation copy of all material on the site is available in the Thatcher MSS (Digital Archive) at Churchill Archive Centre, Cambridge.

Centre, London, 8 Dec 1982). At a tour of Reading, when given an explanation of a new cellular radio system, she said that was "a good reason for denationalising British Telecom" (MTF: *Reading Evening Post*, 28 May 1983). In a speech in which she goes on to praise council house sales for furthering the "link between liberty and property ownership," BT is not mentioned in such terms: "New technology will flourish only in conditions of competition. We have already ended the monopoly in telecommunications and we shall reintroduce the Bill to denationalise British Telecom" (MTF: Hansard HC [44/53–62], 22 Jun 1983). In answer to a friendly question on the privatization of BT, she says, "It is much better for Britain to have less nationalised industry and to put more in the private sector. It is a better bargain for the consumer, and it means that industry can obtain its investment from the market instead of having to rely upon Government sources" (MTF: Hansard HC [46/559–64], 21 Jul 1983). In response to a question on union levies and a suggestion that a pro-management union be created at BT, she resists interfering but takes the opportunity to point out that some union members support privatization: "It is for the chairman of British Telecom to take whatever decisions are in the best interests of the business. I understand that some members of the [union] have been reluctant to pay the levy. That shows that they have made a better assessment than some of their leaders of the benefits of privatisation" (MTF: Hansard HC [49/983–87], 1 Dec 1983).

The tone begins to change in 1984, as the government was planning the sale and preparing its campaign to get workers and the wider public to participate. In July Thatcher equates the BT privatization with the council house sales and speaks of it for the first time ideologically:

> If we look around the world, we see that those countries which deny private property rights also deny other human rights. We seek to redress the balance between the citizen and the state by restoring to private ownership industries that have lain under the pall of nationalisation. . . . We are well on course for the denationalisation of British Telecom and British Airways in the coming year. Most fundamental of all, three quarters of a million families are buying their own council houses . . . freeing themselves from the control of town halls. (MTF: Hansard HC [65/241–52], 31 Jul 1984)

In October, she gives both competition and ownership reasons: "Denationalization has brought greater motivation to managers and workforce, higher profits and rising investment, and what is more, many in industry now have a share in the firm for which they work. We Conservatives want every owner to be an earner and every earner to be an owner. Soon, we shall have the biggest ever act of denationalization with British Telecom . . . ” (MTF: Speech to Party Conference, Conference Centre, Brighton, 12 Oct 1984). In November she just hints at the ownership arguments while justifying the sale with reference to limiting public spending and halting “the expansion of the public sector, which is wealth consuming; . . . we have therefore pursued a programme of returning state industry to the private sector. . . . Shortly the British public will receive a prospectus for British Telecom setting out the terms on which the largest ever transfer of a company from state control is being offered” (MTF: Hansard HC [67/20–31], 6 Nov 1984).

In late November, as the sale is proceeding, this exchange in a House of Commons debate signals the impending change in the way the privatization of British Telecom is viewed:

> [CONSERVATIVE MP:] Did my right hon. Friend hear about the corporation dust cart that screeched to a halt outside the Scottish bank yesterday morning, whereupon the driver leapt out and placed his application for British Telecom shares at five minutes to 10? Is it not good news for Britain that at the beginning of next week probably over 1 million more people will become first-time share owners? Does she agree that one of the things that riles Labour Members is that many of those new shareholders will be Labour supporters, who have ignored threats of renationalisation?
>
> [THATCHER:] Yes, the denationalisation of British Telecom will bring many people into share ownership and independence for the first time. The Labour party cannot tolerate that, because it wants people to be under its thumb and not to be independent with their own shares and their own homes. (MTF: Hansard HC [68/1084–88], 29 Nov 1984)

From this point forward, *every* mention of the privatization of British Telecom over the next six months is justified with reference to the benefits of property ownership for the mass public. The references to competitiveness, efficiency, and benefits for the consumer simply drop out. In December, we hear: “In the coming year we shall build on the success of British Telecom where instead of one giant shareholder, there are now millions of owners” (MTF: New Year Message, 31 Dec 1984, *Conservative Newsline*, January 1985). In January 1985, in response to Labour comments about privatization, we have, “I would rather listen to the millions of our citizens who bought shares in British Telecom" (MTF: Hansard HC [72/427–38], 31 Jan 1985); and in February,

> Did you know that the sale of British Telecom shares a few months ago was the largest ever made in the World? Four times larger than anything in the United States. At one fell swoop, two million people in Britain bought shares. . . . When the Labour Party talk about 'A fundamental and irreversible shift in the balance of power and wealth' they mean more power to the State. We mean more power to the citizen. (MTF: Speech to Young Conservative Conference, Winter Garden, Bournemouth, 9 Feb 1985)

And again, when a friendly questioner asks if Thatcher agrees that "over a third of the employees of British Telecom have agreed to take part in the share option scheme; . . . the ordinary person in this country wishes to belong to a capital-owning democracy," she answers, "Yes. The British Telecom share issue, which was the largest to be conducted on either side of the Atlantic, has been a great success, particularly for the 2 million people who purchased shares and for the people who work in BT. It is a success of capitalism in that it has spread genuine ownership more widely among our people" (MTF: Hansard HC [74/168–72], 26 Feb 1985).

She notes in March that "privatisation is popular; . . . we have denationalised Jaguar, Sealink and British Telecom to name just a few" (MTF: Speech to Conservative Central Council, City Hall, Newcastle, 23 Mar 1985). In May, in response to a question about how high unemployment fit her "dreams of a classless society," she notes the rise in home ownership and adds, "There has been a dramatic extension of share ownership, as shown by the 1.7 million people who now hold shares in British Telecom" (MTF: Hansard HC [78/617–22], 7 May 1985). And again, "We believe also that it should be as common for people to own shares as it is for them to own houses or cars. The privatisation of British Telecom and many other firms extended share-ownership to hundreds of thousands who had never owned shares before" (MTF: Speech to Scottish Party Conference, City Halls, Perth, 10 May 1985). In June she says, "The British Telecom share issue alone has 1.7 million shareholders—a figure equal to the total number of shareholders in 1979" (MTF: Hansard HC [80/1007–12], 13 Jun 1985); and, "In one bold step, over two million people bought shares in British Telecom. And how delighted they must have been with the profits of the first year of privatisation" (MTF: Speech to Welsh Conservative Party Conference, Llandudno Conference Centre, 22 Jun 1985).

Lawson's claim that privatization was always part of the agenda is correct, as shown by the policy work on denationalization done in opposition. Nevertheless, it is clear that the justifications for privatization changed quite suddenly and completely after, and because of, the sale of British Telecom. Before that sale the main complaint had concerned the inefficiency of nationalized industries; after the sale privatization was justified in positive terms, as contributing to a property-owning democracy. Indeed, this phrase (originally a theme of Anthony Eden's) became one of the key chords of Thatcherism; in retrospect, Thatcherism was not about monetarism at all, but about "popular capitalism." And this explains how Thatcher's fear of the floating voter was overcome: the sale of British Telecom was perceived as widely popular, even among some traditional Labour supporters. This, rather than the economic arguments for privatization, cleared the way for the major privatizations to follow. As Joseph said, "I don't think we realised what . . . a winner in national and in political terms we had. We realised that for instance selling council houses would be good for the nation . . . good for individuals, and politically popular. But it's turned out that . . . privatisation is the same" (*Thatcher Factor*, Joseph, box 3).

Both the United States and the United Kingdom made successful attempts to reduce the state's direct role in industry, but policy legacies ensured that the attempts would take different forms in the two countries. After the Second World War the European countries had seen a wave of nationalization of the "commanding heights" of the economy—those firms that, it was thought, could not be left to the private sector because of their crucial position in the national economy. Because the United States had pioneered a unique method of industrial oversight in which firms were left to private ownership, but regulated by the government, the starting point in the two cases was obviously different: the American free marketeers addressed themselves to deregulation; the British, to privatization.

Whereas the early push toward deregulation was brought onto the agenda by outside activists, privatization had to some degree always been on the British Conservative Party's agenda: the promise to reverse Labour's nationalizations had been made in previous manifestos, and even the Labour government of the late 1970s was forced by the International Monetary Fund (IMF) to sell off a small part of British Petroleum. The shift in the privatization program from the narrow to the broad privatizations occurred for non-ideological reasons—as a way to raise capital to modernize the telecommunications infrastructure—and the perceived popularity of the sale led to a renewed emphasis on privatization.

Council House Sales and the British Welfare State

At the end of the Second World War, England had become the first "cradle to grave" welfare state: "Beveridge . . . referred to 'Five Giants on the road to reconstruction'—Want, Disease, Ignorance, Squalor and Idleness. The 'Giant killing' policies [implemented in the closing years of the war] were social security, the National Health Service, Butler's Education Act, town and country planning, and full employment" (Douglas 1989, 403). The Conservative governments of the postwar period occasionally complained about the increasing role of the state in this area, but were able only to check a rise in expenditure. The Heath administration of 1970–1974, which had attempted before the U-turns to institute lower and more regressive taxes, and which had vowed to end state intervention in industry, did not make any similar attempts in welfare policy.

The Thatcher government also failed to reduce spending as a share of national income or significantly alter any of the major programs. Of the major programs, only spending on housing saw a major decline, with a dramatic reduction in public housing stock through the sale of council houses at reduced costs to their tenants.[16] The upshot was a rise in visible homelessness over the course of the decade. The pattern is therefore a familiar one: resilience in the well-established middle-class programs, fragility in the marginal programs. But it is incorrect to argue that Thatcher attempted, and failed, to attack the central elements of the welfare state; in fact, the government self-censored its actions and did not even attempt to target the core programs for cutbacks. Nor is it correct to assume that the attack on housing represented middle-class resentment of welfare scroungers. Council house tenants were not necessarily poor, and council house sales were promoted as helping their tenants rather than punishing them as a conscious political strategy ("We should also not get into a position where we might seem to be attacking council house tenants. We should emphasise those proposals designed to help them" [LCC 76/120, "Minutes of the 120th Leadership Consultative Committee"]). When the policy of council house sales was passed, it was one of Thatcher's most popular policies and was implemented on the assumption that it would attract the floating

16. Scholars often call the council house sales part of the "privatization" program. This seems to follow Thatcher's own attempt to assimilate both as elements of popular capitalism. In this book I reserve the word *privatization* for industrial policy. I do not believe that this semantic question affects the substantive analysis.

voter. Indeed, Thatcher had been initially reluctant to adopt the policy, because she thought it penalized those who had never lived in council housing and who had saved up to buy their own homes. The electoral considerations convinced her, and, like privatization, it became a cornerstone of her program.

Unlike monetarism and denationalization, the party had not engaged in a full-scale rethinking of welfare state policy while in opposition. The wish to partially privatize the National Health Service (NHS) is visible as early as 1975, when Joseph and Maude wrote, "The present strains in the *NHS* will lead to a small increase in the private sector. People are willing to pay for better health for themselves and their families and yet our system penalises this; people wish for some choice and control of health provision; the present system gives neither." They go on to suggest a voucher system for health service (LCC 75/57, "Notes Toward the Definition of Policy"). But although the popular mandate to do something about the unions and to sell council houses was clear, all the systematic evaluations of the middle-class programs shy away from cutbacks. The Conservative Research Department wrote,

> There is no reason to believe that [American-style private health care] offers any attraction to the UK; . . . there is widespread popular dissatisfaction with the system [in the United States]. . . . Even Milton Friedman has expressed his dislike of the present health structure and has called for a transitional programme which would 'assure a safety net for every person in the country, so that no one need suffer distress' ("Free to Choose" 1980). In practice it seems likely that the United States will move towards some system of compulsory health insurance . . . further changes in the US system are clearly on the cards. . . . The introduction of an insurance-based system of health finance in Britain would not only involve a legislative upheaval but an administrative upheaval as well. It would be the biggest internal re-organisation of the welfare state since its creation in 1948 . . . there is little doubt that this would be a matter of profound electoral concern. (CCO 180/30/1/5, Mockler, "The Future of Private Medicine")

The unpopularity of cutbacks in the middle-class programs was brought home to the government in an early episode. Thinking as usual of the PSBR, in 1982 Geoffrey Howe pushed for a comprehensive review of spending patterns and asked the Central Policy Review Staff to suggest ways expenditure might be cut. The CPRS seems to have taken this as a brainstorming exercise, and produced proposals that were clearly politically implausible at the time: education vouchers, introducing private health insurance, canceling a missile program, and so forth. Neither Howe, nor Thatcher, nor any of the other free-marketeers were seriously considering anything like this, and indeed Thatcher was alarmed at the suggestions because of the possibility that they might be leaked. The report produced an uproar both in the Cabinet and, when the Cabinet moderates (the "wets") inevitably leaked it to the *Economist*, in the country, drawing accusations that the government was trying to dismantle the welfare state. Thatcher was forced to promise that the government would not introduce any of the proposals in the paper, and this is when she asserted that "the National Health Service is safe in our hands" (Howe 1994, 257–59; Lawson 1992, 303–4).

Bound by this promise, and even more by the awareness that it brought that the core elements of the welfare state were untouchable, the government postponed significant reform of the welfare state to Thatcher's third term. At that point—emboldened by the victory in the Falklands, by the defeat of the trade unions, and by having become the first postwar Prime Minister in 150 years to have won three consecutive elections—Thatcher became more outspoken in her rhetoric and turned her attention from economic policy and industrial policy to social policy. In 1987 she appointed a free-marketeer, John Moore, as secretary of state for Health and Social Security with a mandate to reform the welfare state. But the fear that these reforms would be unpopular was so great that Thatcher herself was less than committed to them, and on those occasions when a reform was put up to vote, the negative votes of many backbenchers (party members not holding office) combined to dampen the reforming spirit. For example, legislation to freeze universal child benefits only got through with 47 votes in the House, despite a Tory majority of 102 (Campbell 2003, 548), and in 1989 the Tories lost two by-elections in Richmond and Glamorgan because of the perception that they planned to reduce health spending (Webster 1989).

Hemmed in by these proofs of welfare state popularity in the public and on the back benches, in 1988 Thatcher separated Health from Social Security and appointed a moderate with a favorable view of the welfare state, Kenneth Clarke, to lead the attempt to reform the NHS in place of the free-marketeer Moore. Ironically, Clarke's reforms were too radical for Thatcher. He developed a proposal allowing private companies to be NHS providers and allowing patients to go where they thought the service was best, in an attempt to introduce competition and accountability into the system. Thatcher was hesitant about the reforms because the government was so far behind in the polls, but Clarke insisted that it was necessary to save the NHS—a view on which most observers believe he was vindicated (Lawson 1992, 617–19; Campbell 2003, 552–55). Thus, the final result of the health care reform effort was to give up the idea of any kind of privatization and concentrate only on creating an "internal market" to attempt to improve the efficiency of health care delivery (Giaimo 2002; Ruggie 1996).

While middle-class programs could only be reformed, government commitment to public housing was transformed. Council house sales have not been as noticeable on a world-historical level as privatization, simply because Britain's postwar pattern of publicly funded housing at high levels was not prevalent anywhere else. But within Britain during the Thatcher years, the council house sales were taken to be emblematic of Thatcherism; they made a much more substantial difference to the lives of those who participated; and they actually raised much more money—£28 billion over eleven years compared, for example, to £4 billion from the sale of British Telecom (Campbell 2003, 235–36).

Local authorities had always had the discretion to sell council houses to sitting tenants; now the Conservative government passed Right to Buy legislation, which gave tenants the right to decide if they wanted to purchase their houses. Council houses in Britain were quite different from the public housing Americans are familiar with. Inner-city ghettoes did exist, but the program in general did not target the poor: 30 percent of Britons lived in public housing in 1979, while less than 4 percent lived in public housing or received housing subsidies in the United States at the same time (Pierson 1994, 76).

The sale of council houses, which has come to be so closely identified with the Thatcher administration, was originally the idea of a close colleague of Heath's, his Environment Secretary Peter Walker. Although council house sales had taken place as far back as Macmillan, it was Walker who, together with Heath, pioneered the systematic attempt to encourage local authorities to sell their stock of houses to long-term tenants. They were not particularly successful; only 7 percent of housing stock was sold over the course of the Heath administration (Campbell 1993, 379). When Heath narrowly lost the February 1974 election, he concluded that the small size of the loss meant that no radical changes in policy were necessary. In addition, in that election the Tories had actually gained votes over Labour, but they lost because they had lost about a million votes to the Liberals. Thus, the focus of their strategy was to figure out how to win back those middle-class voters who had gone over to the Liberals. The party settled on housing policy as the answer, not only because they felt this was the issue on which voters had felt most abandoned by the Tories (because of rising property taxes and interest rates) but also because it was relatively easy to fashion policies that would tempt back those floating voters, and "there was a risk that the Liberal Party was poised to exploit the issue politically by calling for a statutory right to buy council houses" (CRD 4/8/5, Minutes of the 24 June 1974 Meeting of the Housing Policy Group). According to the minutes of the fifteenth meeting of the Leader's Steering Committee of July 25, 1974,

> Mr. Heath said that the cost of the home ownership proposal would be considerable, but we had to think of it as the main plank of our next programme and ensure that it was an imaginative act of policy along with our policy on rents and mortgage rates. [Whitelaw said] Housing would be crucial at the next election and Mr. Wilson had already started to attack our record. Mr. Walker said that 8–9 million Labour voters were council house tenants. Something imaginative was required to get one million of them to vote Conservative.... A discussion followed about the problem of fair valuation from the point of view of the council house tenant who was going to buy his house and of the nearby private housing estate house owner who might lose capital on the value of his house if council houses were disposed of too cheaply. Mrs. Thatcher felt that we might be endangering our traditional vote in this area. (SC 74/20)

Heath worried that if the manifesto took a "high-line" approach—that is, strong on principles and vague on specific policy prescriptions—then "this would not satisfy people who genuinely felt that politicians were unable to cope with the day to day problems that worried them, such as housing and rates" (LCC 74/22). Heath determined that the manifesto should make three proposals: a reduction and eventual abolition of the property taxes on homeowners (the "rates" that, more than a dozen years later, would lead to Margaret Thatcher's downfall), mortgage subsidies, and council house sales, and he put Thatcher in charge of developing these policies as head of the Department of Environment. Thatcher did not like any of the three proposals; she felt that mortgage subsidies were too interventionist, that no alternative to the rates had been worked out, and that council house sales penalized those who had worked and saved to buy their own houses and never lived in public housing, and she had voiced her concerns about "endangering" the Tories' "traditional vote in this area" from such homeowners.

Nevertheless, when Heath insisted, Thatcher accepted and set to work examining the feasibility of various options (Campbell 1993, 271; 2000,

232–36; Young 1989, 80–83). Thus, council house sales arrived on the agenda for electoral reasons; but the Conservatives lost the 1974 election, and Labour ended the policy of encouraging local councils to sell council houses. Michael Heseltine convinced Thatcher to make council house sales a specific and concrete promise in a 1979 election manifesto that was devoid of many other specificities. But the Thatcher team abandoned Peter Walker's plan to give council houses outright to tenants of twenty years standing, and instead proposed only a substantial discount, because of the fear that current homeowners would consider Walker's proposal unfair:

> The Group firmly believes in a substantial programme of council house sales. . . . Mr. Walker's scheme itself involved transferring to tenants of more than 20 years standing the freehold entitlement to their house or flat. The remaining tenants would pay as mortgage payments a sum equivalent to their current rent payments for whatever time was needed to bring them up to the 20 years qualification for owning their council home. The Group fully understood the considerable political advantages among council house voters for the suggested policy. However it was our judgement that the objections from home owners would be very strong and difficult to overcome. We cannot therefore recommend its acceptance. (LCC 76/118, Raison, "Housing Policy")

In 1978 there is enough concern on the issue of how homeowners will respond to suggest further polling: "We should see if there was any market research to the attitude of existing owner occupiers to generous terms of the purchase of council houses, and, if not, commission some ourselves" (LCC 78/203, "Minutes of the 203rd Meeting, 8 May 1978").

The policy of selling off council houses differed from the policy of privatization of industry in that the government had already developed a coherent program of council house sales before the 1979 election, and it had done so for clearly electoral reasons. Where the popularity—at least among a certain segment of the electorate—of privatization was only discovered after the sale of British Telecom, polls in the late 1970s were already showing that 85 percent of voters wanted council house sales (Pierson 1994, 78). The government began the implementation immediately on taking office, and over the course of Thatcher's administration, public-sector housing expenditure fell by half, while the percentage of Britons owning their own homes grew from 55 percent in 1980 to 67 percent in 1990 (Campbell 2000, 233–34). In addition to the money raised from the council house sales and its social benefits, the Conservatives also liked the policy because of its potential to turn Labour voters into Conservative voters, since the new homeowners would be concerned with keeping down the property taxes and would appreciate the other "pro-homeowner" policies for which the Tories were known.

Council house sales were thus a central feature of the government's strategy to target floating voters and middle-class Labour voters. They were announced in the 1979 manifesto, and the government did not hide its attempt to create a "stakeholder society" and a "popular capitalism" by increasing the percentage of voters depending on private rather than public provision in housing. Indeed, council house sales were so popular that they were an important element in turning Labour into New Labour. The 1983 Labour Manifesto pledged to reverse the policy, and, following the 1983 loss, this was seen as one plank that had made Labour unelectable, and it was one reason for the replacement of Michael Foot with Neil Kinnock (Pierson 1994, 80).

The Popularity of Thatcherism

Council house sales were clearly implemented for electoral reasons, and when the privatization of British Telecom suggested to the government that the policy was popular even with Labour voters, the privatization program was accelerated and expanded. Both of these policies—which together form the cornerstone of the legacy of Thatcherism—were responses to popular and electoral considerations. The story is more complicated in taxation policy, but even there, popular considerations enter the picture at several points: in the decision to cut income tax while raising sales tax and in the ability to use the symbol of monetarism (but not its actual content) in the electoral contest by assuring the public that the Conservatives had an answer to inflation that would avoid the unpopular trade unions.

Whether Thatcherism was supported by the public has become a point of much contention in the scholarship.[17] Mishler, Hoskin, and Fitzgerald

17. See Butler and Pinto-Duschinsky 1971; Clarke, Mishler, and Whiteley 1990; Clarke, Stewart, and Zuk 1986; Crewe 1981; Dunleavy and Husbands 1985; Evans 1993; Franklin 1984; Garrett 1992; Kavanagh 1987; Kerr 1999; King 1981; Lanoue and Headrick 1994; Pimlott 1988; Ranney 1985; Sanders, Marsh, and Ward 1990, 1993; Scarbrough 1987; Studlar, McAllister, and Ascui 1990; and Weakliem 1993.

(1989) see no "evidence that Conservative successes stem from some underlying long-term dynamic in British politics . . . the recent string of Conservative victories owes as much to good timing and luck as to any underlying dynamic" (234; see also Mishler, Hoskin, and Fitzgerald 1988). Crewe and Searing believe that this shows that even in stable democracies it is possible to "successfully implement radical political programs that are unpopular with most political leaders and voters." Other observers argue that "the reason why Mrs Thatcher has secured a third term is that the current of the times still flows with the Conservative Party" (quoted in Butler and Kavanagh 1988, 268).

It is true that there was no full-blown conversion to Thatcherism in the public, and indeed the government was unpopular for most of its time in office (except, of course, during the elections). Nevertheless, there are indications that the public was increasingly receptive to Thatcherite appeals. First, in the general election of 1979, the winter of discontent had made unions remarkably unpopular, giving the Conservatives a slight advantage. Analysts disagree on how important this was: Mishler, Hoskin, and Fitzgerald (1989) find a 1.5 to 2 percent advantage, Clemens (1983) records that days before the election 14 percent of the public mentioned trade union power as an issue that would influence them to vote one way or another. More important, *on those issues that were most salient to them*, voters agreed with Conservative rather than Labour or Alliance positions (Butler and Kavanagh 1980). Most important were the issue of prices and inflation, which 39 percent of voters named, and the issue of high taxation, which 16 percent named (Clemens 1983, 16). Unemployment and law and order rounded out the five issues named most often. Butler and Kavanagh write, "Jobs, prices and law and order are examples of what political scientists call *valence* issues, that is parties and voters are largely agreed on the objectives of more jobs and stable prices. But many voters doubted the capacity of any party to improve the situation. *Position* issues are those on which the parties take different stands, e.g., taxes, trade unions, and de-nationalisation" (1980, 334). Of the top five issues in the 1979 election, only taxation and trade unions are "position" issues, and on both of these voters favored the Conservative position. On issues on which the parties offered clear and opposed courses of action in the 1979 election, the public preferred the Conservative strategy.

Crewe and Searing's data on public support for Thatcherite policies (compiled from British Election Study and Gallup data as well as their own survey) shows that on the eve of Thatcherism the public did support key elements of Thatcher's agenda, but the authors argue that the data show that this support was not sustained:

> While the Thatcher government's trade union reforms have been popular, its more ambitious aim of persuading the electorate that trade unions are undesirable or unnecessary institutions has completely failed. For example, Gallup's annual question of 30 years' standing ("Generally speaking, and thinking of Britain as a whole, do you think that trade unions are a good thing or a bad thing?") has consistently produced only minorities saying "a bad thing," . . . and smaller minorities in 1986 (25 percent) than in 1983 (28 percent), 1979 (41 percent), or 1974 (33 percent). [Although] between 1974 and 1979 the electorate did move to the right on the issue of whether benefits "nowadays have gone too far," by 1983 it had reversed direction and was to the left of its original position in 1974. . . . Asked to choose between tax and social service cuts or tax and social service increases, the public was evenly divided—37 percent apiece—when the Conservatives came to office in May 1979. By 1983 service increasers outnumbered tax cutters by 52 percent to 24 percent, and by May 1987 by the even greater margin of 64 percent to 13 percent. (1988, 377)

But Crewe and Searing are using ordinal data here to reach cardinal conclusions, and they are treating parties as static. Clearly, we should interpret the responses in light of the events of Thatcherism itself. That is, if fewer people respond in 1983 that taxes should be cut, this does not necessarily indicate that respondents' positions have moved; it may indicate that their positions have remained the same but they believe *events* have moved. To ask whether taxes should be cut requires an explicit comparison of the respondent's position with the respondent's sense of whether the actual level of taxation is in accordance with that position. If respondents believe that the actual level of taxation has been cut, then even if their estimation of what the correct level of taxes should be remains the same, they will change their answers in light of the change in level of taxes. Given the highly visible cuts in income taxes of the early budgets (and the fact that sales tax increases tend to become assimilated into the cost of living issue rather than separated out into the tax issue), respondents may well have been satisfied with Thatcher's income tax cuts and, because of those cuts, believed that tax cuts were no longer necessary. Similarly, the fall in responses that trade unions are a "bad thing" may indicate that respondents approved of Thatcher's attack on the unions and felt that, after those attacks, trade unions were *no longer* a "bad thing." Therefore, the change in the opinion data does not clearly indicate volatility in public opinion; it may indicate that in 1979 the public was open to free market reforms—particularly, as shown here, to tax cuts and trade union reform—but by 1983 was satisfied with the reforms that had been accomplished and wanted no *further* move in those directions (i.e., there was stability in public opinion when faced with a period of change).

Mishler, Hoskin, and Fitzgerald make a similar oversight when they find no evidence of party realignment and conclude that there has been no general shift. They write,

> There is little evidence either in the literature or in the analyses reported here of any fundamental realignment of the party system favouring the Conservative party. If such a realignment were in progress, we would expect to find evidence of decreasing volatility in the balance of public support over time and of a substantial and sustained increase in the Conservative share of support. Neither is evident either in our data or elsewhere. (1989, 232)

Their data show that the Conservative Party was about as popular as the Labour Party over the course of the 1980s (with temporary upsurges around election times explaining the Thatcher victories). But their interpretation neglects the fact that the Conservative Party was a much more free-market-oriented party than previously, and that Labour only regained power when it also moved to the right on economic issues. In other words, the whole spectrum had shifted, so that the absence of a large and sustained *drop* in the Conservative vote share is evidence of, at the least, a lack of resistance among the public to the party's rightward shift, and at the most, a ratification of that shift.

We can clarify both of these confusions by noting that although British public opinion data do not record a clear embrace of free market policies among the public, they do record an opening for it in three main realms in the mid-to-late 1970s: Taxation is increasingly unpopular, trade unions are increasingly unpopular, and there is decreasing support for targeted welfare state programs. In 1977, given various options of governmental policy, nearly 48 percent of respondents to a Marplan poll favored cutting the standard rate of income tax (Clemens 1983, 80), while the second most frequently mentioned option polled only 22 percent. In 1979, 53 percent of respondents favored a reduction on direct (income) taxes and an increase in indirect (sales) taxes, while only 27 percent were against (Clemens 1983, 49). In response to a 1979 question of whether to address unemployment by allowing business to keep profits or increasing taxes to create jobs, 74 percent preferred letting business keep profits (Crewe and Searing 1988). Of course, this support for lower taxes only holds (as in the other countries) when taxation is not counterposed to welfare benefits; if services would be cut, support for tax cuts diminishes (Butler and Kavanagh 1984; Crewe and Searing 1988).

On trade union issues, as early as 1974 a panel exercise had concluded that "by far the biggest change compared with 1970 is the frequency of mentions of the strikes/trade unions issue": 37 percent mentioned it in 1974 versus 5 percent in 1970 (ACP 74/12, "Voting Behaviour, 1970–1974"). In 1976 Jim Prior noted that "opinion polls indicate that an increasing number of people—including a clear majority of trade unionists—are disturbed by the extent of union power" (LCC 76/96, "Employment Policy: The Trades Unions and Industrial Relations"). By the time of the "Stepping Stones" exercise of 1978, Thatcher's advisers were providing analyses like the following:

> To compete with Labour in seeking peaceful co-existence with an *unchanged* union movement will ensure continued economic decline.... It may also make failure to win Office more, rather than less likely, for the Tories. There is nothing to gain (except just possibly, Office without authority), and everything to lose by such a 'low risk' approach.... Skilfully handled, however, the rising tide of public feeling could transform the unions from Labour's secret weapon into its major electoral liability, and the fear of union-Tory conflict could be laid to rest.... The programme must... link the Labour Party and the union leadership in the public mind,... [s]how how that partnership ('power at any price') has corrupted the union movement and damaged Britain, [and]... [t]ell the public that they must not fear the union leadership, whose bluff can be called whenever the electorate, *including the rank-and-file*, chooses to do so. (SC 78/61, "Stepping Stones")

Such language was new in the Conservative Party, and it shows the gulf that separated Margaret Thatcher's period in office from those of her Conservative predecessors who had flirted with free market rhetoric earlier in the postwar period.

In the mid-1970s, concern with inflation came to overshadow the concern with the trade unions, but even then—and even before the winter of discontent—in 1977, 62 percent of the public agreed that new laws to control the unions were necessary (CCO 180/18/2/2, "Attitudes to Trade

Unions"). In March 1979 "dealing with trade unions" received the most votes among Conservatives asked to name the three most important problems the government should deal with, and 49 percent of all voters thought trade unions bore the most blame for the country's problems (the next most cited factor was world economic conditions, at only 27 percent), and majorities of up to 87 percent agreed with various aspects of the Conservatives' proposed trade union legislation, which included elements such as secret ballots and rules against the closed shop (CCO 180/18/2/3, "Trade Unions Survey"). In 1980 the Conservative Research Department concluded from a MORI poll that there was even "overwhelming support among trade union members" for the Conservatives' reforms (CRD 4/4/80, Britto to Hoskyns, 5 Sep 1980).

Privatization was never a majority preference, but support for it did increase dramatically during the 1970s, while support for nationalization diminished. In 1974 28.4 percent of respondents believed that industries should be nationalized "a lot more" or "a few more," and 24.8 percent believed that industries should be privatized "some/more." Five years later, in 1979, only 16.9 percent believed that industries should be nationalized "a lot more" or "a few more," while a full 43 percent believed that industries should be privatized "some/more" (Crewe, Day, and Fox 1991, 311). The weight of public opinion had gone from nearly equal numbers supporting nationalization and privatization, with a slight edge for nationalization, to more than twice as many respondents supporting privatization. A poll commissioned by the party in 1980 gave mixed results: "The majority of the electorate think they get better value for money from private companies than from the nationalised industries," and, "There is considerable agreement with the view that because they have a monopoly many public services are wasteful and inefficient, although only a minority feel strongly about it." On the other hand, "On balance the electorate tend to agree that on the whole the nationalised industries do a good job" (CCO 180/9/7/4, "Attitudes to Nationalised Industries and Public Services").

On welfare state issues, the majority of the British public supports universal services strongly and need-based aid weakly: "Most people support maintained or increased spending on the mass services—the NHS, education and pensions—that currently make up over two-thirds of welfare state spending. This support is coupled with a more meagre endorsement of provision for needy social minorities—the unemployed, single parents, the poorer categories of tenants, the homeless—who are often seen as morally undeserving" (Taylor-Gooby 1988, 11). This bifurcation in attitudes toward social spending became particularly strong in the late 1970s. In 1974, 34 percent of respondents in the British Election Studies said welfare benefits had "gone much too far" or "gone a little too far"; in 1979 that figure was 50 percent (Crewe and Searing 1988). In the interim, resentment against recipients of targeted aid had exploded. In 1976, a Liverpool man named Derek Deevey was prosecuted for having received extra benefits; this event catalyzed an extraordinary resentment of "scroungers," and criticisms of the recipients of welfare benefits became a common media theme ("Government Backs Plan to Root Out Benefit Fraud," *Times* [London], 31 Jul 1976; "MPs Demand Public Inquiry after £36,000 Social Security Frauds," *Times* [London], 14 Jul 1976). In a remarkable parallel to the case of the "welfare queen" in the United States, Deevey's exploits were exaggerated in press accounts, where he was reputed to have milked the social security system of £36,000—when in fact the actual charge against him was of receiving £500 extra—and to be living a life of luxury at taxpayer expense (Golding and Middleton 1982; Hodgkinson 1976). In the wake of this media coverage, recipients of welfare benefits found themselves on the receiving end not only of hostile opinion, but even of occasional harassment. The Conservatives throughout the 1970s were aware of the political potential of the issue. In 1975 Keith Joseph and Angus Maude write, "There is an interaction between benefit levels and exemption from taxation on the one hand and earnings on the other. Abuse or scrounging is one of the results—probably not important economically but very important politically. This will be studied" (LCC 75/57, "Notes Toward the Definition of Policy"). The Keith Joseph files contain a letter enclosing a newspaper clipping about a Nigerian immigrant unfairly getting unemployment benefits; the letter writer notes that she and her husband worked very hard, and she now draws a widow's pension: "So now you see why we British [underlined several times] Bred and born people, feel we are unjustly treated. . . . I had a Social Security Officer call on me the other week. Which I might say was Black. . . . There is all this hue & cry about inflation. Tell me who is bringing this about, Coloured or white people" (KJ 29/3, E. Mayhew letter to KJ, 11 Jun 75). Joseph responds by deflecting the racism, but seconding the annoyance of fraud: "I can well understand your annoyance at reading the cutting you sent me. . . . It is absolutely infuriating. There is no reason to think that it is only immigrants who take advantage" (KJ 29/3, KJ to E. Mayhew, 17 Jun 75).

In 1976, in the wake of Deevey, Kenneth Clarke noted in a carefully prepared report that "a few months ago the Party was inclined to play this issue [of welfare abuse] quietly, but this attitude has now been changed, largely as a result of the considerable amount of Press attention to the subject. The Press has made the running in the exposure of fraudulent cases, but the Party has increasingly got itself involved with this concern both in the newspapers and in the House." He worries about the political problems of the issue—the Government might take care of it, "trying to 'shoot our fox,'" and too much attention to it might strengthen the Conservatives' image as heartless to the poor, but he concludes that

> we should continue to join in the exposure of the worst individual cases and the harrying of the Government into taking more serious notice of the level of abuse . . . we should begin to turn more detailed attention to the problem of the relationship between the generous level of untaxed, short-term Social Security Benefits for those out of work as compared with the heavy tax penalties and incidence of means-tested benefits on those in low paid work. (LCC 76/117, "Fraud and Abuse of the Social Security System")

However, although support for targeted programs was decreasing, support for general "social services" was increasing. Between February 1974 and 1979 the percentage of respondents arguing that social services were "extremely important" grew from 6.7 percent to 23 percent, and the percentage responding that social services were "not very important" fell from 44.9 percent to 35.5 percent (Crewe, Day, and Fox 1991, 359). However, when "benefits" were included in the question ("Social services and benefits have gone too far and should be cut back a lot/a bit"), 33 percent agreed in 1974 and 49 percent in 1979 (Taylor-Gooby 1985). Moreover, respondents were almost equally likely in 1974 and 1979 to favor "expenditure to get rid of poverty" and "redistribution of income and wealth in favour of ordinary people" (Taylor-Gooby 1985; Crewe, Day, and Fox 1991). Attitudes toward helping the poor are ambivalent, while support for middle-class welfare spending is strong.

Thus, in several domains public opinion was moving in the direction of free market policies, and two of these domains—trade union reform and taxation—were directly relevant to voters in 1979. After Thatcher's income tax cuts and trade union legislation, support for further change is not evident in the polls, but council house sales were clearly popular, and privatization was seen to be popular.

If public opinion does seem to have been important in the rise of Thatcherism, however, it is also important that Thatcherism in economic realms did not become demagoguery. There were elements of demagoguery in other important policy areas, showing that the British system is not immune to it. For example, Thatcher's stance that Britain's contribution to the European Economic Community budget was excessive, and should be returned, fits the definition of demagoguery rather than political innovation. First, the issue was removed enough from everyday concerns that neither citizens nor interest groups were demanding redress, but it proved quite popular, and internal documents show that the party was well aware of the unpopularity of the EEC in general: "The opinion research shows that around 50 per cent of Conservative supporters favour withdrawal from the EEC and it has been noticeable this year that active Party members are willing to express this view in a way they used not to be" (CRD 4/4/32, Howarth, 15 Jul 1980, "Notes on Strategy"). Second, some elements in Thatcher's insistence that the money was "our money" were demonstrably false: Britain had, after all, agreed to the terms of the budget in 1972. Circumstances had made the terms of the agreement less advantageous for Britain, but it is hard to argue that the Community was therefore obligated to rewrite the terms. Thatcher is often seen as resisting any settlement because she gained political capital back home from being seen as standing up to the Europeans. One of the two members of the Foreign Office responsible for the negotiations wrote, "To her, the grievance was more valuable than its solution" (Ian Gilmour, quoted in Campbell 2003, 67). Christopher Tugendhat noted that Giscard and Schmidt had thought "that she was a new leader, that she was a woman, that therefore she would be a pushover, and they tried to drive her into a corner. . . . We know that they were playing to her strongest suit and that in fact being one against many, being defiant, being able to stand out against the odds was not only something that she rather likes to do, but it's something which she's very good at" (*Thatcher Factor*, Tugendhat, box 5). As the recession worsened, the continuing saga of Maggie being tough on those wily Europeans was a useful distraction and played very well in the tabloid press. In May 1980, Thatcher proved so resistant to any resolution that the Foreign Office decided to accept a compromise without telling her and then leaked the compromise to the press, which called it a great triumph. By the time the issue was finally settled in June 1984, relations between Britain and Europe, and support for Europe within the Tory party, had been damaged, perhaps beyond recovery (Campbell 2003).

This episode not only shows that the British system allows demagoguery, but it also hints at the constraints upon it: where in this case the Foreign

Office put an end to Thatcher's grandstanding, in domestic economic policy too we can explain the results by the constraints that the role of the Treasury and the Bank of England placed upon the process of budget- and policy-making. In tax policy the idea of monetary base control—which would have been a truly radical change—was replaced, because of the influence of the Treasury and the Bank of England, with a fairly nonradical continuation of the previous Labour government's monetary policy instantiated as an insistence on balanced budgets. In addition, although Thatcher herself and many of her constituents deeply resented paying for "welfare scroungers," just as their American counterparts did, the fact that health care was universal prevented politicians from being able to attack it, and even targeted programs were only cut where the support for doing so was clear.

In this case, the main source of political innovation was the Conservative Party's defeats in 1974, which led one faction of the party to turn to the right. In both the U.S. and British cases, the dynamic seen is one of politicians who, for endogenous political reasons, seek out policies that will be politically popular, and a public that, because of the social transformations of the postwar period, ratifies some free market measures but rejects others. The main difference in the political dynamic is that whereas in the United States individual political entrepreneurs brought the main issues onto the agenda, in Britain the Conservative Party as a whole, following the defeat of Heath, engaged in a period of soul-searching that led one faction to formulate a free-market alternative. This faction's electoral victories led the party and the country as a whole to move to the right.

The intense competition in the British political system fed Thatcher's experiment. While the British political system concentrates power in the hands of the prime minister, the workings of that system have made it very hard for one person to keep that power for long (Steinmo 1993). Before Thatcher, postwar prime ministers lasted in office less than four years on average. Compare this to nearly nine years on average for presidents of the French Fifth Republic and nearly eight for chancellors of Germany and unified Germany (nearly seven for West Germany before unification); even U.S. presidents have lasted on average slightly over five years in office in the postwar period. The result of this political competition, combined with the system of a full-fledged Opposition "shadowing" the government, is that in some domains, such as taxation, British economic policy has diverged over the postwar years as different governments have come in with different platforms that they have worked out during their spells in opposition (Steinmo 1993). Moreover, as different governments cast about for likely political issues within this competitive system, the *rhetorics* of Labour and Conservative platforms have always been far apart, and much farther apart than the reality of policy.

For example, Thatcher's immediate predecessor as leader of the Conservative Party, Ted Heath, also had a free-market program when he took office as prime minister in 1970. Heath came to power promising a free market revolution, a "change so radical, a revolution so quiet and so total that it will go beyond the programme of a Parliament.... We were returned to office to change the course and the history of this nation, nothing less" (Heath, quoted in Blake 1985, 309). When Thatcher took office in 1979, the *Economist* ran her program side by side with Heath's earlier program to emphasize their striking similarities. Heath had come to office with a program of lower taxes and less government interference in industry. The revolutionary rhetoric of the party in 1970 was so similar to what Thatcher offered in 1979 that it led to widespread suspicion that Thatcher was more of the same. Two prominent political scientists noted at the time, "When the Conservatives returned to office in 1951 [under Churchill] and 1970 [under Heath] there was similar speculation about a Conservative counter-revolution. The resurrection of the theme in 1979 testifies to the continuities of post-war British politics" (Butler and Kavanagh 1980, 339). Labour attacked the Heath government as the most reactionary in decades, and although this was an exaggeration, between 1970 and 1972 Heath did put into place policies that we would today call Thatcherite, particularly in industrial relations. But beginning in 1972, the Heath administration made what were later characterized as several "U-turns," abandoning free market policies for collectivist policies more in line with the postwar period (Ball 1996; Campbell 1993; Butler and Kavanagh 1974).

Why did Heath abandon the line of policymaking that Thatcher would so successfully take to extremes less than a decade later? This is one of the endlessly fascinating and most discussed questions in the scholarship. Although there is no consensus, it is beyond doubt that at the time that Heath was conducting his "U-turns," few in the Conservative Party publicly objected, not even those who would later rise to power by condemning him for those turns—indeed, Thatcher and Keith Joseph were the highest-spending Ministers in the Heath government (Young 1989). That Thatcher was not thinking in terms of a general reduction of government spending is clear from a 1974 discussion of the unpopularity of the rates that fund local government. Thatcher suggests that the burden of financing local government should simply be shifted onto central taxation, and it takes Keith Joseph to point out that "we had to be careful before deciding to transfer the burden of rates by increasing central government expenditure, which left the total burden of public expenditure unchanged" (LCC 74/22, "Minutes of the 22nd Consultative Committee Meeting"). As late as 1975, Thatcher was suggesting that revenue shortfalls could be made up for by a wealth tax, as it was not taxation itself so much as its distribution that was felt as unfair (SC 75/38/31, "Minutes of the 19th Steering Committee Meeting, 13 Jan 1975"). Young writes, "By his shifts and turns Heath betrayed nothing—because there was no significant body of opinion in the party that wanted him to do anything else. Least of all did he betray the cabinet colleagues who later used betrayal as a pretext for rounding on him. They acquiesced in everything he did, only discovering later, in Joseph's graphic words, how they might be 'converted to Conservatism'" (Young 1989, 80). The right-wing faction that was soon elected only began to develop in a more radical direction as a result of the electoral failure of the Heath government in 1974.

It is at this point that the "ideas" explanation comes in. As Peter Hall writes,

> By 1979 [monetarism] was a fully elaborated alternative to the reigning Keynesian paradigm with a significant base of institutional support in the City, among economists at several universities, and in the media. Thatcher was able to resist massive pressure from inside and outside the government to reverse the course of policy in 1980–81 in large measure because she could draw on the monetarist paradigm to explain what others saw as unanticipated events and to rationalize her resistance to demands for change.
>
> By contrast, when faced with similar pressure to alter his initial policy positions, Heath had no conceptual framework with equivalent coherence or institutional support on which to base his resistance to demands for a reversal of course. Monetarist ideas enjoyed some currency among American and British economists in the early 1970s, but they had no substantial base of institutional support within the British policy-making system. (1992, 97–98)

Similarly, Seldon writes, "There was no alternative and acceptable philosophy available which would have provided the intellectual underpinning for an assault on the prevailing orthodoxy of Keynesianism, . . . [and] Heath lacked the popular, intellectual and media backing for a full frontal assault on Keynesian consensus-type policies, even if he had wanted to do so" (Seldon 1996, 14).

However, the key point to note in a causal analysis of the role of ideology is that the monetarist alternative as practiced by Thatcher did not develop *independently* of Thatcherism; it did not develop in academic contexts removed from the political world and then convince politicians. In fact, British academic economists were overwhelmingly unconvinced by Thatcher's monetarist agenda, as shown by the famous protest by the 364 economists. Monetarism—at least the version practiced by Thatcher—developed in nonacademic contexts close to the centers of power, especially at the Centre for Policy Studies and the Institute of Economic Affairs (IEA). The IEA had been present since the 1950s, but the Centre for Policy Studies was created *by* Thatcher and Keith Joseph during the Opposition years: even more than the IEA, the Centre "became a focal point for the emerging school of monetarism and a 'social market economy,' which underpinned the Conservative manifesto for the 1979 General election and the course of policy of the early Thatcher years in power" (Singer 1993, 77). Other think tanks and institutes were organized to support the monetarist cause, and "these few small research organizations developed a cartel in supplying economic advice that fitted the political needs of the Conservative Party's leader . . . at the end of the 1970s" (78). Hall himself notes that "in the 1970s and early 1980s when British policy turned toward monetarism, the vast majority of British economists, both inside and outside the civil service, remained resolutely Keynesian. In this case the movement of policy preceded, rather than followed, the weight of professional opinion" (Hall 1992, 95–96).

The Thatcherites nurtured into full-fledged existence the economic ideologies that would support their turn to the right. They did not turn to the right because the ideology pushed them to do so, but because the moderate branch of the party had been discredited by the failure of Heath's corporatist attempt at industrial relations (exactly as Labour would be discredited five years later, pushing the party first to the left, then to the right), because the right-wing faction had therefore unexpectedly found itself able to offer an alternative, and because monetarism offered one such alternative that was especially attractive because it was compatible with a set of policies such as lower taxes and an ideal of reduction of state intervention that had always been a minority part of the Conservative agenda. In monetarism—a minority ideology among academics—the right-wing Conservatives found a possible justification for policies that would distinguish them from their failed predecessors; they thus developed the institutional support for the ideology that would in turn support their politics. Joseph himself denied being a "follower" of Friedman in a letter to the *Economist*, which had described him as such:

> Though I have the highest regard for Professor Friedman and now broadly agree with his views, the evolution of my views owes little to him. On the contrary, it stems primarily—as you should know—from critical re-examination of local orthodoxies in the light of our own bitter experiences in the early 1970s. . . . By early this year [1974], we had an historically high rate of inflation, an enfeebled economy, the worst relations with the trade unions movement in decades, and a lost election with the greatest fall in our share of the vote since 1929. Surely this was sufficient incentive to rethink—we are practical people who judge ideas and policies by results. (Keith Joseph, quoted in Cockett 1995, 244–45)

The crucial causal point is that the rise of monetarism did not "cause" Thatcherism; rather, Thatcherism sought out, and justified itself in terms of, monetarist rhetoric. The ascension of Thatcherism is a story of political infighting within the Conservative Party; this political context then nurtured the strain of free market ideology that would support it, even though the ideology was not widely accepted by academic economists. Indeed, the rise of one faction of a party at the expense of another in the wake of electoral defeat is a normal political story.

The political context in which Heath operated when elected party leader in the late 1960s was different from the political context when Thatcher was elected in 1974 in one very crucial way: economic crisis and industrial unrest had intervened. By 1970 there had been no dramatic discrediting of moderate policies, as there would be in 1974 (when Heath lost office because of industrial unrest) and again in 1979 (when Callaghan lost office because of industrial unrest). Moreover, the economic crisis had introduced high inflation in the late 1970s. Because of this, in the late 1970s, the British public was for a brief period extremely hostile to trade unions and receptive to attempts to fight inflation. The party, which paid for a substantial polling operation,[18] was quite aware of this, and it was the

18. "It will be recalled that after each election since 1966 we have commissioned a major market research organisation to re-interview a panel of voters, and we are thus able to measure changes in their actual voting behaviour (so far as this is correctly reported) from election to election. The exercise is, as far as we know, unique (except for the Butler and Stokes work, which is now being continued by a team at the University of Essex)" (LCC 75/70). See also the correspondence on the costs of the polling operation (which was using up the bulk of the CRD budget) between Keith Britto and Alan Howard (CCO 180/9/3/12, 13 Jan 1981).

importance of the new industrial relations context that separated Margaret Thatcher's period in office from those of her Conservative predecessors who had flirted with free market rhetoric earlier in the postwar period.

Finally, it was the example of Heath himself, and the consequences of the disastrous U-turn (as they interpreted it) to which Thatcher and many in her administration were reacting. According to John Biffen, "If there was one thing that haunted her, it was Edward Heath's . . . experience with U-turns, and how not only were they not successful, but their lack of success completely debilitated Conservative morale in its capabilities" (*Thatcher Factor*, Biffen, box 1). As Hoskyns said,

> She made it absolutely clear then, she said she would really rather—she'd really rather go down and be chucked out . . . than do a U-turn. She was ab—in an absolutely sort of burning-the-boats frame of mind on that, and—and that was very important, cos it meant then that people didn't have to waste time wondering whether, with their backs to the wall, so to speak, the wall would suddenly fall down behind them. (*Thatcher Factor*, Hoskyns, box 3)

And Enoch Powell said,

> She had in a sense the good fortune to be swept into the position of leadership upon a determination by the Conservative party not to do a Ted Heath U-turn again. The disaster of . . . a U-turn and the prices and incomes policy and the consequences with which it had been associated was reinforced for her just before she entered upon office by Callaghan's winter of discontent, where Callaghan really tripped over the same obstacle. . . . This gave her an enormous strength in the first few years when the uncomfortable consequences of dealing with inflation were making themselves manifest; that . . . there was nowhere where she could be diverted to. She—into a U-turn, she was not going, and she knew what the consequence of that would be, and so did everybody else; . . . she was well fortified by the circumstances in which she was elected leader of the Conservative party in 1975. (*Thatcher Factor*, Powell, box 5)

The commitment not to make a U-turn had become so important that the government even commissioned a poll on the public's attitude to U-turns (CCO 180/25/1/24).

Another challenge to the argument that Thatcherism represented a general repudiation of collectivist policies in Britain comes from those who argue that Thatcher's reelections were largely accidental: the result of the Falklands victory in 1983 and of the split of the Left in both 1983 and 1987 (Norpoth 1987; Jenkins 1988; Butler and Kavanagh 1988).

First, however, even if the Falklands War did play a key role in the election (and some scholars think that it did not: see Sanders et al. 1987), nevertheless *the role the victory played in British politics was not accidental.* We can see the effect this had on the Thatcher victory of 1983 by comparing it to Churchill's defeat in 1945, despite his extraordinary stewardship of Britain through the Second World War. The first lesson of the comparison is that victory in war does not automatically translate into political victory. The Falklands victory could only have the influence it did, significantly raising the Conservatives' chances of winning, because the British polity had been transformed in the intervening years so that voters were much more likely to vote on particular issues (such as, in this case, the Falklands War) and much less likely to vote based on their class position (see Franklin 1985; Rasmussen 1985). Although scholars disagree on whether the decline of class voting has produced a realignment based on something other than class or simply a dealignment from the political system altogether, they do not disagree on the fact that class voting has declined (Weakliem 1995; Heath, Jowell, and Curtice 1985; Crewe 1986, 1992; Dunleavy 1987). The result has been an electoral context that is more volatile than that of the early postwar period, and in this context the meaning of military victory became tremendously important to the outcome of the election. The point is that, while the timing of the war may have been a contingent event, the fact that *victory in war* led to *political victory* was conditioned on the rise of a newly volatile political context in which short-term issues and the short-term popularity they lead to provided crucial leverage for parties to gain power. This is particularly evident when we examine who was more receptive to the appeal of the Falklands factor. The rise in support for the Conservatives after April 1982 came at the expense of the Liberals and the Alliance—*not* at the expense of Labour, whose support was stable from 1982 to 1983 (Franklin 1985). Voters who were most susceptible to a third-party appeal may also have been those most susceptible to the appeal of the Falklands factor; these are the famous "floating voters" without firm loyalties to major parties based on class position, free to respond to third-party appeals and the appeal of particular issues.

If the Falklands factor is considered important to the 1983 conservative victory, another factor considered to be of prime importance was the split of the Left. Although the Liberals have offered a third-party alternative for most of this century (ever since Labour overtook the Liberals as one of the two main British parties), in 1980 a new party, the Social Democratic Party (SDP) was born to appeal to Liberals and moderate Labour supporters. In 1983 the SDP and the Liberals joined in an alliance that made the election "more than any election since the 1920s, a three-sided race" (Butler and Kavanagh 1984). In the end the Alliance took 25 percent of the popular vote—and most of this came at the expense of Labour; though not all Labour and Conservative defectors voted for the Alliance (some voted for the other major party), most of the Alliance's votes were from Labour (Rasmussen 1985). Crewe and King (1995) note that although the Alliance recruited from across the political spectrum, it

> did indeed advance at the expense of Labour more than the Conservatives. Twice as many Alliance voters identified with the Labour Party (25 per cent) as with the Conservative Party (14 per cent). Vote-switching revealed a similar pattern. Fewer than two in five of the Alliance's 1983 votes came from 1979 Liberals; among the remainder, Labour defections to the Alliance outnumbered Conservative by 32 to 20 per cent. This damage to Labour was reinforced by a somewhat higher rate of defection among 1979 Liberals to the Conservatives (14 per cent) than to Labour (9 per cent). (290)

Although it was less important than in 1983 (Crewe and King 1995, 291), the role of the Alliance was also central in the 1987 election: "In 1987 [Labour] fought what was widely regarded as a good campaign, had an attractive leader, and enjoyed a useful lead on the social issues [but] the existence of the Alliance meant that Labour was no longer the exclusive home for anti-Tory voters" (Butler and Kavanagh 1988, 271).

However, Crewe and King make an important qualification. They note that we cannot simply assume that, in the absence of the Alliance, the Alliance voters would have voted Labour:

> In 1983, when Alliance voters were asked to say which party "had the best policies" and which party "had the best leaders," the minority who did not answer "the Alliance" preferred the Conservatives by an 11 to 5 per cent margin on policies and a 25 to 2 per cent margin on leaders. Not surprisingly, these margins were wider among "not-very-strong" Liberal and SDP identifiers and among Conservative switchers to the Alliance; but even Labour-to-Alliance switchers put the Conservatives a fraction ahead of Labour on policies and comfortably ahead on leaders. Without the Alliance as a safe haven, many of

> these Labour deserters would undoubtedly have gone straight across to the Conservatives, producing an even larger Thatcher majority. (1995, 290)

The Alliance's success was partly a result of the new context of volatility—in which loyalty to the traditional parties was low and voters were open to an appeal from third parties—but it was also a result of Britain's changing class structure. Volatility made the tactical decisions of Michael Foot and Neil Kinnock to take positions on the extreme Left much more significant than they might have been otherwise. In particular, Labour supporters were no longer loyal enough to tolerate a position such as Kinnock's promise to unilaterally disarm Britain of nuclear weapons. But the Left was divided in Britain in the 1980s not only because of certain tactical decisions taken by political actors, but also because of the changing class structure and the fall of the "natural" Labour vote. In 1987, 57 percent of all manual workers owned their own homes, 66 percent did not belong to a union, 40 percent lived in the south (whereas the north and west had been the traditional industrial strongholds), and 38 percent worked in the private sector (Butler and Kavanagh 1988, 276). This "new working class" poorly fit the characteristics associated with the working class that had created the strongest labor movement in western Europe and the party that grew out of this movement. They were less receptive to the traditional Labour stances (e.g., favoring unions) and increasingly more receptive to Conservative policies (e.g., favoring homeowners). These members of the "new working class" are key to the Conservatives' rise: "The steady expansion of home-ownership, the growth of the middle class and a share-owning society, combined with the decline of trade unions, the manual working class and council tenancy, also undermined the traditional institutional supports for Labour voting" (Butler and Kavanagh 1988, 272).

In short, Alliance votes either mask the true extent of Thatcher's popularity, *or* they split the Left to allow Thatcher to win. In either case, the popularity of the Alliance was not an accidental cause of the Conservatives' victory, but a symptom of the crisis of the Left in Britain, caused by an electorate increasingly unwilling to support hard-line leftist positions. That unwillingness led to a struggle on the Left, because Labour, tied both ideologically and financially to socialism and the trade unions, found it difficult to follow the voters. In both of these cases—the decline of class voting leading to the increasing importance of short-term issues like the Falklands War and the fall in the "natural" Labour vote leading to the split of the Left—the ultimate causal factors are the deindustrialization of

British society and the socioeconomic transformation of world-historical scale the country experienced.

Conclusion

This chapter has made the case that Thatcherism—understood both as Margaret Thatcher's acquisition of and hold on power, and her administration's implementation of particular free market policies—was made possible by the postwar transformation of the British public into taxpayers and into non-unionized, home owning workers increasingly drawn to the Conservative policies of lower taxes, incentives for home ownership, and punishment of the unions. The proximate cause was reaction to the defeat of the previous Conservative government, which had started out with a free market platform but abandoned it mid-course.

Margaret Thatcher's decision to adopt a free market platform was not unprecedented in postwar Britain: the Conservative Party had on two previous occasions proposed such platforms, and elements such as lower taxation were consistent Conservative themes.[19] The competitiveness of the British political system kept these themes on the agenda throughout the postwar period and drove political innovation, because every spell out of office forced the parties to rethink their strategies.[20] What was unprecedented was the implementation of Thatcher's platform in the wake of a decade of economic crisis and industrial unrest, which happened to meet a British public that was, because of the crisis as well as several decades of social transformation, increasingly receptive to new political attempts. This receptivity can be measured directly in changes in public opinion at the end of the 1970s and also in indirect ways, such as the dealignment of voters from both parties equally, *despite* the Conservative Party's turn to the right; and the increasing support for a moderate, leftist alternative.

19. Steinmo (1993) and James and Nobes (1981) find that tax policy fluctuated wildly depending on which party was in power, but Karran (1985) finds no effect of party on tax policy, and Rose and Karran (1983) see mostly continuity in the postwar tax system. Whether actual policy changed substantially or not, it is clear that the rhetoric of lower taxes was present before Thatcher.

20. In lobbying Thatcher to be allowed to create the eventually more than ninety policy groups that oversaw the rethinking, James Douglas wrote, "The Conservative Party has found itself in Opposition three times since the war—1945–51, 1964–70, and now. In each of these periods the Party has engaged in extensive policy work to prepare itself for the return to office" (KJ 26/4, "Lobby Brief for Mrs. Thatcher," 18 Jul 1975).

Thus, the competitive political system drove political innovation, and, in the wake of the economic crisis, enough of Thatcher's free market innovations were ratified by voters to keep Thatcher in power long enough to enact her program.

The adversarial elements of the British postwar structure included extraordinarily high tax rates on capital, nationalized industries that generated financial losses—both because frequent Labour governments issued directives that made political rather than economic goals paramount and because strong unions were able to extract concessions from the nationalized industries at the price of efficiency—and the most redistributive welfare state of the four countries examined here. Rooted in this adversarial structure, Thatcherism succeeded in lessening the degree of progressivity of the tax regime and initiating the first major series of privatizations in the world. Although the Thatcher administration did aim at one of the targeted policies, it did not lessen the degree of targeting of the welfare state structure.

The adversarial policies did several things to facilitate neoliberalism: first, when the administration fixated on reducing the PSBR, it decided on increases in sales taxes because the administration believed that income tax increases would be less popular; second, the financial losses of the nationalized industries kept privatization on the table throughout the postwar period in a way that was not the case in France, as we will see; and third, the council house sales offered an opportunity to convert a segment of voters into conservatives. In addition, militant unions had catalyzed the Conservative Party's shift to the right—the strikes of the 1970s were in this sense the political equivalent of the American tax revolts, because they convinced politicians of the Right that here was an issue that it was both necessary and politically profitable to mobilize. In Britain, then, we find adversarial policies similar to those of the United States, but a state structure that is adversarial in quite different ways—instead of individual entrepreneurial politicians mobilizing conflict, the parties themselves have developed an extensive machinery for political innovation in opposition, and the key adversarialism is of the strong unions excluded from the kind of corporatist decision-making structure that we will see in the German case.

CHAPTER THREE

Coalition Politics and Limited Neoliberalism in West Germany

When Helmut Kohl became chancellor of West Germany in 1982, after thirteen years of Social Democratic government, he came to office promising a turn to neoliberal policies. Like Ronald Reagan in the United States and Margaret Thatcher in the United Kingdom, Kohl said his job would be to "reduce the state to the core of its tasks," and in his first government declaration he spelled out that this meant tax cuts, deregulation, and cuts in welfare spending. Kohl was not the only one suggesting such policies in West Germany. It was a neoliberal moment, when the financial pages of the major newspapers had begun to press for policies reducing state intervention in industry, just as British newspapers had done before and during Thatcher's arrival to power. When Thatcher began to implement monetarist policies the *Frankfurter Allgemeine Zeitung* saluted them,[1] deploring "how little confidence the people in [Britain] have in market forces" and concluding, "What's needed today is a moral strengthening of the backbone for Margaret Thatcher's recovery programme" (*FAZ*, 21 Jun 1980, translation from Macauslan to Unwin, 14 Jul 1980, Conservative Research Department file 4/4/32, Conservative Party Archives, Bodleian Library, Oxford University). In the late 1970s the Bundesbank and the Council of Economic Experts had come out in favor of neoliberal ideas, and the Freie Demokratische Partei (FDP) had shifted decidedly toward economic liberalism. Ronald Reagan was happy that Germany had elected a leader who agreed with his economic policies. Observers began to wonder if Kohl

1. Cited hereafter in the text as *FAZ*.

was going to be the German Thatcher or the German Reagan (Esser 1988; Lehmbruch 1994; Zohlnhöfer 1999).

But the neoliberal revolution under Kohl never happened (Webber 1992a; Zohlnhöfer 1998, 1999). Several attempts were made to cut taxes, deregulate, and cut welfare state spending, but the attempts themselves were quite moderate, and even these moderate attempts often as not were blocked. In the end, Kohl distanced himself from Thatcherism, calling it a frightening example of unrestrained capitalism (Geppert 2003, 9).

Had neoliberalism occurred in the 1980s, the history of reunified Germany would be completely different. One of the key problems of the current period is that in the rush to reunify, the substantial welfare benefits of the West German population were extended to East Germans, and the economy—hobbled by the inefficiency of East German enterprise—has not been able to absorb the extra expense. Almost every week another new book arrives with a title like *Can Germany Still Be Saved?* (Sinn 2004),[2] trying to diagnose how it is that one of the richest countries in the OECD two decades ago has become the fifth poorest, in terms of GDP per capita, today (Hank 2004) and often concluding that because of the strains of reunification, the German model of capitalism may be coming to an end. It has become fashionable to blame Helmut Kohl for rushing toward reunification and for doing it at such cost to the West. But at the time, it was not clear how long the Kremlin would display tolerance toward the idea, and the quickest way to override objections was to extend economic benefits to the East. Historians will spend generations wondering if reunification could have been achieved in a different way, and whether Kohl made a mistake or a necessary concession. But another counterfactual deserves exploration: Had those West German welfare benefits been trimmed in the 1980s as part of the promised neoliberal turn, their extension to the East would not have cost so much, probably improving the unified country's economic performance and reducing the strains of reunification.

This chapter examines the history of that lost neoliberal moment under Kohl—the moment in post-oil-crisis history when West Germany was most likely to adopt the neoliberal reforms seen elsewhere, but did not. In retrospect, it is an important might-have-been. To summarize the story told in this chapter, the Kohl government, spurred on by its coalition partner the FDP, did indeed propose a coherent neoliberal program in the 1980s,

2. See also, e.g., Breyer and Franz 2004; Keese 2004; Nolte 2004; Steingart 2004; Walter and Deutsch 2004; Zimmermann 2004.

but a series of institutional factors prevented this program from taking the exaggerated shape that neoliberalism took in the United States and Britain. In particular, resistance during the Kohl era came not from a cultural reluctance to adopt market measures, nor from the *constitutional* veto points of the political system (federalism, separation of powers, and proportional representation), nor from employers who preferred the status quo. Rather, resistance came most often from within the right-wing party, the Christlich Demokratische Union (CDU) itself. And these veto players within the party could not be bought off (as they were in the American case), because the policies under attack displayed three kinds of resilience: taxation was tied to disbursal of revenue; social deregulation was in some areas pro-business and where it was not, it required the agreement of multiple actors (unlike the case of environmental deregulation in the United States); and there were no targeted welfare state policies to scapegoat, while the universal welfare state policies enjoyed the same kind of protection from multiple veto players that universal policies did in the United States. In short, the structure of policies limited the room to maneuver of politicians promoting neoliberalism.

The next section traces the histories of attempts at reform in three policy domains under Kohl: the attempt to cut taxes in 1987; two attempts at social deregulation (and one lack of such an attempt); and the attempt to cut health care spending in the late 1980s. In taxation, the tax reform of 1990 (passed in 1987) was by all accounts the most important tax cut under Kohl before reunification, and in welfare state policy the attempt to reform health care was also the centerpiece of the search to control welfare costs. In industrial policy it is not so easy to pinpoint one major attempt, so I have examined here two minor attempts (the attempt to liberalize the shopping hours regime, and the attempt to deregulate the labor market), asking why they did not become more extensive; and one area where state interventionism increased (environmental regulation), asking why there was no neoliberal attempt.

The second section examines whether three theoretical explanations—those concerning the national culture, veto points, and the varieties of capitalism—can make sense of these histories, arguing that each of these is crucially limited. The third section presents an alternative historical-institutionalist explanation, which argues that the reason neoliberalism was not more extensive in West Germany was that the veto points could not be bought off because of the targeted nature of taxation policy, the pro-business and decentralized nature of industrial policy, and the universal nature of welfare state policy. The attempt throughout is first to show that a veto player *internal* to the party was the main source of resistance and second, through a sustained comparison with the American case, to show the reasons why this veto player could not be bought off or avoided as similar sources of resistance had been in the United States.

Before turning to these questions, the remainder of this introductory section briefly compares the extent of neoliberal change in West Germany in the 1980s with its extent in the United States under Reagan, Britain under Thatcher, and France under Giscard/Barre and Mitterrand/Chirac.

Germany did have a weak neoliberal reform in taxation when Chancellor Helmut Schmidt implemented a substantial tax cut that did not reduce overall revenue levels but stemmed their rising course. As figure 1 in the introduction shows, Germany's tax revenues compare favorably with Britain's and for much of the period charted are actually lower than Britain's. The difference is that Thatcher reoriented the British tax structure in a more regressive direction, increasing the share of total tax revenue that came from (regressive) sales taxes and decreasing the share that came from (progressive) income taxes, while Schmidt cut taxes across the board. Moreover, in sheer terms of revenue loss the German tax cut does not compare with the American one, and it did not produce a deficit. Thus, it is weaker than the other two, but nevertheless substantial, as revealed by comparing German tax revenues to those of France. However, after the Schmidt tax cut, no further change in revenue levels appears until the early 1990s, when various taxes were introduced to finance the reunification. The Kohl tax cuts in the 1980s did manage to prevent total tax revenues from rising, but they did not produce a deficit, and neither did they reorient the tax structure.

In industrial policy, Germany did not see a large privatization program because, like the United States, it has never had a particularly significant nationalized sector. Instead, it has followed the U.S. model of government intervention in industry through regulations—Germany was and is one of the most regulated economies in the developed world. Therefore, instead of comparing it with Britain, it makes more sense to compare it to the U.S. pattern of deregulation. Deregulation was attempted in five areas in West Germany in the 1980s: telecommunications, broadcasting, the labor market, financial services, and shopping hours regulations. It was most successful in telecommunications and broadcasting, failed completely in financial services, and was only trivially successful in shopping hours regulation and labor market regulation. Of the five areas that were deregulated, telecommunications, broadcasting, and financial services involved economic regulations. The ground for regulating these sectors was that they form natural monopolies, so that without regulation the major firm in this sector would be likely to abuse its monopoly position. But technological changes in recent decades had allowed new kinds of competition (for example, satellite telephone technology, cable television) in these sectors and eliminated this need. Labor market regulations and shopping hours regulations, on the other hand, are "social" regulations; their justification is the protection of workers. In the American case, the economic deregulations that generated consensus across the policy spectrum turned into social deregulations that were much more contentious. But this did not take place in West Germany: deregulation of environmental protection—the most successful of the American social deregulations—was not even attempted. Instead, environmental protection was strengthened in the 1980s, and the labor market and shopping hour deregulations did not become as extensive as the neoliberal Right had hoped. The German regime of regulating shopping hours is one of the tightest in the developed world, regulating German everyday life to a greater degree than is done in any of the other developed countries, and German labor market regulation is at the heart of the "German model" and the source of the greatest friction between capital and labor. In comparison with the United States (where funding for the Environmental Protection Agency was severely reduced) and Britain (where privatization became a major policy), the failure of deregulation in shopping hours and labor market policy shows the inability of the German state to reform in the particular area where it was most rigid. In this, it is like France, which has not reduced the taxation or social costs that are its particular rigidities. It is also an exception to the general rule that adversarial policies were fragile: in this case, the regulations were adversarial, but they survived the neoliberal onslaught, and I examine here the conditions that allowed them to do so.

Finally, in terms of welfare state policy, the German experience was no different from that of the other states: as in the United States, Britain, and France, the universal elements of the welfare state resisted major reform. But unlike the United States, Germany lacked means-tested programs, which meant that there was no political advantage to be gained from exploiting hatred of targeted minorities who received benefits from the welfare state. And unlike France, Germany at least made an attempt to reduce costs. The Kohl government tried to control spiraling health care costs, but could not do so. This chapter analyzes the reasons for the failure of the health care reform.

Taxation Policy

Until the mid-1960s, taxes in West Germany had been among the highest in the OECD. The Allies had introduced extremely high tax rates to finance the reconstruction of the country, and these were only gradually reduced over the years. Income tax has been the most important source of revenue in the United States, as sales tax has been in France, but West Germany (like Britain) had a more diversified system, in which social security contributions were the largest single revenue source. In Germany personal income taxes as a share of total tax revenue are lower than in the United States, although higher than in Britain and France. Sales taxes as a share of total tax revenue are much higher than in the United States and about the same as in Britain and France. Capital gains taxes are low, and business profits are taxed only once (rather than twice, as in the United States). As in France, "West German income tax policies have neither sought nor produced a significant redistribution of wealth from the most to the least affluent" (Edinger 1986, 286; see also figures 1–5 in the introduction to this volume).

In the period after the oil crisis, tax cuts moved increasingly center stage when the FDP decided in the wake of election losses that it needed to raise the "free market" part of its profile. The FDP has always vacillated between its economic liberalism and its social liberalism. The economic liberalism of the 1950s and early 1960s allowed the party to enter into coalition with the CDU for the first time, but the program of the late 1960s and early 1970s explicitly repudiated the previous praise of the unbridled free market. In the 1970s the party swung back to neoliberalism, with "the interests of employers and entrepreneurs dominating the party's consideration of social and economic reform" (Padgett and Burkett 1986, 162; see also Søe 1990, 113). In particular, in 1978 the party had suffered devastating electoral losses in Hamburg and Lower Saxony, in the wake of which it had hit upon tax cuts as its best hope of political victory. The argument was that coalition with the left-wing party, the Sozialdemokratische Partei Deutschlands (SPD) had forced the FDP into making too many compromises, and therefore it had lost its free market "profile" with its own social base of small business and the middle class. The party hoped that the issue of tax cuts would give it a "new profile" ("FDP: Graf in Nacken," *Der Spiegel* 32, no. 30 [1978]: 21–22). The wish to increase its free market profile led it out of the coalition with the SPD in 1982, and in the new coalition with the CDU the FDP consistently and vocally pushed for lower taxes (Bohnsack 1983; Irving and Paterson 1983; Merkl 1987, 1990; Schmid 1991; Schmidt 1991).

The man most responsible for championing the revitalization of the economic wing in the late 1970s was Minister of Economic Affairs Count Otto von Lambsdorff. In what has come to be known as the "Lambsdorff paper" (drafted by future Bundesbank President Hans Tietmeyer), Lambsdorff made an argument that will be familiar to readers of the previous chapters: he argued that productive efficiency would result from the reduction of social expenditure and the revitalization of private enterprise. First, he traced the problems of the German economy to the declining return on investment, and he traced this to the rising role of the government in the state, particularly for welfare state expenditures and the high taxes and budget deficits they led to. Then he suggested the following changes in policy: cuts in state spending, tax cuts for business, welfare state restructuring aimed at reducing its costs, and a moderate wage policy. As one commentator wrote, "Obviously, all these suggestions can be summed up as a moderate supply-side programme" (Zohlnhöfer 1999, 150–51). Indeed, in 1978 Lambsdorff quite explicitly gave a supply-side rationale for tax cuts, arguing that they would cost hardly anything because the greater economic growth they unleashed would quickly replenish state coffers ("Konjunktur: Ein bisschen mehr Inflation?" *Der Spiegel* 32, no. 30 [1978]: 19–20). This is exactly the argument that underpinned Ronald Reagan's 1981 tax cut, and constitutes the logic behind the "Laffer curve" that became so popular in the United States.

Schmidt dismissed the supply-side argument as "not serious," but he eventually agreed to tax cuts because the other G7 countries were pressuring West Germany to cut taxes on the theory that this would serve a "locomotive" function—a sort of international Keynesianism that in theory would, by stimulating demand in Germany, pull the whole world out of recession (Roeper 1978; Wood and Jianakoplos 1978; Wörl 1978). Schmidt and other German leaders were not convinced by this line of argument, but in return for tax cuts in West Germany, they could ask Carter to attempt to reduce domestic oil consumption in the United States, which they thought was the main cause of inflation and the weak dollar ("Der Bonner Wirtschaftsgipfel will die USA auf ihre Führungsrolle verpflichten," *Süddeutsche Zeitung*, 13 Jul 1978; Samuelson 1978).

In addition, tax cuts would take an electoral issue away from the CDU, which (especially Franz Josef Strauss's Christlich Soziale Union [CSU]) had been increasingly circling the issue. Opinion polls measuring support for tax cuts in this period found that in November 1975, 59 percent of respondents believed the state squandered tax revenue (69 percent of CDU/CSU-oriented voters, 65 percent of FDP-oriented voters, 49 percent of SPD-oriented voters; Noelle-Neumann 1976, 230). In January 1977, 60 percent thought that the burden of taxes and social spending for old age pensions, health care, and so forth would become a problem in the next year or two (Noelle-Neumann 1977, 93). In 1976, three polls found that the proportion of respondents who thought halting income tax increases was especially important had increased from 63 percent to 73 percent (113), and 30 percent of voters who had switched their votes from the SPD to the CDU gave hindering income tax rises as a reason for their switch (127). In August 1976, 53 percent responded that they found their taxes high (196). Although respondents were not consistent in their preferences (the programs that taxes paid for were also popular), when the issue of taxation was mentioned alone without explicit mention of trade-offs, cuts in income taxes were clearly popular.

Second, Schmidt adopted the tax cut because the opposition to it within the SPD was weak, in that segments of the SPD that did not want it did not have the political power to veto it. Although the most important labor union, the Deutsche Gewerkschaftsbund (DGB), saw in the tax cuts "a positive kernel," most other unions and SPD politicians were against them, and much of the SPD wanted to increase spending ("Opposition verlangt erneut Steuersenkungen Matthöfer dämpft zu grosse Erwartungen," *Süddeutsche Zeitung*, 19 Jul 1978; "Steuersenkung: 'Das Bringt Doch Nichts,'" *Der Spiegel* 32, no. 28 [1978]: 21–23; "Schmidt wird einen Kompromiss suchen müssen," *FAZ*, 19 Jul 1978). But because of the SPD's political structure, those who opposed the tax cut were not in a position to veto it. The SPD was at this time still a significantly hierarchical and centralized party, in which "policy emanates from the top and filters down to the base" (Braunthal 1977, 131). A rebellious attempt by the left wing of the party to democratize it in the 1960s and early 1970s had failed, and so party policy was essentially formulated by two groups: the thirty-six members of the party executive (Parteivorstand) and the party presidium, a core group of nine to eleven high-ranking members. Although in theory the presidium's decisions could be revoked by the party executive, and the executive was in turn beholden to the party convention held every two years—technically the top decision-making body in the SPD—in practice the presidium controlled the executive, and the convention rubber-stamped the decisions of the executive. Thus, although the party convention was theoretically the decision-making organ of the party, "in practice the praesidium [was] the body formulating policy" and "conventions play[ed] a limited role in policymaking" (Braunthal 1983, 21–22).

Many other groups—commissions, councils, committees of various kinds—have been created to advise the policymakers, but "to ensure that their advice will not stray from party principles, most groups are chaired by presidium or executive members" (Braunthal 1994, 53). In 1975 approximately one-third of the party executive was affiliated with the left wing of the party, but the party presidium was predominantly affiliated with the center and the right, and the presidium members were closely tied to the trade unions, which were more conservative. Therefore, because of its partisan composition, control of party policy by the presidium meant control of power by the center and right (Braunthal 1977, 1984, 1994; Dyson 1981; Koelble 1987; Raschke 1974). In 1978, this organizational structure meant that the elements of the party that opposed the tax cuts were not in a position to veto them.

This important principle receives further discussion below. The SPD is a hierarchically organized party, but the CDU is a "coalition of coalitions," and many elements within that coalition have the power to veto policies that they do not like. Therefore, while the SPD is able to push through policies that are not necessarily popular with the rank and file, the CDU is not. This meant that after the arrival of Helmut Kohl to power in 1982, and even after the explicit commitment to a policy of cutting taxes, Kohl did not in fact oversee anything like the dramatic tax cuts seen in the United States or the restructuring of the tax structure seen in Britain.

The consequence is visible in figure 1 of the introduction. Tax revenues in France rose slowly and relentlessly from 1973 to 1985, from less than 35 percent of GDP to almost 45 percent of GDP, but Schmidt's tax reforms kept Germany off of the French path and stabilized revenue at just under 35 percent of GDP. Kohl came to power promising much larger tax cuts, but did not manage to deliver them, although he did keep revenue in West Germany stable in the 1980s. Indeed, Kohl's tax cut was just about equivalent to Schmidt's: the differing institutional structures of the two parties moderated their ideological differences.

The Kohl period from 1982 to the reunification can be divided in two with regard to tax policy: when he first came to office, Kohl was faced with a deficit that made tax cuts difficult. Once the deficit was brought under control, a major effort was made to cut taxes and reform the tax structure, but it diminished as it passed the gauntlet of coalition partners.

In the first period, the story was of a continuing struggle between the impulse to keep the deficit down and the impulse to cut taxes in accordance with the supply-side policies popular in Kohl's coalition. Count Lambsdorff, the new coalition's minister of economic affairs, was committed to a Thatcher-style restructuring of taxes, that is, raising sales taxes to be able to cut income taxes. The act proposing this, however, became caught up in the coalition negotiations at the very beginning of the term, and the left wing of the CDU—the Workers' Wing (Arbeitnehmerflügel), also known as the Christlich-Demokratische Arbeitnehmerschaft (CDA) and the Social Committee (Sozialausschüsse)—demanded that taxes on high earners be raised as an act of solidarity, given that social spending was going to be cut. The coalition also agreed on a small increase in the value-added tax. These tax increases fostered a sustained opposition in the CDU itself, leading to a curious compromise by which the revenues raised from the additional value-added tax income would be "given back" in the form of tax allowances for investment income. Another set of determinedly supply-side measures, such as allowing firms to write off depreciation costs and cuts in income taxes, was modestly successful: income tax cuts were not passed, but the trade tax (Gewerbesteuer) was cut (Zohlnhöfer 1999). The result was a modest tax cut, which was repeated in similar legislation passed in the following year.

This early period of modest tax cuts combined with deeper spending cuts, intended to cut the deficit, had the desired effect: the deficit was brought under control by 1986, and by 1989 had fallen to just over half its 1982 level. From this point on, with no more countervailing pressure, the coalition might have been expected to give itself over to tax cuts. Income taxes were indeed reduced from 1986 to 1990, but the reductions were so minor that Wagschal (1998, 17) places Germany second only to Switzerland as having seen the least tax reform of all the OECD countries between 1986 and 1992. Heinrich (1992, 156) concludes that the government did not reach its stated goals of reducing the complexity of the tax schedule, equalizing the tax burden between indirect and direct taxation, and reducing overall taxation. And Koren (1989) notes that despite the general decline in the tax rate, some changes that made capital gains taxes and family taxes less progressive, and the rise in value-added tax, the overall progressivity of the general tax structure was not changed, and subsidies were increased.

During the 1987 campaign Kohl had boasted that his tax reform was going to be the "largest tax reform in the history of the German republic" (*Die Zeit*, 6 Feb 1987), a "work of the century" (*Jahrhundertwerk*), the planned centerpiece (*Herzstück*) of his next term should he win. On average, he said, every German taxpayer would have to pay 1,000 DM less. The proposed tax reforms included a reduction of the top tax rate, some of it to be paid for by closing various tax loopholes. This became the central arena for the battle over the reform: "Although [the top tax rate] is certainly not the most important problem in a tax reform, . . . [it] became a question of honor" (Findling 1995, 146). Reducing the top tax rate unleashed a battle within the CDU itself, with the Workers' Wing opposing the FDP and the CSU. Labour Minister Norbert Blüm and the CDU General Secretary Heiner Geißler, both associated with the Workers' Wing, thought the policy unfair on principle. Before the 1987 election, Blüm had assured Workers' Wing members that there was no commitment to cutting the top tax rate: "Sink the top tax rate while there's unemployment? I am strictly against it. And by the way there is no such binding Plan for the coalition" (*Soziale Ordnung*, 11 Aug 1986, 2).

Politicians were aware of the argument coming from America that lowering tax rates would raise revenue, but some did not believe it: "A sinking of the top tax rate would to such a degree reduce the funds available to lighten the load of the lower and middle income receivers and thus the largest number of bearers of the [tax] pressure, that a just distribution of the tax cut would be impossible" (*Soziale Ordnung*, 5 Feb 1987). Others thought that cutting the top tax rate would send the wrong signal and would be counter to the value that the strongest members of society should bear the greatest tax burden (interview, Ingrid Sehrbrock, 28 May 2004).[3] As late as October of 1986 the Workers' Wing noted with satisfaction, "Of a sinking of the top income tax rate, a demand that now and again is loud among the rows of the Union, there is no talk in the CDU election program" (*Soziale Ordnung*, 16 Oct 1986, 17).

CSU leader Franz Josef Strauss was so committed to the cut, however, that he threatened to take the CSU out of the coalition if he didn't get it—an almost unthinkable possibility for the party. The resulting conflict became

3. A list of people interviewed appears at the beginning of the references section at the end of the book.

the central issue of the government for weeks, although commentators noted that "the targeting of the top tax rate is more a matter of ideology [*Glaubenssache*] than a reform necessity" (*Die Zeit*, 6 Feb 1987, 22) and called it a "holy war" (*Glaubenskrieg*) over a symbol (*Die Zeit*, 13 Feb 1987, 25). Kohl produced a compromise by reducing the cut severely and also providing various measures for low-income earners. The top tax rate was cut to 53 percent, rather than to less than 50 percent, a level that had been seen as psychologically important. In March 1987 Heinz Soénius of the Workers' Wing recounted with satisfaction, "As for the cut of the top tax rate, 7 billion DM will not, as originally planned, be spent, but only 1 billion DM," and remarked, "What a noise there was in 84/85 and especially in the summer months of 1986. From the FDP, the CSU, and the CDU, yes, even from the house of the Finance Minister, the clear reduction of the top tax rate to below 50 percent was demanded as the highest goal of the reform. We, the Social Committee, had already warned of such one-sidedness" (*Soziale Ordnung*, 10 Mar 1987, 11).

The main opposition to the cutting of the top tax rate came from the Workers' Wing. Scholars of the Workers' Wing have argued that in the early postwar years the Workers' Wing was less influential than the unions (von Winter 1990; *Die Zeit*, 13 Feb 1987 and 6 Mar 1987), but with regard to the issue of cutting the top tax rate, all discussions of the coalition negotiations describe it as a conflict between the FDP and the CSU on one hand and the Workers' Wing on the other. Workers' Wing leaders Norbert Blüm and Heiner Geißler led the resistance: "The negotiations of the coalition over tax reform began with a classic false start. . . . Geißler and Blüm were [primarily] responsible for that. [Finance Minister] Stoltenberg let himself be put on the defensive" (*FAZ*, 5 Feb 1987). The *Frankfurter Allgemeine Zeitung* reported that "the leading economic groups have concluded that [promises to cut taxes] will not become reality. The political responsibility for that is before all given to Labour Minister Norbert Blüm and CDU General Secretary Heiner Geißler" (11 Feb 1987) and commented several days later, "Kohl must make himself seen. Or does he want to let Geißler govern?" (*FAZ*, 23 Feb 1987; see also *FAZ*, 2 Feb 1982 and 3 Feb 1987). The unions were not part of the negotiations, nor were they threatening to strike over the issue. The Workers' Wing's influence came from having its members in key positions, a privilege that I discuss further below.

The reforms also met with opposition from the upper house of Parliament (the Bundesrat), even though it was controlled by the CDU. Although the government had tried to distribute the tax cuts and the closing of loopholes evenly across the states, not all of the states would be equally able to make up for the loss in revenue. Thus even many of the states governed by the CDU were opposed. In particular, Ernst Albrecht of Lower Saxony played a key role, demanding that in exchange for the states' acquiescence, the federal government should take over half of the states' social spending costs. His demand pulled the coalition "into great calamity" just before the issue came to a vote (*Süddeutsche Zeitung*, 29 Jun 1988). Along with the SPD-led states, Albrecht led a coalition of seven of the eleven states that forced a compromise by which the federal government would transfer a subsidy for public investments over the next ten years to the poorer states so that they could invest in infrastructure designed to reduce unemployment (Webber 1991; Zohlnhöfer 1999; "Stoltenbergs Wundertüte ist Leer," *Der Spiegel* 42, no. 18 [1988]: 24–32). Albrecht argued that it was unfair to expect the poorer states of the north to approve the tax reform, which would have brought them into financial difficulties: "Without supplementary financial means from the federal government, . . . it would no longer be possible for Lower Saxony after the tax reform to carry on a budget that would fit within constitutional demands" (*FAZ*, 25 Jun 1988, 1; see also *Die Zeit*, 22 Apr 1988; Tomforde 1988; Woodheart 1988). Politicians from states with local elections planned for 1987 were also wary of alienating the middle classes through a cutting of the top tax rate (Findling 1995, 145; "Arme und Reiche einig gegen die Steuerreform," *Der Spiegel* 42, no. 18 [1988]: 36–45).

These various sources of resistance delayed the implementation of the tax cuts and reduced their overall size (19 million DM instead of the announced 40 million DM—an economist claimed that, given the various rises in sales taxes, the overall tax reduction was not significantly different from zero [*Die Zeit*, 22 Apr 1988]). Resistance also made the final proposal unpopular; only 23 percent of those polled favored it ("Arme und Reiche einig gegen die Steuerreform," *Der Spiegel* 42, no. 18 [1988]: 36–45). Webber writes that Kohl's cut was no larger than the cuts that had "already been carried out by the Social-Liberal coalition . . . in 1978" (1991, 161).

When we compare these events with the tax policies of the period in Britain and the United States, several important differences come to light. First, as in Britain, one of the principal motivations for the shape of the tax policy in the early years was the belief that budget deficits force interest rates to rise; therefore, to allow interest rates to fall, the government was committed to closing the deficit. But whereas inflation and the dramatic discrediting of the previous Conservative prime minister had led British politicians to fetishize the PSBR to such a degree that they severely raised sales taxes, low inflation in Germany led to a pragmatic policy of spending cuts until the deficit was closed. Although the Bundesbank in general supported conservative fiscal policies, its independent role meant that monetary policy could not be as tightly tied with politically driven fiscal policy as it was in Britain. Both Germany and Britain introduced increases in indirect tax to finance reductions in direct tax, rather than simply reducing the direct tax, as was done in the United States. However, this restructuring did not proceed on the same scale as it did in Britain. In the British case, the major increase in sales tax was also seen, in the somewhat convoluted process described in chapter 2, as contributing to the goal of keeping inflation down. Inflation was not a major problem in the postwar period in West Germany, as it was in Britain, so this basis of support for major increases in sales taxes was missing, although they did go up slightly at the end of the decade.

Second, the structure of decision making was different in an important way. Although Lambsdorff himself believed in some version of the Laffer curve, none of the other members of the coalition were convinced. The difference with the United States is not that the supply-side idea did not exist in Germany: it did. As in the United States, its proponents were a minority. But the major difference in the two cases is that in Germany the supply-siders were not given full control of budget-making, as Stockman was for the first year of the Reagan administration, reflecting the more permeable nature of the American state.

What is particularly notable in comparison with the process of tax cuts in the United States is that the need to attract many individual political actors to vote for them *increased* the size of the U.S. tax cuts, whereas in West Germany, the same need *reduced* the size of the tax cuts. In the United States individual members of Congress demanded supplementary tax cuts for their individual states (raising the overall size of the cuts), while in Germany the coalition partners forced Kohl to compromise most of his tax cuts away (reducing the overall size of the cuts). This points to a curious anomaly in the theory that veto points lead to policy stability: Why did they lead to policy stability only in Germany, but to great change in the United States? Why, for example, when faced with opposition in the Bundesrat, did Kohl not try to "sweeten" the tax cut with additional cuts for each of the states, as the Reagan administration did? The answer (as in the British case; see Steinmo 1993) has to do with the link between taxation and spending. In the United States, this link was weakened because the revenue-raising process and the process of passing subsidies from the federal government to the state governments had been decoupled, so that the *individual* states were not specifically harmed by the tax cuts they were receiving (that is, no one knew who would eventually be harmed because of the overall fall in revenue). This produced a classic process of free riding that exaggerated the size of the tax cut beyond what any of its proponents had wanted.

But in West Germany, tax cuts for the states also implied *revenue cuts for each of the states*: first, for certain kinds of taxes the states received in revenue only what had been brought in from taxes in each state, so tax cuts translated into direct loss of revenue for them. This is because of the "derivation" principle, through which the distribution of tax revenue follows the regional origin of the taxes that raised it; that is, "A region receives [in revenue from the federal government] the percentage of tax collected in its particular area" (Maffini 2003, 145; Leibfritz, Büttner, and van Essen 1998). Because the states (*Länder*) do not have independent sources of tax revenue, and because the revenue they receive is proportional to the taxes raised within their borders, tax cuts for the *Länder* are also revenue cuts for them. Second, for other kinds of taxes, although both systems do redistribute from rich states to poor ones, they do it in very different ways. The United States provides no fixed sums to the states; each state can and must bargain on its own for a larger piece of the federal revenues. In West Germany, however, the states collectively bargain for a larger or smaller portion of federal revenues, and only after this general level has been set is there redistribution to the weaker states. The states thus have an incentive to preserve revenue levels (Campbell and Morgan 2005).

Finally, in Germany only a quarter of the value-added tax is distributed according to principles of geographic need. Revenues from all other taxes are distributed according to population, to number of employees resident, or to number of production plants, which weakens the redistributive impulse (Dengel 1987, 267). In short, the link between taxation and revenue is preserved through the way in which German federalism is financed. Moreover, the structure of the tax system ensured that the dynamic seen in the United States—a property tax revolt and the attention to taxation that it brought, as well as reliance on progressive taxes—was absent here. Although income tax cuts did reach the agenda, payroll tax cuts did not, and sales taxes were actually *increased*. As I discuss in more detail in the French case, these regressive taxes either obscure the amounts being paid or are targeted to spending, and they have proved resilient.

Deregulation

Although Germany had a very small nationalized sector, the German market was and is one of the most heavily regulated in the world. Calls for deregulation in the 1980s were strong, and the most spectacular deregulations were in telecommunications and broadcasting. These were economic deregulations (i.e., deregulation involving agencies that had been set up to ensure that natural monopolies do not abuse their position), which were no longer necessary because technological change had made them no longer natural monopolies. In telecommunications, the Bundespost, the powerful public telecommunications firm, was deregulated, but while competition was introduced in supplying terminal equipment, and the market for digital mobile communication was liberalized, the Bundespost retained its monopoly in telephone services, the central element of the market (Dyson 1992; Zohlnhöfer 1999; Müller 2001; Webber 1986).

Broadcasting deregulation was implemented in 1984; until then, the private local media had been restricted to print, and the public service broadcasters to nonlocal broadcasting. This regime had been a response to the Nazi takeover of the film and radio industries. The model that was developed—as elsewhere in the German system—was one of governing bodies of representatives from various societal interests, including churches and trade unions. Technological changes that significantly increased the number of channels available also changed the nature of the broadcasting market so that "niche" broadcasting became a possibility; this meant regulation was no longer necessary. In particular, deregulation was sought to enable competition with American broadcasting. Bundespost Minister Christian Schwartz-Schilling was a champion of the commercial interests pressing for deregulation and had close ties with them. In 1982, he pressed forward with a program of providing cable across the country in the face of intense opposition, and in 1985 he liberalized satellite reception (Dyson 1992; Müller 2001; Humphreys 1992). Deregulation was also attempted in financial services, but it did not succeed in that domain until later (Moran 1992).

Beyond these economic deregulations, social deregulation—cutbacks in regulations that aim to protect workers or the environment in general, with social justice goals—was much less successful in West Germany than in the United States. Environmental deregulation never even entered the agenda and in two areas where social deregulation was attempted—labor market and shopping hours regulation—it was only marginally successful.

Although the Kohl administration had some success in labor market deregulation, the overall achievement here was not particularly radical. The major achievement was the Beschäftigungsförderungsgesetz, the Employment Encouragement Law, which gave firms greater flexibility in hiring apprentices, extending the temporal limits placed on contractual work, and increasing potential working hours for shop workers in certain categories (Leaman 1994, 19; Zohlnhöfer 2001a, 2001b, 2001c; in addition, a major political controversy was set off by a minor change in labor law—see Silvia 1988). Although these were important changes, they did not strike at the core of the protected German labor market, which is underpinned by the Kündigungsschutzgesetz, the law restricting dismissal of workers. This is the heart of the German system's lack of market flexibility, as it leads employers to be hesitant about taking on additional employees and thus directly creates the "insider-outsider" labor market for which Germany is infamous. Employers have always wanted this to be scaled back, and the FDP and the economic wing of the CDU wanted a deregulation of this law to be a part of the Employment Encouragement Law, but the Workers' Wing resisted.

Zohlnhöfer (2001a) has detailed the process through which the Employment Encouragement Law was implemented. First, the FDP and the business wing of the CDU introduced demands for an extension of limited-time work contracts (which saved employers from the long-term commitment implied by regular work contracts), deregulation of the employer's responsibility for an employee "lent out" to a third party (*Arbeitnehmerüberlassung*), and a ceiling on employers' social costs. But the latter two demands did not survive the *Koalitionsrunde* (the meeting between the Chancellor, the chairs of the coalition parties, and various leading politicians and bureaucrats), where the proposal coalesced around a compromise to extend the period of time for which limited-time work contracts could be arranged and to apply them to wider categories of personnel. The next step was to bring this proposal to the coalition as a whole, but here, Norbert Blüm resisted. Blüm threatened to reintroduce a bill mandating that overtime work be paid with time off, which the FDP and business wing had together defeated. This forced a new discussion, which ended in a proposal to extend the duration of limited-time work contracts not beyond eighteen months, and to reexamine the law in a year's time.

The scope for deregulation was also large in the area of shopping hour regulation, because Germany had a highly restrictive regime dating from before the Second World War—in fact, laws regulating shopping hours and forbidding sales on Sundays and holy days on religious grounds can be traced as far back as the thirteenth or fourteenth century (Schunder 1994, 2; George 1995, 7). As Germany industrialized in the nineteenth century, these laws took on a new meaning and were extended with the intent to protect workers. The modern Ladenschlussgesetz (shop-closing law) dates in its current form to 1956. Motivated largely by the wish to protect workers, it was carried through over the opposition of Erhard and the business-oriented segments of the government. It has spawned its own branch of legal expertise, with casuistic arguments over (for example) whether nontravelers have the right to shop at stores that have been allowed to stay open to serve travelers. The law has seen several modifications since 1956 (nearly always in the direction of more liberalization), but as of this writing most shops are still closed on Sundays, and only in 2003 were they allowed to stay open past 2 p.m. on Saturdays and 6:30 p.m. on weekdays—a remarkable contrast to Germany's peers (Täger, Vogler-Ludwig, and Munz 1995, 11). Larger firms have been trying to pry the law apart: in 2004 they argued that they were disadvantaged because they lost business to stores open for travelers, but the high court was not convinced.

A concerted attempt was made in the 1980s to liberalize the tight shopping hours regime, again because of the FDP, which made this a condition of its participation in the coalition after the 1987 election. Opinion polls showed 82 percent of the public supported longer shopping hours (*Financial Times*, 18 Aug 1986). But in the end only marginal changes were made: in 1986 shops for travelers were allowed to stay open longer, and in 1989 other shops were allowed to stay open two hours longer one night a week, but in recompense they were obliged to close earlier one Saturday per month from April to September (Täger, Vogler-Ludwig, and Munz 1995, 11). Douglas Webber calls this "the least radical conceivable alternative to the maintenance of the *status quo*" (1992a, 147; see also Zohlnhöfer 1999). The Social Committee and its head, Norbert Blüm, teamed up with the lobby for retailers and small business, which opposed shopping hours deregulation because of small retailers' fears of losing trade to larger or non-unionized competitors. Unions (whose members opposed longer shopping hours) and churches (who feared a move toward opening stores on Sunday) also joined the resistance (Webber 1992a). In this case, the role of the Workers' Wing was to coordinate and lead the resistance. As a member of the reigning coalition, the Workers' Wing had what we might call lower access costs: it could regularly bring arguments in favor of tighter shopping hours to the attention of the government, and it could remind the coalition that many organized interests were against liberalization.

Note that some employers did support interventionism—but, in contrast to the predictions of the scholars associated with the "varieties of capitalism" school, it was small and medium-sized businesses that resisted deregulating shopping hours. Mares (2001, 2003) predicts that larger firms are more likely to support interventionism, at least in welfare state policy, because they can afford the short-term expense and are more likely to want to pay for predictability in their productive environments. But this thesis does not apply to industrial policy: small firms wanted interventionism in the form of tightly regulated shopping hours because they knew they would lose business to their larger competitors if shopping hours were extended.

Thus, in industrial policy the consensus of scholars is that the changes witnessed in the early 1990s were very small. Markus M. Müller notes, "The kind of change we observe in Germany is, in many respects, both less spectacular than in Britain as well as much more heterogeneous and sector-specific" (2001, 37). And according to Kenneth Dyson, "The general conclusion must be that Germany has not witnessed a radical, wholesale change in the hierarchy of regulatory goals and instruments" (1992, 270).

Attempts at reform were defeated most centrally within the CDU itself. In both labor market and shopping hours reform, the separation of governmental tasks and the veto points thus created worked together with the fragmentation of German society to block change. Because unions and churches predominate in areas of social legislation, they could resist the government's initiative. This is the result of a curious feature of the CDU's policy-making structure that gives responsibility for policymaking within particular domains to specific, identified factions of the party. The business wing is responsible for the Ministry of Finance, while the labor wing is responsible for the Ministry of Labor Affairs: "That means that important parts of the economic policy reforms, for example the legislation concerning the deregulation of the labour market or the restriction of union rights, were prepared in the ministry controlled by the faction of the CDU which was most reluctant to implement far-reaching reforms" (Zohlnhöfer 1999, 154).

This curious division of labor arises because, as the principal social base from which the CDU draws is religious, the CDU represents a significant number of working-class voters who would in other countries vote for the Left (in a dynamic quite similar to the role of religion in the United States). I explore the causes and consequences of this institutional structure below;

the main lesson at this point is that this division of labor and authority creates veto points *internal* to the CDU.

Finally, why did environmental deregulation—the centerpiece of U.S. efforts—not become important in West Germany? Environmental regulations were not a burning issue among business in West Germany after 1973 because employers were themselves responsible for implementing them and because policy elites were committed to the principle of harmonizing economic growth with environmental protection. Unlike the adversarial nature of environmental regulation in the United States, environmental regulation in West Germany was remarkably consensual until the late 1980s. Although the environmental passions of the 1960s and 1970s were as strong, or even stronger, in Germany as in any other country, Germany did not establish a ministry devoted entirely to environmental issues (like the American EPA, established in 1970, which became the focus of much business antagonism) until the Chernobyl accident in 1986. And unlike the adversarial framework in the United States, in which environmental protection and economic growth are zero-sum, in Germany the two came to be seen in positive-sum relation (Weidner 1995).

Although the United States has the reputation of being friendly to business, scholarship comparing business regulation in the United States and Germany (or Europe more generally) overwhelmingly concludes that businesses bear a harsher regulatory burden in the United States. Kagan and Axelrad (1997) interviewed managers of corporations with parallel operations in multiple countries and found general agreement that American social regulations—particularly environmental and safety regulations and liability law—are more stringent. In particular, they found that the American *style* of regulatory enforcement is uniquely adversarial:

> Even when basic American policies and laws are similar to those in other countries, the United States has a distinctive legal style. American methods of implementing legal and regulatory norms and resolving related disputes are often unusually legalistic, adversarial, and expensive. To the direct costs of complying with laws and regulations, therefore, U.S. adversarial legalism, as we label it, generally adds *friction costs* that are not characteristic of other economically advanced democracies. . . . [T]he international differences in legal and regulatory *processes* often are more important to multinational enterprises than are differences in the nominal requirements of national laws and regulations. (146–47)

They cite other studies supporting the conclusion that "The relevant American legal process tends to be characterized by more complex and detailed bodies of rules; more frequent recourse to formal legal methods of implementing policy and resolving disputes; more adversarial and expensive forms of legal contestation; more punitive legal sanctions (including larger civil damage awards); more frequent judicial review, revision, and delay of administrative decision making; and more malleability and unpredictability" (150). Kagan and Axelrad give examples of interviewees who compared the rigidity and uncertainty of American regulatory enforcement with that of Europe:

> Multinational corporate managers repeatedly told us that regulators in Europe and Japan rarely resort to formal punishment in response to relatively trivial or unintentional offenses. Instead, the formal regulators are much more inclined to sit down with company representatives to work out agreements on technically appropriate remedial measures.
>
> U.S. regulatory agencies' hair-trigger resort to formal enforcement is far from uniform, but it is unpredictable. And it is doubly troublesome to corporate officials, given the detail and complexity of U.S. regulations. Firms are often unsure whether they have actually achieved compliance. Officials from a U.S. chemical firm said that when they encountered an ambiguous . . . regulation and sought guidance from the EPA on whether the firm needed to submit certain paperwork, the agency issued a $23 million fine against the company. (160)

Sheila Jasanoff gives another example: "U.S. agencies in the 1970s designated as carcinogens a number of substances that most European regulators did not believe presented a cancer risk to humans. The Environmental Protection Agency (EPA), for example, banned the pesticides aldrin and dieldrin as potential carcinogens, and the Food and Drug Administration (FDA) tried to ban saccharin on similar grounds but failed because of intense public and congressional opposition" (1991, 63–64). The American style of regulation of carcinogens is also more transparent, with procedures established not only for making decisions, but for quantifying how certain those decisions are: "The effect of this strategy is to make the regulator's reasons for finding that substances present (or do not present) a carcinogenic hazard open and accessible to all. Any weaknesses in the scientific argument, as well as any substantial shifts from prior administrative policy, thus become relatively easy to detect. It is hardly surprising, therefore, that the federal government's cancer policies have aroused controversies"

(Jasanoff 1986, 15–16). The European method is to decide "on a case-by-case basis. Such decisions are generally made by expert committees, whose deliberations are usually confidential. As a result, there is no clear record of the principles of scientific interpretation used in individual cases or of changes in these principles over time" (15).

Many comparative studies of regulation have been conducted over the last few decades, and the overwhelming finding is similar. Kelman (1981) on safety regulation, Badaracco (1985) on vinyl chloride regulation, Wilson (1985) on health and safety regulation, and Charkham (1998) on corporate governance all find adversarial procedures in the United States compared to more cooperative procedures in Europe. Daemmrich writes, "First, government officials in the United States closely control the production of information about the safety and efficacy of new medicines, whereas the medical profession has retained greater autonomy to design and oversee clinical testing in Germany. Second, a strict division between testing and marketing prevails in the United States, while German institutions follow a more flexible regime regarding pre- and postmarket regulatory oversight" (2004, 6), and "Restrictive tort laws limit lawsuits in Germany and claims against manufacturers such as drug companies rarely produce large settlements. Scientific and medical experts are generally called as court-appointed witnesses in these and other cases, not as experts for the prosecution or defense. In contrast, American tort law intentionally sets a low barrier to legal access for citizens and different expert witnesses can testify for each side of a case" (8). He also notes that in the United States "[q]uantitative testing methods are imposed by the FDA," while in Germany "[q]ualitative testing methods arise from communal norms and self-imposed standards" (152). Braithwaite found "a strong historical shift away from punitiveness in coal mine safety enforcement" in Europe and "a movement toward punitiveness" in the United States (1985, 4).

Brickman, Jasanoff, and Ilgen studied the regulation of hazardous chemicals in the United States, Britain, France, and Germany, and found that

> American regulatory processes stand apart in the complexity of their procedures, the heavy reliance on formal analysis of risks and benefits, the openness of administrative decision making, and the active supervision of executive agencies by Congress and the Courts. European processes, despite some notable differences among them, share simpler administrative procedures, greater

> informality in the analysis of evidence, less complete public access to decision makers, and relatively little oversight by parliament or the courts. (1985, 23)

Verweij compares water pollution measures in the United States and Western Europe and finds that

> U.S. industry's views have carried less weight in environmental decision-making (at both the federal and state levels) than has been the case in the Rhine valley. Moreover, U.S. pollution values and technological standards have been more detailed and more stringent than European ones. Finally, in the Rhine countries, firms temporarily unable to fulfill their legal obligations toward the environment have sometimes been able to discuss this problem with the authorities. Government officials from these countries have certainly not threatened firms with severe penalties. In similar cases in the United States, the EPA and state environmental departments have shown less understanding. U.S. authorities have sometimes handed out heavy fines to firms and at times have even sought imprisonment for business executives who have not met environmental standards. (2000, 1037–38)

He notes that "although Germany's current effluent standards take up only a few pages, the U.S. effluent standards at present take up 1,592 pages of the U.S. Code of Federal Regulations" (1046).

While some of the scholars finding adversarial legalism in the United States are conservatives who worry about the costs of adversarialism for business and therefore argue that the United States should move toward the European model, at least one is a self-defined progressive scholar who shares sympathies with environmentalists and therefore advocates that Germany should move toward the American model: "Consensual decision-making is appropriate only for a narrow range of issues in environmental law.... Germany should consider adopting the outlines of the American administrative law system.... For environmental issues, Germany needs a policy-making system that operates with constrained openness rather than unconstrained closed consensus" (Rose-Ackerman 1995, 134–39). Although the political implications they draw are different, for our purposes the important point is that scholars from across the political spectrum who have compared regulation in the United States and Germany agree that the American process is full of conflict, whereas the German process is consensual.

There are a few exceptions to this finding, and they are very recent: Bernauer (2003) finds that the United States is much more lax than Europe in regulating agricultural biotechnology, and while Kelemen (2004) agrees that German courts are more restrained regarding environmental regulations than American ones, he finds that they do play an active role. This suggests that in more recent years the conservative revolution in the United States may have had some success in dismantling the adversarial legalism of the postwar period, or that the EU may have brought adversarial legalism to Europe.

Although the dominant finding is of adversarialism in the United States, there is no consensus on whether adversarial procedures lead to either greater costs or different policy outcomes than in Europe. Indeed, the main consequences of adversarialism seem to be not economic, but political: adversarial procedures provide narratives of outrageous regulation around which combatants form; they require the creation of methods for collecting information that put information about costs in the hands of those who pay them; and each success in an adversarial process strengthens the coalition responsible for it. In short, adversarial procedures create adversaries.[4]

In contrast, in Germany in the 1970s businesses largely regulated themselves in environmental protection. This self-regulated structure stems from the *Duldungspflicht* or "duty of toleration" of 1873, which places a priority on economic growth over the inconveniences that it might cause to individuals. In the all-important chemical industry in the early twentieth century, "Business interest associations . . . enjoyed a harmonious relationship with governments of varied complexions. . . . The pattern that developed was one of consultation between the state and industry with the overwhelming emphasis on self-regulation" (Paterson 1989, 73). This tradition led to lack of a universal standard of regulation and, in its absence,

4. Alfred Chandler (1980) traces the beginning of the American adversarial approach to regulation to the nineteenth century. He argues that the arrival of the railroads threatened small business in the United States because the size of the country provided tremendous incentives to railroads to reward economies of scale. For example, twice as much freight could be hauled for much less than twice the cost, so businesses with much larger inventories received discounts. This put small businesses at a disadvantage, and they were able to acquire political protection through the Sherman Antitrust Act and the Interstate Commerce Commission, which established the model of an adversarial approach to business. When government grew after the depression, it grew based on this model. In other countries the smaller size of operations meant that the economies of scale, and therefore the rift between small and big business, were never so great, and in many cases patterns of state intervention had been developed long before the arrival of big business. See also Vogel 1978.

local government officials teamed up with business interests to create associations for self-regulation. In the immediate postwar years, "concern about pollution was lost amid visible symbols of economic growth. After the Second World War and the 'hungry years,' there was satisfaction that the 'chimneys were smoking again'" (Weale 1992, 162). Pressure for regulation in the early postwar years came from businesses worried about the quality of their raw materials as much as from government and citizens. The main business association, the Bundesverband der Deutschen Industrie (BDI), although it resisted the creation of an agency to oversee water, was the main force behind regulations to license the use of water: "Early in the 1950s the BDI ran a campaign for a 'usable environment' which resulted in the Federal Water Resources Act of 1957, which required that users of water resources should obtain an official permit for its use and set norms for discharges" (Weale 1992, 163). Industrial groups played a major role in the formation of policy as well as implementation (Wey 1982; Paterson 1989; Weidner 1995; Aguilar 1993).

When the wave of environmental concern of the 1960s and 1970s hit,[5] this decentralized, self-regulated, and business-supported framework was the foundation upon which the new regulatory regime was built: the federal environmental agencies that emerged provided research and advice, not enforcement. Although several isolated environmental protection laws were passed when the Social Democrats came to power in 1969, the lack of major policy initiatives has been given as one reason for the success of the Green Party in the 1980s: "There is . . . widespread consensus in the literature that the actual reason for the foundation of a Green Party . . . was the deficient responsiveness of the German party system to those political problems which were particularly relevant for potential Green voters" (Poguntke 1992, 338).

The tradition of self-regulation was one reason why business had not made environmental protection a target, as it did in the United States. Another factor producing consensual policies and dampening business resistance is that policy elites had adopted the principle of "ecological modernization," which had become popular in the 1970s. The idea was that pollution control could benefit the economy by protecting the raw materials that businesses need and by fostering new industries devoted

5. Much of it was inspired by American environmentalism—some trace the coining of the word *Umweltschutz* to a direct translation of the term "environmental protection" (Weidner 1995, 3–4).

to producing products to protect the environment, such as catalytic converters for automobiles. "Instead of seeing environmental protection as a burden upon the economy, the ecological modernist sees it as a potential source for future growth. Since environmental amenity is a superior good, the demand for pollution control is likely to increase, and there is therefore a considerable advantage to an economy... [with] the technical and production capacity to produce low-polluting goods or pollution control technology" (Weale 1992, 76). This did not mean that all businesses favored environmental protection (those in directly affected industries of course did not), but it did prevent the kind of generalized and increasingly organized business resistance seen in the United States. The lack of generalized concern with the costs of regulation that arose in the United States meant that Germany experienced no business backlash against environmental regulation.

This was the background for regulatory policy when Kohl took office, and, given the increasing success of the Greens, the regulatory structure was actually strengthened under Kohl. The minister of the interior (responsible for environmental policy until the creation of the Ministry for the Environment in 1986 after Chernobyl), Friedrich Zimmerman, implemented several quite strong environmental protection measures, including an air pollution control act considered one of the strictest in Europe at the time. Zimmerman also called an international conference on air pollution in 1984 and tried to promote EU-level environmental protection. Some argue that Zimmerman adopted a pro-environment line, despite the coalition's overall free market statement of intent, because he came from a state heavily affected by environmental pollution (Weidner 1995). This increasing regulation since the 1980s means that Germany is increasingly adopting the adversarial pattern that characterized the United States in the 1970s.

Welfare State Policy

The political dynamics behind the expansion of the welfare state have been varied, but the institutions of the welfare state have shown a remarkable continuity through Germany's turbulent twentieth century, from the Kaiserreich laying the foundation of income security programs, to the Weimar Republic's expansion to programs for veterans and the unemployed, the rise of the social democratic and Christian worker movements, and the introduction of class politics into social policy. Despite the economic and political crises of the 1930s and 1940s, the welfare state was remarkably durable; rates fluctuated, but there was no major alteration of policy other than the expansion of family policy and health services. After the Second World War the patterns that had already taken shape were expanded upon by both parties; though the SPD was more ideologically committed to expansion of social welfare, the CDU was happy to continue expanding during the boom decades after the war, as this clearly pleased voters and interest groups (Alber 1989; Offe 1999).

The federal structure of the new republic did not prevent the development of an expansive welfare state, an unusual outcome when compared to all other federal states (M. Schmidt 2001). As in France, however, it was a conservative party that oversaw the postwar expansion of Germany's welfare state, and therefore, as in France, the German welfare state's popularity came at the expense of redistributive efficacy. As Esping-Andersen (1990) writes, in the German welfare state social insurance schemes serve to reinforce rather than dissolve status differences: benefits are based on past contributions rather than need, and risks are spread out over the life course rather than across income groups.

Social policy has always been the most difficult area of contention within the CDU: the party's social Catholic branch and its pro-business branch, hurriedly brought together under the banner of Christian Democracy, here go their separate ways. The pro-business elements have tolerated the welfare state as necessary to win votes or to head off more radical policy proposals (Michalsky 1985), and they could afford to do this during the heady days of the economic boom. Since the 1970s, however, the story has been different. Observers from diverse areas—scholars as well as policymakers—have converged on some version of the analysis associated most prominently with Claus Offe: that while the German welfare state was ideally suited to a context of full employment, patriarchy, corporatism, and a growing population, changes in this context have brought the welfare state into crisis:

> The German welfare state model was originally uniquely well designed to generate compliance and effectiveness, and hence stability, within the parameters of this type of industrial social structure, but . . . it is by far less capable to meet these criteria under present structural conditions. . . . [T]he German welfare state can be seen as the present victim of its past success; its perfect adaptation to past conditions and ends hinders its adaptation to present conditions. (Offe 1990, 3)

The welfare state had come in for increasing criticism as early as the mid-1960s, from the Left as well as the Right, for the increase in bureaucratic control it led to, and (following the economic crisis) for the usual reasons of decreasing the competitiveness of the economy (Alber 1989, 314–15; see also Alber 1999; Borchert 1995; Offe 1984). However, Schmidt did not attempt to cut back welfare spending. The Kohl government's most significant attempt to do so was the proposed reform of the health insurance system in 1987, intended to stem the ever-rising tide of health care spending and contributions.

Reform of the health system has been extraordinarily difficult in Germany, despite several attempts over the decades. Webber (1988) shows that even when economic and political considerations seem to favor reform, again and again reform has been blocked by the large number of interests who hold a veto, by the veto rights of the state governments, and by the power of the doctors' lobbies. This was once again the case with the reform attempt of 1987. But why could the veto players not be bought off, as they had been in the case of the U.S. tax cuts?

Even more than taxation and deregulation, health insurance reform was in the hands of the Workers' Wing because of the position of Norbert Blüm as labor minister; indeed, whereas in the former realms the role of the Workers' Wing had been to object to policies pushed elsewhere within the coalition, Blüm was directly and completely in charge of health insurance reform. Moreover, unlike the tax and deregulation cuts, health insurance reform was not brought onto the agenda by the FDP, and the reform was not part of the original discussion when Kohl arrived in office in 1982. Rather, it became a pressing issue only in 1984 as a result of rising health care costs. In 1984, after a few years of stable and even sinking costs, the public health insurance system began to run a deficit. The government felt these costs were undermining its efforts to cut taxes and consolidate the budget deficit, and in September 1984 Blüm convened representatives from the Bundesvereinigung der Deutschen Arbeitgeberverbände (BDA) business lobby and the unions in a meeting resulting in agreement that none of the actors wanted to tolerate the continual increase of health costs, and all wanted to stabilize contributions. The government announced a "structural reform" (*Strukturreform*) to contrast its policies with those of the preceding SPD governments, which had adopted a policy of merely keeping costs down (*Kostendämpfung*). In 1985 Blüm promised that nothing was taboo in the discussion of how best to reform the system, but this did not last long. In the 1987 election the FDP demanded that the structural reform of the health system be explicitly written into the coalition agreements, but the agreement that emerged promised not to touch the principle of free choice of doctors and therapies, and a reform on "pure market economy lines" was categorically rejected. The reform was not actually proposed until after the 1987 election; given support in public opinion for health insurance reform, this was supposed to be the policy that ensured Kohl's reelection in 1990 (Webber 1989; Perschke-Hartmann 1992, 37–39).

As Perschke-Hartmann comments, "The coalition agreements seem to a large part to be borrowed from the health system imaginings of the Social Committee [Workers' Wing] of the CDU, which is certainly no coincidence. It is rather to be traced back to the fact that Blüm was for a long time its head" (1992, 39). Because of the division of labor within the CDU, which places welfare state responsibilities in the hands of the labor minister and places the Labor Ministry in the hands of the left wing of the party, it was Blüm, the head of the Workers' Wing, who was in charge of health insurance reform. In addition to rejecting a reform along "pure market economy" lines, Blüm made his belief clear from the start that previous reform efforts had failed because they had gone "against the doctors," and his would not do so. The reform efforts of the late 1950s and early 1960s, in particular, which had collapsed because of resistance from the powerful doctors' lobby, loomed as a lesson (Webber 1988). But with this self-imposed restriction, the 1987 reform was severely constrained because a significant part of the inflation of costs came from the way in which health care was funded. The health trust funds paid doctors for patients' visits according to the intensity of the problem diagnosed and the care given, but the doctor was alone responsible for determining the intensity of the problem. Doctors routinely exaggerated problems to get more funds. For example, an anonymous doctor wrote to *Der Spiegel* describing how a visit from a woman with bloodshot eyes, leading to a diagnosis of flu that should bring 7.84 marks, could easily be turned into a diagnosis of "danger of suicide" that, with various related diagnoses added to it, would bring 171.50 marks ("Jeder Krankenschein ist ein Blankoscheck," *Der Spiegel* 43, no. 10 [1989]: 56–57). The patient did not pay for care and therefore had no incentive to complain about the diagnosis or cost, and the trust funds had no surveillance system in place. Thus Blüm's concession to the power of the doctors' lobby was an important limitation on the reforms from the very beginning, as it meant that the structure of service delivery could not be touched, and this important cause of the inflation of health care costs was taken off the table. The doctors' association also indicated that it would not tolerate any wholesale introduction of market principles into the health policy domain. Only in the mid-1990s did any change in the direction of greater surveillance take place (Webber 1989, 1992b).

With these limitations in mind, Blüm proposed a three-step reform, which would reform the way health services were funded, reorganize the delivery of services, and require consumers to pay out of pocket for elective health care, with the hospital sector bearing some of the burden of elective health care for those unable to afford it. The first two steps were successfully resisted by a coalition headed by the CSU and composed of state governments that wanted to preserve their electorally popular state-level delivery of services. Furthermore, "a special committee intended to help the social policy experts of the governing parties in the Bundestag and the Ministry of Labor resolve their differences in drafting the bill had the opposite effect. Disagreements between the ministry and the party experts required higher-level meetings, which only created additional points of entry to health care interests, who used these openings to win concessions in the legislation" (Giaimo 2002, 109). Thus, the proposal that took shape simply required consumers to pay for elective health care—not a dramatic overhaul of the system, but still a step in the direction of privatization. In addition, some cuts in benefits at the margins were proposed, particularly regulation of drug prices, which affected the pharmaceuticals sector, but in return the Workers' Wing—including Blüm himself—managed to implement a new program of home health care. Even this mild reform evoked strong protest. The pharmaceutical industry protested, fearing an inability to invest in research and development, and was backed by its political protector the FDP. The FDP also resisted measures that would have hurt chemists and dentists. Despite Blüm's efforts, the doctors' lobbies were offended by measures intended to strengthen surveillance over them, and they campaigned against the reform. Taxi drivers objected because payments for transportation to hospitals were being cut. Undertakers protested because payments to families of the dead were being cut. Blüm struggled against all of these protests, trying to frame the issue as one of making minor cuts to preserve the system from collapse, but more often than not he was forced to give in. The reform that finally emerged regulated drug prices and made marginal benefit cuts, but *extended* health spending by introducing the new program of home health care—quite a curious outcome for a reform that had been triggered by the need to contain cost. The cost-sharing proposals had been reduced to the point where copayments "average[d] DM 3 per prescription, and hardship clauses exempted disadvantaged segments of the population" (Giaimo 2002, 109). And Norbert Blüm, who had been one of the most popular political figures in West Germany in August 1987, with 67 percent of the public wanting him to play an important role in politics, saw that rating plummet to 45 percent the following December and 33 percent by April 1989; jokes began to make the rounds that Blüm wanted to squeeze costs by having families share a set of dentures or by having everyone wear the kind of cheap frames for eyeglasses that Blüm himself wore (Webber 1989, 1992b; Lehmbruch 1992; Giaimo 2002; "Blüm läßt den kleinen Mann bluten," *Der Spiegel* 43, no. 10 [1989]: 36–59).

In short, one or another of the coalition's *own* members picked the reform apart. The FDP resisted measures that would have hurt any of its traditional constituencies. The CSU and the state governments resisted measures that would have reduced their autonomy in providing health service at the state level. And the Workers' Wing resisted any measures that might have been the least bit socially unjust.

Alternative Explanations

How do we explain the limited neoliberalism under Kohl? In this section I test the empirical cases against three popular explanations of German policymaking that emphasize the role of national culture, the role of the veto powers set up by the institutional structure of the policymaking system, and the benefits of the existing system for business (the "varieties of capitalism" explanation).

National Culture

The national culture explanation, as in the case of France, suggests that a collectivist, corporatist German culture, which subordinates market values to the traditional values of solidarity and security, prevents an Anglo-American style of neoliberalism from taking root, and that West Germany did not see an economic change of the order of Reagan or Thatcher because West German national culture sees a large role for state intervention. Kenneth Dyson writes, "The state tradition involves the idea of a set of moral ideas existing apart from the conflicts of interest of social and political life. At the root of this attitude towards public authority is a sense of the importance of unity and order in national life" (1992, 10). He argues that this prevents the adoption of deregulation in Germany.

National culture explanations are more common in popular accounts than in scholarly ones, because such explanations are unsatisfactory for both theoretical and empirical reasons. As Peter Katzenstein writes, "Cultural explanations explain too much. Because they focus on what is distinctive about West Germany in general, cultural explanations are too weak to sort out different outcomes in different policy sectors, [and] in the hands of the unskilled, cultural explanations easily degenerate into labeling phenomena rather than learning about them" (1987, 352). Cultural explanations also cannot explain different degrees of change in different time periods.

Empirically, the evidence for an overarching national culture that channels the behavior of individuals along particular tracks is weak. The evidence is that although there is indeed strong respect for the state in West Germany, there is also a flourishing tradition of market culture that has grown in the postwar period.

West German culture, at both popular and elite levels, saw a minority tradition in favor of the free market gain strength after the discrediting of statist solutions in World War II and the spectacular success of the market economy in comparison with the GDR (Smith 1986). Klaus von Beyme writes that in "some areas Germany has a long tradition of state interference, as in economic policy. But precisely this tradition led to the counterreaction of an exaggerated devotion to neoliberal ideas. The German war economy—praised even by Lenin as a model for central planning under socialism—was abandoned as fast as possible. Germany became the country of non-planning. Neoliberalism became almost a religion" (1985, 14). In particular, a "myth of the miracle" (Padgett and Burkett 1986) arose in postwar Germany, according to which the extraordinary economic growth of the 1950s and 1960s was due to Ludwig Erhard's liberalization measures of the late 1940s. Whether this is true is a complicated issue. There is a great deal of debate in economic history on the precise causes of Germany's extraordinary growth rate (see Bulmer and Humphreys 1989; Braun 1990; Katzenstein 1987; Nicholls 1997).

More important for our purposes than an accurate assessment of the effect of the liberalizations on the economy is the observation that the economic miracle of the postwar period led to a *belief* in the virtues of the market and the importance of adhering to it. "In the course of about two decades of substantial and steady economic growth the new political order became identified for most West Germans with a thriving capitalist economy that might be tempered, but not too much tampered-with, by governmental policymakers" (Edinger 1986, 41). Katzenstein finds in the events of World War II one source of this adherence to the market:

> Although it is true that the Nazis attempted to develop an economy that would differ significantly from both a centrally planned Communist economy as well as from Western liberal market economies, the need to mobilize for war tended to conceal those efforts. In any event, the collapse of Hitler's so-called New Order convinced the West Germans that they wanted the government to play no more than a restricted role in economic life. (1987, 86)

Gerhard Lehmbruch traces the German variant of neoliberalism back before the Second World War to the "Freiburg school" of economics, a neoliberal variant founded by Walter Eucken (one of the founders of the Mont Pèlerin Society, out of which British neoliberalism grew). After the world economic crisis of the 1930s, Eucken, Alfred Müller-Armack, Franz Böhm, and other economists developed their idea of "an economic 'order' based on the dynamics of a competitive market, but 'bound by the state.'... [Even under the Nazi] regime there were always powerful advocates of a competitive market economy based on free enterprise" (Lehmbruch 1992, 33–34).

Indeed, only in the 1970s did the SPD belatedly attempt to develop an alternative principle of stronger intervention (*Strukturpolitik*), but the influence of the FDP kept it from becoming incorporated into policy (Lehmbruch 1992, 30). The German model was seen as so successful that in the years before the Thatcher administration came to power, its members made a careful study of Germany. Although Thatcher later criticized Germany for not embracing the market, in the 1970s the Conservative Party envied Germany's success, particularly its cooperative labor unions. In 1974 Keith Joseph began his rethinking of policy with a specific determination to see what could be learned from West Germany, and in 1988 Chris Patten of the Conservative Research Department wrote, "I think that what the Germans managed to do in the early 1950s was not only... to win the economic case for the market, but to win the moral case for the market as well. And I suspect that we still have to find an overwhelmingly convincing . . . equivalent of the German rhetoric about the social market economy" (*Thatcher Factor*, Patten, box 5).[6] In 1992 Keith Joseph wrote that Germany's problems began when it began to imitate Britain's "statist" policies (Denham and Garnett 2001, 242–43)!

It is important not to overstate the ubiquity of the adherence to the market. Although, compared to other European countries, Germany has almost no public enterprise sector (von Beyme 1985), in terms of actual policy the German market was, and remains, one of the most regulated in the advanced world. As Jeremy Leaman (1988) has argued, despite the myths, the state has always intervened in the economy. And for a brief period immediately after the war, there was consensus that the Great Depression and the instabilities it had led to signaled the failure of *capitalism* (Braun 1990). In terms of ideology, Lehmbruch (1992) concludes that German neoliberals manage to combine respect for the market with defense of the welfare state on the ideological level in a particular way: "The neoliberal theory of *Ordnungspolitik*—as it was further developed after the Second World War—regarded 'secondary' redistribution of incomes through social policy as perfectly legitimate as long as government did not interfere with the ('primary') allocative functions of the *markt wirtschaftliche Ordnung*" (34). A "Scandinavian" type of welfare state was considered "unsocial" because it attempted to interfere with the primary functions of the market and thus "incapacitated its citizens" (Braun 1990, 178). As Müller-Armack, one of the contributors to the German Basic Laws put it, the goal was, "on the basis of the competition economy, to bind free enterprise with social progress—secured precisely through the achievements of a market economy. On the foundation of a market economy a many-shaped and complete system of social protection can be set up" (quoted in Lampert 1992, 87). The appeal of this theory is evident, but it is only possible if the taxation required to achieve social protection does not interfere with the competitiveness of the economy to such an extent that it destroys the market economy's foundations. This seemed to be possible in the flush decades of the 1950s and 1960s, but not so in the 1970s, and since the 1980s, the price of it has been borne by the unemployed. Wolfgang Streeck sums up thus: "The postwar German *state* is neither *laissez-faire* nor *etatiste*, and is best described as an *enabling state*" (1997, 9).

6. The interviews conducted for the documentary *The Thatcher Factor* (Brook Lapping Productions 1991/1992) are collected in the archives of the London School of Economics.

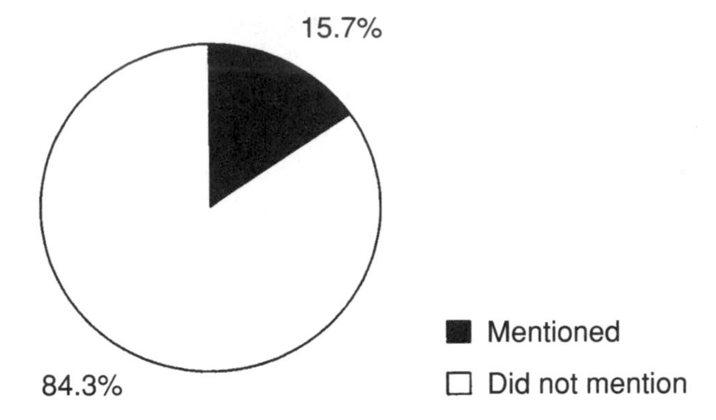

FIGURE 3.1. Presence of the issue of neoliberalism in economics dissertations at Freie Universität, 1982–89

To gain an objective measure of how popular neoliberal ideas were in the 1980s in West Germany, I examined and coded all dissertations written in the field of economics between 1982 and 1989 at the Free University (Freie Universität) in Berlin, one of the more "left-wing" German universities. The total sample consists of 186 theses from all subdisciplines of economics. As with the French dissertations in the following chapter, I read the introduction and conclusion, as well as any pages that, according to the table of contents, dealt with the issue of neoliberalism, and coded the dissertations first as to whether they mentioned the idea that reducing the size of the state (in taxation, industrial policy, welfare state policy, free trade, and monetarism) would improve economic growth, and second, according to the evaluation of neoliberal tenets that the theses gave.

A much smaller percentage than in France mentioned the issue: only 15.68 percent (fig. 3.1). By and large, neoliberalism was a minority preoccupation at the Free University at this time. In general, the discourse of economics dissertations in Germany in this time period was much less polarized than it was in France just a few years earlier (probably because so many students from ex-colonial countries were enrolled at the Sorbonne, many of whom were interested in world systems theory). In comparison, the German dissertations tend to be more value-neutral, choosing small and noncontroversial topics such as the role of technology transfer to Poland in the 1970s or the organization of decisions in particular economic sectors. Obviously the small numbers here are even more cause

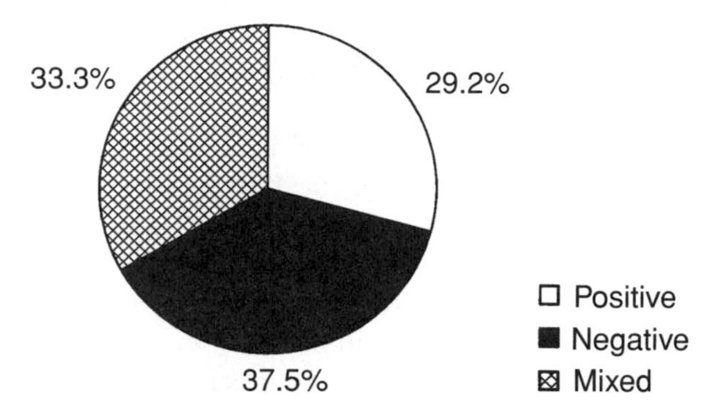

FIGURE 3.2. Evaluation of neoliberal claims as a percentage of theses that mentioned and evaluated them at Freie Universität, 1982–89

for caution than in the French case, but of the twenty-nine dissertations from this period that did discuss neoliberal topics, five did not evaluate the claims, seven gave positive evaluations, nine gave negative evaluations, and eight gave mixed evaluations (fig. 3.2). Thus, of those that mentioned and evaluated neoliberal claims, about a third were positive and about a third were negative—suggesting, at the least, that neoliberal claims were not unthinkable in Germany during this period.

More important than the mere existence of a market tradition is the exaggerated emphasis it receives because of the role of the FDP, the small libertarian party that was the "kingmaker" for almost the whole of the West German state's existence. Because of its exaggerated importance, it had been able to uphold a free market ideal in postwar Germany, particularly during the late 1970s and early 1980s, as discussed above and in more detail below.

In addition, a cultural theme rooted in communal Christian principles—the theme of *subsidiarity*—was fundamental in underpinning German neoliberalism. The principle of subsidiarity is that problems should be resolved by the smallest level of social grouping capable of handling them: thus, the neighborhood should not interfere in what the family can do for itself, the town should not interfere in what the neighborhood can do for itself, the *Land* should not interfere in what the town can do for itself, and the federal government should not interfere in what the *Länder* can do for themselves. Only when the lower-order group proves unable to resolve a particular problem on its own should the higher-order group step in. This particular defense of federalism was used often to favor market principles (Richter 1987).

Finally, another variant of the cultural argument is advanced by Zohlnhöfer (1999), who concludes that the Kohl government's inability to reform was caused by lack of a broad vision outlining the specific changes that were needed. "Apart from the shared view that a budget consolidation was necessary and an elusive belief in market forces, no common concept in economic policy existed within the coalition" (154). He goes on to say, "The federal government failed to implement far-reaching reforms because it lacked programmatic cohesion and a common understanding of what ought to be changed in the relationship between the state and the market" (155). But as we saw in the dynamic of the changes in Britain and the United States, vagueness and lack of cohesion did not prevent large-scale change from taking place in either of those cases. In its early years the Reagan administration was sharply divided over the wisdom of large tax cuts, and the vast scope of privatization under Thatcher—the policy that is in retrospect most associated with "Thatcherism"—was not among the principles with which she began her terms in office. In retrospect, programs that are successfully implemented may seem to have been willed all along as part of a coherent program; in practice, however, in both these cases the coherence of the program developed during the process of implementation itself. Moreover, we should not overstate the vagueness of the Kohl regime's program. As measured by the Lambsdorff paper or by its own early programmatic statements such as the Stuttgart Principles, the regime knew exactly what to do (tax cuts on business, deregulation, cutbacks in social spending), and the policies it proposed were no more vague than those communicated at a similar point by the British or American neoliberals. The reforms that were *attempted* add up to a quite coherent and dramatic neoliberal turn—tax cuts, deregulations, and the cutting of health care costs. "National culture" did not prevent the formulation of neoliberal policies. Such policies were formulated quite often—they just never reached the phase of implementation.

Veto Points

A researcher asking why West Germany did not adopt neoliberal policies in the early 1980s on the scale of the American or British experience is fortunate in having the guidance of Peter Katzenstein's *Policy and Politics in West Germany* (1987), which asks exactly the same question: "How we can account for the absence of large-scale policy change in the face of changes in the composition of government?" (4). Katzenstein comes to this issue out of a wish to turn away from "the German Question" of the Nazi period, and to look "forward . . . to uncover the political structures that make incremental policy change such a plausible political response" (349). Katzenstein is implicitly responding to the question of whether Germany could once again become the powerful state, little-checked by its civil society, that had wreaked such havoc in world history, and he concludes that that state no longer exists. Since Katzenstein's work is so thorough and so widely cited, and has essentially become common sense in discussions of the German polity, I give extended treatment here to his argument. My analysis draws especially on Zohlnhöfer 1999.

Katzenstein's main argument is that the German state is "semi-sovereign"; that is, politicians are constrained in the policies they can pass and implement by the number of checks and balances, or "veto points"—points where any one actor can veto the proposed change—including (1) the political parties and the party system, which favors centrist measures; (2) the system of cooperative federalism, through which state interests are reliably represented at the central level; and (3) parapublic institutions, which tame political initiatives in the implementation. This is an institutional argument; that is, it asserts that the forms of the political decision-making process "introduce their own dynamics into state-society relations" (Bulmer 1989, 17), and it has become the orthodox wisdom concerning Germany. But each of these elements deserves more careful inspection.

PARTY SYSTEM. First, Katzenstein writes that both of West Germany's political parties are centrist:

> The rightist tendency of some segments of the CDU and the CSU toward American-style conservatism in both foreign and domestic policy is held in check by a substantial left wing of social reformers representing reform-minded Catholics and Catholic workers. How far the SPD can move to the left is constrained by the presence of a solid block of parliamentarians who represent union interests and the orthodoxy of the reformist Bad Godesberg program and who are deeply suspicious of the issues—ecology and peace—being raised especially by the younger generation. (1987, 39)

Note that Katzenstein has here defined *centrist* in two quite different ways: for the CDU and CSU, *centrist* in domestic policy means away from free enterprise; for the SPD, it means away from "new social movement" issues.

Second, Katzenstein asserts that the role of the FDP increases centralist tendencies. In coalition with the major parties, the FDP has maintained a position to the right of the SPD and to the left of the CDU/CSU: "During the 1970s the FDP obstructed several Social Democratic reforms. . . . [In 1982] once it had formed the government with the CDU/CSU, the FDP began to articulate its own political position to the left of the CDU/CSU on questions of foreign policy and civil liberties, to the right on many economic and social issues" (1987, 39). Again, *centrist* here is defined as blocking economically leftist policies and socially rightist ones—not as being in the center on both dimensions. But, as noted above, the FDP has vacillated between economic and political liberalism, and during the mid-1970s to 1980s, its economic liberal tendencies were on the ascendant. This means that in economic policies, the FDP was not actually a force for centrism at all, as Katzenstein suggests; it was a force for neoliberalism.

Neither of these first reasons Katzenstein gives constrain turns to the right in economic policy. Third, Katzenstein suggests that coalition governments produce more centrist policies in general, quoting Manfred Schmidt: "One could plausibly argue that the bargaining process within coalitions tends to exclude extreme policy stances and issues which are highly controversial between the partners, and therefore that conditions are conducive to the diminution of policy differences" (41–42). But again, this conclusion is compromised by the tendency to rate the FDP on one left-right scale; in fact, the presence of the FDP in Kohl's coalition largely *reinforced* the economically rightist tendencies. Thus it is not the bargaining process *among different parties* that prevents neoliberalism, although we will see below that (as Katzenstein also notes) the bargaining process *within* one of the parties is crucial and produces exactly the dynamic he defines.

Thus, the argument that the party system restrains extremism needs to be nuanced when we note that the party system—largely because of the role of the FDP—is not "centrist" so much as inconsistent in comparison with Anglo-Saxon party systems, in that the FDP lends weight to the SPD in social issues, but to the CDU/CSU on economic policy issues. In both cases, it checks the adoption of nonliberal economic policy, and promotes the adoption of liberal economic policy. (And in social policy, it restrains the CDU in its attempts to implement nonliberal social policy, such as tighter anticrime measures to combat terrorism, and supports the SPD in promoting liberal social policy.) The CDU/FDP coalition of the early 1960s collapsed when Chancellor Erhard wanted to increase taxes to balance the budget. The SPD/FDP coalition of the 1970s fell apart in 1982 when the FDP adopted an increasingly neoliberal stance. The popularity of the argument that the FDP is centrist may be due to the FDP's own sense of itself as providing a check to the unrestrained power of the larger parties (Søe 1990). But its ability to check the parties is actually bifurcated: it checks the SPD in economic policy, but not social policy; and it checks the CDU in social policy, but not economic policy.

COOPERATIVE FEDERALISM. Katzenstein's second set of reasons to expect lack of dramatic change is "cooperative federalism," through which "divergent [regional] interests are brought together through a policy process that resists central reform initiatives and defies sustained attempts to steer policy developments.... In contrast to the United States, in West Germany the Bundestag must reach agreement with the states represented in the Bundesrat on all major policy initiatives. Furthermore, the federal government relies on the eleven state bureaucracies to administer most federal programs" (1987, 45). The Bundesrat has wide powers, and its approval is necessary to pass a federal budget; more important, it has veto powers over any legislation that affects the *Länder*, which is, of course the majority of federal legislation (Smith 1992, 44). While Katzenstein and Smith are correct in their estimation of the role federalism plays to block major initiatives in Germany in general, and although the resistance of the Bundesrat was important in derailing various reforms under Kohl, there are several reasons why opposition from the Bundesrat was not as important and as continuously present in the stories above as other elements were (particularly the Workers' Wing).

First, the CDU/CSU coalition controlled the Bundesrat until 1990, so it was only in exceptional cases that the state governments went against the wishes of the federal government. Second, in many areas under consideration for neoliberal reform, such as labor market policy, the approval of the Bundesrat was not necessary (Zohlnhöfer 2001b, 659, and 2001c). But a more important point arises from the U.S. case, which shows us that federalism is not by itself a reliable barrier to neoliberal change. In the United States, the individual states entered a sort of "competitive federalism," competing, for example, to see who could acquire the most benefits from the 1981 tax bill, and this inflated the size of that bill beyond what even David Stockman had envisaged. We will examine below why this was not possible in Germany.

PARAPUBLIC INSTITUTIONS. The third feature of West German political economy that Katzenstein singles out as unique are the dozens of institutions that "link the public and private sectors firmly together" (1987, 58). In economic management, industrial relations, and social welfare Katzenstein lists the following parapublic institutions as most important: the Bundesbank, the Council of Economic Experts, the institution of "codetermination" (*Mitbestimmung*), the labor courts, the social security funds, the Federal Employment Office, private welfare associations, and churches. But a closer look at the most important of these institutions gives us cause to hesitate before concluding that they make change—particularly the rise of neoliberalism—impossible. Sturm (1995) points out that the constitutional provisions for the Bundesbank's autonomy are nonexistent; this autonomy is a political convention, and—according to Sturm—may have been undermined by the Kohl regime in the 1980s through Kohl's appointments. More important, Zohlnhöfer (1999) notes that the Bundesbank is more resistant to *some* policies (e.g., the Keynesian pump-priming to reduce unemployment favored by the Left) than others. The Bundesbank in the 1970s and 1980s was quite receptive to neoliberal policy proposals, because the bank "pursued a monetary policy much more compatible with the supply-side-oriented economic policy of the Kohl administrations than with the Keynesian ideas of the SPD-led governments" (149–50). As for the Council of Economic Experts, it was extremely neoliberal—so much so that the Council itself suggested in its 1981–82 report that the tax system should share the risks of entrepreneurship with the entrepreneur (von Beyme 1985, 10). Although not all of the parapublic institutions favored supply-side policies, the most important ones in the domain of economic policy did.

Katzenstein's view of the German state as semi-sovereign because of its multiple sources of power has become the accepted wisdom. Features including the powerful Bundesrat, the independence of ministries and the Bundesbank, the Constitutional Court, and coalition governments all prevent change. These institutional features prevented the SPD from implementing a Keynesian macroeconomic policy during the 1970s. But the point here has been that *these institutions do not resist all kinds of reform equally*, and they may on occasion be arrayed in favor of the government's position. In fact, the Kohl government faced remarkably favorable institutional circumstances for neoliberal reform, including the FDP's support, control of the Bundesrat, and support from the Bundesbank.

In short, "institutions are not necessarily politically neutral" (Zohlnhöfer 1998, 6). As Tsebelis (1999, 2002) points out, it is not only the *number* of veto players that affects policy change, but also their *divergence in preference*. In the 1980s under Kohl, many of the veto players who prevented a full-scale adoption of Keynesianism were actually in favor of neoliberalism. Thus the argument about *institutional* veto points (the veto points entrenched in the constitution) is no more satisfactory than the appeal to national culture as an explanation for the lack of a turn to the right in Germany. What remains of Katzenstein's analysis is his observation that different factions within the parties can restrain extremist policies, which I explore in more detail below.

Varieties of Capitalism

Finally, in recent years comparative political economy has seen a powerful synthesis of institutional and political economic approaches arise in the "varieties of capitalism" literature, which sees firms as the central actors generating persistent differences across countries. The general argument of this school is that some states sustain high taxation, high welfare state spending, and an interventionist industrial policy because firms have found this combination to be *efficient* for the particular types of products in which they specialize. In particular, firms in a country like Germany, which specializes in producing high quality, high-tech, high-cost products, will need a highly skilled labor force. But workers will only invest in the long years of training required for this kind of production if they are confident of lifetime employment in jobs with high wages and high welfare benefits. Employers therefore accept various measures necessary to instill such confidence, such as the law against dismissal, high welfare expenditure, and the taxes that pay for these measures (Estevez-Abe, Iversen, and Soskice 2001; Swenson 1997; Hall and Soskice 2001).

The varieties of capitalism argument is easy to test in this case: when the Kohl administration suggested tax cuts, deregulation, and welfare state cuts, did business oppose them? By and large, the answer is no. Only in the case of shopping hours regulation did a business association oppose a neoliberal measure. The main retailers' association was against the measure because small retailers feared competition from large chains and nonunionized stores. But even here, the pattern was mixed: although the main retailers' association was against the measure, the large financial interests such as Deutsche Bank and Commerzbank were strongly in favor of it (Fisher 1987), as were groups representing discount stores and stores in new sites at the edges of cities, which stood to gain from the measure

(Simonian 1987). The interests and preferences of different segments of business diverged.

In taxation, business interests made great attempts to influence the 1990 tax reform, with mixed success; but in each case, their attempts favored greater neoliberalism, that is, larger tax cuts, larger corporate tax cuts, and larger tax cuts for those with high incomes. (The clearest example of successful business influence on the 1990 tax reform was in the case of the *Kapitalertragsteuer* [tax on capital yields]; see Findling 1995, 194, 284–87.)

Business interests were not so thoroughly organized with regard to health care costs, but in general, business interests supported the Kohl government's neoliberalism, and their most common complaint was that it did not go far enough. When Norbert Blüm approached the business lobbies for input into the health policy reform, the advice offered supported the standard neoliberal position (see Perschke-Hartmann 1992).

Consider the analysis given by Siegfried Mann of the main German employers' association in October 1984:

> It is a mistake to look for the causes of unemployment where old jobs are disappearing. Rather, the causes of unemployment are to be found where, because of a lack of economic dynamism, new jobs are not being created. Market regulations, protectionism, subsidies, demands for protection from rationalization or for a tax on machines cause unemployment merely as a symptom.... [We need] decisive protection from the mentality of redistribution and a consequent strengthening of readiness for individual achievement. (Mann 1987)

Even in the area that scholars of the varieties of capitalism school examine most carefully—industrial policy—employers sometimes preferred the neoliberal alternative. The *Financial Times* claimed for example that "the country's businessmen and managers... in spite of frequent protestations to the contrary, have played a vital backroom role in pushing the present Government to take on the unions" in the case of reforms weakening labor's power in works councils (3 Jun 1986).

The two central business lobbies are the BDA (Bundesvereinigung der Deutschen Arbeitgeberverbände) and the BDI (Bundesverband der Deutschen Industrie): 95 percent of all German businesses are part of the BDI, and 80 percent are part of the BDA, and therefore I follow those who argue that "the official statements of these two umbrella organizations can be taken as representative of business" (Ohneis 1990, 70). Although both groups comment on all aspects of policy, the BDA concerns itself more with social policy, while the BDI focuses on economic policy; moreover, in economic policy, the BDI tends to do policy work, while the BDA concentrates on publicizing business views (70, 82). Both groups were founded in the years after the war, with specifically anticommunist motivations.

Ohneis compares the writings of both groups from the 1950s and the 1980s, and concludes that although both groups' tactics shifted in response to the changing political and economic situation, their principal goals did not change. In the years after the war the BDI and BDA opposed the introduction of workers' councils (*Mitbestimmung*), demanded that firms should have autonomy to set wages, and opposed state-imposed social contributions and any state claims on firms' profits (Ohneis 1990, 73). In the late 1980s, the groups began to argue in terms of globalization—that a structural reform was necessary to keep Germany economically competitive with its neighbors—and argued in particular for "debureaucratization" (*Entbürokratisierung*), deregulation, privatization, more flexibility in worktimes, and the reduction of welfare costs (Ohneis 1990, 76, 79–82). Throughout, despite a willingness to compromise with the state and labor, the general principles are clear: "From the state we demand a boost [*Belebung*] of economic growth potential using market economy means, through the encouragement of private investment. . . . We reject all 'socialist political strategies' as for example—state employment policy—'general, artificial reduction of the volume of work through general shortening of work times'—demand-side monetary policy—raising of taxes and expenses" (Ohneis 1990, 75). The general aim has always been to fight for more autonomy of the firm from the state.

In all three domains considered in this book, the two umbrella business-group organizations in Germany have adopted a neoliberal line. In tax policy, early and late, the business groups argue for the minimum tax possible; in 1952 the goal is to encourage capital accumulation by firms, and in 1987 the business groups demand "noticeable relief" of firms from taxation (Ohneis 1990, 85–86). In industrial policy the business groups oppose state intervention in the firm and argue for deregulation, privatization, and so forth (73–82). In social policy, it is clear that business support for the German welfare state in the early postwar years was motivated not by any premonition that it could function to the advantage of business, but by the fear of communism. In 1952 the BDA writes that social policy is "of the greatest political importance" because only through it can "the dangerous collectivist tendencies of our time and the danger of Bolshevik integration" be met (77). Even during this early phase, however, we can see business fears of wage increases leading to inflation and resistance to the idea of workers participating in setting wages (79–80).

In all of the debates in the foundation of the West German welfare state, business organizations originally took the neoliberal line. In 1956 the BDA warned that the universal system of pensions being considered would threaten economic stability and the value of the currency (Schulz 1999, 15). In 1964 the BDA president warned that the property reform the Workers' Wing wanted was "a decisive step toward collectivism" (18). In social policy the BDA objected to the policy of six weeks' sickness pay on the grounds that it would weaken the country's ability to compete internationally (19). However, in many cases they were completely unsuccessful in resisting interventionist policy, and in other cases they were brought to compromise, and did so to resist the possibility of much greater interventionism. For example, in the case of property reform the BDA eventually accepted and even praised the moderate compromise (18–19). Beyond this basic principle of a moderate welfare state aimed at dampening the attractions of communism, business groups did not support the further growth of the welfare state.

When the welfare state began to grow to unprecedented size in the 1960s and 1970s, business groups began to argue for more autonomy for firms and to demand a reform and reduction of the welfare state (Ohneis 1990, 78). Ohneis concludes, "If we compare the general goals of the business groups at the beginning of the fifties and in the second half of the eighties, we find a high degree of congruence. . . . The belief in the market economy, the emphasis on the property and disposition rights of the entrepreneur, and the rejection of state interventions in entrepreneurial rights represent the kernel of the general political economic norms put forward" (88).

The BDA magazine *Der Arbeitgeber* gives a clear picture of the degree to which in the 1980s business was pushing for a neoliberal agenda. I read and coded articles in the magazine from 1982 to 1989 that give an opinion on any issue involving the proper role of the state in the economy and found that, out of a total of 344 articles, the overwhelming majority took a neoliberal stance. From 1982 to 1989, (1) authors oppose every interventionist proposal suggested in the political arena; (2) authors support every neoliberal proposal of Kohl's; indeed, (3) the usual complaint is that Kohl's neoliberalism does not go far enough and that many other neoliberal policies should be adopted; and (4) authors vigorously and colorfully reject interventionist policies and ideology in general. (5) Only thirteen of the 344 articles take a more interventionist stance.[7] The following sections offer evidence in support of these five findings.

AUTHORS OPPOSE INTERVENTIONIST PROPOSALS. Over the course of the decade, the interventionist policies discussed in *Der Arbeitgeber* include work-time reductions, giving unions codetermination power over the introduction of new technology, nursing insurance, profit-sharing, the dismissal protection law, childcare credits, and minimum pensions. The articles find fault with every one of these issues. On the work protection law:

> The BDA and the BDI have rejected the Labor Ministry's proposal for a work protection law as mistaken. (BDA, "Bundesvereinigung und BDI: Warnung vor schädlichen Eingriffen in den Arbeitsschatz," *DA* 34, no. 8 [1982]: 414)

On work-time reduction:

> General reduction of weekly worktime with full pay was and is, we are convinced, no fitting means to hold or secure jobs. (Otto Esser, "Das Gleichgewicht ist empfindlich gestört," *DA* 37, no. 1 [1985]: 10–11)

> Those who would be the losers if a 35-hour-week were introduced with violence are entrepreneurs *and* workers in those industries which do not move in expanding markets . . . If the work, having been made expensive, cannot be made profitable through investments and increased sales, then work must be given up [i.e., jobs must be lost]. (Burkhard Wellmann, "Die Verlierer stehen schon fest," *DA* 36, no. 5 [1984]: 168)

> Lack of expertise has little to do with training readiness, but much with false labor politics. Through the work-time reduction of 1985 a volume of work was destroyed which represents a potential of 52,000 expert workers. Only through work-time flexibility could the appearance of withdrawal in the form of a loss of economic growth be held within bounds. (Rudolf Geer, "Spätschaden falscher Bildungspolitik," *DA* 38, no. 21 [1986]: 836–88)

7. Full citations are not included in the references section for reasons of space, but they are available—along with the sentences from the articles upon which the coding is based—from the author. *Der Arbeitgeber* is cited as *DA* in the text citations.

> Lack of qualified expert labor was already in 1985 threatening to become a production restraint in some economic fields . . . Given this, a discussion about reducing the weekly work time to 35 hours is absolutely out of place. The available expert labor cannot be replaced without problems, so that the "employment argument" of the 35-hour-week-proponents also does not hold. (Jobst R. Hagedorn, "Die Realität in der Bundesrepublik," *DA* 39, no. 10 [1987]: 385–87)

> All in all it is shown that further work-time reduction increases the problems which allegedly should be solved. It costs jobs and leads to work-condensing. It reduces production times, worsens the lack of expert workers and causes more overtime. (Klaus Murmann, "Vernunft zeigen, nicht die Muskeln spielen lassen," *DA* 41, no. 23 [1989]: 884)

> [F]urther work-time reductions would thus mean considerable dangers for the continuation of the course of economic growth and for the stability of the price level. Thus science warns us away from the way of further work-time reductions. This way was, is and remains a dead end. (Elisabeth Neifer-Dichmann, "Der lange Marsch in die Sackgasse," *DA* 41, no. 24 [1989]: 992–93)

Early retirement is criticized from psychological as well as financial angles:

> For many people early retirement is a Danaer-gift, which one immediately happily agrees to, but whose effects only become clear when it is too late, when this decision can no longer be taken back! For many workers, early retirement can become a curse and cause of a reduction of life quality in old age. (Ursula Lehr, "Lebensarbeitszeitverkürzung: Für viele ein Danaer-Geschenk," *DA* 35, no. 2 [1983]: 73–75)

> The general rule must be that whoever, for whatever reason, takes an early retirement must also bear the corresponding insurance deductions. (Bruno Molitor, "Das Elend der Flickschusterei," *DA* 37, nos. 14–15 [1985]: 518–19)

> The solution of the long-term pension problem demands supplementary individual provision next to the social pension. With the new settlement of the left-behind law [*Hinterbliebenenrechts*], the lawgiver contradicts the incentives to self-provision, in that he rewards he who makes himself needy in old age. (Bruno Molitor, "Anleihe beim Versorgungsstaat," *DA* 38, no. 1 [1986]: 19)

On profit-sharing:

> The [profit-sharing] proposal is in direct contradiction to the commitments of the government in the yearly economic report and in the government declaration of last spring. . . . This rule, dreamed up far from all practical requirements, offers only one way of correction: its striking, without replacement. (Volker Leienbach, "Vermögensbildung: Gesetzentwurf mit einigen Kanten," *DA* 35, no. 18 [1983]: 636)

> *Models of participation in success are no replacement for any form of payment for performance.* (Hans-Günter Guski, "Wer Kapital hält, ist besser motiviert," *DA* 36, no. 1 [1984]: 24–25; emphasis in original)

On the extension of codetermination:

> Sole determination instead of co-determination is evidently the maxim of IG Druck & Papier for the coming wage round. For the entrepreneur there is in this system hardly any place; to him falls the task of taking care of business and also of bearing the financial risk of it. (Peter Klemm, "Alleinbestimmung statt Mitbestimmung," *DA* 36, no. 2 [1984]: 74)

On nursing insurance:

> A general nursing insurance is neither economically nor on humanitarian grounds justified—to the contrary! The only consequences of such a solution would be a hardly estimable cost-avalanche, a step on the way in the direction of unifying general insurance embracing all population circles and in the end also all risks, a further step on the road to a provision state, which we cannot afford. (Volker Leienbach, "Experimente wären gefährlich," *DA* 36, no. 18 [1984]: 689–90)

On childcare credits:

> This certainly is justified with respect to the generational contract. However, the wide-reaching financial duties must be considered. (Werner Doetsch, "Rentenpolitik Fragezeichen," *DA* 36, no. 23 [1984]: 944)

> In a free society the grounding of a family is a process which clearly falls in the private sphere, and must therefore be privately financed. (Gerd Habermann, "Schimärische Tochter des Neides?" *DA* 37, no. 6 [1985]: 202–3)

On the capital gains tax:

> Misallocation of capital cannot be stopped through the introduction of a national capital gains tax alone. If the tax does not exist at equal levels in all the financial locations of the world, then it leads through free capital movement to capital flight from where it has been introduced. For this reason, misallocations of capital would be strengthened. (Werner Dichmann, "Kapitalfehlleitungen II: Die Quellensteuer," *DA* 37, no. 1 [1985]: 16–17)

> The Senate has in its decision of 27 Feb. 1985—GS 1/84—stretched the claim of workers to employment even after the [protections provided by the Dismissal Protection Law have run out], and with that created a new employment restraint. (Rosemarie Winterfeld, "Regierungsarbeit konterkariert," *DA* 37, no. 8 [1985]: 286–89)

> The regulation of overtime leads, and this is even the political intention, to a personnel strength which is greater than the optimum. Certainly no one anymore believes that greater costs can strengthen the economic dynamic. (Burkhard Wellmann, "An den Uberstunden scheiden sich die Geister," *DA* 37, nos. 14–15 [1985]: 488)

On the minimum wage:

> State intervention in wage setting through the minimum wage is well-intentioned. It certainly does not better labor market chances. (Heinz Salowsky, "Mindestlöhne sind oft kontraproduktiv," *DA* 40, no. 9 [1988]: 358–59)

On a small tax increase:

> With this tax resulting from the tax reform law of 1990, . . . the boundary of what may be demanded would clearly have been overstepped. (Kurt Kreizberg, "Beitragspflicht für Essenszuschüsse," *DA* 41, no. 6 [1989]: 200–201)

And, summing up:

> Employment programs which after a flickering as of a straw fire leave behind only the ashes of high state deficits, blown up ABM-programs which do not pay attention to the boundaries of seriousness and replace regular jobs with artificially created ones, work-time reductions which go over the measure of

what is tolerable for economic development, state overtime regulations which cannot do justice to the varied demands of the firm's everyday operations: All these anti-market recipes would not only miss their goal of creating permanent jobs, but in the end would cost such jobs. (Josef Siegers, "Jeder Teilerfolg ist wichtig," *DA* 37, no. 17 [1985]: 598)

AUTHORS SUPPORT KOHL'S NEOLIBERAL PROPOSALS. Kohl's neoliberal program is praised again and again. At a conference in 1982 the president of the BDA says,

> I am convinced the course that the [new Kohl] government is striving for in economic, social, and finance politics [that is, a neoliberal course] in its identifiable foundations accords with the demands of our time. (Otto Esser, "Arbeitszeitverkürzungen: Kostentreibend und beschäftigungsunwirksam," *DA* 35, no. 1 [1983]: 4–5)

Others praise the Employment Encouragement Law as

> a bettering of the frame conditions and an encouraging of the economy. (Rosemarie Winterfeld, "Beschäftigungsförderung durch Sozialplanneuregelung," *DA* 36, no. 22 [1984]: 905–7)

And one writes,

> A recently executed expert survey of the Bundesvereinigung der Deutschen Arbeitgeberverbände shows, that the Employment Encouragement Law has proved itself very well in firm practice.... The law has shown that a somewhat greater liberality in labor law regulations and somewhat greater flexibility can lead the participants of the labor market to more employment. With the background of this experience existing regulations and restrictions should be scrutinized once somewhat more carefully. (Jobst R. Hagedorn, "Beschäftigungsförderung: In der Praxis voll bewährt," *DA* 41, no. 9 [1989]: 320–22)

Particularly popular is the attempt to balance the budget:

> The consolidation of the public and the social budget was a necessity. This process must be continued. (Eugen Müller, "Konsolidierungskurs fortsetzen!" *DA* 38, nos. 14–15 [1986]: 575–78)

> The positive signals should not on that account be overlooked. They are demand and confirmation at the same time, to continue the successful economic-political course: economic growth, budget consolidation, lower growth of labor costs are important elements of the strategy, which until now have led to success. (Fritz-Heinz Himmelreich, "Der Geist, der stets verneint!" *DA* 38, nos. 16–17 [1986]: 600)

> The general economic development of 1988 brought on all sides convincingly positive results and the proof that only with a politics of stabilization and consolidation are lasting economic growth- and employment-successes reachable. (Reinhard Ebert, "Angebot und Nachfrage von Arbeit expandieren," *DA* 41, no. 3 [1989]: 80–81)

A contrast with the preceding regime is common:

> Many program statements awaken the impression, as if the negative experiences of the 1970s had never happened.... By continuing with supply-side policies, we can expect more employment through 1986, as well as continual economic growth and price stability. (Elisabeth Neifer, "Weichenstellung," *DA* 38, no. 24 [1986]: 1024)

The tax cuts are quite popular:

> The tax reform of 1990 must already be clearly considered a success considering the dimension of the planned tax cuts. Certainly the reform concept could be criticized because it does not give enough consideration to the international competition of tax systems in the field of specific firm taxes, and that the top tax rate was not to be reduced below the psychologically important boundary of 50 percent. Even so, it is certain that the introduction of a linear-progressive income tax rate and, along with it, the reduction of the maximum tax burden makes the tax system in the long run friendlier to performance and therefore to economic growth... [and] the hard grip of tax progressivity on the greater earnings of professional achievers is made milder. Performance and private initiative will thus in the future again pay more [*wieder mehr lohnen*]. All in all the tax reform is no wonder drug for the bettering of the labor market situation, but it is without doubt a considerable element of an economic policy strategy set up for more employment in the long term. (Thomas Baum, "Wider die 'Rent-Seeking-Society,'" *DA* 39, no. 18 [1987]: 640)

Privatization is praised:

> The privatization increased efficiency and the carrying capacity [*Ertragskraft*] of firms, brought into the tax coffers high sales proceeds, and made wide classes of the population into stockholders. (Hans-Günter Guski, "Kräftige Impulse für die Wirtschaft," *DA* 40, no. 9 [1988]: 353–54)

AUTHORS ENCOURAGE EVEN MORE NEOLIBERAL PROPOSALS. If Kohl's neoliberalism is criticized, it is only for not going far enough in the direction of market reform:

> A bitter aftertaste remains after the passing of the health reform law through the Bundestag and Bundesrat. The "work of the century" health insurance reform is in many ways a law of missed chances and of deceptive hopes.... Incentives for health deliverers and patients to behave more responsibly or rather with more cost-awareness toward... those who pay the contributions are very thinly sown in the reform law. (Volker Hansen and Gert Nachtigal, "Nicht mehr als ein erster Schritt," *DA* 40, no. 24 [1988]: 960–61)

> Under these circumstances the worry is justified whether the correct steps of the employment encouragement law are not too small and too easily hindered to reach the desired effects. (Alfred Wisskirchen, "Signale gegen das Besitzstandsdenken," *DA* 37, no. 10 [1985]: 360)

Neoliberalism is praised in general terms:

> Businesses have again spoken out in the last year for a supply- and stability-oriented politics through the Bundesbank and the government, and at the same time demanded supporting measures for the consolidation of the public budget.... The counter therapy can only be found in the way of a lasting "Deregulation" [word in English] of these conditions: the welfare state must be freed from its mistaken piloting and profiteering. The dynamic powers of the private economy must start anew to open up. (BDA, "Mitgliederversammlung 1982: Aus dem Gesamtüberblick des Jahresberichts," *DA* 35, no. 1 [1983]: 16–25)

The neoliberal policies of other countries are praised:

> Supply-side politics, in that it wants to create more investment and jobs through cost reductions and increase of proceeds, can be seen to have had worldwide

> success: in the USA, in Japan, and also in England. (Fritz-Heinz Himmelreich, "Zwischen Zweckpessimismus und Zukunftoptimismus," *DA* 36, no. 6 [1984]: 208)

> Given the still tense labor market situation, the message of the hour is to free the work-dismissal protection law from employment-restraining regulations and not to create new additional employment restraints. (Dirk Barton, "Weiterbeschäftigung beim Kündigungsstreit?" *DA* 36, no. 6 [1984]: 215)

The justification for progressivity in taxation is questioned:

> Progressivity is in general a premium for laziness and extravagance. . . . Progressivity destroys its tax source (compare Swiftian tax multiplication tables or the course of the "Laffer Curve"); . . . is "legal" theft any less reproachable, because it is dressed in the form of a "law" or a "tax decree"? (Gerd Habermann, "Was gegen die Progressivsteuer spricht," *DA* 37, no. 4 [1985]: 114)

Private pensions are recommended:

> A reorientation in the direction of a legal minimum insurance, supplemented with voluntary private old age provisions, is the best alternative for reducing the tax burden and maintaining the financial balance of public pensions. (Werner Dichmann, "Abgabenzwang und politisches System III," *DA* 37, no. 19 [1985]: 742–44)

In contrast to the early retirement proposals on the table, some fantasize about later retirement:

> Increasing life expectancies and declining birth rates signal the future crisis of the generational contract. A change in the trend of behavior would bring relief: later retirement. (Volker Hansen, "Länger zu arbeiten muß sich wieder lohnen," *DA* 39, no. 5 [1987]: 173)

> The extension of total lifetime work time is unavoidable over the long term. Easing the transition into retirement and . . . penalties for early pension-income would be helpful and sensible. (Ulrich Schüle, "Verlängerung der Erwerbsphase?" *DA* 39, nos. 13–14 [1987]: 514–16)

Additional tax reductions are suggested:

Without a lasting tax relief for firms, the reform policy would not only remain stuck half way; the competitive conditions for the "investment location West Germany" [Standort Deutschland] would even be worsened, because our neighbors and competitors have already drastically reduced their tax rates. (Klaus Murmann, "Es fehlt an Flexibilität und Investitionen," *DA* 40, no. 1 [1988]: 10–11)

Other areas are mentioned where neoliberalism beyond the degree attempted by Kohl should be implemented:

The need for a specific firm tax reform, which truly earns its name, results from the still multiple, grave, unsolved problems in this important field. Even after 1990—that is, after the conclusion of the "Great Tax Reform"—

- firm profits, the riskiest source of income, will still be taxed higher than all other types of income;
- [because of the incentives of the tax system] resources and economic activities will still be misdirected, for example, from capital accumulation into consumption, from self-financing to financing from other sources, from real capital into finance capital, and, finally, in not inconsiderable amounts, from the official economy into the shadow economy;
- international competitiveness will still not be improved, while other industrial countries, often starting from a lower tax burden level, have reduced their taxes with more courage than is the case in West Germany.

(Winfried Fuest, "Dringender Handlungsbedarf," *DA* 41, no. 10 [1989]: 360–63)

Labor laws regulating weekend and holiday work are criticized:

Regrettably the labor law in operation forces firms in view of Sunday and holiday work into a Procrustean bed of rigid and inflexible regulations, which in the end function to the detriment of all participants. (Ronald Hönsch and Ulrich Siebenmorgen, "Maschinenlaufzeiten verzerren den Wettbewerb," *DA* 40, no. 2 [1988]: 50–51)

Complaints about the comparatively short German work week are a regular feature, as are paeans to flexibility:

West Germany is again the country with the shortest work time. . . . Further, in comparison to other important rival countries, the less flexible work times prove themselves to be a clear competitive disadvantage for the German economy in increasing measure. (Alexandra-Friederike Prinzessin zu Schoenaich-Carolath, "Nicht kürzer arbeiten, sondern flexibler," *DA* 41, no. 4 [1989]: 116–19)

If, despite some employment success, there has until now been no clear breakthrough in the dismantling of unemployment, it is because firms' needs for flexibility have remained unsatisfied. (Jürgen Husmann, "Stimmungsumschwung ersetzt nicht Wachstumsdynamik," *DA* 40, no. 10 [1988]: 368)

Limited work contracts are urged:

When lasting jobs are absent, it should at least be possible to sign a limited work contract with the worker immediately following his professional training . . . a lengthening of limited contract opportunity [Befristungsmöglichkeit] from the year 1990 forward appears urgently needed. (Ronald Hönsch, "Tarifvorrang für Befristungen," *DA* 40, no. 10 [1988]: 376–77)

Easier dismissal is commended:

It must always be possible to terminate the work relationship without insurmountable difficulties, if its continuing duration no longer appears bearable under the consideration of reasonable grounds. (Ronald Hönsch, "Akute Handlungsbedarf wegen Rechtsunsicherheit," *DA* 41, no. 6 [1989]: 203–4)

Even Sunday is entertained as a potential day of work:

It should once again be considered, whether the securing of jobs which would be made possible by working on Sundays should not also be valued as a "service to humanity" [Dienst am Menschen]. (Holger Eisold, "Ausnahmeregelung nicht mehr zeitgemäß," *DA* 41, no. 20 [1989]: 718–23)

AUTHORS STRONGLY REJECT INTERVENTIONIST IDEOLOGY IN GENERAL. In addition to these comments on specific policy proposals, the authors of the articles in *Der Arbeitgeber* sustain a lively anti-interventionist ideology and rhetoric that is completely familiar to anyone who has read American or British neoliberal rhetoric in content but is expressed in its own creative flights of invention:

[People who live off of unemployment money] understand how to trick the social net created for the truly needy and misuse the state as a Heinzelmann [one of the tiny creatures in the fairy tale who come out at night and do all the work].... In a land, in which the state through its tax and social laws punishes achievement and rewards doing nothing, we should not be surprised about lack of a willingness to achieve. (Gerhart Klamert, "Leistungsverweigerer: Arbeiten oder nicht arbeiten—das ist hier die Frage," *DA* 34, no. 5 [1982]: 202)

In the years of lavishness the high art of party-political Machiavellianism consisted in laying social-political gifts on the table for voters, which a third party paid for—the anonymous collective of taxpayers and contributors—at the cost of future generations. (Burkhard Wellmann, "Neue Rentenlasten auf die Häupter der jungen Generation?" *DA* 36, nos. 15–16 [1984]: 568)

If one tries to heal the economic patient with the help of expansive money and tax policy, either the patient becomes addicted, the economic growth programs become more and more extensive, or the whole situation of the patient worsens when one takes the drug away. (Siegfried Utzig, "Wider die aufkeimende Urgeduld," *DA* 39, no. 6 [1987]: 207–8)

The road to Leviathan leads not only through the theory of absolute evil, but also of absolute good in humans. (Arno Krüger, "Freiheit und Ordnung—der verkannte Rechtsstaat—" DA 39, no. 7 [1987]: 240)

Then the health system remains a milk machine, which in the end loses the cow. (Klaus Murmann, "Selbstbeteiligung kein Tabu," *DA* 39, no. 20 [1987]: 740)

[State provision means that individuals are not responsible for each other;] but to bear social burdens gives life meaning, founds community, strengthens the sociality of the person;... the individual cannot be freed of any more social duty and responsibility if society is not to collapse. (Burkhard Wellmann, "Der 'Kapitalismus ohne Klassen' macht den Sozialdemokraten zu schaffen," *DA* 40, nos. 13–14 [1988]: 488)

If, in the end, the one who is most highly valued is not the worthy pioneer, but the most resourceful and unscrupulous cadger, then one must not be surprised that the proportion of cadgers in the economy becomes greater and the proportion of pioneers smaller. (Siegfried Utzig, "Utopie und Wirklichkeit—eine Bestandsaufnahme," *DA* 40, no. 18 [1988]: 636–37)

What was over centuries self-evident seems today to have become a rare good: the community sense of the citizen, the personal responsibility for the well and ill of fellow humans, the way in which property creates a society [*die Sozialbildung des Eigentums*]. (Peter-Claus Burens, "Auch im Sozialstaat sind Stiftungen von Nutzen," *DA* 41, no. 21 [1989]: 814–16)

[Without economic growth, social provision is not possible]: when in the end the economy remains a ruin, noting that we have, however, provided ourselves with a highly modern heating system will bring little political relief. (Rolf Thüsing, "Zum Sinn und Unsinn der 'Sozialen Dimension,'" *DA* 41, no. 24 [1989]: 956)

Perhaps the peak of creativity is a contribution in 1984 that retells the postwar history of Germany as a fairy tale of a land that was hit with "bad weather" but went on to become prosperous through hard work. Later it adopted policies of work-time reduction when hit by a "bad harvest":

A general worktime reduction in country and state reduced the general production of goods and with that a reduction of demand immediately followed a reduction of supply. . . . Most [firms] however already had difficulties finding buyers for the manufactured goods, and they held on to the old numbers of laborers and journeymen. . . . Later good and bad harvests alternated. But because during each bad harvest the work time was further reduced, the people became more and more poor and they quarreled with their destiny. (Ernst Heaß, "Das Märchen von Schlaraffenland," *DA* 36, no. 7 [1984]: 272–73)

ONLY THIRTEEN ARTICLES TAKE AN INTERVENTIONIST STANCE. Finally, although the neoliberal line is clearly dominant, thirteen of the articles do not follow it. Five of these (the largest number on any single issue) defend the principle that unions and employers, rather than the state, should together determine wages. This is in one sense an antistate message, but it is also the kind of "coordinated capitalism" position that the scholars of the varieties of capitalism school think is rampant in German political economy, because the status quo is defended against firms individually deciding wages for themselves (the American, or "liberal capital" model).

The wage contract must keep its general order function also in the future. For firms it provides predictability over time. A fragmentation of existing wage structures into branch and firm regulations would lead to an atomization of wage politics. This would considerably disturb social peace and in the end benefit no one. (Peter Knevels, "Atomisierung der Tarifpolitik," *DA* 37, no. 9 [1985]: 316)

A reporter sums up the conclusion of a colloquium on the issue as follows:

> A realistic alternative to wage autonomy was not recognizable at the colloquium. (Arno Krüger, "Die Zukunft der sozialen Partnerschaft," *DA* 37, no. 9 [1985]: 324–25)

A common argument is that defense of this coordinated manner of wage-setting represents the best alternative to wage-setting initiated by the state:

> The question, whether in the institution of wage autonomy itself lie the causes for the persistent high unemployment, has been popping up with a certain regularity in public discussion for some time. . . . The more responsibility for employment politics is shifted from the wage parties to the state, the less must the [firms and unions] show consideration for the political consequences of their negotiation, with the result that we would have not more moderate but probably more militant unions. (Elisabeth Neifer, " 'Arbeitskartelle' und Beschäftigungskrise," *DA* 38, no. 13 [1986]: 552–53)

> If wage autonomy were given up or were to fail, in the end only state regulation would remain. (Otto Esser, "Das Gleichgewicht ist empfindlich gestört," *DA* 37, no. 1 [1985]: 10–11)

But another author specifically defends the *high* wages that these circumstances produce:

> Wage autonomy is the indispensable foundation of our peaceful social order. . . . Reduced wages mean, from the perspective of the economy, loss of buying power . . . It makes no sense to fight for competitive advantage in a cost-reducing spiral. The European steel industry or the U.S. airlines demonstrate the short-term logic of the politics of price reductions. The German car industry on the other hand is an example of the right strategy. A tremendous wave of investment has not only made automobile workers' wages competitive, it also has had a considerable role in the slender economic growth. . . . The moral of the story: to reduce (firm) costs, we must not reduce wages, but must make wages profitable through investment and innovation. (Burkhard Wellmann, "Der Deflationsbazillus schwächt die Wirtschaft," *DA* 35, no. 24 [1983]: 976)

Clearly this is exactly the logic that the scholars of the varieties of capitalism school expect to find from German employers. Just as clearly, the principle of coordinated wage-setting between industrywide unions and employers is the *only* issue on which such a clear, non-neoliberal position is found in the pages of *Der Arbeitgeber.*

A few other issues receive an occasional treatment contrary to the dominant neoliberal trend. One author defends the idea of full employment:

> Who thinks of full employment has [allegedly] not understood the reality of the time, is [allegedly] an illusionist without hope.... The state must see to it that the unsocial is kept out. Please, can anyone imagine anything more unsocial than mass unemployment? (Horst Friedrich Wünsche, "Rationalisierungsfurcht ist ein schlechter Ratgeber," *DA* 36, no. 1 [1984]: 30–31)

Another writer, while in favor of part-time work, warns that businesses are having a hard time introducing it:

> Above all, middle management advises against the introduction of part-time work. If, however, we succeed in convincing business leaders and management, the advantages will justify the expense. (Günter Bierig, "Teilzeitarbeit—wie führt man sie ein?" *DA* 36, no. 5 [1984]: 194–95)

One defends early retirement:

> Early retirement is not a flop. The numbers climb. And in any case early retirement has an effect on employment by avoiding firings as well as by the hiring of an unemployed person. (Heinz-Dieter Sauer, "Erfolgreicher als vielfach angenommen," *DA* 37, no. 21 [1985]: 800–801)

One defends profit-sharing:

> The duration of our economic order, based on private property, which is at the same time a pillar of our free social order, can only be durably secured if more citizens own property and if access to capital in the economy is made easier for continually more citizens. (Renate Hornung-Draus, "Vermögenspolitik in der Marktwirtschaft," *DA* 38, no. 24 [1986]: 1034–35)

One defends the introduction of new technology as an environmental protection measure:

> The mismanagement of the last decades certainly includes [the fact] that we have increased work productivity too much at the cost of the environment, which is

> unincreasable, and too little at the cost of technology, which is increasable. (Gerhard Fels, "Neue Wachstumsmuster erfordern neue Verteilungsmuster," *DA* 41, no. 22 [1989]: 828)

One author, in the middle of a thoroughly neoliberal defense of tax cuts, comments:

> On the other hand it is clear that, on grounds of justice, the tax according to financial ability to pay cannot be completely left out of consideration. (Jürgen Hasmann, "Steuerreform—Leistungsanreiz und Wachstumsfaktor," *DA* 39, no. 22 [1987]: 856)

There is what is billed as a "scientific controversy"—two articles taking opposing stances on whether Germany should follow the American model of employment. One praises the minimal regulations, and the other argues that

> for Germany, with its strong export dependency, the U.S. employment system is hardly a model worth imitating. For [Germany] competitiveness is tied to product quality, high qualification of the workforce, higher productivity, and co-operative industrial relations. (Werner Sengenberger, "US-Arbeitsmarkt—kein Vorbild für uns! [wissenschaftlich Kontrovers]," *DA* 36, no. 19 [1984]: 735–36)

And, finally, one author displays the following even-handedness:

> Already eight years ago, 1975, Günter Schmölder, citing v. Hayek with agreement, had called attention to the fact that Keynesian politics interprets the economy completely falsely. . . . Now it would be a decline into the illusions of a vulgar paleo-liberalism, if we wanted to remove social problems like unemployment and state deficits from the world only through individual incentive systems. . . . To look for the solution of the labor market problem in the industrial sector and with that to expect a growth in material goods, means to miss the solution. (Burkhard Wellmann, "Wachstum in der Rationalitätenfalle," *DA* 35, no. 20 [1983]: 732)

The dominant trend of these articles is clearly neoliberal. We see the rise of "capital flight" arguments at the end of the 1980s, but even before this, there is a vigorous indigenous resistance to interventionism. The fierce resistance to work-time reductions is clear, as is the general support for the neoliberal measures of Kohl.

How are we to square this evidence of business resistance to interventionist policy with Mares's argument (2001, 2003) that some German employers, particularly small and medium-sized firms, have welcomed interventionist policy? We might wonder first if employers behave differently in the policy sphere than we would predict from the overwhelming neoliberal tenor of these statements—they may not practice what they preach. But all the evidence shows that employers *did* resist work-time reductions and did support the Kohl policies. As discussed above, when invited to health care reform talks, they pushed for cuts in health care costs. There was disunity on the deregulation of shopping hours, but in labor market deregulation and tax cuts the neoliberal measures were brought to the table by the traditional defenders of business, the FDP and the business wing of the CDU. The only exceptions are in labor relations, where the respect for the coordinated model of wage setting leads employers to back down in the face of strikes (see Thelen 1999)—but in fact this matches the rhetoric found in the magazine, which is more tolerant of coordinated wage setting than other non-neoliberal policies and even interprets this as a means of resisting further state intervention. The preference for coordination in labor relations appears to be an exception to the general neoliberal trend of employer sentiment. Because the varieties of capitalism school grows out of a close engagement with the literature on labor relations, it may have generalized this exception into an argument about the entire political-economic structure. Of course, labor relations are a central element in political economy, but its effects do not extend to the areas examined here—tax cuts, deregulation and privatization, and welfare state policy. In all three of these areas, employers clearly supported the neoliberal agenda of Kohl and wanted it to go even further than it did.

The one thing missing from the litany of complaints in *Der Arbeitgeber* is complaint about environmental regulations, the center of the American critique. This may at first seem to vindicate the varieties of capitalism argument, which would predict a business class much more opposed to environmental regulations in the United States than in Germany. But, as discussed above, at this point environmental regulations remained less adversarial in Germany than in the United States, and while in the 1970s the United States had already established an Environmental Protection Agency, in Germany businesses had a strong influence on the way they were regulated. Thus, the absence of complaints from business about environmental regulation does not mean that businesses accepted the need for heavy state intervention in this realm; rather, it indicates that such intervention was nowhere near as onerous for businesses in Germany as it was for their American counterparts.

Another possible reconciliation of the evidence given here with the arguments of the varieties of capitalism school suggests itself from a paragraph in Mares's work:

> Employers were not "agenda setters." They were not responsible for introducing a social policy proposal on the broad agenda of reform (the one exception is the case of disability insurance reform in Germany in the 1880s). The impetus for reforms came from bureaucratic or elected politicians or, in some cases, from the courts. But employers' representatives were involved in the broad political negotiations of social insurance legislation and influenced the minute details of policy design of the legislation that was, ultimately, adopted. (2003, 259)

What Mares and others in this tradition often show is that employers were *involved in* the shape of the legislation. But, as Hacker and Pierson write, evidence of involvement and even evidence of *support* of specific welfare state proposals from business cannot by itself lead us to conclude that "business favors the welfare state," because this support might in fact be acquiescence to an inevitability: "All political participants are in a position to calculate (with at least some degree of accuracy) the reactions of other actors. Given this capacity, a group's actions often will not reveal its preferences but rather its strategic calculations of what is the best that can be accomplished given existing circumstances" (2002, 283).

Indeed, in the German case, we should view much of the postwar expansion of the welfare state as an attempt to ward off the threat of greater state intervention—an ever-present possibility for the newly divided Germany, next door to the Communist block—rather than an embrace of state intervention for itself. The timing of employer support for various elements of postwar political economy supports this conclusion. When codetermination was introduced, for example, employers opposed it but eventually came to accept it. Similarly, employers have resisted all attempts to extend the welfare state until these attempts succeed, at which time employers accept them. They resign themselves to what is possible and come to express this as their preference. By coding employers' preferences out of context, only as favoring or opposing particular political economic principles, the varieties of capitalism thesis neglects to ask what alternatives the employers were reacting to.

While one counterinstance cannot disprove the whole varieties of capitalism thesis, the story examined here is a *crucial* counterinstance: Germany is the paradigmatic "coordinated" economy, and the Kohl era was the key period when neoliberal change might have been expected. If employers in the paradigmatic coordinated economy did favor neoliberalism at the moment when it was most likely, we need to rethink our understanding of what preserves the distinct "varieties of capitalism." I attempt to provide below an alternative to the economic determinism of the varieties of capitalism explanation.

If resistance did not come from national culture, from the various constitutional veto points in the policymaking structure, or from employers, where did it come from? As the preceding stories have shown, one factor was that in some domains West German policies were more favorable to business than those in the United States or Britain. Lower taxes as a percentage of total revenue on capital and income, and self-policing by business in environmental regulations are the most striking examples. However, unlike France, the West German state did include some quite adversarial policies, such as the Dismissal Protection Law, and income taxes were higher than in France. Consequently in the 1970s and 1980s a coherent neoliberal movement did form and did enter politics, through the FDP. When Kohl took office various neoliberal measures were proposed, and the most consistent resistance to them came from within the CDU itself, especially from the Workers' Wing. I turn finally to an analysis of that situation in the next section.

The Integration of Labor and the Structure of Previous Policies

The theories above do not fit the empirical evidence of the case studies of reform attempts in the 1980s. Instead, I suggest that two variables can explain both the rise of moderate change, and the lack of extensive change, in neoliberal directions during the Kohl period from 1982 to 1989: the integration of labor within the decision-making structure, particularly within the right wing of the party, and the moderately pro-growth structure of the political economy. Many of the postwar policies were favorable to business. In areas where policies were not so favorable to business, the important factor was resistance from the Workers' Wing.

Integration of Labor: The Workers' Wing and Norbert Blüm

In all three policy domains—taxation, deregulation, and welfare state policy—one of the key sources of resistance was the Workers' Wing. How did the Workers' Wing come to have such power? And why does the CDU have a Workers' Wing at all if the SPD has no comparably institutionalized "Business Wing"? These questions lead us to the heart of the organizational differences between the two parties and the effects these structural differences have on policymaking style and policymaking capacity.

The history of the CDU begins at Stunde Null, "Zero Hour," the traumatic moment at the end of the war when the devastated country found itself having to create a party system from scratch. To achieve a base of power in a democratic country requires a loyal electoral and financial base, and the most stable of these are rooted in existing social cleavages. After the war the SPD had already begun to transform the growing proletariat into a stable base of this sort. But unlike Britain, where an entrenched aristocracy anchored the beginnings of the Tory party, and the United States, where industrial business interests arrayed themselves in the Republican party in opposition to the farming interests of the Democratic party, West Germany had no such broad middle- or upper-class social cleavage upon which to found a base of power to oppose the Social Democrats. Even before the war, German nonproletarian society was fragmented along economic and regional lines: large estate owners, farmers, and industrialists found little in common, and the strength of Bavarian regional identity led Bavarian farmers (for example) to found their own farmers' party separate from the national farmers' party. Protestants had their own parties, and Catholics had organized into the large Zentrum Party. Many of these parties, including the Zentrum, came to an end when they voluntarily gave up power to Hitler in 1933. Thus, when Hitler was defeated, the political party situation was a patchwork of diverse interests that had arrayed themselves in opposition to each other before the war and had destroyed their own party organizations during the Nazi period. The outlook for a party built on a stable social cleavage was not good. The one stable social cleavage that had remained intact was that of class, but the working class was already being organized by the SPD. The CDU found its opportunity precisely in this lack of clear definition: it became a "catch-all" party, loosely organized around an emphasis on general Christian principles and devoted to developing a program to the right of the SPD (Kaff 1991; Kleinmann 1993; Zohlnhöfer 2001a; Lösche 1994).

In 1945 Christian Democratic Party groupings around the country, mainly at Berlin, Köln, Frankfurt, and Munich, agreed on the following program:

- Christian values as the ground principles of political interaction
- Joint party-political work of Christians of both confessions
- Renewal of Western Christian thought and Christian morality as defense against dictatorship and totalitarian ideologies
- Democracy, rule of law, and federalism
- Freedom and self-responsibility of the individual
- Social justice, equalization between businesspeople and workers, free education for all
- Building a Christian party capable of attaining a majority for the effort of a "storming of the center" and to prevent the splitting of the party, as in the Weimar Republic
- Collection of all party-political groups outside of the social-communist camp (Kaff 1991, ix)

Note that the elements of this program do not clearly come down on one side or the other of the divide between the emphasis on Christian *responsibility*—which would support market-friendly measures—and the emphasis on Christian *solidarity*, which would support more social interventionist measures. But the program was remarkably successful: this party concocted out of the air managed to get up to 38 percent of the votes in local elections in 1946 and 1950.

Thus, since its origin, the CDU has been a coalition of coalitions. From the beginning, the CDU has been not one party, but many—as emphasized in its very name. It is essentially a group of parties from the states, many of which have quite divergent views, and each party is made up of groups that exhibit not only geographical but also professional and religious differences. The Bavarian CSU, which has been the CDU's coalition partner for so long that it is hard to imagine the two not being in coalition together, nevertheless has its own organization, leadership structure, and programmatic preferences. The coalition was held together by the cohesive effects of the economic success led by the CDU. But remarkably, until the arrival of Helmut Kohl on the scene, there was essentially no national organization. By the time Kohl got to work building such an organization, several crucial features of the party had already been institutionalized: its heterogeneity, its voting procedures, and its allocation of tasks to particular factions (Clemens 1998; Huneeus 1996; Pulzer 1999; Saalfeld 1999).

As a party based on a religious cleavage, the CDU attracted many working-class voters: approximately one-third of the working class voted for the CDU/CSU in the postwar period. Much of this support came from workers who were repelled by the SPD's opposition to religion (*Kirchenfeindlichkeit*; interview, Irmgard Blättel, 10 Jun 2004), which weakened only after the Bad Godesberg reforms of 1969. Support from working-class voters for the right-wing party would not in itself be particularly unusual (after all, a similar religious cleavage brings working-class voters into the Republican Party in the United States). But the CDU borrowed from the old Zentrum Party a remarkable principle, by which "factions are . . . integrated in the inner party decision-making process. Decisions . . . are usually taken unanimously, so every faction possesses a veto. Therefore, consensus and proportional representation are the prevailing patterns of decision making in the CDU. . . . This gives those groups inside the party favouring the *status quo* a good opportunity to prevent reforms they dislike or at least to dilute them" (Zohlnhöfer 1999, 153–54). This "proportional" principle of sharing out decision-making power was seen as the only way to make such a diverse party cohere because after 1945 conservatism had been discredited, and after the war there was "an anti-militarist and anti-capitalist consensus, which was directed against conservatism" (Kleinmann 1993, 113). The resulting power-sharing system "evidences a reigning frame of proportion and concordance, while the principle of majority rule was practically given up" (Zohlnhöfer 2001b, 661). Because the CDU took decisions unanimously, reform was easily blocked.

The innovation of sharing power in this way within a party—a stark difference from the more centralized and hierarchical SPD—goes back to the nineteenth century, when the Catholic Zentrum Party took the idea of proportional representation, which usually applies to the representation of parties in parliament, into the structure of the party itself.

> In political Catholicism a model of direct representation was developed [that held that] for effective representation of interests, programmatic or ideological commonality between representative and constituent alone were not enough. Identity of living conditions [*lebensweltliche Identität*] between the electors and the elected was demanded. By that was meant, in the Catholic milieu, not only and not first of all local or regional ties, but rather the same professional and work

> experiences. Workers, artisans, farmers, owners wanted to be represented not by a bourgeois Parliament, lawyers, or clergy, but by workers, artisans, farmers, and owners. (Kühne 1995, 231)

Although the Zentrum Party itself did not survive the war, this idea of proportional representation, extended as an operating procedure of sharing duties between different factions, proved to be the only way that the CDU could integrate its own widely divergent electoral base.

The history of the Workers' Wing, the faction within the party's organizational structure founded to represent the workers, is thus at the center of the history of the CDU: "Former Christian trade unionists, who were organized among themselves, belonged almost everywhere to the base troops of the grounders [of the party]. The Christian Workers had impressed themselves as no other group in the union on the founding of the party, and authoritatively contributed to the fact that the CDU organizationally and programmatically quickly came to its feet" (Kleinmann 1993, 97). Between 1945 and 1946, Social Committees were set up in Köln, Düsseldorf in the Rhineland, Hannover, Braunschweig, and Oldenburg in Lower Saxony, and in Herne in Westphalia. The strength of the Social Committees, as well as of the Junge Union and the Women's Workers' Circle, necessitated a pragmatic politics: "The federative structure of the Union, in which different state developments grew together and heterogeneous interests came together, made practical politics possible only with great concentration. The commonality of the union was made, apart from its Christian fundamental values, in significant part in its pragmatic connection to reality" (Kleinmann 1993, 111).

In the early years, the sense of a common union identity was forged above all in the Economic Advisory Council (Wirtschaftsrat), which was the only place where representatives for all the different Land parties as well as from the different interest groupings came together. Descriptions of the Union's diversity, however, characterized the histories of the party's first decades. The greatest unity within the party is seen in the buildup to an election, when divisions within the party become dormant. In 1981, for example, a dispute between Kohl and the general secretary of the party that had broken into open conflict in the middle of the 1970s was quickly smoothed so as not to endanger the electoral chances. One observer comments,

> What a tremendous achievement the CDU's integration is can be appreciated in international comparison: In no other land has an attempt to bind so many

> different kinds and many-sided segments and currents with one another in one party for a long time been successful, not in France by the Gaullists or in Great Britain by the Conservatives (despite the much lower threshold there for reaching a majority franchise). The CDU is fascinating for party researchers not only because it became a conservative party, but also because it has always had a more or less influential left wing. (Lösche 1994, 113)

The Workers' Wing has always considered itself the "social conscience" of the CDU and is always disagreeing, on grounds of religious principle, with one aspect or another of the party's policy. In the late 1970s and early 1980s, in addition to its role in the episodes considered above, the Social Committee also took the SPD's side against lockouts of striking workers, criticized the market-oriented nature of the Union's energy policy, contradicted the Union's stance on immigration by arguing that Germany should be an immigrant country, argued for public housing while the CDU wanted market housing, and opposed one of its own partners—working women within the CDU—with its stance that "more mother-ness" (*mehr Mütterlichkeit*) was to be encouraged (Kleinmann 1993; Lösche 1994; Glotz 1989; Lenk 1989).

One particular advantage of the position of the Workers' Wing within the coalition is the ability to *coordinate dissent*. It works with a shifting coalition of partners:

> The [Workers' Wing] always had various partners. For example within the coalition the CSU was always a partner when the question was about strengthening family rights. And also in the question of long-term care later. And the FDP was a partner, when the question was about improving immigrants' rights. . . . And then it was fundamentally very important that in the foreground of political work we have a wide spectrum of opinion with the churches, with the unions, and the social groups. . . . When we build an axis with the churches and the unions and the social groups together, then the Union too has to listen to it, . . . so we are certainly a minority within the Union, in numerical terms, but a creator of majorities [*Mehrheitsbeschaffer*] for the Union, through our axes with the churches, with the unions, with the social groups. (interview, Uwe Schummer, 7 Jun 2004; see also Gundelach 1983)

One source of the differences between the American and German cases, therefore, is the *institutionalization* of working-class interests inside the CDU. This means that no matter which party is in power, representatives of the working class will be protecting working-class interests in the government. More important, these factions are not randomly distributed among the structures of power; rather, particular factions control particular policy domains:

> Employment and labor market policy were given to the CDU's Social Committees, . . . which also controlled the responsible Labor Ministry and were overproportionally present in the Bundestag Committee for Labor and Social Order. . . . For [labor and employment policy], that implies that only moderate reforms were to be expected, because the CDU Social Committee was the group in the coalition who were most skeptical of incisive reforms. (Zohlnhöfer 2001b, 661)

Obviously, if policymaking that affects workers is placed in the hands of those most committed to representing the workers, we should not expect great strides toward neoliberalism. The role of the Workers' Wing—both its ability to resist policies suggested elsewhere within the party and its control over policymaking in areas that disproportionately affect workers—is thus one main reason for lack of neoliberal change under Kohl.

In addition, the main difference from the situation in Britain that this structure of decision-making produces is that despite the lower union density in Germany than Britain, German unions did not need to resort to strikes to preserve their interests because the working class was represented in the CDU (see figure 9B in the introduction). Consequently, the temporary extreme unpopularity of unions among voters caused by strikes in Britain, which underpinned the radicalization of the Conservative party, did not arise in Germany. The historical legacy of divided decision making within the CDU not only directly preserved the status quo but also indirectly prevented the rise of electoral dissatisfaction with the political-economic structure, so that the neoliberal reforms coming onto the agenda because of the decentralized state structure could not be anchored in electoral politics.

Nevertheless, even if the Workers' Wing has a reliable veto, what has kept its agreement from being "purchased"? A comparison with the dynamics of the U.S. and British cases is fruitful in answering this question.

The Structure of Previous Policies

In the United States, neoliberal policies were brought onto the agenda by a tax revolt that led entrepreneurial politicians to sense the potential of the issue of income tax cuts; deregulation was pushed by business lobbies and implemented by the executive branch, using the consumers' movement as a smokescreen; and welfare reform generated political capital, but politicians censored themselves from cutting middle-class entitlements. In Britain, labor militancy brought down successive governments and eventually radicalized the Conservative party. When it was in power, this party implemented a redistribution of the tax burden downward, privatization, and council house sales.

The origins of all of these events are in adversarial policies. In the United States these involved the more progressive tax structure, the adversarial social regulations, and the targeted welfare state; in Britain, they concerned the excluded and militant labor unions, who had been able to turn the policy of nationalization to their advantage, and policies of progressive taxation and redistributive welfare states implemented by frequent Labour governments. But in West Germany, as we have seen, labor was included in the decision-making structure and much less militant, so the popular dissatisfaction with labor militancy seen in Britain was therefore unlikely. And the tax and welfare structures were largely pro-growth rather than adversarial, generating the greatest amount of revenue from targeted payroll taxes, which dampened resistance. Environmental regulation, too, at least until the 1980s, was nonadversarial, in that there was a strong element of self-regulation.

However, unlike France, Germany had several policies that were clearly adversarial, and others that contained adversarial elements: shopping hours and labor market regulations made adversaries of business and labor; welfare policies, according to some scholars, did redistribute toward the poor (although they were not targeted); and income tax rates were high. The main element preventing neoliberalism in the 1980s, then, was the role of the Workers' Wing; but to understand why the Workers' Wing could not be bought off or engaged in the kind of competitive neoliberal process seen in the American case, we must examine the specific *shape* of the policies. First, the Workers' Wing could not be engaged in the competitive tax reduction seen in the American case, because of the link between taxation and spending. Second, the Workers' Wing could not be bought off in labor market and shopping hours deregulation because these were discrete policies: unlike the competitive tax reduction in the United States, these policies did not allow a dynamic of purchasing support from veto players by adding a specific amendment for each opponent. Finally, the Workers' Wing could not be bought off in welfare state policy because *it controlled* welfare state policy itself, and the absence of targeted policies meant that politicians did not sense political capital to be made from welfare cuts. The link between taxation and spending and the control of the Workers' Wing over welfare policy are both examples of the political concertation of the postwar period: unlike the American states, which competed against each other, German states bargained collectively with the federal government; and unlike in the United States, where checks and balances were instituted with the intent of *fragmenting power*, in Germany the veto points within the CDU were a by-product of the attempt to *generate power* by forming a coalition in an already fragmented society, which required the odd feature of placing control over welfare state policy in the hands of those most committed to the welfare state.

Conclusion

I have shown in this chapter that although many free market reforms were suggested and attempted under Kohl, very few were implemented.

The CDU itself, as a catch-all party without a strong hierarchy or national organization at this time, was not the source of the free-market innovations; rather, most of them came from the FDP. Following an electoral loss in a provincial election, the FDP decided that raising its "free market profile" would be its way back into power. The party was so convinced of this that it left the coalition with the SPD, fearing that its liberal economic profile was becoming blurred. This is exactly the kind of political innovation, especially with regard to tax cuts, that we also saw in the United States and Britain—it is a remarkable parallel to the way in which a political campaign in the U.S. provinces brought the idea to center stage, and a small-scale version of the way in which electoral losses led to a rethinking and reorientation in the British Conservative party.

The main source of resistance to these proposals was not Germany's antimarket national culture, the checks and balances instituted in the constitution, or employers who found the status quo beneficial. There was a strong pro-market strain in postwar culture, many of the "veto points" had converged on neoliberalism, and employers were in most cases pushing for more neoliberalism. The most important resistance to neoliberal change came from the left of the CDU itself. Because the Workers' Wing was in charge of labor and social policy, it did not itself propose a great deal of neoliberalism, and it could easily block attempts at reform proposed by the FDP. The Workers' Wing is not the only source of resistance—the *Länder* governments occasionally resisted the federal government's proposals—but it is the most consistent and most institutionally strong one. Its institutional position gives it the ability to coordinate and speak on behalf of those who oppose a proposed policy change, such as the medium-sized firms who opposed the liberalization of shopping hours.

However, we saw in the U.S. case that veto points are not decisive. Many sources of resistance to change existed in the American case, but they were either overcome or circumvented in tax and regulatory policy. In tax policy, representatives were bought off by side payments of tax cuts that benefited their particular constituencies. In environmental deregulation, the administration could avoid the checks and balances of the political system because environmental protection was centralized in the executive branch. The veto points could not be overcome in welfare state policy, and thus the main elements of the welfare system did not change, although the targeted portions of the welfare state had no protectors and were scaled back.

In Germany, the coupling of tax collection to revenue dispersal prevented the free riding seen in the American case. The business-appeasing nature of environmental deregulation directed the neoliberal effort down other channels, and shopping hours and labor market deregulation—which might have seen change—could not offer tactical space to overcome the opposition of the Workers' Wing. In welfare policy, the outcome regarding the main elements of the welfare state were similar (lack of rollback) in both countries, while the absence of policies targeting the poor and the historical circumstances that had placed control of welfare policy in the hands of those most committed to the welfare state prevented the minor rollbacks seen in the U.S. case.

One implication of this analysis is that the German resistance to neoliberalism is much more fragile than we had imagined. If it depends to a significant extent on the ability of the Workers' Wing to lead and coordinate dissent in tax and industrial policy, and to control welfare policy, then that resistance is only as strong as the Workers' Wing. But the Workers' Wing was losing absolute membership even before reunification, and after reunification it also lost proportionate strength: business interests in the East joined the CDU, while workers in the East joined the SPD. Lacking the religious basis that has been the foundation for the Workers' Wing, the CDU did not attract workers in the East. This led to a dilution of the strength of the Left in the CDU, which made possible an organizational restructuring that took away the institutionalized power of the Workers'

Wing (Zohlnhöfer 2001a). Unless this is reversed—and currently there are no indications that it will be (interview, Egbert Biermann, 11 Jun 2004)—the most important resistance during the Kohl era will have disappeared, meaning that the next time the CDU is in power, it may be able to take quite extensive action in the direction of a free market. Whether this scenario comes to pass depends on many other circumstances: for example, some CDU politicians want the party to enter into coalition with the Greens, and should this happen, the possibilities for neoliberal change are of course lower (interview, Egbert Biermann, 11 Jun 2004); the Workers' Wing may yet succeed in placing sympathizers in high posts, even if doing so now requires struggle and can no longer be taken for granted (interview, Ralf Brauksiepe, 14 Jun 2004); and even without such institutionalized power, it may be able to lead and coordinate dissent within the party. If the Workers' Wing is unable to do these things, it is likely that the adversarial elements of the political economic structure will be targeted, particularly shopping hours regulation and labor market regulation, as "[i]ncontestably, the German industrial context supports the highest labor costs in the world and, at the same time, the shortest [average annual] labor time" (Theiss 1997, 24; see also Walwei 1994; CEPII 1996).

In these two cases, the churches and the unions may well become the first line of resistance, and without their "protector" within the CDU, they will both have to become much more militant to be successful. Labor market deregulation in particular would have a major effect on dismantling the German insider/outsider economy. Many observers have been puzzled at the way in which what seemed to be strengths in postwar Germany—cooperative unions, a moderate welfare state, a consensual decision-making structure—have become hindrances in the post-oil-crisis period (e.g., Grande 1987). In this chapter I hope to have shown both that the irony of German postwar success is that, once the social market economy had reached its productive potential, it was impossible to mobilize electoral and political support for change precisely *because* of the earlier success and consensualism; and that one of the unintended consequences of reunification—the dilution of the strength of the Left within the CDU—opens up the possibility of a much larger transformation of the German political-economic structure than we have seen to date. (Note: this chapter was written before the 2005 election. The curious result of that election means we will have to wait until the CDU is *fully* in power to test this prediction.)

CHAPTER FOUR

France: Neoliberalism and the Developmental State

In the U.S. and British cases, it is clear that some sort of turn toward free market policies did take place, although the extent of it is debatable. It is equally clear that West Germany under Kohl made several major attempts at neoliberal policies, and they were thwarted. The situation is not quite so straightforward in France. As discussed in the introduction, by all measures of the magnitude of the state, France still retains a larger state presence in the economy than its peers: French tax revenues are among the highest in the world; the proportion of the total workforce working for the state is higher than in the other three countries; the amount the state pays for goods and services is greater as a percentage of GDP in France; the size of the welfare state is slightly larger than in Britain and Germany, and much larger than in the United States (and was much larger than in Germany until the costs of reunification pushed up Germany's social expenditures). An index of state control summarizing public ownership and the state's involvement in industry places France higher than the other three countries.

At the same time, the French state is no longer as interventionist as it was during most of the postwar period: price controls have been abolished, many industries have been privatized, labor and financial markets have been deregulated, and increasing integration with Europe has forced adherence to a more liberal monetary and exchange rate policy (Schmidt 1996; Gordon and Meunier 2001; Levy 1999b). In some cases, such as the size of the public-sector labor force, the size of the state has declined, and the reason for the higher French levels is that the starting point was higher in France when the "neoliberal revolution" hit. However, in other cases (e.g., taxation and total state consumption) the size of the French state has *grown* in the last decades, to a much greater extent than in the other countries.

Fourcade-Gourinchas and Babb (2002) summarize the contradictory indicators by calling the French changes a "pragmatic" neoliberalism, in contrast to the more radical and ideological changes that have taken place elsewhere. The particular shape of this pragmatic neoliberalism is puzzling. An observer in the 1970s who was told that France was about to undergo several neoliberal changes would have predicted that the main change would be reduction in the taxation and the "social costs" that make France one of the most expensive places to run a business. As for the nationalized industries, she would have expected them to remain under state control, because—unlike Britain's nationalized industries—they had support from across the political spectrum (Andrieu, Le Van, and Prost 1987). But thirty years later, privatization has been the most noticeable feature of French neoliberalism, while taxation and social costs remain undiminished. The goal of this chapter is to investigate the specific shape taken by French neoliberalism. Why were tax and welfare costs not reduced, even as the role of the state in industrial policy was transformed?

From the onset of the first oil crisis in 1973 to the signing of the Maastricht treaty in 1992, there were two "neoliberal moments" in France: 1976–81, when President Valéry Giscard d'Estaing had chosen as his prime minister the economist Raymond Barre, and 1986–88, the period of the first "cohabitation" (government with a president and prime minister from opposite parties) between President François Mitterrand and Prime Minister Jacques Chirac. In both periods, industrial policy (the direct intervention of the state in the way firms conduct their business) was reformed: Giscard and Barre oversaw the beginning of the end of price controls, and Chirac began a series of privatizations that has not ended yet. Chirac's tax cuts managed to halt the rise in taxation revenue, but in neither period was welfare state spending substantially reduced.

To understand the French changes, two concepts need clarification. First, a larger state does not necessarily mean a political economy that is oriented toward issues of social justice. In tax, welfare, and industrial policy the French state in the immediate postwar period pursued not social goals but economic growth. France's postwar regime might best be characterized as a strong state at the service of capital, all in the service of nationalism; the French state turned an agricultural and artisanal economy into an economy based on heavy industry like those of its European neighbors. It managed this through a tax structure that was less progressive than that of the United States (and which, in early decades, could therefore avoid heavy corporate taxes), a welfare state aimed at social insurance for the middle classes rather than redistribution, and an industrial policy oriented toward economic growth rather than social goals. In other words, the French postwar policy was a "pragmatic state interventionism" quite unlike the adversarial state interventionism that followed the war in Britain, where the frequent Labour governments instituted redistributive tax and welfare policies, and the strong unions turned nationalized industry to their own purposes, and unlike the approach in the United States, with its progressive tax structure and antibusiness regulations (Steinmo 1993; Kato 2003; Lindert 2004; Vogel 1986). In comparison, the French Left remained out of power until 1981, and the unions were unable to influence nationalized industries; France therefore remained one of the most inegalitarian countries of the advanced capitalist world for most of the postwar period (Cameron 1991; Levy 1999a, 1999b; Ashford 1989).

Second, a conceptual distinction is necessary between the state as the site of policy innovation and the state as the means of policy implementation. These have been confused in the recent literature, which takes the wave of French privatizations and other reorganizations as evidence against a "state-centered" argument: "the statist view appears to neglect what characterized French economic and industrial policy most during the 1980s and 1990s, namely the attempts by the state to retreat from direct economic and industrial policy-making" (Hancké 2002, 24). But the process of this retreat has been state-led, and I argue here that precisely this fact explains the particular shape of the retreat. That is, although the means of policy implementation have changed, so that the state's degree of direct intervention in the economy is much lower, the particular shape of those changes is explained by the effects of previous policies on politics and the effect of the structure of the state on policy innovation—classic "state-centered" variables.

These two conceptual distinctions create a framework for understanding what has happened in France: the orientation toward economic growth (rather than social justice) has remained stable throughout the entire postwar period even as the means to attain growth have changed, and the incentives and resources of state actors (rather than cultural discourses or class interests) have remained the main source of policy innovation. French neoliberalism was "state-led" in that free market innovations were introduced not by the kind of electoral interests we saw in all three of the other cases, but by the technocrats of the state. And because of the electoral resilience of the tax and welfare state structures, French neoliberalism was channeled into industrial policy.

With these distinctions in mind, this chapter suggests that French neoliberalism took a different form than American and British neoliberalism for two reasons. The first is that at the end of the Second World War, France was a much more heavily agricultural economy than the United States, the United Kingdom, and Germany. Therefore, the intensification in state interventionism that followed the war everywhere was implemented in a peculiar manner in France. The difficulties implementing reliable income tax collection in an agricultural economy made France miss the great wave of rapidly rising income taxes that swept other countries (where income taxes went up to finance the war but did not come back down after the war), and so France has remained reliant on indirect sales taxes, which are "invisible" and do not provoke resistance (Wilensky 2002; Cameron 1978; Hibbs and Madsen 1981; Flora and Heidenheimer 1981). Moreover, the welfare state in France was developed by the Right and has been based on the principle of social insurance for the middle classes rather than redistribution of wealth between classes. This has generated loyalty to the welfare state across classes (Esping-Andersen 1990, 1996, 1999; Scharpf and Schmidt 2000; Fournier, Questiaux, and Delarue 1989). Tax policy and welfare state policy have thus been resilient because of the way in which they are rooted in electoral interests. Industrial policy, however, has not been similarly rooted in electoral interests and has been more volatile, but throughout the postwar period it has been guided by the same goal: to make France competitive with its more industrialized neighbors (Schonfield 1965; Hall 1986; Schmidt 1996). These features add up to an extremely resilient "pro-growth" structure that does not display the "adversarial" elements of the American and British states.

The second reason is that several elements of the French political structure made it less innovative than others. Until 1981, no president had ever lost an election in Fifth Republic France, and so the intense political competition that led to major innovation in Margaret Thatcher's Britain was not seen in France. Parties still finance political campaigns, so the entrepreneurship seen in the United States, where a junior congressman hoping to broaden his national reputation brought the issue of tax cuts to political attention, was not necessary. Power is centralized, so the number of points at which innovations can enter the agenda is smaller, making a parallel to the tax cuts in Germany, which entered the agenda because of losses in provincial elections, unlikely. French bureaucracies are staffed by cautious and careful technocrats rather than political appointees, so the haphazard budget making of the Reagan era, which was responsible for the large deficits of the 1980s, did not occur. Finally, interest groups are excluded from routine decision making, so innovations do not get on the political agenda as easily as they did in the case of deregulation in the United States. Innovation in France came from three sources: backlash against the policies of previous governments, imitation of other countries, and the technocracy, and all three of these sources produced moderate innovations.

In sum, the argument of this chapter is that (1) the legacies of state-led industrialization in the postwar period created a resilient political-economic structure that benefits business and the middle classes and increases loyalty to the status quo in France, and (2) the exclusion of interest groups, the continued strength of parties, and other political structures dampen political innovation in France.

Boix (1998) suggests that the French state attempted to pioneer a *different kind* of supply-side policy, an alternative to American-style neoliberalism that would nevertheless strengthen the economy by investing in labor skills and technology. Boix argues that some countries have avoided neoliberalism and adopted a skill- and capital-intensive industrial policy because they were ruled by left-wing governments in the wake of the oil crisis. I find, however, that the pattern of the French experience is more complicated: the cohabitation between Mitterrand and Chirac did produce an *attempt* at Anglo-American style neoliberalism, including tax cuts, less state intervention in industrial policy, and cuts in social spending. Giscard's neoliberalism, although it did not move in an Anglo-American direction, was more hurtful to industry than helpful to it. Rather than creating an environment that would nurture firms, Giscard withdrew state support from them. Thus France's alternative supply-side policy is not the result of left-wing governments being in power, as Boix argues. The alternative supply-side policy that Boix identifies does exist in France, but it has been discovered by firms who have been forced to make the best of the situation given to them by the state. In particular, when faced with high social costs, firms have responded by investing more heavily in technology, leading to a rise in productivity. This was not a coherent program of the state, but an example of French firms turning state policies to their own advantage.

Two Neoliberal Moments

The most neoliberal moment in this time period came during the first years of the cohabitation between Jacques Chirac and François Mitterrand. After devastating electoral defeats in 1981, the Right roared back to win the 1986 legislative elections decisively, so that Mitterrand became the first president of the Fifth Republic to have a Prime Minister not of his own party. Seeing both the failure of Mitterrand's attempt at "socialism in one country," and also the successes of Reagan and Thatcher, the Right had adopted a neoliberal platform. When he took office in 1986, Prime Minister Chirac announced that he wanted to reduce taxes from the 45 percent of GDP at which they currently stood to 35 percent; to reduce spending 1 percent every year; and to privatize a total of sixty-one companies (Levy 1999a, 63). The tax cuts the government passed came nowhere close to this goal, but they did stop the trend of rising tax revenue that France had experienced since the oil crisis. Corporate taxes and individual taxes were cut, and the tax structure was made more regressive, displaced "from business toward households, from the richest households toward those more poor, from already flourishing enterprises toward those not profitable, and from passive revenue (from capital) toward active revenue (from labor)" (Théret 1991, 345). In spending cuts, Chirac never went as far as Reagan (who proposed spending cuts to Congress), or even Kohl (who started out on an overhaul of the health system intended to reduce costs). Chirac took spending cuts off the agenda, probably because he feared their unpopularity, and they were never again mentioned. Although privatizations did not go as far as the prime minister had announced before the stock market crash of 1987 brought them to a halt, thirteen state-owned companies were privatized (and later governments would pick up where Chirac left off; see Attali 1995; Chabanas and Vergeau 1996).

The limited changes in tax and welfare spending, combined with the *way* in which the privatizations were performed (the state decided who could purchase controlling shares in the newly privatized companies and dictated the price, rewarding its political allies; it also, in an attempt to block foreign investors, rigged the sales so that favored investors were sheltered from attempts at takeover by others) led scholars to conclude that "this brand of liberalism was cautious, gradual, and subject to frequent reversal. It was far closer to the conservatism of Helmut Kohl than to the neoliberalism of Margaret Thatcher" (Levy 1999a, 69).

But there is also a period in recent French history when a party much more receptive to an American-style neoliberalism was at the helm. In 1974

France elected as its president, for the first and only time in recent history, a politician receptive to free market ideas—Valéry Giscard d'Estaing. We might expect Chirac's neoliberalism to be limited, given his roots in *dirigisme* (the statist policies of the postwar period), but Giscard had made his name, and a political niche for his party, by advocating a reduced role for the state. He did not in fact greatly reduce the role of the state. Although the abolition of price controls was begun, taxes and social spending were not reduced, and there was no move toward privatization. But Giscard's approach to reducing the role of the state was very interesting. Giscard's neoliberalism was a *punitive* neoliberalism, which sought to reduce the role of the state by removing state subsidies to firms. This was very unpopular among businesses and may have been one factor in Giscard's defeat. It was quite different from the *populist* neoliberalism of Reagan, which sought to reduce the role of the state by making the competitive environment for firms less onerous. But why did Giscard not discover for himself what Reagan or Chirac would discover a few years later—namely, that cutting taxes can be a winning electoral strategy, or that privatization can be popular?

The following sections follow policies from both of these periods to answer these questions. First, I compare the structure of tax policy, industrial policy, and welfare state policy in the United States, Britain, and France to explain why Chirac's neoliberalism between 1986 and 1988 never attained the dynamic quality that pushed the policies of Reagan and Thatcher beyond what had been originally envisioned. Second, I examine in more detail the industrial policy of Giscard, asking why the neoliberal commitment of the one French leader most ideologically committed to a reduced role for the state took a punitive form, and why Giscard did not begin privatizations when Chirac did so only a few years later.

Chirac, 1986–1988

In 1986 Jacques Chirac became prime minister and announced a neoliberal platform of tax cuts, privatizations, and welfare state cuts. The only one of these policies to make headway was privatization. Why did tax and welfare cuts fail, and where did privatization come from?

Tax Policy

As chapter 1 discusses, the 1981 tax cut in the United States was rooted in the anti-property-tax social movement in California, which brought the general issue of taxation to public attention, and in Reagan's wish to ward off the political rivalry of Jack Kemp, who had been making political capital out of the issue of income tax cuts. In addition, recent changes in American government had led to a greater number and variety of political innovations reaching the political agenda because "policy entrepreneurs" were seeking out and mobilizing issues that had the potential to be popular with the public, and the federal "multi-actor" structure of the American government inflated the size of the tax cut because each politician had to be individually convinced to vote for it with an attachment of tax cuts for her own district.

Such a movement was unlikely in France because French tax policies taxed income, capital, and property much less than did American tax policies (see figures 10–11 and tables 2–3 in the introduction). As many scholars have pointed out, France, like the other large welfare states of Europe, has a *regressive* tax structure (taking proportionately more taxes from the lower portions of the income distribution; see Steinmo 1993; Kato 2003; Lindert 2004) based on payroll and sales taxes. While property taxes hit those with property, and income taxes are structured so that those with higher incomes pay higher percentages, sales taxes are regressive because the same absolute amount is paid on an item regardless of income or wealth (which means lower income workers pay a higher percentage of their income for the tax). Payroll taxes are regressive because

> [f]irst, only wages are taxed, whereas earnings from capital or real estate, which accrue overwhelmingly to the wealthy, escape imposition. Second, social security contributions are deductible, and since tax rates are progressive, the size of the deduction increases with income. For example, those in the top income bracket, with a marginal tax rate of 56 percent, pay only 44 percent of their social security charges. Third, many social security programs do not tax earnings above a certain ceiling ($2,300 per month in 1997). Not surprisingly, in the early 1990s, it was estimated that a minimum-wage worker contributed 13.6 percent of his or her salary to the social security system, whereas a manager earning $60,000 per year paid only 7.5 percent. (Levy 1999a, 250)

Throughout the course of the Fifth Republic France has had a regressive tax structure. This is a holdover from the eighteenth century. Under Napoleon, the French government had decided that the benefits of indirect taxes (namely, their invisibility) outweighed their drawbacks (their regressivity). Moreover, Montesquieu—sounding exactly like Thatcher several centuries later—wrote, "The tax per head is most appropriate to servitude; the tax on goods is most appropriate to liberty, because it relates in a less direct way to the person" (cited in Schnerb 1973c)—that is, income taxes are coercive, but sales taxes are voluntary. In addition, sales taxes are simply much easier to collect, especially where the bulk of the population is engaged in agricultural production. Like other countries, France introduced an income tax in the early twentieth century, and its levels increased directly after the Second World War. However, income tax never generated the proportion of revenue that it did in some of France's peer countries. One reason for this is that at the end of the war France had a much more agricultural economy than others did, and therefore income taxes could be reliably levied only on a much smaller proportion of the population. The ideological leanings of the postwar government were another factor. De Gaulle's primary concern was to keep taxes on business low: "All taxes, without exception—taxes on business volume [*chiffre d'affaires*], indirect taxes, registration taxes, direct taxes—were concerned to reduce the fiscal burden weighing on enterprise, or indeed to suppress it altogether" (Nizet 1991, 267). So taxes on consumption, partly by design and partly by default, had to pay for the steadily increasing postwar role of the state. Since the oil crisis, the general trend has been toward a more progressive tax structure, although ironically the bulk of this change took place under Giscard (Schnerb 1973a, 1973b; Wolff 1973; Nizet 1991; Bertoni 1995; Neurrisse 1996).

The key political implication of progressive versus regressive taxation is that progressive and regressive taxes structure the flow of information quite differently (Wilensky 2002). Progressive taxes give taxpayers very precise information about how much they are paying and no information at all on what the tax revenues purchase. Sales and payroll taxes, on the other hand, work the other way: Sales taxes are collected *invisibly*, and payroll taxes are *targeted* to spending. In both cases, the tax-collection procedures structure the flow of information to French and American taxpayers in opposite ways.

In France in the postwar period indirect taxes such as sales taxes (particularly the value-added tax) have consistently generated approximately 60 percent of total tax receipts. Sales taxes are "invisible" because taxpayers lack a precise sense of how much of a product's price is made up of taxes. The taxes are collected in small amounts from many exchanges over a long period of time, and consumers often assimilate them into the cost of living (Wilensky 2002). Moreover, welfare costs in France are paid by targeted payroll taxes; these structure information so that the welfare services provided to workers are made visible and linked precisely to the taxes that they pay (see fig. 4.1):

> [P]eople think that they have "bought" their own social benefits through the social contribution they have paid. In France, each *branche* (health, old age, unemployment insurance, family benefits) has its own contribution which appears on every French employee's pay slip. The link between payment and entitlement is very visible. When you pay health insurance contribution, for instance, you "buy" your right to health care;... social contribution is perceived as a "deferred wage" which will come back when the insured person will be sick, unemployed or aged. (Palier 2000, 121)

This is, of course, the reason analysts often give for why Social Security is so popular in the United States; it extends to other domains of social policy in France.

Thus Wilensky notes: "[I]t is not the *level* of taxes that creates tax-welfare backlash but the *type* of taxes—property taxes and income taxes with their visibility and perceived pain. Conversely, consumption taxes and social-security payroll taxes keep things cool" (2002, 391). While in the United States highly visible property and income taxes take money from taxpayers at infrequent intervals, so that they know precisely how much they are paying but not precisely what they are getting for it, France's reliance on invisible consumption taxes and targeted payroll taxes dampens antitax sentiment (see also Kato 2003; Lindert 2004).

In short, French tax structures were less conducive to reform because of the kinds of taxes that make up the French tax regime and the ways in which they are collected; consequently there was no "sales tax revolt" to parallel the role of the American property tax revolt in bringing taxes to political attention; and because cutting payroll taxes would have required cutting welfare spending in an extremely transparent manner, politicians did not sense any political capital to be made as American politicians did with income tax cuts. Moreover, France had no equivalent to the American political entrepreneurs. As Wilson (1983, 1987) shows, party structures have actually been getting stronger over the course of the Fifth Republic: French parties "are more cohesive, better organized, better able to form durable coalitions, and more popular in the eyes of the citizens than at any time since the end of World War II" (266; see also Kesselman 1992)—and they have been more able to finance the campaigns of ambitious politicians. This prevents the dynamic of individual politicians seeking out issues as a

BULLETIN de SALAIRE

N° MATRICULE	N° SECURITE SOCIALE	DATE ENTREE
		30.05.97

STATUT	SALAIRE MINIMUM
EMPLOYES	

QUALIFICATION	
COMMIS DE CUISINE	

CONVENTION COLLECTIVE	POSITION
HOTELS, CAFES, RESTAURANTS	

SECTION	DATE DE SORTIE	PERIODE DE REFERENCE	PERIODE DE PAIE DU	PERIODE DE PAIE AU	DATE DE PAIE
		DECEMBRE	01.12.98	31.12.98	31.12.98

	RUBRIQUES	BASE OU NOMBRE	PART PATRONALE TAUX OU PRIX	PART PATRONALE MONTANT	TAUX OU PRIX	A DEDUIRE	A PAYER
1060	Salaire mensuel	9.860,79			186,330		9.860,79
1400	Taux horaire				52,920		
3130	Nourriture prise	46,00			18,390		845,94
3989	** TOTAL BRUT **						10.706,73
3998	*********TOTAL BRUT EURO						1.647,18
4020	CSG non imposable	10.171,39			5,100	518,74-	
4060	Assurance maladie	10.706,73	14,400	1.541,77	0,850	91,01-	
4070	Assurance V.V. FNAL	10.706,73	8,300	888,65	6,550	701,29-	
4080	FNAL + 9	10.706,73	0,400	42,83			
4090	Accident du travail	10.706,73	2,280	244,11			
4130	URSSAF Transport	10.706,73	2,500	267,67			
4260	Allocations familiales	10.706,73	5,400	578,16			
4790	ASSEDIC TrA	10.706,73	3,970	425,05	2,210	236,61-	
4800	ASSEDIC Struct. Fin. TrA	10.706,73	1,160	124,19	0,800	85,65-	
4830	FNGS	10.706,73	0,250	26,76			
5050	ret circo sal total	10.706,73	3,438	368,10	3,437	367,99-	
5890	R.D.S. et C.S.G.imposabl	10.171,39			2,900	294,97-	
5989	** TOTAL COTISATIONS **					2.296,76-	
5999	NET IMPOSABLE	8.705,44					8.705,44
6530	Transport 2 zones	271,00			0,500		135,50
7130	Nourriture prise	46,00			18,390	845,94-	
8200	Remise 1,28 Hotellerie	46,00	1,280	58,88-			
9700	Taxe d'apprentissage	10.706,73	0,500	53,53			
9710	Aide à la construction	10.706,73	0,450	48,18			
9720	Formation continue	10.706,73	1,500	160,60			
9730	Médecine du travail	10.706,73	0,400	42,82			
9835	** NET IMPOS. Francs **			1,00			8.705,44
9836	*********NET IMPOS. EURO			1,00			1.339,29
9837	** NET A PAYER Francs **			1,00			7.700,03
9838	********NET A PAYER EURO			1,00			1.184,61

MODE DE PAIEMENT	NET A DEVOIR	NET A PAYER

Dans votre intérêt et pour vous aider à faire valoir vos droits, conservez ce bulletin de paie sans limitation de durée.

CONGES PAYES EN COURS	CONGES PAYES ACQUIS ANCIEN SOLDE	COMPLEMENT	PRIS	NOUVEAU SOLDE			REPOS COMPENSATEUR ANCIEN SOLDE	ACQUIS	PRIS	NOUVEAU SOLDE

	PLAFOND S.S. HEURES PAYEES	BASE C.S.G. BASE R.D.S.	BRUT IMPOSABLE BRUT COTISABLE	COTISATIONS SALARIALES COTISATIONS PATRONALES	NET IMPOSABLE	NON IMPOSABLES AVANTAGES EN NATURE	COÛT SALARIAL
MOIS							
CUMUL							

IMPACTS - CCMX Ref D960105

FIGURE 4.1. Pay stub of a French worker, showing taxes pegged to government programs *Note*: The second column shows the name of the program; the second-to-last column shows the amount of tax withheld.

route to power. When Chirac took office in 1986, tax cuts were a part of his platform, and he did halt the growth of tax revenue; but there were no obvious ways to anchor the tax cuts in electoral interest, and fewer people were involved in the search to do so, so they never attained the dynamic that caused tax cuts to explode in the United States.

Industrial Policy

In industrial policy in the United States, neoliberalism involved deregulation of industry, particularly, reductions in health and environmental protections. The cause of "deregulation" was brought onto the policy agenda by social movements, particularly the consumers' movement led by Ralph Nader, which pushed for economic deregulation in the interest of lower prices for consumers. But the Ford and Reagan administrations took over the deregulation idea and turned it in a direction the original proponents did not favor: "social" deregulation. Business lobbies had by this point been complaining of social regulations for a decade, and there is some evidence that the Ford administration cynically used the popularity of economic deregulation as a cover for the policy of social deregulation.

Like French tax policy—and unlike American social regulation—French industrial policy throughout the postwar period has been favorable to business. France has been the European state most associated with state-led industrial growth, and this is responsible for its socialist image. Directly after the Second World War key industries were nationalized, and the Planning Commission was founded with the intention of directing economic growth. But many observers have pointed out that the nature of this state intervention was to turn France into a world-class *capitalist* economy (Hall 1986; Schmidt 1996; Zysman 1983). Neither the nationalized industries nor the Planning Commission were focused on social justice; rather, intervention was aimed at reducing the role of agriculture in the French economy and increasing the role of industry, with the goal of improving aggregate economic growth compared to France's much more heavily industrialized neighbors.

The plans were largely oriented toward economic growth: only two of the nine postwar plans—the Seventh and Ninth, introduced long past the heyday of planning—concentrated on attaining full employment. The first four plans, which laid the foundations for the postwar period, concentrated on ways to stimulate economic growth. Social goals were a minor component of the Fifth Plan in 1965, but that was overshadowed by new attention to international competitiveness, which the Sixth and Eighth Plans also took as their main theme (Hall 1986). Thus, the plans only began to address social goals as the planning era was coming to an end, and seven of the nine postwar plans were market-oriented; that is, they explicitly advocated generating a favorable climate for industry. Planning was abandoned not because the state became less socialist—the plans were never very socialist to begin with—but because the increasing integration of the French economy into the world made economic prediction nearly impossible, rendering attempts to control the direction of the French economy through domestic policies unfeasible.

Nationalization, too, was not used in the interest of full employment or egalitarian redistribution of incomes. An early observer noted that, with a few exceptions, "nationalization has replaced a fluctuating and uncertain income [for the former owners of the nationalized enterprises] by a guaranteed and constant income in a reasonably fair way;... nationalization, therefore, has failed to make a substantial contribution to the socialist objective of achieving a more equalitarian distribution of income" (Sturmthal 1953, 48). Nationalization simultaneously provided direct access to key state sectors and prevented "capital flight." During the postwar period the French state controlled about half of the capital being invested in French industry and could provide a continuous stream of capital even during economic downturns. But this prevention of capital flight was not used as leverage with which to institute worker-friendly policies or income redistribution; rather, it was used to transform the French economic structure from one dominated by rural and artisanal production into one dominated by heavy industry and big business: "Nationalized industries—the banks, the transport industry, the energy industry—would serve as the spearheads in the postwar economic battle. They would help to 'relaunch' France as a great economic power" (Smith 2004, 71). De Gaulle's strategy was to create firms large enough to compete on a European, and worldwide, scale—"national champions." Although measuring productivity in the nationalized industries across countries is difficult, it seems that French nationalized industries were more productive than British nationalized industries throughout the postwar period, except for the decade of 1958 to 1968 (see Pryke 1971, 1981). Estrin and Pérotin (1987, 1991) suggest that this is because a firm's productivity depends more on management than on ownership, and they discuss various mechanisms that ensured that French nationalized firms were consistently managed with the goal of productivity, unlike British nationalized firms.

Comparative assessments of the performance of nationalized industries are rare, but those that have been conducted generally find French nationalized industries performing better than their British counterparts, and performing more *consistently* over the course of the postwar period. Thuong compared the performance of nationalized railways and concluded that technical efficiency in the British railways was "[l]owest and least improved" of the studied countries, whereas in the French railways it was "[h]ighest and most improved" over the period of nationalization (1980, 255). Curiously, according to Thuong, the attempt to provide a "buffer" between government and the nationalized industry in Britain by creating a strong Board of Directors backfired. The board came to dominate the nationalized firm, whereas in France the executive management of the firm remained dominant. Policy on British Rail vacillated with the party in power, while the French Société Nationale des Chemins de Fer (SNCF) followed a continuous and stable policy. In terms of performance,

> The British Transport Commission, viewing itself as "guardians of public interests," shied away from assuming its managerial responsibilities, thus giving way to a misconceived investment program in steam locomotives and, shortly after, to another hastily planned and poorly costed modernization scheme.... In contrast to the foregoing, the management of the SNCF, through its close coordination with ministerial officials, was able to coordinate its modernization efforts with national development plans. This, coupled with strict financial scrutiny on railroad investment by French public authorities, brought about a series of well-formulated and executed modernization plans for the SNCF. (260)

British Rail was more successful at rationalization than the SNCF, but in a familiar adversarial pattern. In backlash to the "tradition of self-imposition of public service obligations" and the failed modernization that it caused, in 1961 Harold Macmillan's Conservative government appointed a board chairman with a mandate to close less heavily utilized lines, a plan which sparked much resistance and outcry at the time but eventually increased efficiency. This is what is being picked up in Pryke's figures of decreased efficiency in the 1950s in Britain and increased efficiency in the 1960s. Meanwhile, Gourvish's history of the British railways shows operating deficits every year between 1948 and 1973, with only one exception

(1986, 585–87). Gourvish writes "Scratch a railway manager, it is said, and he will complain that post-war governments have greatly harmed the railways by continually organising or reorganising nationalised transport, thereby creating a permanent climate of uncertainty" (569). Because the French SNCF's modernization plan was more successful, no dramatic rationalization was deemed necessary. Introduction of new technology and a steady reduction in the number of employees had led to a 60 percent increase in productivity between 1938 and 1952 (Meunier 2002, 23). SNCF also ran a deficit, but it met this by beginning a program of closing rail lines as early as 1950 (56). In 1963 only 5 percent of the public held a negative opinion of SNCF, and that had increased to only 11 percent in 1971 (98).

In electricity, O'Mahony and Vecchi (2001) show that the nationalized French electricity industry was more productive than the nationalized British electricity industry. Regarding nationalized electricity in France, Frost writes,

> The nationalization of electricity yielded not a socialist France but a far more efficient capitalist one. EDF [Electricité de France] became the largest and one of the most cost-effective, fully integrated power systems in the West, and ultimately helped to build a society of abundance, yet it failed to foster greater social equality. Productive triumphs, Promethean language, and mathematical modeling obscured the fact that by 1970 EDF managers were allied with the "trusts" that the nationalization of electricity was supposed to have undermined. (1991, 2)

Frost found that although EDF had initially operated with an alliance of union workers and managers, between 1954 and 1962 that alliance "eroded, and it was slowly—indeed, for the CGT, imperceptibly—replaced by quiescent labor and economistic managers, held together by a strong mythology of high technology. The unions preserved the right to have a voice in determining the character of the daily life of the firm, but those who enjoyed that voice found increasingly that the most important issues were decided before they were presented in the participationist forums" (247). Meanwhile, in Britain the nationalized electricity industry was almost continuously reorganized and continuously forced to adhere to politically determined goals. The government controlled overall investment levels and heavily influenced how investments would be allocated, and the government required rural electrification, which "led to a diversion of scarce capital resources into investments which were known to be unremunerative and in fact turned out to be so" (Hannah 1982, 75). In addition, many engineers lacked university training, which led to a conservatism that caused the industry to fall behind that of France: "French engineers, facing similar difficulties of a wartime investment backlog [chose less conservative investments, so that the] average thermal efficiency of French steam power stations, which had been well below that in Britain initially, was to overtake it in the later 1950s, as the more advanced French sets were commissioned; and France caught up with American levels of thermal efficiency, while Britain remained behind" (110).

A comparative assessment of French and British nationalized iron and steel industries shows that the French industries were more productive than the British (U. S. Congress 1980). An in-depth study of British Steel suggests that the problem was that it was taken in and out of nationalization several times, nationalized in 1951, denationalized in 1953, renationalized in 1967:

> On return to nationalisation [in 1967] there was a great gap in technological efficiency between Britain and its competitors; . . . there had existed a general unwillingness in the industry to adopt . . . new techniques. . . . This can be attributed to the uncertainty of the individual company managers and owners as to whether their firm would be nationalized again. And with this feeling of uncertainty there was an unwillingness to adopt the new techniques, as they rightly assumed that the industry would return to governmental control and that they would not be rewarded for their expenditure by the public purse. (Blair 1997, 574–75)

Worse than either a steady policy of private ownership *or* a steady policy of nationalization was the uncertainty caused by the constant reversals of policy.

In the coal industry, British unions were more able to turn the nationalized industry to their advantage than French unions were. In France, two strikes in 1947 and 1948 had ended in defeat for the coal miners and

> marked the end of the social and economic reforms of the postwar period. . . . Modernization of equipment helped raise production while reducing the number of mine workers. This improved productivity and allowed the state to keep coal prices low. The CGT [Confédération Générale du Travail, the strong Communist-dominated labor union that had initiated the nationalizations] complained that merging the coal industries of western Europe could

lower standards for French miners and lead to mine closings. But the labor movement, weakened by the 1948 strike and divided into political and religious factions, no longer possessed much influence within the decision-making process in the mines. (Holter 1992, 200)

The astonishing scope of the defeat—two thousand strikers were dismissed, and almost eighty thousand mineworkers left the mines in that year alone (Holter 1982, 47)—led some to see the result as a sign of the "defeat of the French working class" (Alexander Werth, quoted in Holter 1982, 47). After this, the industry rapidly retreated from commitment to social goals:

The miners union claimed that the nationalization no longer corresponded to the needs of the workers or the nation and that the state directed the industry to serve industrialists and businessmen. . . . In 1949, the Marshall Plan provided funds for new mining equipment, and the number of mineworkers was substantially reduced. The housing program launched in 1946 was curtailed. By the early 1950s, the industry had made such strides in productivity that it was able to subsidize indirectly the coal-consuming industries by selling cheap coal. Business newspapers and journals saluted the coal industry. . . . [While the CGT withdrew its support,] the two leaders of the major employers' organization . . . withdrew their earlier opposition to nationalization and commended the leaders of the coal industry. (Holter 1982, 48–49)

Successive pit closures in 1959, 1968, 1980, and 1984–88 reduced the total number of mineworkers in France from three hundred thousand soon after the war to twenty-eight thousand in 1989 (Scargill 1991, 173).

Meanwhile, in the nationalized coal industry in Britain, government was less sure of what it wanted, and the unions were more able to get what they wanted:

It seems to have been the case that governments did not clearly think out what they wanted from nationalization; that, nevertheless, they wanted a degree of control, however uncertain they were of its specific uses, which was bound to limit the commercial autonomy of a nationalized board; and that from time to time they varied both the requirements which they sought from boards and the way they expected them to be fulfilled. . . .

. . . The disputes of party politics, which became sharper in the late seventies than they had been for more than twenty years, spilled over into industrial

> relations, and the restraint of employees was diminished by experience of access to the public purse. (Ashworth 1986, 657–58)

This happened because unions had discovered that the government was willing to subsidize higher wages in the coal industry than a private industry could have supported.

In short,

> The [French] nationalized companies [in the 1950s] were expansionist in their own operations and in their effect on the French economy. Electricité de France (EDF) and the state railways led the way in applying econometric techniques. The uniform purchasing procedures of state firms fostered the standardization of equipment supply. In a few instances a public enterprise, such as Renault, served as a model for private firms and sharpened competition. The directors of the nationalized companies successfully pressed for higher productivity, new technology, and more investment. The result was a large expansion of capacity (e.g., EDF) and rising productivity (e.g., coal mines and railways). . . . The example of public enterprise contributed to leading private industry toward a pattern of high investment and a decisive break with prewar behavior. An economist surveying the machine tool industry of Renault, the Caravelle jet, and EDF's high-voltage power grid, concluded that "much of the stimulus for technological change came from nationalized industry." (Kuisel 1981, 266; see also Adams 1989)

Unlike the social regulations found in the United States, which generated hostility from capital, French industrial policy has in general aimed to help large capitalist firms in the interest of nationalism. These policies both reflected the Right's role as part of the coalition that implemented nationalization and ensured that the Right would be committed to nationalization throughout the postwar years. Thus, when privatization came on the agenda, it was not for the same reasons as in Britain. There, privatization had remained on the agenda throughout the postwar period because of disappointment with the performance of the nationalized industries. In France, however, Chirac's privatizations were initiated for tactical political reasons, "intended for the short-term political benefit of those backing the policy" (Feigenbaum and Henig 1994, 196). Feigenbaum and Henig point out that profit-and-loss statements show that state-run enterprises were increasingly profitable in France, casting doubt on the economic arguments for privatization. The Gaullists seized on privatization as a political response to the socialists' nationalizations: "Since 1983 the socialists had slowly deregulated the economy, reduced taxes, and liberalized capital markets. While they had deregulated for pragmatic reasons, largely because they had no other ideas after the failure of the 1981 economic program, this left the conservatives with little to call their own. Thus they blamed France's problems on the public sector, especially on the nationalizations of the socialists" (197). Because the Socialists had already made a significant political U-turn and moved toward the center, they forced the Gaullists even further to the right. Therefore the privatizations did not stop with returning the industries that Mitterrand had nationalized to the private sector; once privatization was on the agenda, the Gaullists went on to an extremely broad privatization program, because Mitterrand's economic difficulties caused a rethinking within the Gaullist party of the idea of nationalized industry as a whole. One wonders if large tax cuts and cuts in social spending would also have arrived on the agenda in 1986 if Mitterrand had significantly raised taxes or social spending in 1981.

Welfare State Policy

In the domain of social policy in the United States, the ideologically motivated Reagan administration originally intended to cut all manner of spending. In the early years, it was not particularly concerned with antipoverty policies, because they made up such a tiny part of the budget (less than 1 percent). The main focus was middle-class entitlements, particularly Social Security, the largest social spending expenditure. Congress would not touch Social Security, however, because of the political costs of cutting a popular universal program—but no one protested the antipoverty cuts. Moreover, although antipoverty policies could provide little in the way of financial savings, a tremendous amount of political capital could be made from them. Because the beneficiaries of antipoverty policies were disproportionately black, an attack on antipoverty policies could mobilize racial resentment particularly from working-class whites; in this sense cutting antipoverty policies was an extension of the Republicans' "Southern Strategy" that could be generalized all over the country (see chapter 1 for more detail).

These dynamics were not possible in France: as many scholars of the welfare state have pointed out (e.g., Korpi and Palme 1998), welfare state policies there do not separate and stigmatize, and so they are not a source of political capital. This is not because of a lack of racism in France; plenty of racism exists, and politicians do not hesitate to make political capital out

TABLE 4.1 **After-tax household income, as percentage of national wealth, decile, early 1970s**

	First decile (poorest 10%)	Second decile (second poorest 10%)	Ninth decile (second richest 10%)	Tenth decile (richest 10%)
France (1970)	1.4	2.8	16.6	30.5
W. Germany (1973)	2.8	3.7	15.7	30.6
U.K. (1973)	2.4	3.7	15.4	23.9
U.S. (1972)	1.7	3.2	16.0	26.1

Source: Smith 2004, 135.

TABLE 4.2 **Percentage of transfer payments received, 1950–1975**

	Britain (%)	France (%)
Received by top 20% of income distribution	7.2	24
Received by bottom 20% of income distribution	47.3	18

Source: Smith 2004, 128.

of it, as is evident from recent immigration policy. Rather, the same political mobilization against welfare state policies has been difficult because, as Esping-Andersen (1990) notes, the French welfare state is a *middle-class* welfare state, redistributing risk within classes rather than between them. Poverty is addressed through programs that benefit everyone, *including* the poor, such as universal health care and child care (Bergmann 1996). Moreover, much of the French welfare state is actually *reverse-redistributive*, benefiting the upper portion of the income distribution proportionately more.

The largest portion of the high level of social spending for which France is known goes to old-age pensions and health and education spending, all of which benefit the middle classes to a greater extent than the poor. The wealthiest 15 percent of retirees receives one-third of all pension disbursements; the next wealthiest 25 percent receives another one-third; and the bottom 60 percent receive one-third (Smith 2004, 165). This is because pensions are linked to earned income, as are unemployment benefits and sickness pay (Ambler 1991, 12). Moreover, because the wealthy tend to live longer, they take greater advantage of universal health care, and the middle and upper classes are also more likely to take advantage of spending on higher education. Together, the top of the income distribution actually received more than the bottom over the period 1950–75, making the welfare system reverse-redistributive (see tables 4.1 and 4.2; also see figure 12 in the introduction). As Cameron sums up, "[H]igh levels of social spending, if distributed in a proportional manner throughout the society rather than concentrated among the poorest households, and if unaccompanied by significantly higher levels of [progressive] income taxation, will do little to mitigate the inequalities endemic in any capitalist economy" (Cameron 1991, 90; see also Levy 1999a; Smith 2004).

Because the welfare state benefits the majority, and especially the powerful, there is little room for neoliberal ideologists to appeal to the majority middle classes for a scaling back of hugely popular welfare services. This is also true in terms of *costs*. As discussed above, the French welfare state is financed through the *cotisations sociales*, payroll taxes pegged to welfare spending; because these taxes are precisely identified with the programs they pay for, they are difficult to cut. But these taxes are at least partly coming at the expense of the creation of new jobs, particularly for the less skilled.[1] This means that French welfare state policies benefit a sheltered core of the population at the expense of an excluded minority (see Smith 2004 for more on this argument). The political implication of a welfare

1. That is, for any firm, payroll taxes must by definition come from a combination of employer profits, wages, firm growth, and higher prices; since wages in France are as high, or higher, than in comparable countries, the taxes may at least partly be coming at the expense of the firm's growth and thus at the expense of potential employees. In particular, French firms can avoid hiring expensive unskilled labor by investing in capital-intensive technology, so the French unemployment rate among the unskilled is much higher than among skilled workers who are less easily replaced by technology. Henry Sneessens (1994) has made this argument most forcefully; investigating the causes for the much higher rate of unemployment among the unskilled, he writes, "Given the composition of the active population, one finds that a substantial reduction (20% or more) of the relative cost of unskilled labor would be necessary to eliminate the gap between the unemployment rates of skilled and unskilled workers and to create the conditions for a return to full employment" (29). That is, the *cotisations sociales* add to the cost of work, making employers less likely to hire new workers, especially when they lack essential skills (on this much-discussed issue, see also Cohen and Michel 1987; Dormont 1997; Dormont and Pauchet 1997; Drèze 1997; *Economie et Prévision* 1994; Fourçans 1980; Hamermesh 1994; Malinvaud 1998; Sneessens 1993). This leads to the French state's "dual" character—highly beneficial for those in the system, but very difficult to break into for those not in it, notably immigrants, the young, and unskilled workers. As Edmond Malinvaud sums up the mainstream—though far from consensus—position, "[W]e are not so far from reality when we claim that all modes of financing . . . make employment pay the cost of social protection" (1998, 70). To tolerate a high level of unemployment is one thing when the unemployed receive welfare protections, and when unemployment is evenly distributed throughout the population; it is quite another when welfare protections are linked to employment, and when their cost is concentrated upon certain underprivileged segments. In recent years the French state has taken steps to address both unemployment and the linkage of welfare with employment; most notably, the *cotisations sociales* have been reduced for *unskilled* workers and their employers, in the hope that the reduction of the cost of unskilled work will lead to the creation of new unskilled jobs. In addition, the Revenu Minimum d'Insertion (employment benefits inaugurated under Mitterrand), the Couverture Maladie Universelle (health insurance not linked to employment), and a new tax funding non-contributory benefits help to dismantle the dual character of the French welfare state (Palier 2005).

state system that redistributes within rather than between classes and is even reverse-redistributive is that "welfare" is not identified with weak populations. As Walter Korpi (1980; Korpi and Palme 1998) and others have spent several decades demonstrating, this makes the French welfare state highly resilient. Given all of these sources of political resilience, under Chirac the program to reduce spending by 1 percent every year was never backed up by a committed effort to do so.

In sum, the dominant tendency in tax policy, industrial policy, and welfare policy was neither egalitarianism nor anticapitalist state intervention— a surprising observation, given the country's egalitarian reputation and self-image. The book explaining when and why France acquired such a durable reputation as an anticapitalist state, despite the evidence, remains to be written.

The pro-growth elements of the political structure meant that a political actor who announced a plan to reduce the size of the state could find no political traction in adversarial resentment of progressive taxes or in adversarial resentment of redistributive welfare policies. There was no adversarial resentment of nationalization, either, so privatizations reached the political agenda only as political backlash.

Of course, Chirac was a representative of the old order who was arguably never committed to neoliberalism, adopting it only for political reasons:

> Economic liberalism was as foreign to the right in France as it was to the left. . . . For loyal Gaullists, *dirigisme* was not simply an economic program: it constituted a core component of their identity, the translation into the economic arena of General de Gaulle's belief that only a strong, activist, modernizing state could restore France to greatness. Chirac and Balladur had both been forged in this ethos. (Levy 1999a, 66)

Thus, the next section examines another neoliberal moment in France after the oil crisis, when a neoliberal party was at the helm of the concentrated state structure.

Giscard and the Neoliberal Moment

Between 1947 and 1981 Valéry Giscard d'Estaing, the top politician most committed to reducing the size of the state, was president of France. Giscard's small Union pour la Démocratie Française (UDF) party was the closest thing in France to a neoliberal party. Between 1976 and 1981 his prime minister was Raymond Barre, an economist. With such men at the head of a state structure that has very few checks and balances, one might have expected a neoliberal turn in France in the wake of the oil crisis. Giscard himself spoke of reducing the powers of the state and freeing the individual:

> If we want the individual to become master of his own destiny and free to take an increasing number of decisions, here is what should *not* be done: increase the powers or the dimensions of an already multi-tentacled administration; nationalize enterprises which do not perform a public service—to do so would be either to deliver them to the technocracy, or to "etatize" them and have them be directed by a small number of bureaucrats of the central administration not responsible to anyone; planify the economy, which would be the same as to give a few men the power to decide for several millions; suppress initiative and competition. (1979, 16–17)

What should be done is to "deepen liberties: not only the fundamental political liberties, but also the new liberties of everyday life, such as educational freedom, free medical choice, freedom of information; conserve the market economy, the only manner of assuring the responsibility of directors and managers, and the efficacity of the enterprise; decentralize boldly in enterprise, and toward local life" (17).

This list of Giscard's concerns—concentration of power, the market as the preserver of individual freedoms—would not be out of place coming from an American or British politician of the period. The language does not prescribe specific policies, but in the 1970s neoliberals were also writing in vague terms in both the United States and the United Kingdom. As Théret notes, "Neoliberalism is not a coherent doctrine furnishing a formal system of rules of action . . . but rather a 'global referent' . . . which should be seen as an ensemble of practical receipts and of common representations of a certain number of concrete political actors" (1991, 343). He summarizes this "global referent" as consisting of three main principles: "that market exchange is the most optimal method of production; that a structural distribution of revenues favorable to entrepreneurs is necessary for economic growth; and the strengthening of the state passes through its disengagement from the economy" (359). This is a set of general principles against state intervention rather than specific policies of what kinds of state intervention to attack.

These general principles drove both Reagan and Thatcher, but were only embodied in specific policies through the vagaries of the processes of policy formation. For example, as we have seen, Reagan was a late convert to the idea of broad middle-class tax cuts, and when Thatcher was Education Minister, she presided over an expansion of the education budget. However, their rhetoric was antistate, and used the same general terms as the elements quoted here from Giscard. It is teleological to assume from the outcomes of the Reagan and Thatcher administrations their preferences in the 1970s. As noted in chapters 1 and 2, the historical record shows that in the 1970s the Republicans were still the party of fiscal responsibility (it was the Keynesian Democrat Kennedy who had lowered taxes and created a deficit), and the Conservative party offered only weak support for Thatcherism when Thatcher took office. The most radical elements of the Reagan and Thatcher agendas developed after each had taken office and snowballed as a result of events.

The Giscard period, then, presents us with a moment when a politician receptive to free market aims presided over a centralized state apparatus. Moreover, because of France's unique dual executive system, Giscard's government held power longer than any other government of the Right in the post-oil-crisis period, and he had five full years with a prime minister of his own party—a record unequaled by the Gaullists even today.[2] Although he never had a majority in the Parliament, the French Constitution gives the president several ways to outmaneuver Parliament, and, at the limit, to bypass Parliament altogether.[3] Giscard made use of these powers to pass other laws, but not to implement sharp tax cuts, as Reagan did, or major privatizations, as did Thatcher. He reigned on the eve of Reaganism and Thatcherism but oversaw very different outcomes. Given this, the lack of scholarly attention to the Giscard period is remarkable, as it seems to present an important counterexample to the Reagan and Thatcher episodes. The remainder of this chapter aims to remedy that gap by providing a comparative historical study of neoliberalism under Giscard, to ask both how neoliberalism arose in his administration and why it did not become more extensive. Because it is (as far as I am aware) the first

2. A constitutional amendment synchronizing presidential and legislative elections ensures that starting in 2002, five-year governments with cohesive executives will be the rule rather than the exception.

3. One way is Constitutional Article 49.3, the "guillotine," which cuts off debate on a bill and considers the bill passed unless a motion of no confidence is introduced within a specific period of time (Huber 1992).

comparative historical study of the Giscard period, part of the goal is to illuminate the main elements of the episode for future researchers and to show that closer examination of this historical period is worthwhile. The claim is not that this period is more crucial than later periods, but that examining what happened during the one moment when a non-Gaullist party was in power can give insights into the variables other than party ideology that may be at work in contemporary French political economy.[4]

Perhaps the most popular explanation of why France resists Anglo-American style neoliberalism is that French national culture emphasizes egalitarianism, solidarity, and collectivism. In recent years we have witnessed a resurgence of cultural arguments in the social sciences, and the cultural explanation for the French pattern is common in both popular as well as scholarly accounts. Defining the independent variable to include "world views, cultures, societal scripts, norms, models, and causal beliefs" (Bleich 2002, 1063), proponents of the cultural argument make the reasonable claim that actors' cognitive processes influence their actions. This is intended as a corrective to structural theories, in which human agents seem to follow blindly the dictates of material incentives. Several theorists take this argument one step further, arguing that particular cultures can be identified within geographically bounded units. Frank Dobbin argues that "national traditions influence policy-making by contributing to collective understandings of social order and instrumental rationality. History has produced distinct ideas about order and rationality in different nations, and modern industrial policies are organized around those ideas" (1994, 2). In the French case, a cultural tradition such as "the Jacobin obsession with equality, universalism, and national unity . . . negates particularism based on locality, corporate membership, and birth, thereby weakening the probability of people drawing boundaries on the basis of ascribed characteristics" (Lamont 1992, 137). The "Jacobin" tradition identifies the state as the defender of the general interest, in opposition to the particular interests advanced by interest groups (Schmidt 1999). This tradition is said to underpin policies of state intervention in industry that aim for "equality, universalism, and national unity," and makes the competitive, individualistic, and antistate rhetoric of neoliberalism unpalatable, particularly in the domain of welfare state policy, because "the welfare state constitutes

4. On Giscard and the Giscardian era see Bothorel 1983; Cohen 1992; Duhamel 1980; Ferenczi 1981; Flamant 1992; Frears 1981; Giroud 1979; Giscard d'Estaing 1979, 1984, 1988; Laverdines 1979; Robin 1979; Todd 1977.

a kind of common meeting ground or lowest common denominator that symbolizes republican unity and a collective commitment to providing a strong safety net, values to which the Left has historically assigned priority; state responsibility for promoting the common good, a value that the Left and Gaullism championed; and Christian solidarity" (Kesselman 2002, 181).

There are many advantages to cultural explanations, not least the way in which they demand a detailed engagement with historical context, challenge the dominant social scientific trend of assuming a universal human nature, and attempt to produce explanations "from the inside," beginning with actors' understandings of their situations. To some degree, cultural explanations have been accepted as one tool in the arsenal of social scientific explanations. But there is considerable evidence against the proposition that a "national culture" sustained the French pattern of a weak adoption of neoliberal measures in the Giscard period.

First, many sources of support for neoliberal positions, particularly among the elite, existed in the 1970s in France. Kesler (1985) writes that the Ecole Nationale d'Administration (ENA), which feeds the Grands Corps of the French state, had already been "conquered" by neoliberal thought in the 1970s, even if this teaching was not quite hegemonic. Instruction was overseen by the "brilliant leader of fundamentalist neo-liberalism . . . Professor Jean-Jacques Rosa [who] considered western economies sick because of their bulimic states, and considered the Welfare State to have failed" (374). "The high bureaucrats issued from the ENA or from the Ecole Polytechnique believe that there is a limit to the state's intervention and to the tax burden. The state can't do everything, it has already done too much, it should stop. They believe that France has lived for twenty years a social democratic experience and that it should from now on bend to the constraints of international competition" (395). Indeed, Kesler writes that after the Socialist victory of 1981, the ENA was the "protector" in France of neoliberal ideas.

A similar situation was occurring at the Institut d'Etudes Politiques (Sciences Po), from which almost the whole of France's leadership class emerges. There economics was taught under the auspices of Jacques Rueff, one of the most ardent postwar defenders of the market. Rueff is known as one of the few leading economists to resist the increasingly interventionist direction of the postwar French state. He was the architect of a liberalization effort under de Gaulle, and he is responsible for analyses such as the following: "If you aid the unemployed, you make durable a condition which would have been only temporary had you not intervened... you have falsified the mechanisms.... And you have done more bad than good" (quoted in Hatzfeld 1971, 55). Along with economists and social scientists Jean Fourastié (1978), Jean-Marie Benoist, Lionel Stoleru (1974), Jean-Pierre Fourcade (1979), Jean-Jacques Rosa, André Fourçans (1978, 1980), and several others, Rueff was part of a group, dubbed the "new economists," who carried the neoliberal flame in France in the postwar period.

In the 1970s antistatist arguments had also received a renewed boost from an unexpected quarter. Following the publication in French of Alexander Solzhenitsyn's *Gulag Archipelago*, a new strain of anti-Marxist argument emerged among the French intelligentsia: "At some point between 1973 and 1978 marxism, and the study of its theoretical implications and resonances, lost its stranglehold upon the intellectual imagination in France, a grip it had exercised unbroken for a generation. In the space of less than a decade it became fashionable to be not just non-Marxist, but anti-Marxist. The French discovered Popper, Hayek, and, with embarrassment at the oversight, their own Raymond Aron" (Judt 1986, 170). Thus in the mid-to-late 1970s, at just the time that France had elected a politician favorable to reducing state intervention, French political culture was rediscovering for its own reasons a rejection of collectivism.

I do not argue here that neoliberalism was dominant, but that it was an important minority position, with exponents in the highest reaches of the French state. To develop an objective measure of how popular neoliberal ideas were among academics in the 1970s under Giscard, particularly when he had chosen as his prime minister the economist Raymond Barre, I examined and coded all doctoral theses (Doctorats d'Etat) defended between 1976 and 1981 in economics at the Sorbonne (Paris I), following the methodology of Babb's (2001) work on Mexico. The total population consists of 152 theses, ranging across all subdisciplines in economics. I chose Paris I because it is reputed to be *less* neoliberal than the other leading producers of academic work on economic subjects, ENA, Sciences Po, and the Ecole Polytechnique (Kesler 1985) and thus provides a "tough test" of the thesis that neoliberal ideas were already "thinkable" by the late 1970s. (Although the Ecole des Hautes Etudes en Sciences Sociales was also a possible candidate for the analysis, too few dissertations were produced there during this period to make such an analysis meaningful.)

I read the introduction and conclusion of each dissertation as well as any pages that, according to the table of contents, dealt with the issue of

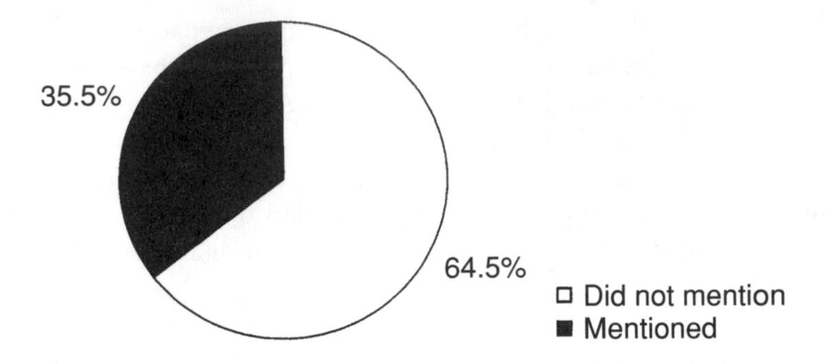

FIGURE 4.2. Presence of the issue of neoliberalism in economics dissertations at Paris I (Sorbonne), 1976–81

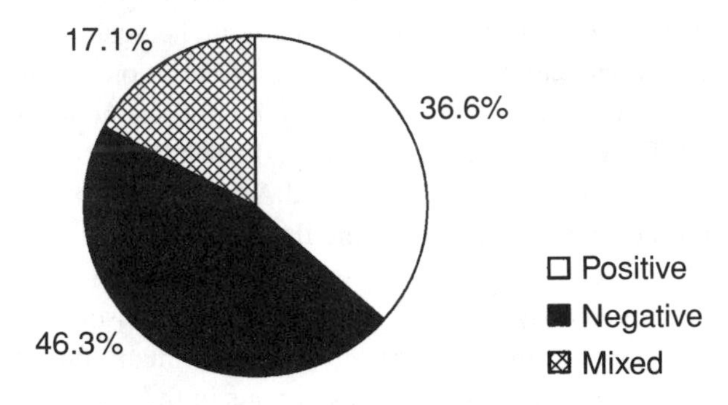

FIGURE 4.3. Evaluation of neoliberal claims as a percentage of theses that mentioned and evaluated them at Paris I (Sorbonne), 1976–81

neoliberalism. The specific issue was defined as the question of whether state intervention in the form of high taxes, high welfare spending, nationalization of firms, or tariff barriers prevents economic growth, and whether monetarist policies are preferable to Keynesian policies.

I coded the dissertations first as to whether they mentioned any of these issues at all. This provides a first glimpse of whether the issue of state interventionism was on the agenda, which it was (fig. 4.2): 35.5 percent of the dissertations mentioned one of these issues, either in the introduction or conclusion, or in a section important enough to be labeled in the table of contents. (I did not include in this count several dissertations that simply mentioned the words *neolibérale* or *neoclassique*; the specific theme of less state intervention had to be mentioned.) The most heated debate during this period concerned the question of free trade: a substantial number of dissertations praised the virtues of low tariff barriers, while an equally large number condemned free trade for leading to the "underdevelopment" of the periphery.

Second, I coded the evaluation of neoliberal tenets that the theses gave. Of the group that mentioned neoliberal tenets, 24.1 percent did not attempt a normative evaluation of them at all. This group largely consisted of dissertations that in the United States would be written in departments of history rather than departments of economics, in that their intent was historical and descriptive rather than evaluative. For example, one dissertation on the history of antipoverty policy in the United States between 1964 and 1974 refrained from evaluating the *effect* of these policies on the economy. Because the intent of this project is to examine how neoliberal tenets were evaluated, I exclude this group from the calculations below.

Of the group that mentioned and evaluated neoliberal tenets, a large number (17.1 percent) gave mixed evaluations, as might be expected in academic work at this level. The largest group—though not quite the majority—of the theses that mentioned and evaluated neoliberal tenets evaluated them negatively: 46.3 percent. (The largest subgroup of these examined the question of underdevelopment, particularly in the countries formerly colonized by France, and among these theses world-systems theory was by far the strongest intellectual influence in the late 1970s.) And, of dissertations that mentioned and evaluated neoliberal tenets, 36.6 percent evaluated them positively (fig. 4.3). The small numbers involved mean that the findings must be interpreted modestly, but it is worth noting that I examined the whole *population* of dissertations (not just a sample) for a specific time period at the institution most likely to be opposed to neoliberalism.

What these numbers show is that in the late 1970s in Paris, at an institution not reputed to be particularly favorable to neoliberal ideas, such ideas were mentioned regularly, and they were evaluated favorably quite often. The tendency is clearly anti neoliberal: almost half of the dissertations that mentioned such ideas evaluated them negatively. But more than one-third of the dissertations that mentioned such ideas evaluated them positively, suggesting that even at the educational institution least in favor of the free market, neoliberalism was a significant minority presence among economists in the late 1970s.

For comparison, consider figures 4.4 and 4.5, which perform a similar coding on the sixty-eight dissertations submitted to the Economics Department of the University of Chicago between 1980 and 1983. Chicago's

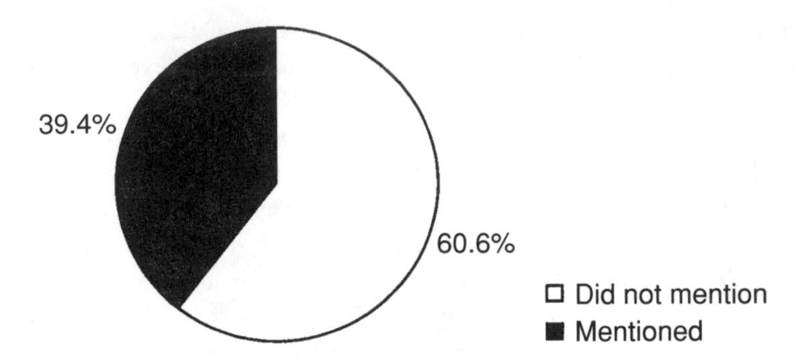

FIGURE 4.4. Presence of the issue of neoliberalism in economics dissertations at the University of Chicago, 1981–83

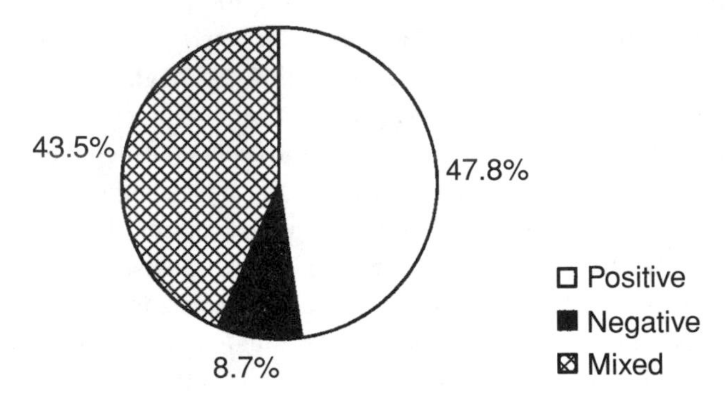

FIGURE 4.5. Evaluation of neoliberal claims as a percentage of theses that mentioned and evaluated them at the University of Chicago, 1981–83

Economics Department is usually considered the scholarly ground most favorable to neoliberal policies and ideas, so this is an indication of one extreme among the economics profession.[5] Negative evaluations of neoliberalism as defined above were clearly quite rare at the University of Chicago; on the other hand, positive evaluations were not in the majority: the majority of dissertations at this, the department most favorable to such ideas, did give either mixed or negative evaluations of them.

5. Obviously, comparing the department at the Sorbonne—the most "Left" elite department in France—with a similarly positioned department in the United States, such as Harvard or MIT, would be more useful, but resources did not permit this; so what we have here are the two extremes of the spectrum—the institution held to be the most anti-neoliberal in France, and the one held to be the most pro-neoliberal in the United States.

Finally, opinion polls suggest that the French embrace of the state and of egalitarianism during this period was ambivalent, as seen in responses to questions on taxation, nationalization, egalitarianism, and trust in government. On taxes, the vast majority of respondents favored a tax on "great fortunes": in 1977 Gallup found 86 percent in favor of a tax on fortunes greater than two million francs, and 69 percent in favor of a tax on fortunes greater than one million francs. On the other hand, 68 percent of French respondents in 1970 and 55 percent in 1974 found taxes "excessive or unbearable" (Gallup 1976).

On nationalization, views were mixed: 30 percent of respondents thought nationalized enterprises were rather less efficient than private enterprises in 1977, with 26 percent responding the reverse; but 36 percent believed the nationalization of banks and large enterprises would play a positive role in the resolution of the economic crisis, with only 20 percent anticipating a negative role (Gallup 1976).

Although support for the welfare state has always remained high (V. Schmidt 1999, 2001, 2002), this does not extend to support for egalitarianism. Although repeated surveys on this measure are not available for this period, in 1978 the Société Française d'Enquêtes par Sondage (SOFRES) posed a set of questions on egalitarianism to those who identified themselves as on the left of the political spectrum. One question asked respondents to place themselves on a scale from 1 to 6, with 1 representing the position "It is necessary to conserve a large measure of inequality of revenues, to foster imitation" and 6 the position "It is necessary to give the same revenue to everyone, whatever their context or aptitudes." Those identifying themselves as on the "extreme left" were the most egalitarian (83 percent placed themselves at levels 4 to 6, the egalitarian half of the spectrum), but those who identified with the Communists, Socialists, Left Radicals, and Ecologists showed considerably more mixed responses: respectively, 54 percent, 45 percent, 43 percent, and 40 percent at levels 4 to 6 (SOFRES 1978, 60). In other words, the majority of Socialists, Left Radicals, and Ecologists fall in the more *in*egalitarian half of the scale.

Trust in government is actually *lower* in France than in other countries, particularly for the time period examined here. Scholars of France have often noted this distrust: Crozier wrote of it as long ago as 1964. Ambler (1975) reports the results of a survey conducted in the early 1970s showing that the French give trustful responses less often than respondents in other countries: when asked "Speaking generally, what are the things about this country that you are most proud of as a Frenchman?" only 29 percent spontaneously reported pride in the political system; this compares with 85 percent in the United States, 46 percent in the United Kingdom, and 7 percent in Germany (results for the latter three taken from Almond and Verba 1963). Ambler concludes that these findings show "the significance of political alienation in France, as well as the instrumental nature of loyalties to the Fifth Republic" (1975, 40). Levels of trust in authorities are similar in the United States and France (53 percent vs. 47 percent) but belief in the efficacy of elections varies. To the question "How much do you feel that having elections makes the people who govern (the government) pay attention to what the people think?" 24 percent of French respondents but only 8 percent of American respondents said "not at all" or "not very much," while 66 percent of French respondents but 90 percent of American respondents said "some" or "a good deal." Crozier's (1964) classic analysis of the ambivalent French relation to government is that the French desire bureaucracy *because* they fear the authority of government, that is, a formally stated set of rules frees the individual from the unpredictability of personal dependency on superiors. Ambler believes that the peace and prosperity brought by de Gaulle's Fifth Republic ameliorated this mistrust, but did not erase it, and that "a tradition of political cynicism continues to show through" (1975, 54).

I conclude from these various sources first that collectivist or statist culture may have been dominant, but was certainly not hegemonic, in France in the 1970s, and space had opened for a possible neoliberal moment under Giscard. The president had committed himself publicly to reducing the size of the state, and a minority culture of questioning state intervention was developing among the elite as well as professional economists. The public was ambivalent about high taxes, nationalization, egalitarianism, and the efficacy of the state—often evidencing what psychologists call attitudinal inconsistency (Plous 1993): the tendency to express contradictory preferences depending on which aspect of a phenomenon is salient in a question (e.g., preference for a large welfare state, but discomfort with the taxes that finance that welfare state), making it difficult to predict behavior from expressed attitudes.

Differences in public opinion among different countries on the issue of the proper role of government do exist, but the question is complicated enough that scholars have taken opposing sides as to whether the general trend is difference or similarity. Tom Smith (1987) surveys results from the International Social Survey Programme's modules on the role of government, social support, and social inequity in five countries and concludes,

"Americans have a less elaborated welfare system because they want and demand less, while Europeans have more because they want more" (407–8). On the other hand, Coughlin (1980) examines individual polls in eight countries and concludes,

> Americans are not alone in their sanctification of the values of individualism; similar tendencies exist even among the "welfare leaders" of Western Europe. In the same fashion, collectivism is not restricted to nations with strong social-democratic traditions; Americans as well as Canadians accord great respect to the values of security and social protection. The prevailing ideological climate in each of the eight nations is mixed and is not dominated by extremes of ideology. (1980, 31)

Wilensky (2002) suggests that the discrepancy in these conclusions is explained by the fact that although persistent cross-national differences exist on abstract questions of *principles and values*, issue-specific questions yield similar responses across nations. For example, although American respondents distrust government, they overwhelmingly support increases in Medicare and Social Security, as well as increases or maintenance of spending on Medicaid, unemployment compensation, AFDC, and food stamps. Less than 16 percent of respondents favored decreasing spending on AFDC, the most unpopular of the American state's welfare programs. These findings about support for specific programs are typical (see also Free and Cantril 1968; Kluegel and Smith 1986; McClosky and Zaller 1984; Shapiro and Young 1989; Weaver, Shapiro, and Jacobs 1995).

In addition, answers to such questions show extreme sensitivity to the precise framing of the question: for example, Americans are hesitant to say that it should "definitely" or even "probably" be the government's responsibility to "provide" jobs for everyone who wants them, yet, in a separate question, the majority states that it is an "essential" or "important" responsibility of the government to "see to it" that everyone who wants a job has one (Smith 1987). More spectacularly, Americans have always been distrustful of "welfare," but they have always overwhelmingly favored "aid to the poor" (Gilens 1999). Finally, "American exceptionalism" does not hold on questions of taxation: about two-thirds of citizens of all the countries find their own income taxes too high. Interestingly, Americans are much more likely than respondents in other countries to believe that taxes on business are too *low* (Smith 1987).

TABLE 4.3 **European countries ranked in ascending order of income inequality**

European countries ranked in ascending order of income inequality (Gini coefficient)		European countries ranked in ascending order of income inequality (Theil statistic)	
1970	1992	1970	1992
U.K.	Spain	Norway	Norway
Sweden	Finland	Finland	Denmark
Belgium	Belgium	Denmark	Finland
Netherlands	Netherlands	Germany	Netherlands
Finland	Italy	Netherlands	Sweden
Germany	Germany	U.K.	U.K.
Denmark	U.K.	Belgium	Germany
Greece	Sweden	Sweden	Belgium
Spain	Denmark	Greece	Austria
Norway	Norway	France	Greece
Portugal	France	Austria	Portugal
Italy	Greece	Italy	France
France	Portugal		Spain
			Italy

Source: Conceição, Ferreira, and Galbraith 1999, 18.

Wilensky (2002) sums up as follows: "Survey data show that whatever national ideological differences appear in response to abstract questions, the issue-specific attitudes toward taxing, spending, and the welfare state are very similar across countries and over time" (2002, 269–70). This seems to be the case because, as scholars of American politics have noted, an enduring feature of American politics is that Americans are "ideologically Republican and programmatically Democrat"—suspicious of government, but supportive of every *specific* thing that government does. Thus abstract questions find American suspicion of government—and lead scholars to conclude that the United States is exceptional—while questions on specific policies find American support for policies, and lead scholars to emphasize the similarities between countries. For our purposes, the main point to take away from this review of the surveys is that this ambivalence of public opinion and the existence of inconsistencies mean that public opinion is not determinist. Perhaps more important, even if a culture of egalitarianism existed, it did not prevent France from being, for most of the postwar period, one of the most inegalitarian countries of Europe (see table 4.3).

There are also several theoretical reasons why the "national culture" explanation is unsatisfactory. First, as the evidence above makes clear, the national culture argument ignores the presence of contradictory cultural trends, conflict and struggle, and of often vital subcultures. (In the French case, egalitarianism has been in tension with nationalism: for example, nationalist reasons led de Gaulle to keep taxes on French businesses low, so that they could compete internationally.) Second, the national culture argument also ignores the presence of cultural diffusion across national boundaries, an increasingly important phenomenon (Simmons, Garrett, and Dobbin 2003). Third, it ignores the fact that cultural concepts are malleable, and can usually be interpreted in multiple ways, which makes it impossible to read policy off of culture. As anthropologists teach us: "If culture is not an object to be described, neither is it a unified corpus of symbols and meanings that can be definitively interpreted. Culture is contested, temporal, and emergent" (Clifford 1986, 19), "contradictory, loosely integrated, contested, mutable, and highly permeable" (Sewell 1999, 52). This is the understanding of culture that is also emerging in cognitive psychology. Summarizing recent psychological research, DiMaggio (1997) asks whether culture is best conceived of as a "latent variable"—that is, a "tight network of a few abstract central themes and their more concrete entailments, all instantiated to various degrees in a range of symbols, rituals, and practices"—or a cultural toolkit, "a pastiche of mediated representations, a repertoire of techniques, or a toolkit of strategies." He concludes,

> Research in cognitive psychology strongly supports the toolkit over the latent-variable view and suggests that the typical toolkit is very large indeed. . . . This work has several important implications for students of culture. First, it refutes the notion that people acquire a culture by imbibing it (and no other) through socialization. . . . Third, the research explains the capacity of individuals to participate in multiple cultural traditions, even when those traditions contain inconsistent elements. Fourth, it establishes the capacity of people to maintain distinctive and inconsistent action frames, which can be invoked in response to particular contextual cues . . . recent cognitive research . . . places the burden of proof on those who depict culture as strongly constraining behavior or who would argue that people experience culture as highly integrated, that cultural meanings are strongly thematized, that culture is binding, and that cultural information acquired through experience is more powerful than that acquired through other means. (267–68)

The "national culture" explanations, with their talk of "distinct ideas about order and rationality" pervading entire territorial units, are at odds with this research. There are indeed aggregate differences in the way populations respond to specific questions, but both attitudinal inconsistency and the ability of actors to participate in and invoke multiple cultures depending on contextual cues mean that we cannot directly extrapolate from national differences in survey responses to policymaking.

If national culture cannot explain the French resistance to neoliberalism, another popular explanation suggests that the French labor movement has prevented neoliberalism, but for the period under study here, this too is unconvincing. First, the French unions in the postwar period have been fragmented and excluded from routine decision-making authority. As figure 9 in the introduction shows, a lower proportion of the workforce is unionized in France than in Britain, Germany, or even the United States, and France had fewer working days lost per thousand employees in this period than Britain and the United States. Moreover, the French labor movement has been characterized by a lack of ties between parties of the Left and the trade union movement, meaning that the ability of the unions to affect policy is limited to extreme instances when they can mobilize thousands of demonstrators (Howell 1992a, 1992b). Although in recent years the public sector unions have been able to resist or amend reform by striking, leading some analysts to argue that "labor still matters" (Béland 2001; Palier 2000), the much larger private sector, where unionization rates are as low as 5 percent, has been unable to resist reform. Related to this is the question of how and whether the strength of labor translates into policy: in postwar France the left was split between the Communists and Socialists, a split which kept both parties excluded from power.

If the working class is weak, a new trend in the scholarship associated with the "varieties of capitalism" perspective argues that business interests are at the heart of policymaking. A look at the work of Bob Hancké (2001, 2002), who has been instrumental in applying this approach to the French case, shows both the insights it yields and its limits. Hancké studies the response of the French political economy to the profitability crisis of the early 1980s. He argues that all of the attempts of the state—through the reform of labor relations, through the Auroux laws on workplace decentralization, and through financial reform—failed. He then shows how large firms turned varying aspects of each of these state-implemented reforms to their own ends, but could only do so by keeping the state at arm's length. Hancké's work is an elegant and entirely convincing explanation of industrial adjustment in the 1980s, but it falters when it tries to generalize from this case to the French political economy as a whole. Other features of French neoliberalism—e.g., privatizations, abolition of price control, and financial deregulation—were all initiated by the state. Privatization began as a tactical political response to Mitterrand's nationalizations, abolition of price controls was undertaken by Prime Minister Barre in the face of business opposition (both discussed further below), and financial deregulation was (in Hancké's own term) the "brainchild" of a senior minister. If the "firm-centered" explanation cannot be generalized to other aspects of industrial policy, much less can it be generalized to other policy domains: French firms are not unified on the question of whether to oppose expensive social policy and the high taxation that it requires. (See Mares [2001] for discussions of why some firms have historically supported social policy and high taxes.) And as we will see below, Giscard's neoliberalism, although it did not move in an Anglo-American direction, was more hurtful to industry than helpful to it—rather than creating an environment that would nurture firms, Giscard withdrew state support from them.

Punitive Neoliberalism

Although he did not institute a neoliberalism of the kind and intensity seen elsewhere, Giscard did introduce several measures in this direction—neoliberalism *à la française* (interview, Michel Poniatowski, 1 Jun 2001).[6] These included an attempt to end subsidies to lame duck industries; the end of price control; the beginning of the process that would result in the Euro; and efforts to control health care costs (interviews: Fernand Icart, 10 Jun 2001; Pierre Lelong, 8 Jun 2001; René Monory, 18 Jul 2001; Michel Poniatowski, 1 Jun 2001; Jean Sérisé, 20 Jun 2001; Simone Veil, 26 Jun 2001). In particular, even if the comparison of the policy structures explains why French neoliberalism did not take the shape that American neoliberalism did, we still have to explain a curious element of French neoliberalism under Giscard: its *punitive* character.

Neoliberalism for Giscard meant above all three things: making French industry more competitive by opening it to external competition, ending subsidies to "lame duck" industries, and encouraging firms to make their own decisions (Wright 1984):

6. A list of people interviewed appears at the beginning of the references section at the end of the book.

> The three objectives were translated into policies in a number of ways: nationalised industries were forced to adopt a more "realistic" economic pricing policy; price controls in the private sector were dramatically abolished or considerably eased (in August 1978 the price of bread was decontrolled for the first time since 1791); certain restrictions on capital investment abroad were lifted; and private shareholders were given (albeit limited) access to state industries, banks and insurance companies. (18)

These measures had the intended effects—they "rationalized" industry, driving unprofitable firms out of the market—but because the world economic climate had turned difficult in the late 1970s, workers who lost their jobs when these unprofitable firms closed down did not find new jobs, driving unemployment to record heights.

The political unpopularity of this position (see, e.g., "Barre s'explique sur tout," *Le Figaro Magazine*, 7 Oct 1978; "Raymond Barre: 'Je suis un premier ministre des temps difficiles,'" *Le Matin*, 4 Sep 1979) soon created pressure to continue the tradition of subsidizing key industries, especially steel, shipbuilding, and textiles, to which Giscard bowed. Many Gaullists criticized the policy to such an extent that by 1979 rumors were circulating that the prime minister would resign; he did not do so, but the punitive policies could not withstand the criticism (Schwarz 1979). Moreover, for reasons of defense as well as international symbolism, Giscard invested heavily in high-tech industries such as aerospace and nuclear power. These two policies—politically generated continuation of subsidies plus symbolically important investment in certain industries—combined to *increase* the size of the state: "By the end of Giscard d'Estaing's presidency one worker in four was employed by the state administration, in local authorities, the public service industries (for example, the electricity industry), or the public enterprises (such as Air France, Renault, and Seita)" (Wright 1984, 18–19).

Where Giscard did succeed was in making the environment "more competitive" for French companies that could not exert pressure for subsidies:

> One of the most direct and far-reaching consequences of Giscardian industrial policies is the radical rationalisation which took place. A number of well-known companies disappeared in mergers (often as an alternative to liquidation) (for instance, Boussac and Kléber-Colombes), and many of the big industrial groups moved out of some of their traditional (and often loss-making) activities into new ones.... The costs of this belated and accelerated rationalisation were high.

> The number of bankruptcies rose dramatically, increasing 70 per cent over the seven years of the Giscardian presidency. (Green 1984, 147–48)

These changes were encouraged by the forced confrontation of French industry with the international field, and resulted in the demise of uncompetitive firms.

As Green notes, however, these changes were not popular with the French. The immediate result of this rapid rationalization was increasing unemployment: "It could be argued that rather than constituting a failure, the attempt to encourage industrial adjustment... was too successful. More specifically, the consequences of Giscardian industrial policy (in the shape of the disappearance, at too rapid a rate, of sectors, firms, and jobs) proved to be electorally unacceptable" (Green 1984, 152). When confronted with external competition, French firms that had counted on state aid but could not pressure the state to continue that aid folded. Note the curious role that "globalization" plays in this story. The usual argument is that globalization hinders state actors who want to pass leftist, redistributive policies by forcing states to attract capital with low taxes, weak labor organizations, harsh antilabor laws, and minimal welfare payments. But under Giscard, globalization forced the abandonment of neoliberal policies because external competition led to increased folding of firms. By contrast, American neoliberalism in industrial policy included attempts to *make* firms more competitive across the board by lowering the costs of regulatory compliance—a populist neoliberalism. By 1980 56 percent of French business leaders were calling Raymond Barre's policies a failure (*Quotidien de Paris*, 11 Jan 1980).

This punitive neoliberalism was also an innovation in France—but where did it come from? To explain the particular shape of French neoliberalism, this section develops another point in my critique of theories of path dependence. The path-dependence model assumes that innovations arise randomly, and that the key moment to analyze is the moment of implementation, at which point these innovations will be blocked because of the costs of reversal. But one key difference in analyzing change across societies is that innovation itself is systematically structured: Social structures may determine the rate of innovations and the *kind* of innovations that are brought onto the agenda. This is clear from a comparison of the sources of innovation in the two countries.

In the U.S. case, the weakening of party structures in the 1960s increasingly forced candidates to turn away from dependence on parties and to oversee their own campaigns. For most of the century, the mass party was the medium through which politicians acquired and used power; by the 1970s, however, parties were no longer financially strong enough to continue in this role, and politicians increasingly enlisted social sources of support to help build their own personal campaign machines and conduct their campaigns themselves. In this system, candidates are "in business for themselves" (Davidson 1981, 131). Many politicians became "policy entrepreneurs," because one technique for ensuring visibility in voters' eyes is immediate engagement with substantive issues. The quest for political office became a stable source of political innovation, as discussed in chapter 1.

Another source of innovations was the decentralized nature of the polity. It has become scholarly orthodoxy that decentralization of power hinders policy change. Immergut (1992) introduced the idea that veto points—sites in the policymaking process where minorities can block change—can lead to policy stability, and Tsebelis (1995, 1999, 2002) has attempted to turn the idea into a basis for the reorganization of comparative politics. But in the study of organizations, the orthodox view is that decentralized systems lead to rapid innovation. Stark (1999) writes,

> [I]n relentlessly changing organizations where, in extreme cases, there is uncertainty even about what product the firm will be producing in the near future, the strategy horizon of the firm is unpredictable and its fitness landscape is rugged. To cope with these uncertainties, instead of concentrating its resources for strategic planning among a narrow set of senior executives or delegating that function to a specialized department, firms may undergo a radical decentralization in which virtually every unit becomes engaged in innovation. (159)

Decentralized organizations have several advantages that lead to greater innovation, the most important of which is the greater number of workers involved in innovative activities, including those closest to and most knowledgeable of the production process. Damanpour (1991) examined studies conducted between 1960 and 1988 on organizational innovation and reports a routine finding of a negative correlation between centralization and innovation. What decentralization does is bring a larger range of actors into contact with the production or policymaking process, which increases the rate of innovations, although the decentralized nature of the organization may make implementing those innovations difficult.

With its entrepreneurial politicians and its decentralized innovation, the American case fits the model of politics described by William Riker: "New alternatives, new issues, are like new products. Each one is sponsored as a test of the voting market, in the hope that the new alternative will render new issues salient, old issues irrelevant, and, above all, will be preferred by a majority to what went before. This is the art of politics: to find some alternative that beats the current winner" (1982, 209).

But, just as economic markets are socially constructed, so are political markets: Riker's description does not fit French politics in the postwar period very well. There, politics is reminiscent not of a market, but of a bureaucracy, with many of the classical features of bureaucracies identified by Weber. Most important among these are entry based on competitive exams (instead of on loyalty, popularity, or ideological similarity, as in the American system) and a centralized hierarchy (strong parties, and with the legislature firmly subordinate to the executive in this period). Rather than through becoming an "entrepreneurial politician," the path to success for a French politician is through the formalized system of schools of administration (Sciences Po, ENA) followed by civil service. Parties still finance political campaigns, so individual politicians do not need to seek new issues to make a name for themselves; and centralization of power means fewer points at which innovations can enter the political agenda. This combination of characteristics leads to a distinctive pattern of policy innovation. Reliance on experts leads to policy innovations that are tightly coupled to innovations in the academic world, as well as to a methodical process of search for the most successful practices; and hierarchy leads to political innovations at the level of the national party rather than at the level of the local individual politician. Although there is innovation at the level of the party, no president had ever lost an election in Fifth Republic France before Giscard, so the parties of the Right had not set up an apparatus for policy rethinking of the kind seen, for example, in British parties when they are out of power.

Technocracy

The most prominent source of innovations in France, cited by the majority of my interviewees, is the academy, or more narrowly, the technocracy that funnels students through particular elite schools and into government office. The French executive is staffed to a great degree by graduates of the Ecole Nationale d'Administration (ENA), entrance to which, and exit from which, are governed by competitive exams. Dogan (1979) found that this path of "mandarin ascent" was the predominant means into ministerial office for the Giscard ministers. He describes the typical such minister as follows: "He is representative neither of a current of thought nor of a political force. He owes his appointment entirely to the confidence that the president or possibly the prime minister has in him.... He incarnates no legitimacy of his own" (16). A characteristic of innovations that arise from the academy is that they are constrained by the evolution of academic expertise; this explains both the punitive nature of some of the innovations (they were born autonomously of what would be politically popular) as well as their moderate degree (they were constrained by the rationalist ethos of the technocracy; see Fourcade-Gourinchas and Babb 2002 for a similar argument about the influence of the French technocracy). Note that it would be misleading to argue that because French state actors are more enamored of academic expertise than American state actors, there must be a national cultural difference at work; the United States has plenty of academically trained professionals, but the difference is that they do not control the state.

Imitation

A second result of staffing the state with trained professionals, rather than through mechanisms of loyalty or ideology, is that policy innovation is fed to a greater degree by a search for the most successful practices among neighboring states. For example, in discussing the origins of her attempt to control health costs, Simone Veil, Giscard's minister of Health, Social Security, and the Family, said,

> It was in 1974 that, when I arrived at the Ministry,... I began to say that medicine has a cost, "health is priceless but medicine has a cost" ["la santé n'a pas de prix mais... la médecine a un coût"], and that one could not avoid being interested in costs.... [Q: What were the influences on the development of your thinking in this domain?] At the very beginning of my ministry, I made a very interesting voyage to Canada. They did very interesting things, very experimental.... Then, I kept up with the evolutions in the other European countries, those that had the same standard of living, for example, Germany, the English system... we

were all agreed on the fact that the population didn't realize that our other colleagues from the Economy said that we managed badly, "You spend too much." (interview, 26 Jun 2001)

Raymond Barre invoked similar experiences during his tenure as vice-president of the Commission of the European Communities in Brussels, and a secretary of state recounted an episode where he disguised himself as part of a team of OECD experts to inspect Germany's vocational training system (interviews: Barre, 28 June 2001; Jacques Legendre, 20 Jun 2001).

Backlash

A third source of innovation becomes evident when we examine why Giscard did not move to privatize, when Chirac, only a few years later, did. The postwar nationalizations had been undertaken by a very wide political spectrum, including de Gaulle himself, and the Gaullist party remained within this understanding of nationalization in the interest of modernization. But when Mitterrand nationalized further, he broke this implicit coalition; in reaction, the Gaullists rethought their views on nationalized industry. As discussed above, Chirac's privatizations were initiated for tactical reasons, "intended for the short-term political benefit of those backing the policy" (Feigenbaum and Henig 1994, 196; see also Feigenbaum, Henig, and Hamnett 1999). Thus, the kind of searching for political space that happened at an individual level in the United States occurred at the level of the party in France—decreasing the number of actors involved in political innovation. Moreover, because until 1971 no president had lost an election, in Giscard's time the Right had not developed a policy machinery for political innovation when in opposition, as seen in Britain; this meant that political innovation at the level of the party was not as systematic as in Britain.

In sum, we see a very different picture of policy innovation in France. In the United States innovation was generated by candidates engaged in intense political competition and intensified because parties could not fund candidates; in addition, tight informal linkages, a tradition of amateurs in politics, and decentralized state structures combined to bring new ideas into the American polity. In France, the process of policy innovation during this period was more moderate, constrained by the bureaucratic features of the French state, particularly entrance based on competitive exams and hierarchy.

Conclusion

Putting these observations together, we can explain why the Giscard period—when all of the signs seemed to favor a neoliberal direction—did not see pro-market reform of the Anglo-American kind. First, an appeal to French national culture cannot explain French resistance to neoliberalism: French cultural traditions, like the cultural traditions of all complex societies, are flexible enough to include the possibility of free market measures. But despite this, and despite the autonomy of the state, the weakness of labor, the economic crisis that had opened a space for new solutions to be tried, and the president's stated intentions to reduce state intervention, France did not see the kinds of changes in the late 1970s that the United Kingdom and the United States would see just a few years later.

Rather, the source of the different fates of the United States and France is found in the ways in which the postwar political economy mobilized support or opposition, and in the structures that led to innovation in each country. First, the legacies of state-led industrialization in the postwar period—turning an agricultural country into an industrial power—created a pro-growth economic structure that was popular with both business and the public. The state was concerned in the postwar period to keep direct taxes on business low, French planning was largely used in the interests of industry, and the unions were not able to turn nationalized industries to their advantage (as the strong British labor unions had been able to), so no antistate business coalitions formed. The one exception to the pro-business nature of the state was in the welfare state taxes, the *cotisations sociales*, but the universal nature of the welfare state and the specific manner of tax collection—with taxes visibly targeted to benefits—generated loyalty from the majority of citizens. In addition, the largest portion of state revenue comes from "invisible" indirect taxes, which do not generate political protest.

The neoliberal innovations that did arrive on the agenda arose mainly from the technocracy and from imitation of other countries—which meant they were autonomous from popular will and explains the punitive nature of Giscard's industrial policy—and, later, from backlash to the policies of Mitterrand. Because nationalization was a main element of Mitterrand's policies, privatization became the leitmotif of the Gaullists afterward. Throughout this episode these innovations were constrained by the evolution of economic expertise.

What is not visible is the kind of intensely innovative, populist, and entrepreneurial process—not at all constrained by economic expertise—seen in the American case. Evident in the histories of neoliberalism under both Thatcher and Reagan is a remarkable degree of improvisation, with events moving in unpredictable fashion, and earlier events opening horizons of possibility that had not been envisioned, so that the neoliberal impulse becomes more clearly defined and exaggerated as time passes. In the United States this dynamism was catalyzed by a set of structures—weak parties, decentralized state structures, permeable bureaucracies—that made politics more like a competitive market by bringing a wider range of actors into the policymaking process. This allowed politicians to discover a way to make free market policies appeal to the majority. The structurally induced absence of similar dynamism made it difficult for French policymakers to find a way to entrench neoliberal policies in public opinion, and the punitive neoliberalism they came up with through their technocratic means of innovation withered at the next election.

This observation allows us to resolve the anomaly of rapid change occurring in the fragmented American state, rather than the centralized French state. While fragmentation and decentralization of power are obstacles to rapid implementation of policy, they aid policy innovation. Centralized states see less innovation, and technocratic states see different kinds of innovation: innovation comes from close familiarity with academic expertise, and from imitation of other states. In addition, in strong party systems, political innovation happens at the level of the party rather than the level of the individual politician.

Both of these elements—the pro-growth policies, and the technocratic structure—arise from the same historical dynamic, the postwar attempt to create a political economy that would turn France from an agricultural economy into an industrial one. This attempt was instantiated in a regressive tax structure, nationalized industries oriented toward economic growth, and reverse-redistributive welfare policies, as well as in a decision-making structure that was able to dampen social conflict by passing it through the filter of a state tightly tied to academic expertise, in contrast to states in which politicians found it advantageous to exaggerate social conflicts and bring them into the policymaking process.

Conclusion

Theories that see neoliberalism as caused by globalization, business-group power, the rise of ideas, or national culture—the "society-centered" explanations of neoliberalism—miss the essential role of the political process itself in policy outcomes. In the wake of the Second World War, France and Germany established a consensual decision-making structure and pro-growth policies, whereas the United States and United Kingdom implemented an adversarial decision-making structure and adversarial policies. Consequently, the four countries experienced the socio-economic transformations of the next several decades in very different ways. In the United States and United Kingdom the majority of the population crossed the "adversarial divide" (e.g., the majority began to pay an increasing level of visible, progressive taxes, and the majority moved out of union membership and into homeownership). This created a potential dissatisfaction with the status quo in these two countries, and politicians were able to turn this dissatisfaction into neoliberal policies. In France and West Germany, less visible taxes, pro-growth industrial policies, and less redistributive welfare state policies generated a consensus with the status quo that was resilient in the wake of the oil crisis, and a technocratic state apparatus and corporatist decision-making structure dampened political conflict.

In particular, the postwar structure did two things to separate the paths traveled by the United States and United Kingdom from those traveled by France and West Germany. First, the former two adopted *adversarial policies*, including more progressive tax structures, adversarial industrial policies, and more egalitarian welfare states; the latter adopted *pro-growth policies*, including more regressive tax structures, pro-growth industrial policies, and less redistributive, even reverse-redistributive, welfare states.

These policies had three main effects. (1) They defined categories—for example, adversarial policies defined the middle classes separately from the poor, and business separately from the state. (2) They structured information flows to reinforce these categories, for example by delivering to taxpayers precise information on how much taxes they were paying. (3) They strengthened the coalitions that struggled to get them passed—for example, the postwar coalition that produced nationalizations in France took privatization off of the agenda, while the fact that only Labour was involved in nationalizations in Britain meant the Conservatives kept the privatization flame burning throughout the postwar period. All of these dynamics provided opportunities for political gain to politicians who exploited these divisions, such as the episode of Reagan and the welfare queen, or Thatcher demonizing the unpopular unions as the "enemy within."

Second, the postwar structure saw a set of institutional divergences that sped neoliberal policies onto the political agenda in the United States and Britain, and prevented them in France and West Germany. In the weak labor countries, the key was the way in which new innovations arrive on the agenda or fail to do so. In France, the *technocracy*—state actors constrained by the evolution of economic expertise—restrained the development of neoliberalism, whereas in the United States *entrepreneurial politicians* sought out new issues. In the strong labor countries, the *integration of labor* within the decision-making apparatus was the key. In West Germany, the working class formed a faction of the right-wing party with an institutionalized (but not constitutionally guaranteed) veto, and labor was a corporatist partner, while in Britain, the working class was excluded from the right-wing party and this excluded and adversarial labor movement radicalized the Conservative Party and turned policies in an adversarial direction.

Critics who decry the potential of democracy to dissolve into a tyranny of the majority usually come from the right of the political spectrum, from Burke and Tocqueville to Fareed Zakaria. They are often concerned with the ability of the masses to *resist* free market policies, and they therefore often counsel resistance to the extension of democracy. One of my aims in this work has been to show that the tyranny of the majority can work the other way too: when the extension of democracy weakens the ability of the government to protect the rights of minorities, economic minorities suffer. This is the story of the rise of neoliberalism in the United States and Britain. Free market policies in advanced industrial democracies therefore raise a fundamental concern that lies at the heart of the meeting of democracy and late capitalism: how to protect the interests of the minority who lose in late capitalist market competition when the majority benefits from such competition (or can be brought to believe that it does) and the majority rules.

The consequences of the extension of democracy are therefore a concern that transcends traditional partisan distinctions of left and right. Concerns over the potential of democracy to devolve into tyranny of the majority have led to two distinct schools of thought on how to resolve the problem, which may be called the *republican* and the *democratic* solutions. I use *republican* here to invoke the concept of representative government, in which the power to rule is given to those most capable of ruling on behalf of all the people and in the interests of all (however such capability may be defined), and *democratic* is meant to invoke the concept of direct rule by the people themselves.

The republican solution is that to defend against the potentially chaotic results of democracy, actual power must be delegated by the people to wise guardians who have been chosen to deliberate in the interest of all the people. This model assumes that the guardians have either a greater capacity to deliberate and decide upon the wisdom of various courses of action, or more information and time with which to do so; they will therefore come to better conclusions and should implement them even when these conclusions conflict with the opinions of the majority who chose them. Edmund Burke provides what is still the best argument for this view: "Your representative owes you, not his industry only, but his judgment; and he betrays instead of serving you if he sacrifices it to your opinion" (quoted in Zakaria 2003, 168). A representative is not delegated simply to follow public opinion slavishly, but is delegated the task of *thinking about issues* and acting on them in accordance with her best judgment, even when this contradicts public opinion.

The attractions of this model are evident. It is empirically the case that public opinion is often ill-informed and ambivalent about issues, and selecting as a representative a person with the ability to examine issues and the time and information necessary to do so may yield better results for the society as a whole. As support for this argument Zakaria (2003) gives the examples of the U.S. Supreme Court and the Federal Reserve, two institutions that have retained public trust despite their nondemocratic natures.

The failings of the republican solution are also evident: if the history of the twentieth century has taught us any lasting lesson, it is surely that power delegated to the state and exercised in the name of the people can be shockingly abused. It is not clear what factors prevent the wise guardians, the state actors, from behaving in their own interest. Zakaria suggests that it is possible to restrain the guardians through codes of conduct, such as the values of "fair play, decency, liberty, and a Protestant sense of mission . . . that helped set standards for society" (2003, 236) earlier in the century. Aside from the question of whether these values did have the function ascribed to them, it does not seem that the sense of restraint advocated here is compatible with capitalism; the elite Zakaria identifies as having exercised their power with a sense of social responsibility—the business elite, lawyers, the press—are today engaged in a struggle for survival in which such values may place their proponents at a competitive disadvantage.

The "democratic" solution to the demagogic potential of democracy is to educate citizens to become capable of the same kind of deliberation that a representative would provide for them. "Deliberative democracy" has become something of a rallying cry among a small subset of political theorists. The basic idea is that preferences are formed and transformed (and not just aggregated) by the process of voting itself or by the process of coming to a decision in general. It should therefore be possible to influence the process by making available a higher quality of information and plenty of time to the voter or decision maker, such that the end result is a better decision. Ackerman and Fishkin (2004) suggest the introduction of a new national holiday, "Deliberation Day," that

> will be held one week before major national elections. Registered voters will be called together in neighborhood meeting places, in small groups of 15, and larger groups of 500, to discuss the central issues raised by the campaign. Each deliberator will be paid $150 for the day's work of citizenship, on condition that he or she shows up at the polls the next week. All other work, except the most essential, will be prohibited. (1)

On Deliberation Day voters would be exposed to arguments on various issues from both parties and given time to consider the arguments in small groups. Research has indeed shown that specific kinds of information can dramatically alter respondents' opinions (Althaus 1998; Bartels 1996; Gilens 2001), but *regardless* of the outcome—even if votes and decisions did not change as a result of the deliberation—many theorists in this tradition believe that some such process would be the truest incarnation of democracy because it creates citizens who participate actively in the process of self-government.

The idea should not be dismissed simply because it seems so utopian; all new political ideas seem utopian when first suggested, but some eventually get assimilated into common sense. The political systems of all the countries examined here—including the British and the American—have undergone radical transformation that would have seemed impractical and utopian to an observer in 1900, such as the extension of the franchise to women and minorities, and there is no particular reason why deliberative approaches cannot be tried.

Still, several problems in the perspective need to be worked out. First, what constitutes "true information"? Much political debate hinges on what the true facts of a case are and on how to interpret those facts. Second, is there a "true" opinion that the rationally deliberating citizen would necessarily adopt? What about the problems of cognitive bias, charisma, and ideological dominance in small-group decision making? What about the unwieldy nature of decision making by deliberation? Is it truly possible in a short stretch of time to allow information absorption as well as true deliberation? Ackerman and Fishkin's proposal guarantees only ten minutes of speaking time to each participant, rigorously measured by stopwatches; it is not clear that these are the best conditions for deliberation. And finally, is it not possible that a politicized public would actually be *more*, rather than less, polarized? Those who participate in the political process today tend to hold more extreme views than those who do not. While to some degree this must be a selection effect, it is also possible that political participation itself crystallizes extreme views; the politically unaware may be more willing to accept that both sides have good arguments. Is it possible that one reason complex societies are governable at all is that most people don't pay attention?

Research must continue on how and whether to implement republican and democratic solutions. For example, we need research on "how to guard the guardians," in the form of historical investigations into the functioning of nondemocratic institutions such as the Federal Reserve or the Bundesbank. When do such institutions function in the general interest, and when do they begin to function to the benefit of their members instead? This question lies at the border of historical sociology, political sociology, and the sociology of organizations. A lively research tradition is already growing around the question of whether deliberative democracy is possible or desirable; part of the research in this tradition might focus on when voters assimilate new information and when they resist it. Are there institutional contexts that can turn "motivated reasoning"—the phenomenon of seeking out information that reinforces one's prior beliefs and resisting contradictory information (Kunda 1987, 1990)—into "Bayesian updating," that is, the process of assimilating new information, including contradictory information, and updating one's beliefs accordingly (Gerber and Green 1999)? This question engages political sociology as well as social psychology.

But between these two alternatives, we can also use the investigations in this book to propose a third angle of investigation of the demagogic potential of democracies. I have suggested here that the politics we have seen recently in the United States and Britain are underpinned by an adversarial political context that has by now taken on a life of its own and that, for reasons specified in chapters 1 and 2, this adversarialism can lead to demagoguery in the United States. This suggests that demagoguery is not inherent in democracy but is generated in very specific circumstances having to do with the incentive structure of politicians, and it may be possible to alter those specific circumstances. As we have seen, adversarial politics has many benefits, including rapid entry of new issues onto the political agenda through intense political competition; the ability to engage many social actors, including non-elites, in the political process; a transparent mode of decision making; and the ability to encourage social debate about issues resulting from the length of time that an issue spends in the public sphere before resolution. On the other hand, adversarial politics can also have considerable costs. The inability to reach a social consensus on providing health care to the population is perhaps the American state's greatest current weakness, leading to a stunning waste of collective resources and reduced life-chances for a large minority of Americans. The anger and distrust that areas of state failure generate in turn lead to a punitive governmental structure in more tractable realms, such as environmental regulation, where businesses are punished in ways they find hard to understand. This in turn leads businesses to resent governmental intrusion and organize against the state, which makes state action even more difficult, and the cycle begins again. Adversarial politics magnify the harm to those who are already socioeconomically disadvantaged, and in the United States they have also had the unusual effect of requiring businesses to struggle under a heavier regulatory burden.

In explaining why the United States and Britain saw neoliberal policies in the wake of the oil crisis, while France and Germany did not, this book has raised many additional questions: Why did the United States and Britain adopt such unusually progressive tax codes? What role did contingent factors (such as the presence in power of Left parties for greater periods of time in the early postwar years) have on the development of adversarial structures in the United States and Britain, and what role did institutional factors (like the fragmentation of power, or the exclusion of labor) play? In normative terms, are the costs of regressive policies worth their benefits? The regressive tax and welfare structure of the French state underpins a remarkably stable political economy, the effects of which include outstanding health care for the entire population. Is it possible or desirable to shift from an adversarial mode to a pro-growth mode, or vice versa? Is the EU introducing adversarial politics into Europe?

I do not answer any of these questions here, but I hope to have made the case that these are the important questions to ask in any investigation of the history and evolution of capitalist democracy.

References

Interviews

Interviews with Members of the Workers' Wing (Christlich-Demokratische Arbeitnehmerschaft, or CDA) of the CDU

Egbert Biermann, Member of the Administration
Irmgard Blättel, Former Deputy Chair
Ralf Brauksiepe, Member of Parliament, Deputy Chair, Regional Chair (North Rhein-Westphalia)
Rainer Eppelmann, Member of Parliament, Honorary Chair
Joachim Krüger, Regional Chair (Berlin)
Karl-Josef Laumann, Member of Parliament, Deputy Chair
Uwe Schummer, Member of Parliament, Member of the Administration
Ingrid Sehrbrock, Deputy Chair

Interviews with Members of Giscard's Government

Raymond Barre, Prime Minister
Michel Durafour, Minister of Labor
Jean François-Poncet, Minister of Foreign Affairs
Robert Galley, Minister of Voluntary Services ("Ministre de la Cooperation")
Fernand Icart, Minister of Public Works and Town and Country Planning
Jacques Legendre, Secretary of State for the Minister of Labor
Pierre Lelong, Secretary of State in Posts and Telecommunications
Maurice Ligot, Secretary of State for the Prime Minister, Public Services
Pierre Mehaignerie, Minister of Agriculture
René Monory, Minister of Industry, Commerce, and the Artisanat, and Minister of the Economy
Jacques Pelletier, Secretary of State for the Minister of Education
Monique Pelletier, Secretary of State for the Guardian of the Seals, and Minister Delegate of the Prime Minister, in charge of the Condition of Women
Maurice Plantier, Secretary of State for Veterans

Michel Poniatowski, Minister of State, Minister of the Interior
Christiane Scrivener, Secretary of State for Minister of Economy and Finance (Consumption)
Jean Sérisé, Secretary to Giscard
Olivier Stirn, Secretary of State of Departments and Territories
Pierre-Christian Taittinger, Secretary of State for Minister of Foreign Affairs
Simone Veil, Minister of Health, Social Security, and the Family

Books and Articles

Abbott, Andrew. 1992. "From Causes to Events: Notes on Narrative Positivism." *Sociological Methods and Research* 20 (4): 428–45.

———. 1997. "On the Concept of Turning Point." *Comparative Social Research* 16:85–105.

———. 2000. *Time Matters: On Theory and Method*. Chicago: University of Chicago Press.

Ackerman, Bruce, and James Fishkin. 2004. *Deliberation Day*. New Haven, CT: Yale University Press.

Adam, Thomas. 1997. "Rettung der Geschichte—Bewahrung der Natur: Ursprung und Entwicklung der Historischen Vereine und des Umweltschutzes in Deutschland von 1770 bis zur Gegenwart." *Blätter für Deutsche Landesgeschichte* 133:239–77.

Adams, William James. 1989. *Restructuring the French Economy: Government and the Rise of Market Competition since World War II*. Washington, DC: Brookings Institution.

Aguilar, Susan. 1993. "Corporatist and Statist Designs in Environmental Policy: The Contrasting Roles of Germany and Spain in the European Community Scenario." *Environmental Politics* 2 (2): 223–47.

Akard, Patrick. 1989. *The Return of the Market: Corporate Mobilization and the Transformation of U.S. Economic Policy, 1974–1984*. PhD diss., University of Kansas.

———. 1992. "Corporate Mobilization and Political Power: The Transformation of U.S. Economic Policy in the 1970s." *American Sociological Review* 57:597–615.

Alber, Jens. 1989. *Der Sozialstaat in der Bundesrepublik, 1950–1983*. Frankfurt/New York: Campus Verlag.

———. 1999. "Draft Version of a Lecture Given at the European Forum of the European University Institute, Florence, 16 March 1999." San Domenico, Italy: European University Institute.

Aldrich, John H., and Richard G. Niemi. 1996. "The Sixth American Party System: Electoral Change, 1952–1992." In *Broken Contract? Changing Relationships between Americans and Their Government*, ed. Stephen G. Craig. Boulder, CO: Westview Press.

Alexander, Herbert E. 1983. *Financing the 1980 Election*. Lexington, MA: Lexington Books.

Almond, Gabriel A., and Sidney Verba. 1963. *The Civic Culture*. Boston: Little, Brown.
Althaus, Scott L. 1998. "Information Effects in Collective Preferences." *American Political Science Review* 92:545–58.
Ambler, John S. 1975. "Trust in Political and Nonpolitical Authorities in France." *Comparative Politics* 8 (1): 31–58.
———, ed. 1991. *The French Welfare State: Surviving Social and Ideological Change*. New York: New York University Press.
Andrieu, Claire, Lucette Le Van, and Antoine Prost. 1987. *Les nationalisations de la libération*. Paris: Presses de la Fondation Nationale des Sciences Politiques.
Arthur, W. Brian. 1994. *Increasing Returns and Path Dependence in the Economy*. Ann Arbor: University of Michigan Press.
Ashford, Douglas. 1989. "L'Etat-providence à travers l'étude comparative des institutions." *Revue Française de Science Politique* 39 (3): 276–95.
Ashworth, William. 1986. *The History of the British Coal Industry*. Vol. 5. *1946–1982: The Nationalized Industry*. Oxford: Clarendon Press.
Attali, Jacques. 1995. *Verbatim II, 1986–1988*. Paris: Fayard.
Babb, Sarah. 2001. *Managing Mexico: Economists from Nationalism to Neoliberalism*. Princeton, NJ: Princeton University Press.
Bachrach, Peter, and Morton Baratz. 1962. "The Two Faces of Power." *American Political Science Review* 56:947–52.
Badaracco, Joseph L., Jr. 1985. *Loading the Dice: A Five-Country Study of Vinyl Chloride Regulation*. Boston, MA: Harvard Business School Press.
Baker, Ross K. 1985. "Party and Institutional Sanctions in the U.S. House: The Case of Congressman Gramm." *Legislative Studies Quarterly* 1985:315–37.
Ball, Stuart. 1996. "The Conservative Party and the Heath Government." In Ball and Seldon 1996.
Ball, Stuart, and Anthony Seldon, eds. 1996. *The Heath Government 1970–74: A Reappraisal*. London: Longman.
Balz, Dan. 1985. "Kennedy Challenges Party to Change: Speech Nudges Democrats Toward the Political Center." *Washington Post*, March 30, sec. A.
Barone, Michael, and Grant Ujifusa. 1982. *Almanac of American Politics*. New York: E. P. Dutton.
Bartels, Larry M. 1996. "Uninformed Votes: Information Effects in Presidential Elections." *American Journal of Political Science* 40:177–207.
Bass, Jack, and Walter DeVries. 1995. *The Transformation of Southern Politics*. Athens: University of Georgia Press.
Béland, Daniel. 2001. "Does Labor Matter? Institutions, Labor Unions and Pension Reform in France and the United States." *Journal of Public Policy* 21 (2): 153–72.
Bell, Daniel. 1963. *The Radical Right: The New American Right*. Expanded and updated ed. Garden City, NY: Doubleday.
Bergmann, Barbara. 1996. *Saving Our Children from Poverty: What the United States Can Learn from France*. New York: Russell Sage.
Bernauer, Thomas. 2003. *Genes, Trade, and Regulation: The Seeds of Conflict in Food Biotechnology*. Princeton, NJ: Princeton University Press.

Bertoni, Pascale. 1995. *Les politiques fiscales sous la cinquieme république: Discours et pratiques (1958–1991)*. Paris: Editions L'Harmattan.
Blair, Alasdair M. 1997. "The British Iron and Steel Industry since 1945." *Journal of European Economic History* 26 (3): 571–81.
Blake, Robert. 1985. *The Conservative Party: From Peel to Thatcher*. London: Methuen.
Blank, Rebecca M. 1997. *It Takes a Nation: A New Agenda for Fighting Poverty*. Princeton, NJ: Princeton University Press.
Bleich, Erik. 2002. "Integrating Ideas into Policymaking Analysis: Frames and Race Policies in Britain and France." *Comparative Political Studies* 35 (9): 1054–76.
Blumenthal, Sidney. 1986. *The Rise of the Counter-Establishment: From Conservative Ideology to Political Power*. New York: Times Books.
Blyth, Mark. 2002. *Great Transformations*. Cambridge: Cambridge University Press.
Bohnsack, Klaus. 1983. "Die Koalitionskrise 1981/1982 und der Regierungswechsel 1982." *Zeitschrift für Parlamentsfragen* 14:5–32.
Boix, Carles. 1998. *Political Parties, Growth, and Equality: Conservative and Social Democratic Strategies in the World Economy*. New York: Cambridge University Press.
Borchert, Jens. 1995. *Die konservative Transformation des Wohlfahrtsstaates*. Frankfurt: Campus Verlag.
Bothorel, Jean. 1983. *Histoire du septennat giscardien, I: Le pharaon, 19 mai 1974–22 mars 1978*. Paris: Bernard Grasset.
Bourgeois, Paulette. 1978. "Toward a Shorter Work Week." *Labour Gazette* 78 (9): 411–12.
Bouvier, Jean, and Jacques Wolff, eds. 1973. *Deux siècles de fiscalité française XIXe–XXe siècle: Histoire, économie, politique*. Paris: Mouton.
Braithwaite, John. 1985. *To Punish or Persuade: Enforcement of Coal Mine Safety*. Albany: State University of New York Press.
Branson, William H., and Martin Neil Baily. 1981. "The Thatcher Experiment: The First Two Years. Comments and Discussion." *Brookings Papers on Economic Activity*, no. 2: 368–79.
Braun, Hans-Joachim. 1990. *The German Economy in the Twentieth Century*. London: Routledge.
Braunthal, Gerard. 1977. "The Policy Function of the Social Democratic Party." *Comparative Politics* 9 (2): 127–45.
______. 1983. *The West German Social Democrats, 1969–1982: Profile of a Party in Power*. Boulder, CO: Westview Press.
______. 1984. "The West German Social Democrats: Factionalism at the Local Level." *West European Politics* 7 (1): 47–64.
______. 1994. *The German Social Democrats since 1969: A Party in Power and Opposition*. Boulder, CO: Westview Press.
Breyer, Friedrich, and Wolfgang Franz. 2004. *Reform der sozialen Sicherung*. Berlin: Springer-Verlag.

Brickman, Ronald, Sheila Jasanoff, and Thomas Ilgen. 1985. *Controlling Chemicals: The Politics of Regulation in Europe and the United States*. Ithaca, NY: Cornell University Press.

Brownlee, W. Elliot. 1996a. "Tax Regimes, National Crisis, and State-Building in America." In Brownlee 1996b.

———. 1996b. *Funding the Modern American State, 1941–1995: The Rise and Fall of the Era of Easy Finance*. Cambridge: Cambridge University Press.

Buiter, Willem H., and Marcus Miller. 1981. "The Thatcher Experiment: The First Two Years." *Brookings Papers on Economic Activity*, no. 2: 315–67.

———. 1983. "Changing the Rules: Economic Consequences of the Thatcher Regime." *Brookings Papers on Economic Activity*, no. 2: 305–65.

Bulmer, Simon, ed. 1989. *The Changing Agenda of West German Public Policy*. Aldershot, Hants, UK: Dartmouth Publishing.

Bulmer, Simon, and Peter Humphreys. 1989. "Kohl, Corporatism and Congruence: the West German Model under Challenge." In Bulmer 1989.

Burnham, David. 1975. "Issue and Debate; Regulatory Agencies and Competition." *New York Times*, September 20.

Butler, David, and Dennis Kavanagh. 1974. *The British General Election of February 1974*. London: Macmillan.

———. 1980. *The British General Election of 1979*. London: Macmillan.

———. 1984. *The British General Election of 1983*. London: Macmillan.

———. 1988. *The British General Election of 1987*. New York: St. Martin's Press.

Butler, David, and Michael Pinto Duschinsky. 1971. *The British General Election of 1970*. London: Macmillan.

Bykerk, Loree, and Ardith Maney. 1991–92. "Where Have All the Consumers Gone?" *Political Science Quarterly* 106 (4): 677–93.

Cameron, David. 1978. "The Expansion of the Public Economy: A Comparative Analysis." *American Political Science Review* 72 (4): 1243–61.

———. 1991. "Continuity and Change in French Social Policy: The Welfare State under Gaullism, Liberalism, and Socialism." In Ambler 1991.

Campbell, Andrea Louise, and Kimberly Morgan. 2005. "Federalism and the Politics of Old-Age Care in Germany and the United States." *Comparative Political Studies* 38 (8): 887–914.

Campbell, John. 1993. *Edward Heath: A Biography*. London: Random House.

———. 2000. *Margaret Thatcher*. Vol. 1. *The Grocer's Daughter*. London: Random House.

———. 2003. *Margaret Thatcher*. Vol. 2. *The Iron Lady*. London: Random House.

Cannon, Lou. 1991. *President Reagan: The Role of a Lifetime*. New York: Simon and Schuster.

Cassidy, John. 2000. "The Price Prophet." *New Yorker*, February 7.

CEPII (Centre d'Etudes Prospectives et d'Informations Internationales). 1996. "Les couts salariaux en France, en Allemagne et aux Etats-Unis." *La Lettre du CEPII*, no. 151 (November).

Cerny, Karl H., ed. 1990. *Germany at the Polls: The Bundestag Elections of the 1980s*. Durham, NC: American Enterprise Institute for Public Policy Research.

Chabanas, Nicole, and Eric Vergeau. 1996. "Nationalisations et privatisations depuis 50 ans." INSEE Première No. 440. Paris: Institut Nationale de la Statistique et des Etudes Economiques.

Chandler, Alfred D., Jr. 1980. "Government Versus Business: An American Phenomenon." In *Business and Public Policy*, ed. John T. Dunlop. Cambridge, MA: Harvard University Press.

Charkham, Jonathan. 1998. *Keeping Good Company: A Study of Corporate Governance in Five Countries*. Oxford: Oxford University Press.

Clarke, Harold D., William Mishler, and Paul Whiteley. 1990. "Recapturing the Falklands: Models of Conservative Popularity, 1979–83." *British Journal of Political Science* 20 (1): 63–81.

Clarke, Harold D., Marianne C. Stewart, and Gary Zuk. 1986. "Politics, Economics and Party Popularity in Britain, 1979–83." *Electoral Studies* 5 (2): 123–41.

Clawson, Dan, Alan Neustadtl, and Mark Weller. 1998. *Dollars and Votes: How Business Campaign Contributions Subvert Democracy*. Philadelphia, PA: Temple University Press.

Clayton, Richard, and Jonas Pontusson. 1998. "Welfare-State Retrenchment Revisited: Entitlement Cuts, Public Sector Restructuring, and Inegalitarian Trends in Advanced Capitalist Societies." *World Politics* 51 (1): 67–98.

Clemens, Clay. 1998. "Party Management as a Leadership Resource: Kohl and the CDU/CSU." *German Politics* 7 (1): 91–119.

Clemens, John. 1983. *Polls, Politics, and Populism*. Aldershot, Hants, UK: Gower.

Clifford, James. 1986. "Introduction: Partial Truths." In *Writing Culture: The Poetics and Politics of Ethnography*, ed. James Clifford and George E. Marcus. Berkeley and Los Angeles: University of California Press.

Cockett, Richard. 1995. *Thinking the Unthinkable: Think-Tanks and the Economic Counter-Revolution, 1931–1983*. London: HarperCollins.

Cohen, Daniel, and Philippe Michel. 1987. "Théorie et pratique du chômage en France." *Revue économique* 38 (3): 661–75.

Cohen, Elie. 1992. "Dirigisme, politique industrielle et rhétorique industrialiste." *Revue Française de Science Politique* 42 (2): 197–218.

Cohen, Richard E. 1981. "A Reagan Victory on His Tax Package Could be a Costly One Politically." *National Journal*, June 13, 1058–62.

———. 1986. "Why Kennedy Chose Labor Over Judiciary." *Los Angeles Times*, November 16, part 5.

Collier, Ruth Berins, and David Collier. 1991. *Shaping the Political Arena*. Princeton, NJ: Princeton University Press.

Collins, Chris, ed. 1998. *Complete Public Statements of Margaret Thatcher on CD-ROM, 1945–1990*. Oxford: Oxford University Press.

Conceição, Pedro, Pedro Ferreira, and James K. Galbraith. 1999. "Inequality and Unemployment in Europe: The American Cure." University of Texas Inequality Project Working Paper no. 11.

Congressional Quarterly. 1982. *Congressional Roll Call 1981: A Chronology and Analysis of Votes in the House and Senate, 97th Congress, First Session*. Washington, DC: Congressional Quarterly.

Cook, Fay Lomax, and Edith J. Barrett. 1992. *Support for the American Welfare State: The Views of Congress and the Public*. New York: Columbia University Press.

Coughlin, Richard M. 1980. *Ideology, Public Opinion and Welfare Policy: Attitudes toward Taxes and Spending in Industrialized Societies*. Berkeley and Los Angeles: University of California Press.

Cowley, Philip, and Matthew Bailey. 2000. "Peasants' Uprising or Religious War? Re-examining the 1975 Conservative Leadership Contest." *British Journal of Political Science* 30 (4): 599–629.

Crafts, Nicholas. 2001. "Supply-Side Policy and British Relative Economic Decline." In *Economic Growth and Government Policy*, ed. HM Treasury, 23–30. London: HM Treasury.

Craig, F. W. S., ed. 1990. *British General Election Manifestos 1959–1987*. Aldershot, Hants, UK: Dartmouth Publishing.

Creighton, Lucy Black. 1976. *Pretenders to the Throne: The Consumer Movement in the United States*. Lexington, MA: Lexington Books.

Crenson, Matthew A. 1971. *The Unpolitics of Air Pollution*. Baltimore, MD: Johns Hopkins University Press.

Crewe, Ivor. 1981. "Why the Conservatives Won." In *Britain at the Polls: A Study of the General Election*, ed. Howard R. Penniman. Washington, DC: American Enterprise Institute for Public Policy Research.

———. 1986. "On the Death and Resurrection of Class Voting." *Political Studies* 34:620–38.

———. 1992. "Changing Votes and Unchanging Voters." *Electoral Studies* 11:335–45.

Crewe, Ivor, Neil Day, and Anthony Fox. 1991. "The British Electorate 1963–1987: A Compendium of Data from the British Election Studies." Cambridge: Cambridge University Press.

Crewe, Ivor, and Anthony King. 1995. *SPD: The Birth, Life, and Death of the Social Democratic Party*. Oxford: Oxford University Press.

Crewe, Ivor, and Donald D. Searing. 1988. "Ideological Change in the British Conservative Party." *American Political Science Review* 82 (2): 361–84.

Crozier, Michel. 1964. *The Bureaucratic Phenomenon*. Chicago: University of Chicago Press.

Daemmrich, Arthur A. 2004. *Pharmacopolitics: Drug Regulation in the United States and Germany*. Chapel Hill: University of North Carolina Press.

Damanpour, Fariborz. 1991. "Organizational Innovation: A Meta-Analysis of Effects of Determinants and Moderators." *Academy Of Management Journal* 34 (3): 555–90.

Daunton, Martin. 2002. *Just Taxes: The Politics of Taxation in Britain, 1914–1979*. Cambridge: Cambridge University Press.

Davidson, Roger H. 1981. "Subcommittee Government: New Channels for Policy Making." In *The New Congress*, ed. Thomas E. Mann and Norman J. Ornstein. Washington, DC: American Enterprise Institute for Public Policy Research.

Dengel, Annette. 1987. "Federal Republic of Germany." In *Comparative Tax Systems*, ed. Joseph A. Pechman. Arlington, VA: Tax Analysts.

Denham, Andrew, and Mark Garnett. 2001. *Keith Joseph*. Chesham, Bucks, UK: Acumen.

Derthick, Martha, and Paul J. Quirk. 1985. *The Politics of Deregulation*. Washington, DC: Brookings Institution.

Dilnot, A. W., and C. N. Morris. 1983. "The Tax System and Distribution 1978–83." *Fiscal Studies* 4 (2): 54–64.

DiMaggio, Paul. 1997. "Culture and Cognition." *Annual Review of Sociology* 23:263–87.

Dobbin, Frank. 1994. *Forging Industrial Policy: The United States, Britain, and France in the Railway Age*. Cambridge: Cambridge University Press.

Dogan, Mattei. 1979. "How to Become a Cabinet Minister in France: Career Pathways, 1870–1978." *Comparative Politics* 12 (1): 1–25.

Dormont, B. 1997. "L'influence du coût salarial sur la demande de travail." *Economie et Statistique*, nos. 301–302: 95–109.

Dormont, B., and M. Pauchet. 1997. "L'élasticité de l'emploi au coût salarial dépend-elle des structures de qualifications?" *Economie et Statistique*, nos. 301–302: 149–70.

Douglas, James. 1989. "The Changing Tide: Some Recent Studies of Thatcherism." *British Journal of Political Science* 19 (3): 399–424.

Drèze, Jacques H. 1997. *Europe's Unemployment Problem*. Cambridge, MA: MIT Press.

Duhamel, Alain. 1980. *La Republique Giscardienne*. Paris: Grasset et Fasquelle.

Dunleavy, Patrick. 1987. "Class Dealignment in Britain Revisited." *West European Politics* 10:400–419.

Dunleavy, Patrick, and C. T. Husbands. 1985. *British Democracy at the Crossroads: Voting and Party Competition in the 1980s*. London: George Allen and Unwin.

Dyson, Kenneth H. 1981. "The Politics of Economic Management in West Germany." *West European Politics* 4 (2): 35–55.

———, ed. 1992. *The Politics of German Regulation*. Aldershot, Hants, UK: Dartmouth Publishing.

Economie et Prévision. 1994. "Sécurite sociale en France, 1850–1940." No. 116. Paris: Librairie Armand Colin.

Edinger, Lewis J. 1986. *West German Politics*. New York: Columbia University Press.

Edsall, Thomas Byrne. 1984. *The New Politics of Inequality*. New York: W. W. Norton.

Eichengreen, Barry, ed. 1985. *The Gold Standard in Theory and History*. New York and London: Methuen.

Eisner, Marc Allen. 1993. *Regulatory Politics in Transition*. Baltimore, MD: Johns Hopkins University Press.

Ellwood, David T., and Mary Jo Bane. 1984. "The Impact of AFDC on Family Structure and Living Arrangements." Washington, DC: Department of Health and Human Services. (Grant No. 92A-82)

Esping-Andersen, Gøsta. 1990. *The Three Worlds of Welfare Capitalism*. Princeton, NJ: Princeton University Press.

———. 1996. *Welfare States in Transition: National Adaptations in Global Economies*. London: Sage.

———. 1999. *Social Foundations of Post-Industrial Economies*. Oxford: Oxford University Press.

Esser, Josef. 1988. "'Symbolic Privatisation': The Politics of Privatisation in West Germany." *West European Politics* 11:61–73.

Estevez-Abe, Margaret, Torben Iversen, and David Soskice. 2001. "Social Protection and the Formation of Skills: A Reinterpretation of the Welfare State." In Hall and Soskice 2001.

Estrin, Saul, and Virginie Pérotin. 1987. "The Regulation of British and French Nationalised Industries." *European Economic Review* 31:361–67.

———. 1991. "Does Ownership Always Matter?" *International Journal of Industrial Organization* 9 (1): 55–72.

Evans, Geoffrey. 1993. "The Decline of Class Divisions in Britain? Class and Ideological Preferences in the 1960s and the 1980s." *British Journal of Sociology* 44 (3): 449–71.

Evans, Peter B., Dietrich Rueschemeyer, and Theda Skocpol. 1985. *Bringing the State Back In*. Cambridge: Cambridge University Press.

Feigenbaum, Harvey, and Jeffrey Henig. 1994. "The Political Underpinnings of Privatization: A Typology." *World Politics* 46 (2): 185–208.

Feigenbaum, Harvey, Jeffrey Henig, and Chris Hamnett. 1999. *Shrinking the State: The Political Underpinnings of Privatization*. Cambridge: Cambridge University Press.

Ferenczi, Thomas. 1981. *Le prince au miroir: essai sur l'ordre giscardien*. Paris: Albin Michel.

Ferguson, Thomas, and Joel Rogers. 1986. *Right Turn: The Decline of the Democrats and the Future of American Politics*. New York: Hill and Wang.

Findling, Marion. 1995. *Die Politische Ökonomie der Steuerreform*. Aachen, Germany: Shaker.

Fisher, Andrew. 1987. "West German Industry Sends Cold Blast Whistling through Bonn." *Financial Times*, December 29.

Flamant, Maurice. 1992. *Histoire du libéralisme*. Paris: Presses Universitaires de France.

Flora, Peter, and Arnold J. Heidenheimer. 1981. *The Development of Welfare States in Europe and America*. New Brunswick, NJ: Transaction.

Fourastié, Jean. 1978. *La réalite économique: Vers la révision des idees dominantes en France*. Paris. Laffont.

Fourcade, Jean-Pierre. 1979. *Et si nous parlions de demain*... Paris: Arthème Fayard.

Fourcade-Gourinchas, Marion, and Sarah Babb. 2002. "The Rebirth of the Liberal Creed: Paths to Neoliberalism in Four Countries." *American Journal of Sociology* 108 (3): 533–79.

Fourçans, André. 1978. *Sauver l'Economie*. Paris: Calmann-Lévy.

———. 1980. "L'impact du S.M.I.C. sur le chômage: Les leçons de l'expérience." *Revue d'économie politique* 90 (6): 881–93.

Fournier, Jacques, Nicole Questiaux, and Jean-Marie Delarue. 1989. *Traité du Social: Situations, Luttes, Politiques, Institutions*. 5th ed. Paris: Jurisprudence Générale Dalloz.

Franklin, Mark N. 1984. "How the Decline of Class Voting Opened the Way to Radical Change in British Politics." *British Journal of Political Science* 14 (4): 483–508.

———. 1985. *The Decline of Class Voting in Britain: Changes in the Basis of Electoral Choice, 1964–1983*. Oxford: Clarendon Press.

Frears, J. R. 1981. *France in the Giscard Presidency*. London: George Allen and Unwin.

Free, Lloyd A., and Hadley Cantril. 1968. *Political Beliefs of Americans*. New York: Simon and Schuster.

Friedman, Barry D. 1995. *Regulation in the Reagan-Bush Era: The Eruption of Presidential Influence*. Pittsburgh, PA: University of Pittsburgh Press.

Frost, Robert L. 1991. *Alternating Currents: Nationalized Power in France, 1946–1970*. Ithaca, NY: Cornell University Press.

Galbraith, James K. 1998. *Created Unequal: The Crisis in American Pay*. New York: Free Press.

Galbraith, John Kenneth. 1977. "Galbraith Suggests . . . Big Business Brings on Socialism." *Industry Week* 193 (4): 70.

Gallup, George, ed. 1976. *The Gallup International Public Opinion Polls: France 1939, 1944–1975*. Vol. 2. *1968–1975*. New York: Random House.

Gamble, Andrew. 1994. *The Free Economy and the Strong State*. Houndsmills, Basingstoke, UK: Macmillan.

Garrett, Geoffrey. 1992. "The Political Consequences of Thatcherism." *Political Behavior* 14 (4): 361–82.

———. 1998. *Partisan Politics in the Global Economy*. Cambridge: Cambridge University Press.

Gaventa, John. 1980. *Power and Powerlessness*. Oxford: Clarendon Press.

Genschel, Philipp. 2002. "Globalization, Tax Competition, and the Welfare State." *Politics and Society* 30 (2): 245–75.

George, Torsten. 1995. *Das Ladenschlußgesetz auf dem Prüfstand*. Berlin: Deutscher Universitäts Verlag.

Geppert, Dominik. 2002. *Thatchers konservative Revolution: Der Richtungswandel der britischen Tories, 1975–1979*. Munich: R. Oldenbourg Verlag.

———. 2003. *Maggie Thatchers Rosskur—Ein Rezept für Deutschland?* Berlin: Siedler.

Gerber, Alan, and Donald Green. 1999. "Misperceptions about Perceptual Bias." *Annual Review of Political Science* 2:189–210.

Gerston, Larry N., Cynthia Fraleigh, and Robert Schwab. 1988. *The Deregulated Society*. Pacific Grove, CA: Brooks/Cole.

Giaimo, Susan. 2002. *Markets and Medicine: The Politics of Health Care Reform in Britain, Germany, and the United States*. Ann Arbor: University of Michigan Press.

Gilens, Martin. 1999. *Why Americans Hate Welfare: Race, Media, and the Politics of Antipoverty Policy*. Chicago: University of Chicago Press.

———. 2001. "Political Ignorance and Collective Policy Preferences." *American Political Science Review* 95:379–96.

Gilhaus, Ulrike. 1995. "Vom Konfrontationskurs zur Lobbyarbeit: Umweltprobleme, Unternehmerische Lösungsstrategien und Industrielle Verbandsarbeit bis zum Ersten Weltkrieg." *Zeitschrift für Unternehmensgeschichte* 40 (3): 143–57.

Gilmour, Ian. 1992. *Dancing with Dogma: Britain under Thatcherism*. London: Simon and Schuster.

Giroud, Francoise. 1979. "La pratique giscardienne de la politique, ou l'art de l'anesthesie." *Pouvoirs* 9:105–14.

Giscard d'Estaing, Valéry. 1979. *Démocratie Française*. Paris: Arthème Fayard.

———. 1984. *Deux Français Sur Trois*. Paris: Flammarion.

———. 1988. *Le Pouvoir et la Vie*. Paris: Compagnie Douze.

Glotz, Peter. 1989. *Die Deutsche Rechte*. Stuttgart: Deutsche Verlags-Anstalt.

Golden, Miriam, Peter Lange, and Michael Wallerstein. 2002. "Union Centralization among Advanced Industrial Societies: An Empirical Study." Dataset available at http://www.shelley.polisci.ucla.edu/data. Version dated September 19, 2002.

Golding, Peter, and Sue Middleton. 1982. *Images of Welfare: Press and Public Attitudes to Poverty*. Oxford: Martin Robertson.

Gordon, Philip, and Sophie Meunier. 2001. *The French Challenge: Adapting to Globalization*. Washington, DC: Brookings Institution.

Gottschalk, Peter T. 1988. "Retrenchment in Antipoverty Programs in the United States: Lessons for the Future." In Kymlicka and Matthews 1988.

Gourevitch, Peter Alexis. 1984. "Breaking with Orthodoxy: The Politics of Economic Policy Responses to the Depression of the 1930s." *International Organization* 38 (1): 95–129.

Gourvish, T. R. 1986. *British Railways, 1948–73: A Business History*. Cambridge: Cambridge University Press.

Grande, Edgar. 1987. "Neoconservatism and Conservative-Liberal Economic Policy in West Germany." *European Journal of Political Research* 15:281–96.

Grant, Susan. 1994. *UK Fiscal Policy*. Oxford: Heinemann.

Green, Diana. 1984. "Industrial Policy and Policy-Making, 1974–82." In Wright 1984.

Greider, William. 1981. "The Education of David Stockman." *Atlantic Monthly*, December.

———. 1982. *The Education of David Stockman and Other Americans*. New York: E. P. Dutton.

Gundelach, Herlind. 1983. *Die Sozialausschüsse zwischen CDU und DGB: Selbstverständnis und Rolle, 1949–1966*. Bonn: Friedrich-Wilhelms-Universität.

Hacker, Jacob S. 2004. "Privatizing Risk without Privatizing the Welfare State: The Hidden Politics of Social Policy Retrenchment in the United States." *American Political Science Review* 98 (2): 243–60.

Hacker, Jacob S., and Paul Pierson. 2002. "Business Power and Social Policy: Employers and the Formation of the American Welfare State." *Politics and Society* 30 (June): 277–325.

Hall, Peter A. 1986. *Governing the Economy: The Politics of State Intervention in Britain and France*. New York: Oxford University Press.

———. 1992. "The Movement from Keynesianism to Monetarism: Institutional Analysis and British Economic Policy in the 1970s." In Steinmo, Thelen, and Longstreth 1992.

———. 1993. "Policy Paradigms, Social Learning, and the State: The Case of Economic Policymaking in Britain." *Comparative Politics* 25 (3): 275–96.

Hall, Peter A., and David W. Soskice. 2001. *Varieties of Capitalism: The Institutional Foundations of Comparative Advantage*. New York: Oxford University Press.

Hamermesh, D. 1994. *Labor Demand*. Princeton, NJ: Princeton University Press.

Hammond, Thomas H., and Jack H. Knott. 1988. "The Deregulatory Snowball: Explaining Deregulation in the Financial Industry." *Journal of Politics* 50 (1): 3–30.

Hancké, Bob. 2001. "Revisiting the French Model: Coordination and Restructuring in French Industry." In Hall and Soskice 2001.

———. 2002. *Large Firms and Institutional Change*. Oxford: Oxford University Press.

Hank, Rainer. 2004. "Rezepte für den kranken Mann." *Frankfurter Allgemeine Zeitung*, March 28, 42.

Hannah, Leslie. 1982. *Engineers, Managers, and Politicians: The First Fifteen Years of Nationalised Electricity Supply in Britain*. Baltimore, MD: Johns Hopkins University Press.

Hansen, Susan. 1983. *The Politics of Taxation: Revenue without Representation*. New York: Praeger.

Hartman, Robert W. 1982. "Congress and Budget-Making." *Political Science Quarterly* 97 (3): 381–402.

Hartz, Louis. 1955. *The Liberal Tradition in America: An Interpretation of American Political Thought since the Revolution*. New York: Harcourt, Brace.

Harwood, Richard, ed. 1980. *The Pursuit of the Presidency, 1980*. Washington, DC: Washington Post Co.

Hatzfeld, Henri. 1971. *Du pauperisme à la Sécurité sociale: Essai sur les origines de la Sécurité sociale en France, 1850–1940*. Paris: Armand Colin.

Hay, Colin. 2001. "Globalization, Economic Change and the Welfare State: The 'Vexatious Inquisition of Taxation'?" In *Globalization and European Welfare States: Challenges and Change*. New York: Palgrave.

Hays, Samuel P. 1987. *Beauty, Health, and Permanence: Environmental Politics in the United States, 1955–1985*. Cambridge: Cambridge University Press.

Heady, Ferrel. 1988. "The United States." In *Public Administration in Developed Democracies: A Comparative Study*, ed. D. C. Rowat. New York and Basel: Marcel Dekker.

Heath, Anthony, John Curtice, Roger Jowell, Geoff Evans, Julia Field, and Sharon Witherspoon. 1991. *Understanding Political Change: The British Voter 1964–1987*. Oxford: Pergamon Press.

Heath, Anthony, Roger Jowell, and John Curtice. 1985. *How Britain Votes*. Oxford: Pergamon Press.

Heinrich, Martin Leo. 1992. *Steuerpolitik zwischen systematischer und wirtschafts-politischer Orientierung*. Pfaffenweiler: Centaurus-Verlagsgesellschaft.

Hibbs, Douglas, and Henrik Jess Madsen. 1981. "Public Reactions to the Growth of Taxation and Government Expenditure." *World Politics* 33:413–35.

Hicks, Alexander. 1999. *Social Democracy and Welfare Capitalism*. Ithaca, NY: Cornell University Press.

Himmelstein, Jerome. 1990. *To the Right: The Transformation of American Conservatism*. Berkeley and Los Angeles: University of California Press.

Hodgkinson, Neville. 1976. "Public hysteria fuels drive by the Government to tackle social security frauds." *Times* (London), September 22.

Holter, Darryl. 1982. "Mineworkers and Nationalization in France: Insights into Concepts of State Theory." *Politics and Society* 11 (1): 29–49.

______. 1992. *The Battle for Coal: Miners and the Politics of Nationalization in France, 1940–1950*. DeKalb: Northern Illinois University Press.

Hornblower, Margaret. 1979. "Businessmen Launch Drive to Soften Clean Air Rules." *Washington Post*, January 9, sec. 1.

Hoskyns, John. 2000. *Just in Time*. London: Aurum Press.

Howe, Geoffrey. 1994. *Conflict of Loyalty*. London: Macmillan.

Howell, Chris. 1992a. "The Contradictions of French Industrial Relations Reform." *Comparative Politics* 24 (2): 181–97.

______. 1992b. *Regulating Labor: The State and Industrial Relations Reform in Postwar France*. Princeton, NJ: Princeton University Press.

Huber, Evelyne, Charles Ragin, and John D. Stephens. 1997. *Comparative Welfare States Data Set*. Northwestern University and University of North Carolina. http://www.lisproject.org/publications/welfaredata/welfareaccess.htm.

Huber, Evelyne, and John D. Stephens. 2001. *Development and Crisis of the Welfare State: Parties and Policies in Global Markets*. Chicago: University of Chicago Press.

Huber, John. 1992. "Restrictive Legislative Procedures in France and the United States." *American Political Science Review* 86 (3): 675–87.

Humphreys, Peter. 1992. "The Politics of Regulatory Reform in German Telecommunications." In Dyson 1992.

Huneeus, Carlos. 1996. "How to Build a Modern Party: Helmut Kohl's Leadership and the Transformation of the CDU." *German Politics* 5 (3): 432–59.

Hunt, Albert R. 1978. "Dollar Bill vs. the Tax Revolt." *Wall Street Journal*, September 27, 22.

Immergut, Ellen. 1992. "The Rules of the Game: The Logic of Health Policy-making in France, Switzerland, and Sweden." In Steinmo, Thelen, and Longstreth 1992.

International Labour Organization (ILO). 2002. *Yearbook of Labour Statistics*. Geneva, Switzerland: International Labour Office.

International Monetary Fund (IMF). 1971–1996. *Balance of Payment Statistics Yearbook*. Computer file. Washington, DC: International Monetary Fund.

Irving, R. E., and W. E. Paterson. 1983. "The Machtwechsel of 1982–1983." *Parliamentary Affairs* 36:417–33.

Iversen, Torben, and Thomas R. Cusack. 2000. "The Causes of Welfare State Expansion: Deindustrialization or Globalization?" *World Politics* 52 (April): 313–49.

James, Simon R., and Nobes, Christopher. 1981. *The Economics of Taxation*. London: Phillip Allen.

Jasanoff, Sheila. 1986. *Risk Management and Political Culture*. New York: Russell Sage Foundation.

———. 1991. "American Exceptionalism and the Political Acknowledgment of Risk." *Daedalus* 119 (4): 61–81.

Jenkins, Peter. 1988. *Mrs. Thatcher's Revolution: The Ending of the Socialist Era*. Cambridge, MA: Harvard University Press.

Joe, Tom. 1982. *Profiles of Families in Poverty: Effects of the FY 1983 Budget Proposals on the Poor*. Washington, DC: Center for the Study of Social Policy.

Joe, Tom, and Cheryl Rogers. 1985. *By the Few for the Few: The Reagan Welfare Legacy*. Lexington, MA: Lexington Books.

Judt, Tony. 1986. *Marxism and the French Left: Studies in Labour and Politics in France, 1830–1981*. Oxford: Clarendon Press.

Kaff, Brigitte, ed. 1991. *Die Unionsparteien 1946–1950: Protokolle der Arbeitsgemeinschaft der CDU/CSU Deutschlands und der Konferenzen der Landesvorsitzenden*. Düsseldorf: Droste Verlag.

Kagan, Robert A., and Lee Axelrad. 1997. "Adversarial Legalism: An International Perspective." In *Comparative Disadvantages? Social Regulations and the Global Economy*, ed. Pietro S. Nivola. Washington, DC: Brookings Institution.

Karran, Terence. 1985. "The Determinants of Taxation in Britain: An Empirical Test." *Journal of Public Policy* 5 (3): 365–86.

Kato, Junko. 2003. *Regressive Taxation and the Welfare State: Path Dependence and Policy Diffusion*. New York: Cambridge University Press.

Katz, Michael B. 1989. *The Undeserving Poor: From the War on Poverty to the War on Welfare*. New York: Pantheon Books.

———. 1996. *In the Shadow of the Poorhouse: A Social History of Welfare in America*. New York: Basic Books. Orig. pub. in 1986.

Katzenstein, Peter. 1985. *Small States in World Markets*. Ithaca, NY: Cornell University Press.

———. 1987. *Policy and Politics in West Germany: The Growth of a Semisovereign State*. Philadelphia, PA: Temple University Press.

Kavanagh, Dennis. 1987. *Thatcherism and British Politics: The End of Consensus?* Oxford: Oxford University Press.

Keegan, William. 1984. *Mrs. Thatcher's Economic Experiment*. London: Penguin.

Keese, Christoph. 2004. *Rettet den Kapitalismus. Wie Deutschland wieder an die Spitze kommt*. Berlin: Hoffmann und Campe Verlag.

Kelemen, R. Daniel. 2004. *The Rules of Federalism: Institutions and Regulatory Politics in the EU and Beyond*. Cambridge, MA: Harvard University Press.

Kelman, Steven. 1981. *Regulating America, Regulating Sweden: A Comparative Study of Occupational Safety and Health Policy*. Cambridge, MA: MIT Press.

Kerr, Peter. 1999. "The Postwar Consensus: A Woozle That Wasn't?" In *Postwar British Politics in Perspective*, ed. David Marsh, Jim Buller, Colin Hay, Jim Johnston, Peter Kerr, Stuart McAnulla, and Matthew Watson. Cambridge: Polity Press.

Kesler, Jean-François. 1985. *L'ENA, la société, l'Etat*. Paris: Berger-Levrault.

Kessel, John H. 1984. "The Structures of the Reagan White House." *American Journal of Political Science* 28 (2): 231–58.

Kesselman, Mark. 1992. "France." In *European Politics in Transition*, by Mark Kesselman, Joel Krieger, Christopher S. Allen, Joan Debardeleben, Stephen Hellman, Jonas Pontusson. Lexington, MA: D. C. Heath.

———. 2002. "The Triple Exceptionalism of the French Welfare State." In *Diminishing Welfare: A Cross-National Study of Social Provision*, ed. Gertrude Schaffner Goldberg and Marguerite G. Rosenthal. Westport, CT: Auburn House.

Kinder, Donald R., and Lynn M. Sanders. 1997. *Divided by Color: Racial Politics and Democratic Ideals*. Chicago: University of Chicago Press.

King, Anthony. 1981. "Politics, Economics, and Trade Unions." In *Britain at the Polls: A Study of the General Election*, ed. Howard R. Penniman. Washington, DC: American Enterprise Institute for Public Policy Research.

Kingdon, John W. 1995. *Agendas, Alternatives, and Public Policies*. 2nd ed. New York: HarperCollins College.

Kleinmann, Hans-Otto. 1993. *Geschichte der CDU 1945–1982*. Stuttgart: Deutsche Verlags-Anstalt.

Kluegel, James R., and Eliot R. Smith. 1986. *Beliefs about Inequality: Americans' Views about What Is and What Ought to Be*. Hawthorne, NY: Aldine de Gruyter.

Koelble, Thomas A. 1987. "Trade Unionists, Party Activists, and Politicians: The Struggle for Power over Party Rules in the British Labour Party and the West German Social Democratic Party." *Comparative Politics* 19 (3): 253–66.

Koren, Stefan. 1989. *Steuerreformen im internationalen Vergleich*. Berlin: Duncker and Humblot.

Korpi, Walter. 1980. "Social Policy and Distributional Conflict in the Capitalist Democracies: A Preliminary Comparative Framework." *West European Politics* 3 (3): 296–316.

———. 1989. "Power, Politics, and State Autonomy in the Development of Social Citizenship: Social Rights during Sickness in Eighteen OECD Countries since 1930." *American Sociological Review* 54 (3): 309–28.

Korpi, Walter, and Joakim Palme. 1998. "The Paradox of Redistribution and Strategies of Equality: Welfare State Institutions, Inequality, and Poverty in the Western Countries." *American Sociological Review* 63 (5): 661–87.

Kraft, Michael E., and Normal J. Vig. 1984. "Epilogue." In Vig and Kraft 1984.

Kramnick, Isaac. 1987. Introduction to *The Federalist Papers*, by James Madison, Alexander Hamilton, and John Jay. Ed. Isaac Kramnick. London: Penguin.

Kühne, Thomas. 1995. "Zur Genese der deutschen Proporzkultur im wilhelminischen Preußen." *Politische Vierteljahresschrift* 36:220–42.

Kuisel, Richard F. 1981. *Capitalism and the State in Modern France: Renovation and Economic Management in the Twentieth Century*. Cambridge: Cambridge University Press.

Kunda, Ziva. 1987. "Motivation and Inference: Self-serving Generation and Evaluation of Evidence." *Journal of Personality and Social Psychology* 53:636–47.

———. 1990. "The Case for Motivated Political Reasoning." *Psychological Bulletin* 108:480–98.

Kuttner, Robert. 1980. *Revolt of the Haves: Tax Rebellions and Hard Times*. New York: Simon and Schuster.

———. 1994. "A Liberal Loved by Economic Conservatives." *Baltimore Sun*, June 14.

Kymlicka, B. B., and Jean V. Matthews, eds. 1988. *The Reagan Revolution?* Chicago: Dorsey Press.

Kymlicka, Will. 1991. *Liberalism, Community, and Culture*. New York: Oxford University Press.

Laitin, David D. 1985. "Hegemony and Religious Conflict: British Imperial Control and Political Cleavages in Yorubaland." In Evans, Rueschemeyer, and Skocpol 1985.

Lamont, Michèle. 1992. *Money, Morals, and Manners: The Culture of the French and the American Upper-Middle Class*. Chicago: University of Chicago Press.

Lampert, Heinz. 1992. *Die Wirtschafts- und Sozialordnung der Bundesrepublik Deutschland*. Munich: Günter Olzog Verlag.

Lanoue, David J., and Barbara Headrick. 1994. "Prime Ministers, Parties, and the Public: The Dynamics of Government Popularity in Great Britain." *Public Opinion Quarterly* 58 (2): 191–209.

Lave, Lester B., and Gilbert S. Omenn. 1981. *Clearing the Air: Reforming the Clean Air Act*. Washington, DC: Brookings Institution.

Laverdines, George. 1979. "Le liberalisme organisé, ou le combat de Jacob." *Pouvoirs* 9:17–26.

Lawson, Nigel. 1992. *The View from No. 11*. London: Bantam.

Layard, R., and S. Nickell. 1989. "The Thatcher Miracle?" *American Economic Review* 79 (2): 215–19.

Leaman, Jeremy. 1988. *The Political Economy of West Germany 1945–85*. London: Macmillan.

———. 1994. "Regulatory Reform and Privatization in Germany." In *Privatization and Regulatory Change in Europe*, ed. Michael Moran and Tony Prosser. Buckingham and Philadelphia: Open University Press.

Lehmbruch, Gerhard. 1992. "The Institutional Framework of German Regulation." In Dyson 1992.

———. 1994. "République Fédérale d'Allemagne: Le Cadre Institutionnel et les Incertitudes des Stratégies Néo-libérales." In *Le Tournant Néo-Libéral en Europe*, ed. Bruno Jobert. Paris: Editions L'Harmattan.

Leibfritz, Willi, Wolfgang Büttner, and Ulrich van Essen. 1998. "Germany." In *The Tax System in Industrialized Countries*, ed. Ken Messere. Oxford: Oxford University Press.

Lenk, Kurt. 1989. *Deutscher Konservatismus*. Frankfurt: Campus Verlag.

Levitan, Sar A., and Richard S. Belous. 1977. "Thank God It's Thursday: Could Shorter Workweeks Reduce Unemployment?" *Across the Board* 14 (3): 28–31.

Levy, Jonah D. 1999a. *Tocqueville's Revenge: Dilemmas of Institutional Reform in Post-Dirigiste France*. Cambridge, MA: Harvard University Press.

———. 1999b. "Vice into Virtue? Progressive Politics and Welfare Reform in Continental Europe." *Politics and Society* 27 (2): 239–73.

Lieberman, Robert C. 2001. *Shifting the Color Line: Race and the American Welfare State*. Cambridge, MA: Harvard University Press.

Lindert, Peter. 2004. *Growing Public: Social Spending and Economic Growth since the Eighteenth Century*. New York: Cambridge University Press.

Lindsey, Robert. 1980. "What the Record Says about Reagan." *New York Times*, June 29, sec. 6, p. 12.

Lipset, Seymour Martin. 1996. *American Exceptionalism: A Double-Edged Sword*. New York: W. W. Norton.

Lipset, Seymour Martin, and William Schneider. 1979. "The Public View of Regulation." *Public Opinion* 2 (1): 6–13.

Lo, Clarence. 1990. *Small Property versus Big Government*. Berkeley and Los Angeles: University of California Press.

Locke, Richard, and Thomas Kochan. 1995. "Conclusion: The Transformation of Industrial Relations? A Cross-National Review of the Evidence." In *Employment Relations in a Changing World Economy*, ed. Richard Locke, Thomas Kochen, and Michael Piore. Cambridge, MA: MIT Press.

Loomis, Burdett. 1988. *The New American Politician; Ambition, Entrepreneurship, and the Changing Face of Political Life*. New York: Basic Books.

Lösche, Peter. 1994. *Kleine Geschichte der deutschen Parteien*. Stuttgart: Verlag W. Kohlhammer.

Lukes, Steven. 1974. *Power: A Radical View*. London: Macmillan Education.

MacAvoy, Paul W. 1979. *The Regulated Industries and the Economy*. New York: W. W. Norton.

Mackay, Robert J., and Carolyn L. Weaver. 1983. "Commodity Bundling and Agenda Control in the Public Sector." *Quarterly Journal of Economics* 98 (4): 611–35.

Madelin, Alain, ed. 1997. *Aux sources du modèle liberal français*. Paris: Librairie Academique Perrin/Association d'Histoire de l'Entreprise.

Madison, James, Alexander Hamilton, and John Jay. 1987. *The Federalist Papers*. Ed. Isaac Kramnick. London: Penguin. Orig. pub. in 1788.

Maffini, Giorgia Chiara. 2003. "Germany." In *Tax Systems and Tax Reform in Europe*, ed. Luigi Bernardi and Paola Profeta. London and New York: Routledge.

Mahler, Vincent, and David Jesuit. 2004. "State Redistribution in Comparative Perspective: A Cross-National Analysis of the Developed Countries." Luxembourg Income Study Working Paper Series, Working Paper no. 392. http://www.lisproject.org/publications/liswps/392.pdf.

Mahoney, James. 2000. "Path Dependence in Historical Sociology." *Theory and Society* 29:507–48.

———. 2001. *The Legacies of Liberalism*. Baltimore, MD: Johns Hopkins University Press.

Malinvaud, Edmond. 1998. *Les cotisations sociales à la charge des employeurs: analyse économique*. Paris: La documentation Française.

Malone, Julia. 1980. "Murky Outlook for Clean Air Act." *Christian Science Monitor*, November 24.

Mann, Siegfried. 1987. "Herausforderung der 80er Jahre—ordnungspolitische Gefahren für die deutsche Industrie." In *Der Bundesverband der Deutschen Industrie*, ed. Georg Brodach and Hermann Freiherr von Wolff-Metternich. Düsseldorf: Droste Verlag.

Mares, Isabella. 2001. "Firms and the Welfare State: When, Why, and How Does Social Policy Matter to Employers?" In Hall and Soskice 2001.

———. 2003. "The Sources of Business Interest in Social Insurance: Sectoral versus National Differences." *World Politics* 55 (2): 229–58.

Marshall, T. H. 1950. *Citizenship and Social Class*. Oxford: Oxford University Press.

Martin, Cathie Jo. 1991. *Shifting the Burden: The Struggle over Growth and Corporate Taxation*. Chicago: University of Chicago Press.

Martin, David Dale. 1977. "Does Nationalization Hold Any Promise for the American Economy?" *Journal of Economic Issues* 11:327–38, 369–73.

Martin, Isaac. 2003. "The Political Opportunity for Property Tax Limitation in the United States, 1964–1990." Paper presented at the Annual Meetings of the American Sociological Association, Atlanta, Georgia, August 19.

Maxwell, Glen. 1980. "Free Spenders: The 'Other' Campaign for Reagan Chooses Its Targets." *National Journal*, September 13, 1512–15.

Mayer, Kenneth R. 1999. "Executive Orders and Presidential Power." *Journal of Politics* 61 (2): 445–64.

Mayer, Robert N. 1989. *The Consumer Movement: Guardians of the Marketplace*. Boston, MA: Twayne.

McClosky, Herbert, and John Zaller. 1984. *The American Ethos: Public Attitudes toward Capitalism and Democracy*. Cambridge, MA: Harvard University Press.

McCraw, Thomas K. 1984. *Prophets of Regulation*. Cambridge, MA: Belknap.

McDowell, Edwin. 1981. "OSHA, EPA: The Heyday Is Over." *New York Times*, January 4.

Mead, Lawrence. 1986. *Beyond Entitlement: The Social Obligations of Citizenship*. New York: Free Press.

Meese, Edwin III. 1992. *With Reagan: The Inside Story*. Washington, DC: Regnery Gateway.

Meier, Kenneth. 1988. *The Political Economy of Regulation: The Case of Insurance*. Albany: State University of New York Press.

Merkl, Johannes. 1987. "Klar zur Wende?—Die FDP vor dem Koalitionswechsel in Bonn 1980–1982." *Politische Vierteljahresschrift* 28:384–402.

Merkl, Peter H. 1990. "Adenauer's Heirs Reclaim Power: The CDU and CSU in 1980–83." In Cerny 1990.

Messere, Ken C. 1993. *Tax Policy in OECD Countries: Choices and Conflicts*. Amsterdam: International Bureau of Fiscal Documentation Publications.

Meunier, Jacob. 2002. *On the Fast Track: French Railway Modernization and the Origins of the TGV, 1944–1983*. Westport, CT: Praeger.

Michalsky, Helga. 1985. "The Politics of Social Policy." In *Policy and Politics in the Federal Republic of Germany*, ed. Klaus von Beyme and Manfred G. Schmidt. Aldershot, Hants, UK: Gower.

Miller, Norman C. 1978. "Tax-Cut Plan Gives GOP a New Issue and a New Face; Ex-Quarterback Jack Kemp Stars as Republicans Catch the Proposition-13 Fever." *Wall Street Journal*, September 19.

Mishler, William, Marilyn Hoskin, and Roy G. Fitzgerald. 1988. "Hunting the Snark: Or Searching for Evidence of the Widely Touted but Highly Elusive Resurgence of Public Support for Conservative Parties in Britain, Canada, and the United States." In *The Resurgence of Conservatism in Anglo-American Democracies*, ed. Barry Cooper, Alan Kornberg, and William Mishler. Durham, NC: Duke University Press.

———. 1989. "British Parties in the Balance: A Time-Series Analysis of Long-Term Trends in Labour and Conservative Support." *British Journal of Political Science* 19 (2): 211–36.

Moe, Terry. 1985. "Control and Feedback in Economic Regulation: The Case of the NLRB." *American Political Science Review* 79:1094–1116.

———. 1993. "Presidents, Institutions, and Theory." In *Researching the Presidency: Vital Questions, New Approaches*, ed. George C. Edwards III, John H. Kessel, and Bert A. Rockman. Pittsburgh: University of Pittsburgh Press.

Moffitt, Robert. 1992. "Incentive Effects of the U.S. Welfare System: A Review." *Journal of Economic Literature* 30 (1): 1–61.

Moran, Michael. 1992. "Regulatory Change in German Financial Markets." In Dyson 1992.

Moravcsik, Andrew. 1998. *The Choice for Europe: Social Purpose and State Power from Messina to Maastricht*. Ithaca, NY: Cornell University Press. European edition, London: Routledge/UCL Press.

Morris, Stan. 1974. "Activities to Reform Governmental Regulation, Including Strengthening Competition." Paul McCracken Files, Box 4, Gerald Ford Presidential Library, Ann Arbor, Michigan.

Müller, Markus M. 2001. "Reconstructing the New Regulatory State in Germany: Telecommunications, Broadcasting, and Banking." *German Politics* 10 (3): 37–64.

Murray, Charles. 1984. *Losing Ground: American Social Policy, 1950–1980*. New York: Basic Books.

———. 1993. "Welfare and the Family: The U.S. Experience." *Journal of Labor Economics* 11 (1): S224–62.

Nadel, Mark V. 1971. *The Politics of Consumer Protection*. Indianapolis, IN: Bobbs-Merrill.

Nathan, Richard P., and Fred C. Doolittle. 1985. "Federal Grants: Giving and Taking Away." *Political Science Quarterly* 100 (1): 53–74.

National Election Studies Cumulative Datafile. 1952–1992. Consulted via Survey Documentation and Analysis Archives, http://csa.berkeley.edu:7502/archive.htm.

Neurrisse, Andre. 1996. *Histoire de la fiscalité en France*. Paris: Economica.

Nicholls, A. J. 1997. *The Bonn Republic: West German Democracy, 1945–1990*. London and New York: Longman.

Nicoletti, Giuseppe, Stefano Scarpetta, and Olivier Boylaud. 2000. "Summary Indicators of Product Market Regulation with an Extension to Employment Protection Legislation." Organization for Economic Cooperation and Development, Economics Department Working Paper no. 226. Paris: OECD.

Nizet, Jean-Yves. 1991. *Fiscalité, économie, et politique*. Paris: Librairie Generale de Droit et de Jurisprudence.

Noble, Charles. 1986. *Liberalism at Work: The Rise and Fall of OSHA*. Philadelphia: Temple University Press.

———. 1997. *Welfare as We Knew It: A Political History of the American Welfare State*. New York: Oxford University Press.

Noelle-Neumann, Elisabeth, ed. 1976. *Allensbacher Jahrbuch der Demoskopie 1974–1976: Band VI*. Vienna, Munich, Zurich: Verlag Fritz Molden.

———. 1977. *Allensbacher Jahrbuch der Demoskopie 1976–1977: Band VII*. Vienna, Munich, Zurich: Verlag Fritz Molden.

Nolte, Paul. 2004. *Generation Reform. Jenseits der blockierten Republik*. Berlin: C. H. Beck Verlag.

Norpoth, Helmut. 1987. "Guns and Butter and Government Popularity in Britain." *American Political Science Review* 81 (3): 949–59.

Novak, William. 1996. *The People's Welfare: Law and Regulation in Nineteenth-Century America*. Chapel Hill: University of North Carolina Press.

Nozick, Robert. 1974. *Anarchy, State, and Utopia*. New York: Basic Books.

Offe, Claus. 1984. *Contradictions of the Welfare State*. Cambridge, MA: MIT Press.

———. 1990. "Smooth Consolidation in the West German Welfare State: Structural Change, Fiscal Policies, and Populist Politics." ZeS-Arbeitspapier Nr. 4/90. Bremen: Zentrum für Sozialpolitik.

———. 1999. "The German Welfare State: Principles, Performance, Prospects." In *The Postwar Transformation of Germany*, ed. John S. Brady, Beverly Crawford, and Sarah Elise Wiliart. Ann Arbor: University of Michigan Press.

Office of Management and Budget. 1968–1997a. *Budget of the United States Government*. Washington, DC: U.S. Government Printing Office.

———. 1968–1997b. *Historical Tables*. Washington, DC: U.S. Government Printing Office.

Ohneis, Gerhard. 1990. *Wandel in den Zielsetzungen der Deutschen Unternehmerverbände—Eine Systemtheoretische Analyse am Beispiel von BDI und BDA*. Stuttgart: Institut für Sozialforschung der Universität Stuttgart.

O'Mahony, Mary, and Michela Vecchi. 2001. "The Electricity Supply Industry: A Study of an Industry in Transition." *National Institute Economic Review* 177: 85–99.

Organization for Economic Cooperation and Development. 1965–2002. *Revenue Statistics of OECD Member Countries*. http://www.sourceoecd.org.

———. 1974–1997. *National Accounts*. Paris: OECD.

———. 1980–1999. *Social Expenditure Database: Public Expenditure*. http://www.sourceoecd.org.

———. 2001. "Public Sector Pay and Employment Data." OECD Public Management Service. http://www.oecd.org/document/1/0,2340,en_2649_37457_2408769_1_1_1_37457,00.html.

Padgett, Stephen, and Tony Burkett. 1986. *Political Parties and Elections in West Germany: The Search for a New Stability*. New York: St. Martin's Press.

Paige, Jeffrey. 1999. "Conjuncture, Comparison, and Conditional Theory in Macrosocial Inquiry." *American Journal of Sociology* 105 (3): 781–800.

Palier, Bruno. 2000. "'Defrosting' the French Welfare State." *West European Politics* 23 (2): 113–36.

———. 2005. "Ambiguous Agreement, Cumulative Change: French Social Policy in the 1990s." In *Beyond Continuity: Institutional Change in Advanced Political Economies*, ed. Wolfgang Streeck and Kathleen Thelen. Oxford: Oxford University Press.

Paterson, William. 1989. "Environmental Protection, the German Chemical Industry, and Government: Self-Regulation under Pressure." In Bulmer 1989.

Paul, Rep. Ron, and Lewis Lehrman. 1982. *The Case for Gold: A Minority Report of the U.S. Gold Commission*. Washington, DC: Cato Institute.

Pepper, Gordon. 1998. *Inside Thatcher's Monetarist Revolution*. Houndsmills, Basingstoke, and London: Macmillan.

Perry, James M. 1980. "Fund Flap: Reagan's Backers Plan to Spend Big for Him, and His Foes Cry Foul." *Wall Street Journal*, June 19, 1.

Perschke-Hartmann, Christiane. 1992. "II. Geschichte des Auseinandersetzungsprozesses um das GRG." In *Das Gesundheits-Reformgesetz—Eine gescheiterte Reform der Gesetzlichen Krankenversicherung?* ed. Karl-Jürgen Bieback, 37–54. Sankt Augustin: Asgard Verlag.

Pertschuk, Michael. 1982. *Revolt against Regulation: The Rise and Pause of the Consumer Movement*. Berkeley and Los Angeles: University of California Press.

Peterson, Cass. 1983. "President Needs a Nominee for EPA Who Will Defuse the Issues." *New York Times*, March 14.

Pierson, Paul. 1993. "When Effect Becomes Cause." *World Politics* 45:595–628.

———. 1994. *Dismantling the Welfare State? Reagan, Thatcher, and the Politics of Retrenchment*. Cambridge: Cambridge University Press.

———. 2000. "Path Dependence, Increasing Returns, and the Study of Politics." *American Political Science Review* 94 (2): 251–67.

Pierson, Paul, and Theda Skocpol. 2002. "Historical Institutionalism in Contemporary Political Science." In *The State of the Discipline*, ed. Ira Katznelson and Helen Milner. New York: W. W. Norton.

Pimlott, Ben. 1988. "The Myth of Consensus." In *The Making of Britain: Echoes of Greatness*, ed. L. M. Smith. London: Macmillan.

Pine, Art. 1981. "DuPont's Irving S. Shapiro." *Washington Post*, February 8.

Piven, Frances Fox, and Richard A. Cloward. 1982. *The New Class War: Reagan's Attack on the Welfare State and Its Consequences*. New York: Pantheon Books.

Plous, Scott. 1993. *The Psychology of Judgment and Decision Making*. New York: McGraw-Hill.

Poguntke, Thomas. 1992. "Between Ideology and Empirical Research: The Literature on the German Green Party." *European Journal of Political Research* 21 (4): 337–56.

Pollard, Sidney. 1992. *The Development of the British Economy, 1914–1990*. 4th ed. London: Edward Arnold.

Pryke, Richard S. 1971. *Public Enterprise in Practice*. London: MacGibbon and Kee.

———. 1981. *The Nationalised Industries: Policies and Performance since 1968*. Oxford: Martin Robertson.

Pulzer, Peter. 1999. "Luck and Good Management: Helmut Kohl as Parliamentary and Electoral Strategist." *German Politics* 8 (2): 126–39.

Quadagno, Jill S. 1994. *The Color of Welfare: How Racism Undermined the War on Poverty*. New York: Oxford University Press.

Ranney, Austin, ed. 1981. *The American Elections of 1980*. Washington, DC: Washington Post Co.

———. 1985. *Britain at the Polls, 1983: A Study of the General Election*. Washington, DC: American Enterprise Institute for Public Policy Research.

Raschke, Joachim. 1974. *Innerparteiliche Opposition*. Hamburg: Hoffman und Campe.

Rasmussen, Jorgen. 1985. "The Alliance Campaign, Watersheds, and Landslides: Was 1983 a Fault Line in British Politics?" In Ranney 1985.

Reay, Michael John. 2004. *Economic Experts and Economic Knowledge*. PhD diss., Department of Sociology, University of Chicago.

Rhodes, Martin. 1996. "Globalization and the Welfare State: A Critical Review of Recent Debates." *European Journal of Social Policy* 6 (4): 305–27.

Rhodes, Martin, and Bastiaan van Apeldoorn. 1997. "The Transformation of West European Capitalism?" European University Institute—Robert Schuman Centre Working Papers, no. RSC 97/60. Florence, Italy: European University Institute, Economics Department.

Richter, Emanuel. 1987. "Subsidiarität und Neokonservatismus. Die Trennung von politischer herrschaftsbegründung und gesellschaftlichem Stufenbau." *Politische Vierteljahresschrift* 28 (3): 293–314.

Riddell, Peter. 1989. *The Thatcher Decade: How Britain Has Changed during the 1990s*. Oxford: B. Blackwell.

Riker, William H. 1982. *Liberalism against Populism. A Confrontation Between the Theory of Democracy and the Theory of Social Choice*. W. H. Freeman and Co.

Roberts, Paul Craig. 1984. *The Supply-Side Revolution: An Insider's Account of Policymaking in Washington*. Cambridge, MA: Harvard University Press.

Robin, Maurice. 1979. "Ideologie(s) de Valery Giscard d'Estaing?" *Pouvoirs* 9: 5–16.

Robinson, Colin. 1998. Introduction to *Inside Thatcher's Monetarist Revolution*, by Gordon T. Pepper. Houndsmills, Basingstoke, and London: Macmillan Press.

Robinson, Michael J. 1981. "The Media in 1980: Was the Message the Message?" In Ranney 1981.

Rochefort, David A. 1986. *American Social Welfare Policy: Dynamics of Formulation and Change*. Boulder, CO: Westview Press.

Rodrik, Dani. 1997. *Has Globalization Gone Too Far?* Washington, DC: Institute for International Economics.

Roeper, Hans. 1978. "Die Lokomotive auf dem Gipfel." *Frankfurter Allgemeine Zeitung*, July 14.

Rose, Richard, and Terence Karran. 1983. *Increasing Taxes, Stable Taxes, or Both? The Dynamics of United Kingdom Tax Revenues since 1948*. Glasgow, Scotland: University of Strathclyde Centre for the Study of Public Policy.

———. 1987. *Taxation by Political Inertia: Financing the Growth of Government in Britain*. London: Allen and Unwin.

Rose-Ackerman, Susan. 1995. *Controlling Environmental Policy: The Limits of Public Law in Germany and the United States*. New Haven, CT: Yale University Press.

Rothstein, Bo. 1998. *Just Institutions Matter: The Moral and Political Logic of the Welfare State*. New York: Cambridge University Press.

Rudder, Catherine E. 1983. "Tax Policy: Structure and Choice." In *Making Economic Policy in Congress*, ed. Allen Schick. Washington, DC: American Enterprise Institute for Public Policy Research.

Ruggie, Mary. 1996. *Realignments in the Welfare State: Health Policy in the United States, Britain, and Canada*. New York: Columbia University Press.

Saalfeld, Thomas. 1999. "Coalition Politics and Management in the Kohl Era, 1982–98." *German Politics* 8 (2): 141–73.

Sachs, Jeffrey D., and William H. Branson. 1983. "Changing the Rules: Economic Consequences of the Thatcher Regime. Comments and Discussion." *Brookings Papers on Economic Activity*, no. 2: 366–79.

Sale, Kirkpatrick. 1993. *The Green Revolution: The Environmental Movement, 1962–1992*. New York: Hill and Wang.

Samuelson, Paul A. 1978. "Post-Summit Problems." *Newsweek*, July 31, 58.

Sanders, David, Dave Marsh, and Hugh Ward. 1990. "A Reply to Clarke, Mishler, and Whiteley." *British Journal of Political Science* 20 (1): 83–90.

———. 1993. "The Electoral Impact of Press Coverage of the British Economy, 1979–87." *British Journal of Political Science* 23 (2): 175–210.

Sanders, David, Hugh Ward, David Marsh, and Tony Fletcher. 1987. "Government Popularity and the Falklands War: A Reassessment." *British Journal of Political Science* 17 (3): 281–313.

Särlvik, Bo, and Ivor Crewe. 1983. *Decade of Dealignment: The Conservative Victory of 1979 and Electoral Trends in the 1970s*. Cambridge: Cambridge University Press.

Saunders, Peter, and Colin Harris. 1994. *Privatization and Popular Capitalism*. Buckingham, UK: Open University Press.

Scarbrough, Elinor. 1987. "The British Electorate Twenty Years On: Electoral Change and Election Surveys." *British Journal of Political Science* 17 (2): 219–46.

Scargill, D. Ian. 1991. "French Energy: The End of an Era for Coal." *Geography* 76 (2): 172–75.

Scharpf, Fritz W., and Vivien A. Schmidt. 2000. *Welfare and Work in the Open Economy*. Oxford: Oxford University Press.

Schmid, Josef. 1991. "Der Machtwechsel und die Strategie des konservativ-liberalen Bündnisses." In Süß 1991.

Schmidt, Manfred G. 1991. "Machtwechsel in der Bundesrepublik (1949–1990)." In *Die Alte Bundesrepublik*, ed. Bernhard Blanke and Helmut Wollmann. Opladen: Westdeutscher Verlag.

———. 2001. "Still on the Middle Way? Germany's Political Economy at the Beginning of the Twenty-First Century." *German Politics* 10 (3): 1–12.

Schmidt, Vivien A. 1996. *From State to Market? The Transformation of French Business and Government*. Cambridge: Cambridge University Press.

———. 1999. "The Changing Dynamics of State-Society Relations in the Fifth Republic." *West European Politics* 22 (4): 141–65.

———. 2001. "The Politics of Adjustment in France and Britain: When Does Discourse Matter?" *Journal of European Public Policy* 8 (2): 247–64.

———. 2002. "Does Discourse Matter in the Politics of Welfare State Adjustment?" *Comparative Political Studies* 35 (2): 168–93.

Schneider, William. 1981. "The November 4 Vote for President: What Did It Mean?" In Ranney 1981.

———. 1983. "The Environment: The Public Wants More Protection, Not Less." *National Journal* 15 (13): 676.

Schnerb, Robert. 1973a. "Les vicissitudes de l'impôt indirect de la Constituante à Napoleon." In Bouvier and Wolff 1973. Orig. pub. in 1947.

———. 1973b. "Quelques observations sur l'impôt en France dans la première moitié du XIXe siècle." In Bouvier and Wolff 1973. Orig. pub. in 1954.

———. 1973c. "Technique fiscale et parties pris sociaux: L'impôt foncier en France depuis la Revolution." In Bouvier and Wolff 1973. Orig. pub. in 1938.

Schonfield, Andrew. 1965. *Modern Capitalism: The Changing Balance of Public and Private Power*. New York: Oxford University Press.

Schulman, Paul R. 1988. "The Politics of 'Ideational Policy.'" *Journal of Politics* 50 (2): 263–91.

Schulz, Günther. 1999. "Sozialpolitik in der Bundesrepublik und die Mitwirkung der BDA." In *50 Jahre BDA—50 Jahre Politik für die Wirtschaft*, ed. Reinhard Göhner. Korbach: Wilhelm Bing.

Schunder, Achim. 1994. *Das Ladenschlußgesetz—heute*. Munich: Verlag Franz Vahlen.

Schwarz, Walter. 1979. "Barre to Resign: Rumours as Discontent Grows." *Guardian*, February 22.

Seldon, Anthony. 1996. "The Heath Government in History." In Ball and Seldon 1996.

Sewell, William H. 1996a. "Historical Events as Transformations of Structures: Inventing Revolution at the Bastille." *Theory and Society* 25:841–81.

———. 1996b. "Three Temporalities: Toward an Eventful Sociology." In *The Historic Turn in the Human Sciences*, ed. Terence McDonald. Ann Arbor: University of Michigan Press.

———. 1999. "The Concept(s) of Culture." In *Beyond the Cultural Turn*, ed. Victoria Bonnell and Lynn Hunt. Berkeley and Los Angeles: University of California Press.

Shabecoff, Philip. 1981. "Environmental Action Enters New Arena." *New York Times*, January 20, sec. A.

———. 1983. "Politics and the E.P.A. Crisis: Environment Emerges as a Mainstream Issue." *New York Times*, April 23.

Shanahan, Eileen. 1975. "Regulatory Reform: A Roundtable Discussion. (Phonotape-cassette). Eileen Shanahan, moderator [with] Hubert H. Humphrey [and others]." Washington, DC: American Enterprise Institute for Public Policy Research.

Shapiro, Robert Y., and John M. Gilroy. 1984a. "The Polls: Regulation—Part I." *Public Opinion Quarterly* 48:531–42.

———. 1984b. "The Polls: Regulation—Part II." *Public Opinion Quarterly* 48:666–77.

Shapiro, Robert Y., Kelly D. Patterson, Judith Russell, and John T. Young. 1987. "The Polls: Public Assistance." *Public Opinion Quarterly* 51 (1): 120–30.

Shapiro, Robert Y., and John T. Young. 1989. "Public Opinion and the Welfare State: The United States in Comparative Perspective." *Political Science Quarterly* 104 (1): 59–89.

Shultz, George P., and Kenneth W. Dam. 1977. "Reflections on Wage and Price Controls." *Industrial and Labor Relations Review* 30 (January): 139–51.

Silvia, Stephen J. 1988. "The West German Labor Law Controversy: A Struggle for the Factory of the Future." *Comparative Politics* 20 (2): 155–73.

Simmons, Beth, Geoffrey Garrett, and Frank Dobbin. 2003. "The International Diffusion of Democracy and Markets." Paper presented at the Annual Meeting of the American Political Science Association, Philadelphia, August.

Simon, Donald. 1977. "Senator Kennedy and the Civil Aeronautics Board." Case prepared by Donald Simon under the supervision of Professors Stephen G. Breyer and Philip B. Heymann for use at the John Fitzgerald Kennedy School of Government, Harvard University, and at the Harvard Law School. Distributed by the Intercollegiate Case Clearing House, Soldiers Field, Boston, MA 02163.

Simonian, Haig. 1987. "W[est] Germans Still Waiting to Ring in Changes in Shop Hours." *Financial Times*, December 22.

Sinclair, Molly. 1985. "Consumer Groups Seek New Focus for Action: Nader Attacks Docility." *Washington Post*, February 7.

Singer, Otto. 1993. "Knowledge and Politics in Economic Policy-Making: Official Economic Advisers in the USA, Great Britain and Germany." In *Advising West European Governments: Inquiries, Expertise, and Public Policy*, ed. B. Guy Peters and Anthony Barker. Edinburgh: Edinburgh University Press.

Sinn, Hans-Werner. 2004. *Ist Deutschland noch zu retten?* Berlin: Econ Verlag.

Skocpol, Theda. 1979. *States and Social Revolutions*. Cambridge: Cambridge University Press.

———. 1985. "Bringing the State Back In: Strategies of Analysis in Current Research." In Evans, Rueschemeyer, and Skocpol 1985.

———. 1992. *Protecting Soldiers and Mothers: The Political Origins of Social Policy in the United States*. Cambridge, MA: Belknap Press of Harvard University Press.

Skocpol, Theda, and Margaret Weir. 1985. "State Structures and the Possibilities for 'Keynesian' Responses to the Great Depression in Sweden, Britain, and the United States." In Evans, Rueschemeyer, and Skocpol 1985.

Smith, Gordon. 1986. *Democracy in Western Germany: Parties and Politics in the Federal Republic*. Aldershot, Hants, UK: Gower.

———. 1992. "The Nature of the United State." In *Developments in German Politics*, ed. Gordon Smith, William E. Paterson, Peter H. Merkl, and Stephen Padgett. Durham, NC: Duke University Press.

Smith, Hedrick. 1983. "Movement to Center." *New York Times*, March 22.

Smith, Mark. 1999. "Public Opinion, Elections, and Representation within a Market Economy: Does the Structural Power of Business Undermine Popular Sovereignty?" *American Journal of Political Science* 43 (3): 842–63.

———. 2000. *American Business and Political Power*. Chicago: University of Chicago Press.

Smith, Timothy B. 2004. *France in Crisis: Welfare, Inequality and Globalization since 1980*. Cambridge, UK: Cambridge University Press.

Smith, Tom W. 1987. "The Polls: The Welfare State in Crossnational Perspective." *Public Opinion Quarterly* 51:404–21.

Sneessens, Henri. 1993. "Penurie de main d'oeuvre qualifiée et persistance du chômage." Rapport au Commissariat General du Plan.

———. 1994. "Croissance, qualifications, et chômage." *Revue française d'économie* 9 (4): 1–33.

Søe, Christian. 1990. "The Free Democratic Party: Two Victories and a Political Realignment." In Cerny 1990.

SOFRES. 1978. "L'opinion française en 1977." Paris: Presses de la fondation nationale des sciences politiques.

Stark, David. 1999. "Heterarchy: Distributing Intelligence and Organizing Diversity." In *The Biology of Business: Decoding the Natural Laws of Enterprise*, ed. John Clippinger. San Francisco: Jossey-Bass.

Stein, Herbert. 1990. *The Fiscal Revolution in America*. Washington, DC: AEI Press.

———. 1994. *Presidential Economics*. Washington, DC: American Enterprise Institute for Public Policy Research.

———. 1996. "The Fiscal Revolution in America, part 2: 1964–1994." In Brownlee 1996b.

Steingart, Gabor. 2004. *Deutschland—Der Abstieg eines Superstars*. Berlin: Piper Verlag.

Steinmo, Sven. 1989. *Taxes, Institutions, and the Mobilization of Bias*. PhD diss., University of California, Berkeley.

———. 1993. *Taxation and Democracy: Swedish, British, and American Approaches to Financing the Modern State*. New Haven, CT: Yale University Press.

Steinmo, Sven, Kathleen Thelen, and Frank Longstreth. 1992. *Structuring Politics: Historical Institutionalism in Comparative Analysis*. Cambridge: Cambridge University Press.

Steuerle, Eugene. 1992. *The Tax Decade: How Taxes Came to Dominate the Public Agenda*. Washington, DC: Urban Institute Press.

Stockman, David. 1986. *The Triumph of Politics: How the Reagan Revolution Failed*. New York: Harper and Row.

Stoleru, Lionel. 1974. *Vaincre la pauvreté dans les pays riches*. Paris: Flammarion.

Strahan, Randall. 1990. *New Ways and Means: Reform and Change in a Congressional Committee*. Chapel Hill: University of North Carolina Press.

Streeck, Wolfgang. 1997. "German Capitalism: Does It Exist? Can It Survive?" In *The Political Economy of Modern Capitalism: Convergence and Diversity*, ed. Colin Crouch and Wolfgang Streeck. London: Sage.

Studlar, Donley T., Ian McAllister, and Alvaro Ascui. 1990. "Privatization and the British Electorate: Microeconomic Policies, Macroeconomic Evaluations, and Party Support." *American Journal of Political Science* 34 (4): 1077–1101.

Sturm, Roland. 1995. "How Independent Is the Bundesbank?" *German Politics* 4 (1): 27 41.

Sturmthal, Adolf. 1953. "Nationalization and Workers' Control in Britain and France." *Journal of Political Economy* 61 (1): 43–79.

Süß, Werner. 1991. *Die Bundesrepublik in den achtziger Jahren*. Opladen: Leske and Budrich.

Swank, Duane. 1998. "Funding the Welfare State: Globalization and the Taxation of Business in Advanced Market Economies." *Political Studies* 46 (4): 671–92.

Swank, Duane, and Sven Steinmo. 2002. "The New Political Economy of Taxation in Advanced Industrial Democracies." *American Journal of Political Science* 46 (3): 642–55.

Swann, Dennis. 1988. *The Retreat of the State: Deregulation and Privatization in the UK and US*. Ann Arbor: University of Michigan Press.

Swenson, Peter. 1997. "Arranged Alliances: Business Interests in the New Deal." *Politics and Society* 25 (1): 66–116.

Täger, Uwe Christian, Kurt Vogler-Ludwig, and Sonja Munz. 1995. *Das deutsche Ladenschlußgesetz auf dem Prüfstand*. Berlin and Munich: Duncker and Humblot.

Tanzi, Vito. 1969. *The Individual Income Tax and Economic Growth*. Baltimore, MD: Johns Hopkins University Press.

Taylor-Gooby, Peter. 1985. *Public Opinion, Ideology and State Welfare*. London: Routledge and Kegan Paul.

———. 1988. "The Future of the British Welfare State: Public Attitudes, Citizenship and Social Policy under the Conservative Governments of the 1980s." *European Sociological Review* 4 (1): 1–19.

———. 1989. "Welfare, Hierarchy and the 'New Right': The Impact of Social Policy Changes in Britain, 1979–1989." *International Sociology* 4 (4): 431–46.

Teske, Paul. 1991. "Interests and Institutions in State Regulation." *American Journal of Political Science* 35 (1): 139–54.

Thatcher, Margaret. 1993. *The Downing Street Years*. New York: HarperCollins.

Thayer, Frederick. 1997. "The U.S. Civil Service: 1883–1993 (R.I.P.)." In *Modern Systems of Government: Exploring the Role of Bureaucrats and Politicians*, ed. Ali Farazmand. Thousand Oaks, CA: Sage.

Theiss, Ulrich. 1997. "Allemagne: Site industriel en danger?" In *La Fin du Modèle Allemand*, ed. Alois Schumacher and Hans Brodersen. Paris: Chambre de Commerce et d'Industrie de Paris.

Thelen, Kathy. 1999. "Why German Employers Cannot Bring Themselves to Dismantle the German Model." In *Unions, Employers, and Central Banks: Wage Bargaining and Macro-Economic Regimes in an Integrating Europe*, ed. Torben Iversen, Jonas Pontusson, and David Soskice. New York: Cambridge University Press.

Théret, Bruno. 1991. "Néo-libéralisme, inégalites sociales et politiques fiscales de droite et de gauche dans la France des années 1980." *Revue Française de Science Politique* 41 (3): 342–81.

Thuong, Le Trung. 1980. *A Comparative Study of Administration of Nationalized Railroads in the United Kingdom, France, West Germany, and Japan*. PhD diss., Michigan State University.

Tocqueville, Alexis de. 1969. *Democracy in America*. Tr. George Lawrence, ed. J. P. Mayer. New York: Harper and Row. Orig. pub. in 1835.

Todd, Olivier. 1977. *La marelle de Giscard, 1926–1974*. Paris: Robert Laffont.

Tolchin, Martin. 1983. "Recent Trends Hint Deregulatory Zeal Is Waning." *New York Times*, December 1, sec. B.

Tomforde, Anna. 1988. "CDU Forced to Confront Economic Divide." *Guardian*, April 25.

Trattner, Walter I. 1999. *From Poor Law to Welfare State: A History of Social Welfare in America*. New York: Free Press. Orig. pub. in 1974.

Tsebelis, George. 1995. "Decision Making in Political Systems: Veto Players in Presidentialism, Parliamentarianism, Multicameralism, and Multipartyism." *British Journal of Political Science* 25:289–326.

———. 1999. "Veto Players and Law Production in Parliamentary Democracies." *American Political Science Review* 93:591–608.

———. 2002. *Veto Players*. Princeton, NJ: Princeton University Press.

Uekötter, Frank. 2002. "Umweltschutz in den Händen der Industrie—Eine Sackgasse? Die Geschichte der Hamburger Vereins für Feuerungsbetrieb und Rauchbekämpfung." *Zeitschrift für Unternehmensgeschichte* 47 (2): 198–216.

U.S. Congress. 1977. Senate, Committee on Environment and Public Works. *Public Works Employment Act of 1977*. Hearings before the Subcommittee on Regional and Community Development, 2–4 Feb 1977. Washington, DC: U.S. Government Printing Office.

———. 1978a. House of Representatives. *Leading Economists' Views of Kemp-Roth*. Washington, DC: U.S. Government Printing Office.

———. 1978b. Senate, Committee on Banking, Housing, and Urban Affairs. *The President's New Anti-Inflation Program*. Hearing, 3 Nov.

———. 1978c. Senate, Committee on Environment and Public Works. *Labor Intensive Public Works Act of 1978*. Hearings before the Subcommittee on Regional and Community Development, 15 June–13 July 1978. Washington, DC: U.S. Government Printing Office.

———. 1980. Office of Technology Assessment. *Technology and Steel Industry Competitiveness*. Washington, DC: U. S. Government Printing Office.

U.S. Senate. 1977. Committee on the Judiciary. Subcommittee on Administrative Practice and Procedures. *Oversight of the Civil Aeronautics Board*. Washington, DC: U.S. Government Printing Office.

Vaughan, Roger J. 1976. *Public Works as a Countercyclical Device: A Review of the Issues*. Santa Monica, CA: Rand Corporation.

Vernez, Georges. 1977. *Public Works as Countercyclical Fiscal Policy*. Santa Monica, CA: Rand Corporation.

Verweij, Marco. 2000. "Why Is the River Rhine Cleaner Than the Great Lakes (Despite Looser Regulation)?" *Law and Society Review* 34 (4): 1007–54.

Vig, Norman J., and Michael E. Kraft. 1984. *Environmental Policy in the 1980s: Reagan's New Agenda*. Washington, DC: Congressional Quarterly Press.

Vogel, David. 1978. "Why Businessmen Distrust Their State: The Political Consciousness of Corporate Executives." *British Journal of Political Science* 8 (1): 45–78.

———. 1986. *National Styles of Regulation: Environmental Policy in Great Britain and the United States*. Ithaca, NY: Cornell University Press.

———. 1989. *Fluctuating Fortunes: The Political Power of Business in America*. New York: Basic Books.

Volkerink, Bjørn, and Jakob de Haan. 2000. "Tax Ratios: A Critical Survey." http://www.volkerink.net/papers/taxratio.pdf.

von Beyme, Klaus. 1985. "Policy-Making in the Federal Republic of Germany: A Systematic Introduction." In *Policy and Politics in the Federal Republic of Germany*, ed. Klaus von Beyme and Manfred G. Schmidt. Aldershot, Hants, UK: Gower.

von Winter, Thomas. 1990. "Die Sozialausschüsse der CDU: Sammelbecken für Christdemokratische Arbeitnehmerinteressen oder linker Flügel einer Partei?" *Leviathan* 18 (3): 390–416.

Wagschal, Uwe. 1998. "Schranken staatlicher Steuerungspolitik: Warum Steuerreformen Scheitern können." Bremen: Zentrum für Sozialpolitik Arbeitspapier Nr. 7/98.

Walter, Norbert, and Klaus Günter Deutsch. 2004. *Mehr Wachstum für Deutschland: Die Reformagenda*. Berlin: Campus Verlag.

Walwei, Ulrich. 1994. "Ist die Arbeit zu teuer und inflexibel?" In *Standort Deutschland*, ed. Hans-Georg Wehling. Stuttgart: W. Kohlhammer Verlag.

Waterman, Richard W. 1989. *Presidential Influence and the Administrative State.* Knoxville: University of Tennessee Press.

Weakliem, David L. 1993. "Class Consciousness and Political Change: Voting and Political Attitudes in the British Working Class, 1964 to 1970." *American Sociological Review* 58 (3): 382–97.

______. 1995. "Two Models of Class Voting." *British Journal of Political Science* 25 (2): 254–70.

Weale, Albert. 1992. "Vorsprung durch Technik? The Politics of German Environmental Regulation." In Dyson 1992.

Weaver, R. Kent. 1988. *Automatic Government: The Politics of Indexation.* Washington, DC: Brookings Institution.

Weaver, R. Kent, Robert Y. Shapiro, and Lawrence R. Jacobs. 1995. "Trends: Welfare." *Public Opinion Quarterly* 59 (4): 606–27.

Webber, Douglas. 1986. "Die ausbleibende Wende bei der Deutschen Bundespost." *Politische Vierteljahresschrift* 27 (4): 397–414.

______. 1988. "Krankheit, Geld und Politik: Zur Geschichte der Gesundheitsreformen in Deutschland." *Leviathan* 16 (2): 156–203.

______. 1989. "Zur Geschichte der Gesundheitsreformen in Deutschland—II. Teil: Norbert Blüms Gesundheitsreform und die Lobby." *Leviathan* 17 (2): 262–300.

______. 1991. "Das Reformpaket." In Süß 1991.

______. 1992a. "Kohl's *Wendepolitik* after a Decade." *German Politics* 1 (2): 149–80.

______. 1992b. "The Politics of Regulatory Change in the German Health Sector." In Dyson 1992.

Webster, Charles. 1989. "The Health Sector." In *The Thatcher Effect*, ed. Dennis Kavanagh and Anthony Seldon. Oxford: Oxford University Press.

Weidner, Helmut. 1995. "Twenty-Five Years of Modern Environmental Policy in Germany: Treading a Well-Worn Path to the Top of the International Field." Discussion paper. Berlin: Wissenschaftszentrum für Sozialforschung, FS II 95–301.

Weisman, Steven R. 1981. "Stockman's Views Touch Off Furor." *New York Times*, November 12.

______. 1983. "Uproar over an Agency." *New York Times*, February 17.

Wey, Klaus-Georg. 1982. *Umweltpolitik in Deutschland: Kurze Geschichte des Umweltschutzes in Deutschland seit 1900.* Opladen: Westdeutscher Verlag.

Whiteman, Charles H. 1978. "A New Investigation of the Impact of Wage and Price Controls." *Federal Reserve Minneapolis* 2 (Spring): 2–8.

Wicks, Malcolm. 1987. "The Decade of Inequality." *New Society* 79:10–12.

Wilensky, Harold. 2002. *Rich Democracies: Political Economy, Public Policy, and Performance.* Berkeley and Los Angeles: University of California Press.

Wilson, Frank L. 1983. "Les groupes d'intérêt sous la cinquieme république: Test de trois modèles théoriques de l'interaction entre groupes et gouvernement." *Revue Française de Science Politique* 33 (2): 220–54.

______. 1987. *Interest-Group Politics in France.* Cambridge: Cambridge University Press.

Wilson, Graham K. 1985. *The Politics of Safety and Health.* Oxford: Oxford University Press.

Wolff, Jacques. 1973. "Fiscalité et développement en France entre 1919 et 1939." In Bouvier and Wolff 1973.

Wood, Geoffrey E., and Nancy Ammon Jianakoplos. 1978. "Coordinated International Economic Expansion: Are Convoys or Locomotives the Answer?" *Federal Reserve Bank of St. Louis Review* (July): 11–19.

Woodheart, David. 1988. "Struggle to Take the Political Long View in Bonn." *Financial Times*, May 23.

Wörl, Volker. 1978. "Das Spiel mit den Steuern." *Süddeutsche Zeitung*, July 3.

World Bank. 1960–1999. *World Development Indicators*. Computer file. Washington, DC: World Bank.

Wright, Vincent, ed. 1984. *Continuity and Change in France*. London: Allen and Unwin.

Young, Hugo. 1989. *One of Us: A Biography of Margaret Thatcher*. London: Macmillan.

Zahariadis, Nikolaos. 1995. *Markets, States, and Public Policy: Privatization in Britain and France*. Ann Arbor: University of Michigan Press.

Zakaria, Fareed. 2003. *The Future of Freedom: Illiberal Democracy at Home and Abroad*. New York: W. W. Norton.

Zimmermann, Klaus F. 2004. *Reformen—jetzt! So geht es mit Deutschland wieder aufwärts*. Berlin: Gabler Verlag.

Zohlnhöfer, Reimut. 1998. "Politikwechsel nach Machtwechseln: Das Beispiel der christlich-liberalen Wirtschaftspolitik in den achtziger Jahren." Working paper no. 12/98. Bremen: Zentrum für Sozialpolitik.

———. 1999. "Institutions, the CDU and Policy Change: Explaining German Economic Policy in the 1980s." *German Politics* 8 (3): 141–60.

———. 2001a. "Der Einfluss Innerparteilicher Vereinigungen auf die Regierungspolitik der CDU am Beispiel der Finanz- und Arbeitsmarktpolitik in der Ära Kohl." Paper presented at the conference entitled "Innenansichten der deutschen Parteien." http://www.rzh.uni-hd.de/pdf/01%20Forschung/04%20Parteifl%FCgel.pdf.

———. 2001b. "Parteien, Vetospieler und der Wettbewerb um Wählerstimmen: Die Arbeitsmarkt- und Beschäftigungspolitik der Ära Kohl." *Politische Vierteljahresschrift* 42:655–82.

———. 2001c. *Die Wirtschaftspolitik der Ära Kohl: Eine Analyse der Schlüsselentscheidungen in den Politikfeldern Finanzen, Arbeit und Entstaatlichung, 1982–1998*. Opladen: Leske and Budrich.

Zysman, John. 1983. *Governments, Markets, and Growth: Financial Systems and the Politics of Industrial Change*. Ithaca, NY: Cornell University Press.

Index